STAGING THE SOUL
ALLEGORICAL DRAMA AS SPIRITUAL PRACTICE IN BAROQUE ITALY

LEGENDA

LEGENDA is the Modern Humanities Research Association's book imprint for new research in the Humanities. Founded in 1995 by Malcolm Bowie and others within the University of Oxford, Legenda has always been a collaborative publishing enterprise, directly governed by scholars. The Modern Humanities Research Association (MHRA) joined this collaboration in 1998, became half-owner in 2004, in partnership with Maney Publishing and then Routledge, and has since 2016 been sole owner. Titles range from medieval texts to contemporary cinema and form a widely comparative view of the modern humanities, including works on Arabic, Catalan, English, French, German, Greek, Italian, Portuguese, Russian, Spanish, and Yiddish literature. Editorial boards and committees of more than 60 leading academic specialists work in collaboration with bodies such as the Society for French Studies, the British Comparative Literature Association and the Association of Hispanists of Great Britain & Ireland.

The MHRA encourages and promotes advanced study and research in the field of the modern humanities, especially modern European languages and literature, including English, and also cinema. It aims to break down the barriers between scholars working in different disciplines and to maintain the unity of humanistic scholarship. The Association fulfils this purpose through the publication of journals, bibliographies, monographs, critical editions, and the MHRA Style Guide, and by making grants in support of research. Membership is open to all who work in the Humanities, whether independent or in a University post, and the participation of younger colleagues entering the field is especially welcomed.

ALSO PUBLISHED BY THE ASSOCIATION

Critical Texts
Tudor and Stuart Translations • New Translations • European Translations
MHRA Library of Medieval Welsh Literature

MHRA Bibliographies
Publications of the Modern Humanities Research Association

The Annual Bibliography of English Language & Literature
Austrian Studies
Modern Language Review
Portuguese Studies
The Slavonic and East European Review
Working Papers in the Humanities
The Yearbook of English Studies

www.mhra.org.uk
www.legendabooks.com

ITALIAN PERSPECTIVES

Editorial Committee
Professor Simon Gilson, University of Oxford (General Editor)
Dr Francesca Billiani, University of Manchester
Professor Manuele Gragnolati, Université Paris-Sorbonne
Dr Catherine Keen, University College London
Professor Martin McLaughlin, Magdalen College, Oxford

Founding Editors
Professor Zygmunt Barański and Professor Anna Laura Lepschy

In the light of growing academic interest in Italy and the reorganization of many university courses in Italian along interdisciplinary lines, this book series, founded by Maney Publishing under the imprint of the Northern Universities Press and now continuing under the Legenda imprint, aims to bring together different scholarly perspectives on Italy and its culture. *Italian Perspectives* publishes books and collections of essays on any period of Italian literature, language, history, culture, politics, art, and media, as well as studies which take an interdisciplinary approach and are methodologically innovative.

APPEARING IN THIS SERIES

20. *Ugo Foscolo and English Culture*, by Sandra Parmegiani
21. *The Printed Media in Fin-de-siècle Italy: Publishers, Writers, and Readers*, ed. by Ann Hallamore Caesar, Gabriella Romani, and Jennifer Burns
22. *Giraffes in the Garden of Italian Literature: Modernist Embodiment in Italo Svevo, Federigo Tozzi and Carlo Emilio Gadda*, by Deborah Amberson
23. *Remembering Aldo Moro: The Cultural Legacy of the 1978 Kidnapping and Murder*, ed. by Ruth Glynn and Giancarlo Lombardi
24. *Disrupted Narratives: Illness, Silence and Identity in Svevo, Pressburger and Morandini*, by Emma Bond
25. *Dante and Epicurus: A Dualistic Vision of Secular and Spiritual Fulfilment*, by George Corbett
26. *Edoardo Sanguineti: Literature, Ideology and the Avant-Garde*, ed. by Paolo Chirumbolo and John Picchione
27. *The Tradition of the Actor-Author in Italian Theatre*, ed. by Donatella Fischer
28. *Leopardi's Nymphs: Grace, Melancholy, and the Uncanny*, by Fabio A. Camilletti
29. *Gadda and Beckett: Storytelling, Subjectivity and Fracture*, by Katrin Wehling-Giorgi
30. *Caravaggio in Film and Literature: Popular Culture's Appropriation of a Baroque Genius*, by Laura Rorato
31. *The Italian Academies 1525-1700: Networks of Culture, Innovation and Dissent*, ed. by Jane E. Everson, Denis V. Reidy and Lisa Sampson
32. *Rome Eternal: The City As Fatherland*, by Guy Lanoue
33. *The Somali Within: Language, Race and Belonging in 'Minor' Italian Literature*, by Simone Brioni
34. *Laughter from Realism to Modernism: Misfits and Humorists in Pirandello, Svevo, Palazzeschi, and Gadda*, by Alberto Godioli
35. *Pasolini after Dante: The 'Divine Mimesis' and the Politics of Representation*, by Emanuela Patti

Managing Editor
Dr Graham Nelson, 41 Wellington Square, Oxford OX1 2JF, UK
www.legendabooks.com

Staging the Soul

*Allegorical Drama as
Spiritual Practice in Baroque Italy*

Eugenio Refini

Italian Perspectives 48
Modern Humanities Research Association
2023

Published by Legenda
an imprint of the Modern Humanities Research Association
Salisbury House, Station Road, Cambridge CB1 2LA

ISBN 978-1-78188-437-9 (HB)
ISBN 978-1-78188-440-9 (PB)

First published 2023

All rights reserved. No part of this publication may be reproduced or disseminated or transmitted in any form or by any means, electronic, mechanical, photocopying, recording or otherwise, or stored in any retrieval system, or otherwise used in any manner whatsoever without written permission of the copyright owner, except in accordance with the provisions of the Copyright, Designs and Patents Act 1988, or under the terms of a licence permitting restricted copying issued in the UK by the Copyright Licensing Agency Ltd, Saffron House, 6–10 Kirby Street, London EC1N 8TS, *England, or in the USA by the Copyright Clearance Center, 222 Rosewood Drive, Danvers MA 01923. Application for the written permission of the copyright owner to reproduce any part of this publication must be made by email to legenda@mhra.org.uk.*

Disclaimer: Statements of fact and opinion contained in this book are those of the author and not of the editors or the Modern Humanities Research Association. The publisher makes no representation, express or implied, in respect of the accuracy of the material in this book and cannot accept any legal responsibility or liability for any errors or omissions that may be made.

Trademark notice: Product or corporate names may be trademarks or registered trademarks, and are used only for identification and explanation without intent to infringe.

© *Modern Humanities Research Association 2023*

Copy-Editor: Richard Correll

CONTENTS

Acknowledgements		ix
List of Illustrations		xi
Notes on the Text and Translations		xiii
Introduction: From the Stage of the World to the Stage of the Soul		1
1	Bodiless Objects in Human Shape: Personification across Rhetoric and Drama	19
	Image-Making and Allegory's Loophole	22
	Across Thought and Speech: Personification in Classical Rhetoric	28
	Personification in Early Modern Rhetoric and Poetics	41
	From the Verbal to the Visual: Personified Allegories as Images	54
	From the Visual to the Theatrical: Personified Allegories on Stage	59
2	The Tragedy of Human Life: *Ars Moriendi* and *Theatrum Mundi* in Fabio Glissenti's *Discorsi morali* (1596)	81
	Physician, Philosopher, Playwright	82
	Setting the Stage for the Dialogue	86
	A Little Bit of Everything	89
	Making Death Visible	97
	Venice, Theatre of the World	114
	Converting (through) Drama	124
3	Anatomy of the Soul: Morality Plays as Spiritual Exercises in Early Seicento Venice	135
	School Drama in the Venetian *ospedali* and Beyond	138
	The Poetics and Performance of Purgation	147
	Spiritual *topoi*	155
	The Theatre of Vanity	166
	The Theatre of Conscience	183
	The Performance of Virtue	199
Conclusion: Death in the Mirror		209
Bibliography		221
Index		236

ACKNOWLEDGEMENTS

Research for this book has accompanied me for a long time. It all began when I was working on my doctoral dissertation devoted to the use of allegorical personifications in early modern drama. It was during a productive summer spent doing research at the British Library that I first encountered the works of Fabio Glissenti. Intrigued by the title of his philosophical dialogue on the art of dying well, *Athanatophilia*, I quickly found out that the Venice-based physician was also the author of some curious morality plays written at the outset of the seventeenth century for the female orphans of the Venetian hospitals. Emboldened by the truly unique features of a virtually unexplored corpus, I embarked on a project that, even after the completion of my dissertation, continued to raise more questions than I anticipated. I was not expecting to deal with the educational agendas of Venice's hospitals; I was not planning on chasing information about the life and spiritual training of the *putte*; I was not foreseeing the numerous intersections of drama, allegory, and iconography which would eventually prove key to the writing of this book. Undoubtedly beneficial to the project was my involvement with other post-doctoral endeavours, which made me leave my work on allegorical drama on the side — they call it spare time! Going back to it at regular intervals, I was able to revisit my early findings from a distance and, above all, to identify sources that had previously escaped my radar.

If I owe the British Library's extraordinary collections of early prints my first encounter with Glissenti, it was the manuscript collection of the Marciana Library that gave me both the opportunity to shed light on the place of school drama in the hospitals of Venice and the very idea to write this book. I am grateful to the staff of both libraries for their assistance at various stages of my research, particularly Stephen Parkin and Orfea Granzotto.

Over the years, my work has benefited from numerous exchanges with colleagues and friends. I especially wish to thank Virginia Cox for the many conversations on this project and for encouraging me to explore the many facets of the literature and culture of the Counter-Reformation. Many thanks to Patrizia De Capitani, Shannon McHugh, Sara Miglietti, Matthias Roick, and Anna Wainwright, who, on different occasions, have allowed me to present parts of this research at conferences and panels they organised. Further opportunities for invaluable feedback were facilitated by Ambrogio Camozzi Pistoja, Massimo Scalabrini, Andrea Rizzi, and Alessandro Vettori, whom I thank for inviting me to give lectures on these topics at their institutions. I am also grateful to other individuals who have provided me with most useful insights into specific aspects of this project: Marco Arnaudo, Gaia Benzi, Abigail Brundin, Monica Calabritto, Claudio Ciociola, Davide Daolmi,

Luca D'Onghia, Marco Faini, Marco Guardo, Ullrich Langer, Nerida Newbigin, Federica Pich, Matteo Residori, Lucia Simonato, Claudia Tardelli, Andrea Torre, Caroline Van Eck, Elissa Weaver, Gabriella Zarri.

Finally, I wish to thank Simon Gilson for accepting this book as part of Legenda's Italian Perspectives series; Graham Nelson for his assistance throughout the editorial process; and the anonymous peer reviewers for their generous comments and useful suggestions.

I dedicate this book to my mentor, Lina Bolzoni. Among the innumerable teachings I owe her, there is one which I am most grateful for and which, ironically, counterbalances the somewhat sombre topic of this volume: *primum vivere*.

E.R., New York, September 2022

LIST OF ILLUSTRATIONS

Fig. I.1. Jean-Jacques Boissard, *Theatrum Vitae Humanae*. Frankfurt: Abraham Faber, 1596, p. 1. Courtesy of The Rare Book & Manuscript Library, University of Illinois at Urbana–Champaign (Emblems 096.1 B636t).

Fig. I.2. Boissard, *Theatrum Vitae Humanae*, title page.

Fig. I.3. Francesco Pona, *Cardiomorphoseos sive ex corde desumpta emblemata sacra*. Verona: 1645, p. 1. Courtesy of the Getty Research Institute, Library, Special Collections (BV4515 P66 1645).

Fig. 1.1. Giovan Battista Andreini, *L'Adamo sacra rappresentatione*. Milan: Girolamo Bordone, 1617, title page. Courtesy of the Getty Research Institute, Library, Special Collections (PQ4562.A7 A66 1617).

Fig. 1.2. Andreini, *L'Adamo*, fol. [c4]^v.

Fig. 1.3. Andreini, *L'Adamo*, p. 123.

Fig. 1.4. Andreini, *L'Adamo*, p. 149.

Fig. 1.5. Bonaventura de Venere, *Rappresentatione spirituale dell'anima e del corpo, con alcune laudi, et altre ottave, fatte dal Pellegrino Romito*. Rome and Perugia: Bartoli and Laurenzi, 1644, foldable illustration between fols. A2–A3. Courtesy of Università degli Studi di Torino — Biblioteca Storica di Ateneo Arturo Graf (Coll T 190).

Fig. 1.6. Troilo Lancetta, *La scena tragica d'Adamo e d'Eva, estratta dalli primi tre capi della sacra Genesi, et ridotta a significato morale*. Venice: Giovanni Guerigli, 1644, fol. ★4^v. Courtesy of Università degli Studi di Torino — Biblioteca Storica di Ateneo Arturo Graf (Coll T 499).

Fig. 2.1. Fabio Glissenti, *Discorsi morali contra il dispiacer del morire*. Venice: Domenico Farri, 1596, title page. Florence, Biblioteca Nazionale Centrale (Pal. 7.7.5.7). Reproduced with permission of Ministero della Cultura. Reproduction forbidden.

Fig. 2.2. Glissenti, *Discorsi morali*, title page's *verso*.

Fig. 2.3. Glissenti, *Discorsi morali*, fol. 5^r.

Fig. 2.4. *Les simulachres et faces historiées de la mort*. Lyon: Trechsel, 1538, fol. Dii^v. Courtesy of Harvard University, Countway Medicine Library, Rare Books (1.Mx.63).

Fig. 2.5. Glissenti, *Discorsi morali*, fol. 7^r.

Fig. 2.6. Glissenti, *Discorsi morali*, fol. 22^v.

Fig. 2.7. Glissenti, *Discorsi morali*, fol. 43^v.

Fig. 2.8. Glissenti, *Discorsi morali*, fol. 107^r.

Fig. 2.9. Glissenti, *Discorsi morali*, fol. 135^v.

Fig. 2.10. Glissenti, *Discorsi morali*, fol. 138^v.

Fig. 2.11. Glissenti, *Discorsi morali*, fol. 127^r.

Fig. 2.12. Glissenti, *Discorsi morali*, fol. 87^v.

Fig. 2.13. Glissenti, *Discorsi morali*, fol. 245^r.

Fig. 2.14. Glissenti, *Discorsi morali*, fol. 339^r.

Fig. 2.15. Glissenti, *Discorsi morali*, fol. 341^r.

Fig. 2.16. Glissenti, *Discorsi morali*, fol. 446^v.

Fig. 2.17. Glissenti, *Discorsi morali*, fol. 77^v.

FIG. 2.18. Glissenti, *Discorsi morali*, fol. 99^r.
FIG. 2.19. Giacomo Franco, *Habiti delle donne venetiane*, undated print, title page. Courtesy of The Metropolitan Museum, New York.
FIG. 2.20. Glissenti, *Discorsi morali*, fol. 58^v.
FIG. 2.21. Giovanni Manenti, *Opera nuova in versi volgare, intitulata Specchio de la Giustitia*. Venice: Giovanni Antonio Nicolini da Sabbio, 1539, title page. Vienna, Österreichische Nationalbibliothek (*38.G.84). Reproduced with permission of the Österreichische Nationalbibliothek.
FIG. 2.22. Manenti, *Opera nuova*, fol. D[1]^v.
FIG. 3.1. Fabio Glissenti, *Il Diligente overo il Sollecito favola morale*. Venice: Giovanni Alberti, 1608, p. 1. Courtesy of Università degli Studi di Torino — Biblioteca Storica di Ateneo Arturo Graf (Coll T 457).
FIG. 3.2. Pona, *Cardiomorphoseos*, p. 21.
FIG. 3.3. Antonio Glissenti, *L'assoluta conclusione dell'humana libertà*. Venice: Rampazzetto, 1597, fols. B3^v–[B4]^r. Courtesy of the Department of Special Collections, Stanford University Libraries (BJ1464 .G55 1597).
FIG. 3.4. Fabio Glissenti, *La Ragione sprezzata favola tragica morale*. Venice: Marco Claseri, 1606, fol. 10^{r-v}. Rome, Biblioteca Universitaria Alessandrina (N b 43). Reproduced with permission of Ministero della Cultura. Reproduction forbidden.
FIG. 3.5. Pona, *Cardiomorphoseos*, p. 17.
FIG. 3.6. Hans Baldung, *Three Ages of the Woman and the Death* (1510), Vienna, Kunsthistorisches Museum. © KHM-Museumsverband.
FIG. 3.7. Anonymous, *Death and the Maiden* (c. 1570), Shakespeare Trust Birthplace, Hall's Croft, Stratford-upon-Avon. © Shakespeare Trust Birthplace.
FIG. 3.8. Jacques de Gheyn II, *Still Life* (1603), The Metropolitan Museum, New York. Courtesy of The Metropolitan Museum, New York.
FIG. 3.9. Jan van Hemessen, *Vanity* (1535–1540), Palais Beaux Arts, Lille. © RMN-Grand Palais / Art Resource, NY.
FIG. 3.10. Maarten van Heemskerck (1498–1574), *Allegory of Innocence and Guile*, The Bowes Museum, Barnard Castle. © Bowes Museum / Bridgeman Images.
FIG. 3.11. Lorenzo Lippi (1606–1665), *An Allegory of Innocence* (c. 1640), Oxford, The Ashmolean Museum. © HIP / Art Resource, NY.
FIG. C.1. Scene from the production of *La Morte innamorata*, Teatro di Documenti, Rome, June 1987.
FIG. C.2. *La Morte innamorata* and *Amor nello specchio*, poster of Luca Ronconi's production for the Accademia Nazionale d'Arte Drammatica (1987).

NOTES ON THE TEXT AND TRANSLATIONS

❖

Part of the section 'Personification in Early Modern Rhetoric and Poetics' re-elaborates and expands the article 'Prologhi figurati: appunti sull'uso della prosopopea nel prologo teatrale del Cinquecento', *Italianistica*, 35.3 (2006), 61–86. Preliminary remarks on the entanglements of allegory and drama were published in the article '"Quasi una tragedia delle attioni humane": le tragique entre allégorie et édification morale dans l'œuvre de Fabio Glissenti (1542–1615)', *Cahiers d'études italiennes*, 19 (2014), 185–98. The section 'Converting (through) Drama' in Chapter 2 re-elaborates the book chapter 'Reforming Drama: Theater as Spiritual Practice in the Works of Fabio Glissenti', in Shannon McHugh and Anna Wainwright, eds, *Innovation in the Italian Counter-Reformation* (Newark: University of Delaware Press, 2020), pp. 169–89.

Unless indicated otherwise, all translations from languages other than English are mine.

INTRODUCTION

From the Stage of the World to the Stage of the Soul

A perk of serving as ambassador in Venice in the early seventeenth century was certainly given by the variety of entertainments available in town. For diplomats coming from other cities with vibrant theatre scenes, Venice would likely make up for what they missed in their home countries while on duty in the Serenissima. Sir Henry Wotton (1568–1639), who served as the English ambassador in Venice from 1604 to 1624, missed most of the plays, authored by William Shakespeare and others, that were staged in London during his time overseas. Yet, as far as we know, he did attend theatrical performances in Venice and, according to his Venetian acquaintances, he enjoyed them. In 1607, for instance, he saw the morality play *La Morte innamorata* [Smitten Death], which was performed by the female orphans (the so-called *putte*) of the Ospedale di San Giovanni e Paolo, also known as Ospedale dei Derelitti or Ospedaletto.[1] The play was authored by Fabio Glissenti (1542–1615), a physician trained in Padua who worked as a doctor in the hospitals of Venice, where he was also involved with the education of orphans. It probably reminded Wotton of morality plays such as *Everyman*, a genre that had been spreading widely north of the Alps since the late Middle Ages.[2]

La Morte innamorata, which was later printed and dedicated to the English ambassador himself, tells the parable of Man, married to Human Life and pursued by Death, who, as the title suggests, is in love with him.[3] Man's servants are Discourse and Sense; further characters include World, Fraud, Adulation, and Illness. The psychological and physiological components of human life are thus anatomised and brought on stage. As indicated by a manuscript copy of the play now in Venice's Marciana Library, *La Morte innamorata* was performed amidst the enthusiasm of the attendees in spite of its tragic ending, which, apparently, filled the audience with

---

1   Fabio Glissenti, *La Morte innamorata favola morale* (Venice: Giovanni Alberti, 1608).
2   For an overview of morality plays as codified within the British medieval tradition, see Pamela M. King, 'Morality Plays', in *The Cambridge Companion to Medieval English Theatre*, ed. by Richard Beadle (Cambridge: Cambridge University Press, 1994), pp. 240–64; more broadly, on the transnational reach of the genre across the Middle Ages and early modernity, see Blair Hoxby, 'Allegorical Drama', in *The Cambridge Companion to Allegory*, ed. by Rita Copeland and Peter Struck (Cambridge: Cambridge University Press, 2010), pp. 191–208.
3   See the dedication letter penned by the author's niece, Elisabetta Glissenti Serenella, dated 1st March 1608, in Glissenti, *La Morte innamorata*, fol. A2r.

fear and dread.⁴ Along with other plays of the same kind — school dramas with moral and spiritual undertones, which proliferated in Italy around 1600 (Glissenti alone wrote ten of them) — *La Morte innamorata* stages the world: the action takes place in the land of 'Lungavita' [Longlife], 'dinanzi l'albergo del Mondo', literally, in front of the World's Inn, where the double acceptation of 'Mondo' refers to both 'World' as a character (the innkeeper) and 'the world' as a location.

Works such as Glissenti's plays have been virtually overlooked by scholarship due to long-standing prejudices based on aesthetic arguments. Yet, they share the transnational poetics of their own time, particularly ideas, images, and commonplaces that have been made famous by the masterworks of William Shakespeare and Pedro Calderón de la Barca, among others. The Spanish playwright is the author of allegorical plays that immortalised the exquisitely Baroque trope of the *theatrum mundi* [theatre of the world] some twenty years after the Venetian staging of *La Morte innamorata*: one could think of *El gran teatro del mundo* [The Great Theatre of the World] (1633–36) and *El gran mercado del mundo* [The Great Market of the World] (1635–40), 'autos sacramentales' that bring the world on stage through the interaction of personified allegories.⁵ Shakespeare is instead often associated with proverbial statements, uttered not by allegorical personifications but by human characters, that translate the allegorical image of the *theatrum mundi* into a metaphor to comment upon human life.

'All the world's a stage', as per Jacques's monologue on the seven ages of man in *As You Like It*, though the bitter implications of the trope come more poignantly to the fore in Macbeth's words after his wife's death:

> [...] Out, out, brief candle.
> Life's but a walking shadow, a poor player
> That struts and frets his hour upon the stage,
> And then is heard no more. It is a tale
> Told by an idiot, full of sound and fury,
> Signifying nothing.⁶

Macbeth compares human life to the ephemeral performance of an actor. According to the metaphor, the world is a stage; life is a meaningless play; men and women are players; death is the epilogue. The kinship among these different theatrical uses of the *theatrum mundi* is too evident to require proof. Indeed, as indicated by seminal studies of the trope by Ernst R. Curtius, Richard Bernheimer, Frances A. Yates, Mario Costanzo, and Lynda G. Christian, the *theatrum mundi* is

---

4   Venice, Biblioteca Nazionale Marciana, MS Ital. IX.316. For a discussion of this manuscript copy of the play, see Chapter 3, p. 141–42.

5   On the tradition of the Spanish *autos sacramentales*, with a focus on Calderón de la Barca, see Barbara Ellen Kurtz, *The Play of Allegory in the 'Autos Sacramentales' of Pedro Calderón de la Barca* (Washington, DC: Catholic University of America, 1991).

6   William Shakespeare, *Macbeth*, Act v, Scene 5, 22–27, in *The Oxford Shakespeare: The Complete Works*, ed. by John Jowett, Stanley Wells, Gary Taylor, and William Montgomery (Oxford: Oxford University Press, 2005), p. 992; for the famous quote of Jacques, see William Shakespeare, *As You Like It*, Act II, Scene 7, 139 ff. ('All the world's a stage, | And all the men and women merely players. | They have their exits and their entrances, | And one man in his time plays many parts, | His acts being seven ages.'), in *The Oxford Shakespeare*, p. 666.

one of the most enduring commonplaces that modernity inherited from classical antiquity through the Latin Middle Ages. From Plato and Petronius through John of Salisbury's influential *Policraticus*, the trope had been circulating widely, mostly in non-dramatic contexts.[7] In the aftermath of the humanist rediscovery of classical theatre, the image of the *theatrum mundi* shaped the theatricality and performativity that, as brilliantly indicated by William Egginton, among others, have informed the modern world.[8] At this cultural juncture, the world is at once earthly sphere and the *cosmos* that surrounds it, emblematically represented by the image of the globe held by Hercules while Atlas fetches the apples of the Hesperides for him. In this all-encompassing capacity, the world becomes one and the same with the theatre. It is then all too fitting that the Herculean image, painted on a flag alongside the Latin motto 'totus mundus agit histrionem' [all the world plays the part of the actor], allegedly fluttered at the top of the Globe Theatre in London, where the protagonists of Shakespeare's plays delivered their monologues.[9]

Therefore, similarities that are in full sight, and which are not necessarily related to one another in direct ways, are not the scope of this book, though one of the benefits of studying the history of texts and ideas is to be constantly reminded that both texts and ideas travelled with people. From this standpoint, the case of the English ambassador Henry Wotton, who was familiar with the cultural lives of both London and Venice in the years that interest us in the present study, is evocative of the transnational patterns that contributed to the shaping of Europe's imagination. The reader of Wotton's works collected in the posthumous 1651 edition of *Reliquiae Wottonianae* (if also aware of Wotton's attendance of *La Morte innamorata* at the Ospedale dei Derelitti) will not resist the charm of what is likely just a serendipitous coincidence. The anthology includes a poetical piece in Latin entitled 'De Morte' [On Death] attributed to one 'Ignoto'. (The pseudonym led some scholars to assign it to Walter Raleigh, but it is not possible to exclude Wotton's authorship

---

7   Ernst R. Curtius, *European Literature and the Latin Middle Ages* [1953], trans. by Willard R. Trask (Princeton, NJ: Princeton University Press, 2013), pp. 140–42; Richard Bernheimer, 'Theatrum Mundi', *The Art Bulletin*, 38.4 (1956), 225–47; Mario Costanzo, *Il 'Gran Teatro del Mondo': schede per lo studio dell'iconografia letteraria nell'età del Manierismo* (Milan: All'insegna del pesce d'oro, 1964); Frances A. Yates, *Theatre of the World* (Chicago, IL: University of Chicago Press, 1969); Lynda G. Christian, *Theatrum Mundi: The History of an Idea* (New York: Garland, 1987). Further insights into the metaphoric value of the *theatrum mundi* with a focus on the French tradition are found in *Theatrum mundi: Studies in Honor of Ronald W. Tobin*, ed. by Claire L. Carlin and Kathleen Wine (Charlottesville, VA: Rookwood Press, 2003); for the British context, see *'If Then the World a Theatre Present...': Revisions of the Theatrum Mundi Metaphor in Early Modern England*, ed. by Björn Quiring (Berlin and Boston, MA: De Gruyter, 2014).
8   William Egginton, *How the World Became a Stage: Presence, Theatricality, and the Question of Modernity* (Albany: State University of New York Press, 2003); and *Theatricality*, ed. by Tracy C. Davis and Thomas Postlewait (Cambridge: Cambridge University Press, 2005).
9   On the vexed question of the Globe's motto, see Richard Dutton, '*Hamlet, An Apology for Actors,* and The Sign of the Globe', in *Shakespeare Survey*, ed. by Stanley Wells (Cambridge: Cambridge University Press, 1989), pp. 35–44; Tiffany Stern, 'Was *Totus Mundus Agit Histrionem* ever the motto of the Globe Theatre?', *Theatre Notebook*, 51.3 (1997), 122–27; and, more recently, the point made by Thomas Postlewait, 'Theatricality and Antitheatricality in Renaissance London', in *Theatricality*, ed. by Davis and Postlewait, pp. 90–126 (p. 99).

altogether.) A variation on the trope of the *theatrum mundi*, the poem outlines the progress of human life according to a multi-section structure that evokes the division in prologue, acts, and epilogue typical of classical drama:

> Man's life's a Tragedie. His mother's womb
> (From which he enters) is the tyring room.
> This spacious earth the theater. And the stage
> That country which he lives in: Passions, Rage,
> Folly, and Vice are actors. The first cry
> The Prologue to th' ensewing Tragedy.
> The former act consisteth of dumb showes:
> The second, he to more perfection growes:
> I' th' third he is a man, and doth begin
> To nurture vice, and act the deeds of sin.
> I' th' fourth declines. I' th' fifth diseases clog
> And trouble him: the Death's his Epilogue.[10]

From birth to death, men and women play their part on the stage of the world. Their life is marked by tragedy, for human kind's perfection is inevitably corrupted by passions, rage, folly, and vice. The poem revisits the same ideas that were at the core of Macbeth's monologue, which, by the time of Wotton's return to London from Venice was available in the 1623 folio. At the same time, the poem touches upon the very concept that inspired the morality plays written by Fabio Glissenti for the orphans of the Venetian hospitals, including *La Morte innamorata*: namely, the allegorical dramatisation of everyman's struggle with life and the importance of committing to the salvation of the soul. Serendipitous coincidences continue when one considers that this variation on the trope of the *theatrum mundi* was also the overarching concern of another work by Fabio Glissenti, the *Discorsi morali contra il dispiacer del morire*, an *ars moriendi* [art of dying well] published in Venice in 1596, a book that, as I will show, is entirely conceived according to theatrical metaphors.[11] Eminently didactic in their aim, both the *Discorsi morali* and Glissenti's plays pursue a process of literalisation of the *theatrum mundi* metaphor that captures the very essence of the trope, bridging across drama as a performative event and theatre as a tool able to promote spiritual practice, discipline, and meditation.

As such, the *theatrum mundi* metaphor illustrates the porosity of two notions — drama and theatre — that, while undoubtedly interrelated, index different features of early modern performative culture. In the present study, I use the terms 'drama' and 'dramatic' to refer to works conceived as texts for the stage (in other words, texts whose full fruition entails the idea of a dramatic action performed by actors, no matter whether or not the staging actually takes place). By 'theatre' and 'theatrical' I refer instead to the broader notion of theatre as a space that, be it real or metaphorical, allows for the framing of performative events while also evoking

---

10   *Reliquiae Wottonianae. Or, a collection of lives, letters, poems; with characters of sundry personages: and other incomparable pieces of language and art. By the curious pensil of the ever memorable Sir Henry Wotton* (London: Thomas Maxey, 1651), pp. 539–40.

11   Fabio Glissenti, *Discorsi morali contra il dispiacer del morire. Detto Athanatophilia* (Venice: Domenico Farri, 1596) [henceforth, *DM*]; for a detailed discussion of this work, see Chapter 2.

ideas of spectatorship and vision. As this distinction suggests, while dramatic works, at least in principle, tend to fall under the purview of theatre, the breadth of the 'theatrical' may encompass writings that are not necessarily dramatic or conceived for the stage. Yet, it is the intersection of the 'dramatic' and the 'theatrical' that, as this book aims to show, proves particularly fertile when it comes to assessing the interplay of allegorical drama and spiritual practice. My own analysis thus contributes to recent developments in theatre and performance studies that, by complicating the terms 'drama' and 'theatre', have made room for the study of hybrid forms of theatricality in which the boundaries between the texts themselves and their performative consumption wear thin.[12]

★ ★ ★ ★ ★

By making works such as Glissenti's speak to other sources, either explicitly conceived as theatrical or deeply informed by theatrical structures, this book focuses on a feature of the *theatrum mundi* trope, largely overlooked by scholars, that is — I argue — key to new uses of the metaphor at the outset of modernity: namely, the potential unleashed by a strictly performative treatment of the metaphor itself. More precisely, I contend that it is through its own staging that the *theatrum mundi* metaphor displays its most substantial meaning: not simply a trope suggesting a correspondence between the world and the theatre, but a framework within which to effect various forms of discipline (moral, political, religious, etc.). Crucial to this dynamic is the attempt to promote the inner staging of the world on the spiritual stage of the soul, which was systematically pursued by allegorical drama in the decades around 1600. A case in point is that of Fabio Glissenti's morality plays, which were composed to be performed as part of the pedagogical entertainments of the female orphans of the *ospedali* of Venice. The plays move from the staging of the world to the staging of the soul in a double sense. First, the action moves gradually from the stage of the world (in fact, the world is explicitly indicated as the scene upon which most dramas are set) to the stage of one's soul or conscience (which, as we will see, is the other setting — indeed, a scene — that Glissenti imagines for his moralities). Second, the interiorisation of the performative experience is further enabled by the consumption of the plays beyond the performances, specifically as books to be read, meditated upon, and, so to speak, staged by readers in their own minds, a post-performance afterlife that turns them into spiritual exercises.

In this particular acceptation, the *theatrum mundi* and its counterpart, the *theatrum animae*, entail the paradoxical coincidence of the setting (either the world or the soul) and the protagonists of the action. Not only does the World appear as a character while also being the space upon which the action unfolds, but he also shares the stage with personified allegories representing the various functions of the human soul, which are given dramatic shape. Thus, I maintain that the intersection of these inward and outward dynamics counts among the features peculiar to the use of the

---

12   For a lucid assessment of the problem, see Michael Meere, 'Introduction', in *French Renaissance and Baroque Drama: Text, Performance, Theory*, ed. by Michael Meere (Newark: University of Delaware Press, 2015), pp. xv–xxi.

theatrum mundi metaphor in the late Renaissance and throughout the Baroque age. Paramount to these dynamics and to the possibility of staging the metaphor are the spatial implications that it entails. Literally a *topos*, the *theatrum mundi* is indeed a 'place'; in fact, a double one, in that it evokes both the theatre and the world.

Theatre, since classical antiquity, is the space that, by bringing some sort of action onto some sort of stage, opens up a window onto the world and human life. As indicated by its etymology, which goes back to the Greek verb θεάομαι ('to view', 'to watch', 'to be a spectator of something'), theatre *is* about vision, in that it shows things to the audience. The kind of vision entailed by theatre, though, is not merely the one that involves the physical eyes. As Aristotle puts it in the *Poetics*, the actual spectacle (what the audience *does* see on stage) is certainly important, but not essential to the profound work that a dramatic text is meant to do.[13] More important is the inner vision (not necessarily a 'visual' one) that drama triggers in the audience. The eyes of the mind, according to classical rhetoric from Aristotle and Demetrius to Cicero, Quintilian, and Pseudo-Longinus, are those which any effective form of verbal communication should be targeting. In this interplay between 'sight' and 'vision' (the same interplay that, by the way, informs another keyword germane to theatre, 'theory') lies the mirroring effect that ties theatre to the other space implicated by the metaphor of the *theatrum mundi*: the world.[14]

Due to the lexical ambiguity of the term *theatrum* throughout the Middle Ages, only partially cleared by the humanist recovery of ancient theatre, the metaphor revolved around the basic idea of men and women performing their lives in front of a judging audience.[15] According to the moral understanding of the metaphor, men and women are deemed to be facing a life of misery and struggle, drawn into a *ludus* (game) like the victims in a Roman amphitheatre more than treading the boards like actors on stage. When the philosophical legacy of this tradition merged with the theological perspective of Christian doctrine, the metaphor became a crude eschatological warning. In conjunction with its metaphorical use in book titles that echoed the rediscovery of theatre as an architectural structure suitable for shaping and organising knowledge, the *theatrum mundi* lent itself to expressing the misery of human life.[16]

---

13   Aristotle, *Poetics*, 1449b 31–32; in the Aristotelian lexicon of drama, spectacle includes all the things that fall under the category of *opsis*, 'sight'; on Aristotle's *opsis*, see G. M. Sifakis, 'The Misunderstanding of *opsis* in Aristotle's *Poetics*', in *Performance in Greek and Roman Theatre*, ed. by George Harrison and Vayos Liapis (Leiden and Boston, MA: Brill, 2013), pp. 45–62.
14   On recent developments about the cultural and etymological intersections of 'theatre' and 'theory', see Ramona Mosse, 'Thinking Theatres beyond Sight: From Reflection to Resonance', *Anglia*, 136.1 (2018), 138–53.
15   A detailed account of this tradition is offered by Christian, *Theatrum mundi*; on notions of theatre and drama in the European Middle Ages, with a focus on the material features of theatrical events, see the canonical work of William Tydeman, *The Theatre in the Middle Ages: Western European Stage Conditions, c. 800–1576* (Cambridge: Cambridge University Press, 1978).
16   On the metaphorical use of theatre as a framing device for encyclopaedic and scientific works in early modernity, see Ann Blair, *The Theater of Nature: Jean Bodin and Renaissance Science* (Princeton, NJ: Princeton University Press, 1997).

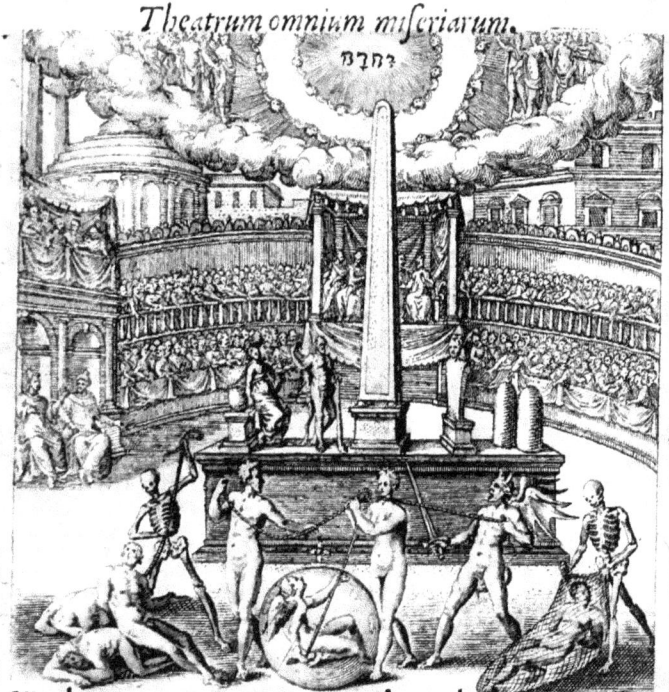

FIG. I.1. Boissard, *Theatrum Vitae Humanae* (1596), p. 1

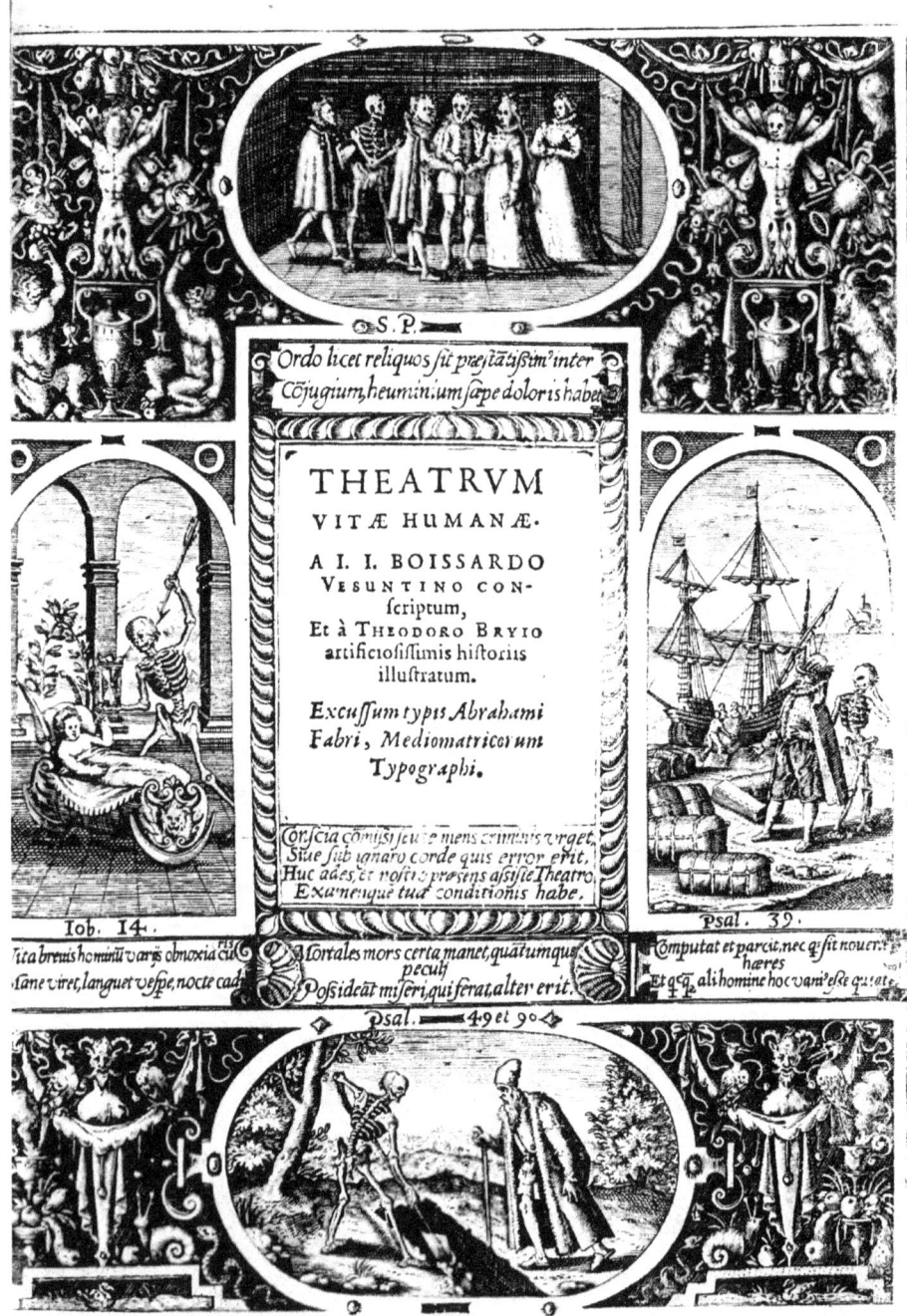

FIG. I.2. Boissard, *Theatrum Vitae Humanae* (1596), title page

The idea of life-as-a-tragedy thus acquired a truly emblematic status. Its allegedly universal value is captured most effectively by the use of personifications such as those evoked in the aforementioned poem 'De Morte'. The protagonist of life, Man — who stands for the whole human kind — shares the stage of the poem (that is, the stage of the world) with 'actors' (Passions, Rage, Folly, Vice, now duly capitalised) that lead him to 'act the deeds of sin'. The situation described by the poem is very similar to plays such as the ones that Henry Wotton attended in Venice (*La Morte innamorata* being a case in point), but it also resonates with actual emblems that poets of Wotton's generation were familiar with. To stick to felicitous coincidences, an instructive example comes from Jean-Jacques Boissard's beautifully illustrated *Theatrum Vitae Humanae*, first printed in 1596, the same year in which Fabio Glissenti published his own *ars moriendi*.[17] Boissard's first chapter reminds the reader that 'Vita humana est tanquam theatrum omnium miseriarum' [human life is like the theatre of all miseries]. In the accompanying image [Fig. I.1], which functions as a prologue to Boissard's history of the human kind from God's creation of the world to the Last Judgment, men and women in a circus are not vexed by gladiators.

As explained in the Latin verses below the image, they are tormented by Flesh, Sin, Death and Satan.[18] In the allegorical representation of life as a fight between the human soul and sinful temptations, which revives the late antique tradition of the psychomachia canonised by Prudentius, sinners are chained to Evil and are hardly able to free themselves.[19] Their earthly performance, judged by an unforgiving audience, determines their fate. The 'theatre of human life' thus showcases a play, whose protagonist (Man) shares the stage of the world with dangerous co-protagonists that pester him till the end of the performance. This sinister theatre promotes a meditation on life as an inexorable race towards death, a *memento mori* powerfully summarised by the frontispiece of Boissard's *Theatrum*, which pictures the stages of human life, from birth to death, all characterised by the looming presence of the Grim Reaper, according to an iconographic trope that is at work in Glissenti's own literary production as well [Fig. I.2].

In Boissard's emblem book, the *theatrum mundi* metaphor is not only alluded to, but fully staged and used as a systematic lens through which to look at human life. The staging visualised by the illustration is meant to provide the reader with a visual prompt for a meditation that, eventually, ought to be processed by the eyes of the mind. The spiritual relevance of the image, its being a 'play' to be performed in one's mind (or, to turn to the lexicon of spirituality and devotional literature, to be

---

17   Jean-Jacques Boissard, *Theatrum Vitae Humanae* (Metz: Abraham Faber, 1596).
18   Boissard, *Theatrum*, p. 1: 'Vita hominis tanquam circus, vel grande theatrum est: | Quod tragici ostentat cuncta referta metus. | Hoc lasciva caro, peccatum, morsque, Satanque | Tristi hominem vexant, exagitantque modo'. See Björn Quiring, 'Introduction', in, *'If Then the World a Theatre Present...'*, ed. by Quiring, p. 8.
19   On the seminal role played by Prudentius in the establishment of the psychomachia tradition, see Rita Copeland and Peter Struck, 'Introduction', in *The Cambridge Companion to Allegory*, pp. 1–11 (pp. 6–7). On the ensuing iconographic tradition, see Joanne S. Norman, *Metamorphoses of an Allegory: The Iconography of the Psychomachia in Medieval Art* (New York: Peter Lang, 1988).

performed in one's heart) resonates with other iconographic treatments of the trope. An eloquent example is the first emblem from Francesco Pona's *Cardiomorphoseos* (1645), a book of sacred emblems devoted to the metamorphosis of the heart.[20] The image [Fig. I.3] is an overtly theatrical version of the psychomachia, in which the heart symbolises the human soul: it is represented on stage, being freed from the chains of vice and, as per the Latin motto 'Liber En ad Te Redeo' [eventually freed, I return to you], ready to return to God. The theatrical inspiration of the emblem is unveiled in the accompanying poem, which focuses on the allegorical fight between Heart, Flesh, World, and Satan, the same dangerous jailers that harassed men and women in Boissard's *Theatrum*.[21]

These scattered examples suggest that, by regaining its literal meaning, the metaphor of the *theatrum mundi* triggers an understanding of human life *sub specie theatri*, while also reviving the idea of theatre as a device that enables a kind of vision different from eyesight. This dynamic is captured by a variety of sources that demonstrate the productive link between the idea of theatre as a building and theatre as a mental projection, that is, an inner space within which thoughts can be made visible to the eyes of the mind. Experiences as diverse as those of Giulio Camillo (1480–1544) in Italy and Robert Fludd (1574–1637) in England indicate that the architectural design of the theatre provided philosophers with an instrument of knowledge based on the spatiality of theatre itself. In both Camillo and Fludd, theatre is not about visualising what is staged, but about using the space to arrange and increase one's knowledge. An oft-quoted description of Camillo's theatre, found in a letter sent from Venice by Wigle van Zwichem to Erasmus of Rotterdam in 1532, is worth quoting here:

> The author has different names for his theatre: artificial soul and mind, or endowed with windows. He says, in fact, that all the things that the human mind conceives [*omnia quae mens humana concipit*] but that cannot be seen with the eyes of the body [*quaeque corporeis oculis videre non possumus*] can, however, with careful consideration, be expressed with some bodily signs [*signis deinde quibusdam corporeis*], so that everyone can see directly with his own eyes all that which otherwise is submerged in the depths of the human mind [*in profundo mentis humanae*].[22]

---

20 Francesco Pona, *Cardiomorphoseos sive ex corde desumpta emblemata sacra* (Verona: n.pub., 1645); see Armando Maggi, 'Visual and Verbal Communication in Francesco Pona's *Cardiomorphoseos* (1645)', *Word & Image*, 16.2 (2000), 212–24; Irene Gallinaro, 'Il "Cardiomorphoseos" di Francesco Pona', *Lettere italiane*, 56.4 (2004), 570–601.

21 The Latin poem that illustrates the emblem is entitled 'Peccator ad se reversus. Rhythmus Apodos'. For the allegorical personifications mentioned in it, see the following passage in Pona, pp. 1–2: 'Errabam coecus, devius, | Septus hinc inde sordibus. | Mancipium hostis inferi, | Catenis vinctus horridis. || Forti (heu nimis) imperio, | Caro iam Carni insederat: | Mundusque iam seduxerat | Palantem (vafer) animum. || Retia saepe Diaboli | Subivit desiderium: | Foedo Voluntas aucupi | Praedam se dedit miseram' [I wandered, sightless and lonely, surrounded by filth everywhere; slave to the infernal enemy, tied to horrible chains. My body leaned against Flesh's too forceful power; the cunning World lured my wandering spirit; Devil's trap often penetrated my desire; my will gave itself as a miserable prey to the deceitful goat].

22 The passage is quoted and discussed by Lina Bolzoni, *La stanza della memoria: modelli letterari e iconografici nell'età della stampa* (Turin: Einaudi, 1995), p. 161; for the English translation, see *The*

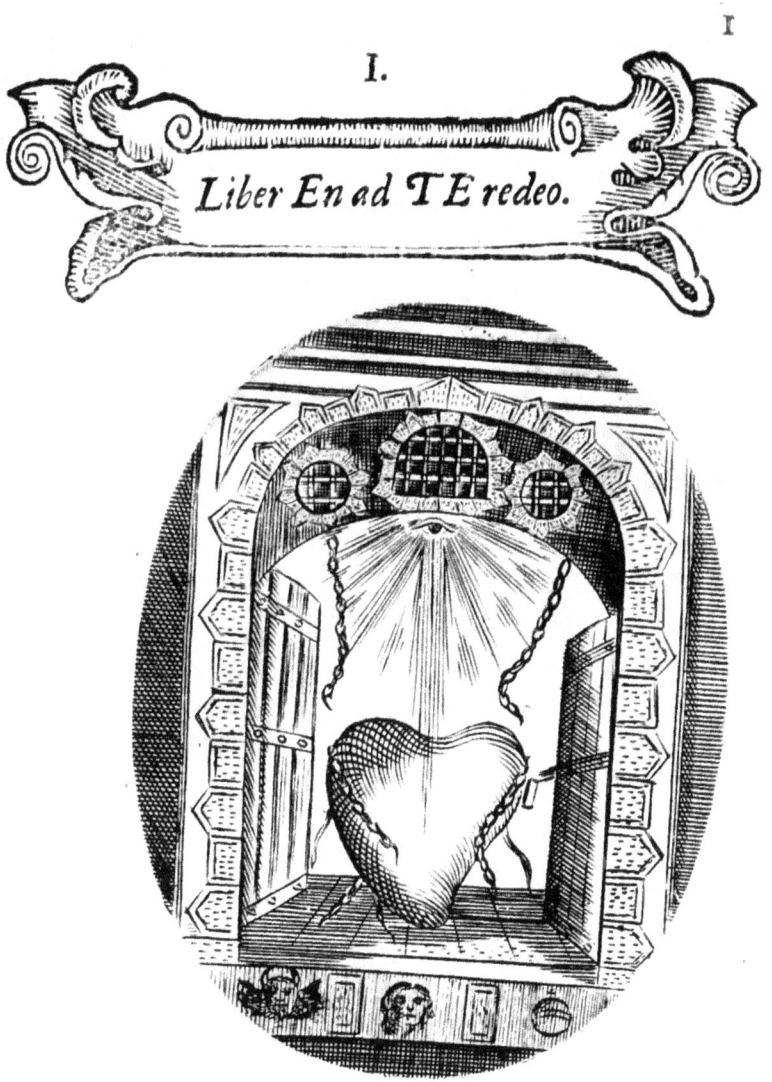

Peccator ad se reuersus.
Rythmus Apodos.

TE laudamus Dominum,
  Celsum Cęlorum Principem;
  Tibi vouemus Canticum:
Tibi Triumphum canimus.

Potentię tu fastigium,
  Tu Sapientię culmina
  Tu Bonitatis apices
  Tenes, regnans in secula.
          A   Errabam

FIG. I.3. Pona, *Cardiomorphoseos* (1645), p. 1

As suggested by Zwichem's insightful description, Camillo is not concerned with the pessimistic tradition of the *theatrum mundi*. The theatre, at the centre of which the actor achieves the union of microcosm and macrocosm, is what makes visible the invisible. It is a window open on the human soul. It allows man to perform a mental (one could say spiritual) exercise that makes it possible for the individual to find, and eventually reveal, what is buried deep in the human mind.[23] Even if Camillo's theatre had or was meant to have some sort of material existence, it was not made for staging theatrical performances. One could say that Camillo made the metaphor of the *theatrum mundi* as literal as it can be: the world is indeed made fit the theatre's space, with the focus shifting from the theatrical stage to the theatre as a whole, which does become a substitute for the world. While Camillo's project remains exceptional, the tension between outer and inner worlds that informs it is also at the core of further uses of the *theatrum mundi* throughout the sixteenth and seventeenth centuries.

The relationship between the metaphor and the theatrical culture of early modernity has been explored, notably by Frances A. Yates in her comparative study of Robert Fludd's Memory Theatre and Shakespeare's Globe, as well as in the important scholarly tradition that, since Yates and through the studies of Lina Bolzoni, has shed light on Giulio Camillo's own 'teatro della memoria'.[24] Paradoxically, however, one question has been overlooked: how does the metaphor of the 'world as a stage' work when it is returned to the materiality of the theatrical performance? In other words, what happens when the *theatrum mundi* metaphor is actually staged? What happens when the metaphor ceases to be a statement uttered by a character and becomes the structuring and spatial framework of a play?

★ ★ ★ ★ ★

By raising these questions, this book aims to reassess our understanding of early modern theatricality, arguing that the use of theatrical metaphors *within* dramatic genres unveils both their deeper implications and the reasons for the fascination they exert in the modern world. More precisely, by looking at the *theatrum mundi* not only as a metaphor entailing a correspondence between the world and the theatre, but as the very object brought on stage, I contend that the metaphor becomes a framing device conducive to forms of moral and spiritual disciplining. Essential to this argument is the second feature of allegorical drama that this monograph

---

Gallery of Memory: Literary and Iconographic Models in the Age of the Printing Press, trans. by Jeremy Parzen (Toronto: University of Toronto Press, 2000), p. 159.
23 Corrado Bologna, 'Esercizi di memoria. Dal "Theatro della sapientia" di Giulio Camillo agli "Esercizi spirituali" di Ignazio di Loyola,' in *La cultura della memoria*, ed. by Lina Bolzoni and Pietro Corsi (Bologna: il Mulino, 1992), pp. 169–221.
24 Frances A. Yates, *The Art of Memory* (London: Routledge and Paul, 1966), pp. 129–72, 320–69; Lina Bolzoni, *La stanza della memoria*; but see also Lina Bolzoni, *Il teatro della memoria. studi su Giulio Camillo* (Padua: Liviana editoriale, 1984); eadem, 'Le tecniche della memoria e la costruzione degli spazi interiori fra Medioevo e Rinascimento', *Lettere italiane*, 55.1 (2003), 26–46; and Giulio Camillo, *L'idea del theatro con 'L'idea dell'eloquenza', Il 'De transmutatione' e altri testi inediti*, ed. by Lina Bolzoni (Milan: Adelphi, 2015).

addresses: the use of personified allegories, particularly when understood as a rhetorical tool aimed at promoting the inner staging of the world on the spiritual stage of the soul. As we shall see, allegorical drama shared such a device with the ever-growing corpus of literature concerned with practices of meditation and self-examination, powerfully revamped in Italy by the cultural agenda of the Catholic Counter-Reformation.[25]

Bearing in mind the examples mentioned so far, one could rephrase the main question at stake here as follows: what happens when instead of characters such as Jacques and Macbeth, who mention the metaphor in their monologues, the audience is faced with personifications that, as in the poem 'De Morte' or in Boissard's *Theatrum*, perform the metaphor? And, even more relevant to the present discussion: what happens when the metaphor is performed on stage? By addressing the question in these terms, I seek to illustrate the work done by allegorical drama and, more specifically, the systematic use of personified allegories in theatre at a key moment in the cultural history of Europe. While allegorical theatre was not new to the decades around 1600 (indeed, morality plays and other genres of allegorical drama flourished throughout the Middle Ages and the Renaissance), the pervasive theatricality peculiar to the period fostered a re-appropriation of theatrical metaphors within the context of drama that, as I show in this study, enhanced the performative potential of the allegorical code itself.[26]

It is fair to assume that Henry Wotton, the dedicatee of *La Morte innamorata*, recognised in the play the features of allegorical drama, a genre that had been very popular in his own country since the medieval period. If it is all too easy (and, after all, somewhat gratuitous) for us to diminish the aesthetic quality of plays such as *La Morte innamorata* vis-à-vis dramatic masterworks such as Shakespeare's *Macbeth*, it is certainly more fruitful to reflect on the fact that these works inhabited the same world and that their production and consumption demand a holistic approach. Moralities such as *La Morte innamorata* bear witness to the process of theatricalisation of the allegorical code that, for both didactic and spiritual purposes, blossomed through late antiquity and the Middle Ages. Based on influential models such as Prudentius's *Psychomachia*, and propagated by works as diverse as Boethius's *Consolation of Philosophy* and the *Roman de la Rose*, among others, narrative texts featuring personified allegories provided the medieval and early modern imagination with a set of situations easily transferable to the stage. The point was made convincingly by Armand Strubel in his pioneering study of the French *moralités*, where he identified a direct connection between the rise of allegorical theatre and the long-standing tradition of allegorical narratives. Along with highlighting the continuity that, in this respect, characterises the Middle Ages and the Renaissance, Strubel identifies the dynamics that inform allegorical drama

---

25 For a recent reassessment of the entanglements of allegory and theatre, see Elisabetta Selmi and Enrico Zucchi, eds, *Allegoria e teatro tra Cinque e Settecento: da principio compositivo a strumento esegetico* (Bologna: Emil, 2016), particularly Elisabetta Selmi, 'Prolegomeni all'allegoria teatrale: "Nel labirinto delle idee confuse". Alcune considerazioni', pp. i–xxx.
26 Particularly useful to my use of the lexicon of performance and performativity is the theoretical framework outlined by Egginton, *How the World Became a Stage*.

in terms that are worth reviewing:

> Le corpus des Moralités constitue un aboutissement de la tradition allégorique: il offre une anthologie des motifs et schémas de la littérature des deux siècles antérieurs, et les montre sous une forme immédiatement accessible. Dans la Moralité, on a l'impression que se réalise le rêve de l'écriture allégorique, la figuration par le visuel et le concret, de l'invisible. Sans doute représente-t-elle la forme la plus naïve et la plus efficace de la création allégorique.[27]

> [The corpus of moralities stems from the allegorical tradition: it offers a collection of motifs and patterns from the literature of the two previous centuries, and it reshapes them in a form that is immediately accessible. Moralities seem to achieve the dream of allegorical writing, that is, the visualisation of the invisible. They undoubtedly are the most naïve and effective kind of allegorical creation.]

The forcefulness of the allegorical code lies in the possibility of giving visual shape to what would otherwise be invisible. The appeal of such a device, whose rhetorical and poetical status will be discussed in Chapter 1, is didactic in the first place, providing models and dramatic patterns ready for the stage. On the one hand, the personification acts in front of the audience: conveyed by the body of the actor, a given concept becomes tangible; on the other, the personification is given a voice and, through words, it gives shape to thoughts. Speaking about themselves, as well as by describing their attributes, personifications as diverse as Fortune, Nature, Reason, and Death achieve the status of *imagines agentes*: by 'doing something', as per the definition found in *Rhetorica ad Herennium*, these active images bring in front of the audience's eyes the theatre of human life that all men and women are asked to engage with.[28] If rhetorical efficacy is, as I will suggest, what contributes to making the images 'performative', it is by personifying abstract notions and making them act in front of the audience that performativity is achieved in its fullest sense. Similarly, the personifications of *La Morte innamorata* are performative in a double sense: they 'perform' on stage at once with 'performing' the functions entailed by their names.[29]

One of the reasons why we enjoy today Macbeth's inner struggles more than the self-explanatory arguments dramatised by medieval and early modern moralities lies in our perception of the artificial mechanisms that inform allegory. Even a markedly negative character such as Iago in Shakespeare's *Othello* (a character that, as indicated by Shakespeare scholars, is much indebted to the mono-dimensional features traditionally assigned to the personification of Vice) proves more interesting to modern sensibility than his allegorical counterparts in the moralities of the time. The paradoxical tension that distances the artificial dichotomies of the allegorical code (Reason–Sense, Virtue–Vice, Soul–Flesh, Life–Death, etc.) from the ambiguous complexity of human nature (where the distinction between

---

27 Armand Strubel, *'Grant senefiance a': allégorie et littérature au Moyen Âge* (Paris: Champion, 2002), p. 319.
28 *Rhetorica ad Herennium*, 3.37; for a discussion of this passage, see Chapter 1, pp. 24–25.
29 For an overview of the lexical clusters of performance and performativity, see *Performativity and Performance*, ed. by Andrew Parker and Eve Kosofsky Sedgwick (New York: Routledge, 1996).

Good and Evil is far from unclouded) gradually made the language of allegorical personifications obsolete.

According to Ernst H. Gombrich's discussion of the 'icones symbolicae' [symbolic images] that populated early modern imagination, the Age of the Enlightenment is the chronological limit beyond which personifications went irremediably out of fashion.[30] In spite of the problematic nature of any chronological generalisation, Gombrich's point holds. Moving from personifications such as those found in the Milanese library of Sant'Alessandro and described by the Barnabite preacher Cristoforo Giarda (1595–1649) in a sermon that inspired the title of his own essay, Gombrich builds a compelling argument about the peculiar function that those images performed in the early seventeenth-century context in which they were created. In Giarda's own words, the images are not mere 'signs' built on a set of conventions (though conventions, as I shall recall shortly, inform their very essence), but the tangible (or, better, visible) translation of the concepts that they represent. As such, they are directly related to the realm of ideas and offer the observer a bridge to reconnect with the ideas themselves.[31] Thanks to a system of allegedly reliable representation, humans can gain at least some partial access to the domain of the higher intelligences, from which they are normally excluded. According to the markedly Neoplatonic nuance of the preacher's theoretical framework, the symbolic value of those images lies in their being a substitute for the intellectual objects that they signify. Their performative function is set in motion by the gap that separates the perception-based experience of the images and the intellectual content of the abstract notions that they embody: it is in fact thanks to such divide that knowledge's desire is instilled in the observer.

Giarda's Neoplatonic approach is not the only one at work in the early modern context that this book explores. In fact, it coexists and, to some extent, merges with a more properly Aristotelian tradition, which privileges the role of conventions in the establishment of any lexicon, including the language of images. The slippery distinction between the two traditions, which, for clarity's sake, can be summarised by the juxtaposition of symbol and allegory, fuels a most diverse corpus of texts and images that, throughout the Middle Ages and early modernity, filled the European imagination with innumerable personifications.[32] Be they deemed 'symbolic' (hence bearers of some essential connection with the ideas) or 'allegorical' (hence the result of a conventional translation of concepts into signs), such images share the same goal: they make visible what is *per se* devoid of visual substance; they give a body to what is bodiless; they give a voice to what is voiceless. By doing so, they

---

30   Ernst H. Gombrich, 'Icones Symbolicae: Philosophies of Symbolism and their Bearing on Art', in Ernst H. Gombrich, *Symbolic Images: Studies in the Art of the Renaissance* (London: Phaidon Press Limited, 1972), pp. 123–91.
31   Cristoforo Giarda, *Bibliothecae Alexandrinae Icones Symbolicae* (Milan: Melchiorre Malatesta, 1626), p. 1.
32   On the historical, cultural, and theoretical intricacies that characterise discussions of allegory and symbol, see Angus Fletcher, *Allegory: The Theory of a Symbolic Mode* (Ithaca, NY: Cornell University Press, 1965); Simon Brittan, *Poetry, Symbol, and Allegory: Interpreting Metaphorical Language from Plato to the Present* (Charlottesville, VA, and London: University of Virginia Press, 2003); Jeremy Tambling, *Allegory*, The New Critical Idiom (London: Routledge, 2010).

participate in an anthropomorphic system of signs that expose their performative dimension.

* * * * *

In order to address the performative turn that, as I argue, fuels the early modern interplay of theatrical metaphors and allegorical discourse across theatre and spiritual practice, this book follows two main axes. First, I engage with the rhetorical tradition, deep-rooted in classical antiquity, that contributed to the early modern theoretical codification of allegorical personification as a figure of speech and thought. In particular, I focus on the ways in which personification was conceptualised as a 'performative' figure, exploring the place it held in theories of image-making and drama. Second, by turning to literary and theatrical works from the decades around 1600, I show that the systematic use of personified allegories in conjunction with theatrical metaphors such as the *theatrum mundi* transformed drama into a device able to open a window on the soul while also offering a space for the 'staging' (or 'performance') of one's conscience.

In Chapter 1, I look at personification as a figure of speech and thought that, first theorised by Greek and Latin rhetoricians, gained particular importance in early modern rhetoric, when its fluid theoretical status intersected multiple areas of knowledge and artistic production, including drama. I follow theoretical discussions of the figure in debates about the communicative power of words and images, focusing on those treatments that were especially relevant to the use of personification in theatre. By doing so, I show that the making of personified allegories in the early modern period was informed by theoretical concerns that were also at the core of concurrent discussions about the rhetoric and poetics of the visual arts. The entanglement of these various domains is illustrated through select examples from the broad corpus of morality and spiritual plays produced in Italy within the first half of the seventeenth century. After reviewing theoretical works by intellectuals as diverse as Francesco Bonciani, Giovanni Andrea Gilio, Gabriele Paleotti, and Emanuele Tesauro, among others, I turn to dramas by Giovan Battista Andreini, Agostino Manni, Bonaventura de Venere, Bonaventura Morone, and Troilo Lancetta, which, in different ways, speak to the interconnections of theatre, image-making, and spiritual practice. By explaining in what sense the *imagines agentes* of classical rhetoric may be understood and described as truly performative, Chapter 1 paves the way for the case studies explored in the following sections of the book.

Chapter 2 looks at the ways in which the performative framing of the *theatrum mundi* metaphor enabled forms of experimentation in spiritual literature. The example at the core of this section draws on the tradition of the *ars moriendi*: namely, Fabio Glissenti's *Discorsi morali contra il dispiacer del morire detto Athanatophilia*, published in Venice in 1596. After introducing the author — a doctor originally from Brescia, who studied medicine in Padua before settling in Venice, where he worked in the local *ospedali* — I dwell on this work that stands out as a most bizarre product of the Venetian printing industry. Conceived as a five-day dialogue involving a

Courtier and a Philosopher, it is presented by the author as a mirror of the 'tragedy of human life'. Entirely built according to theatrical tropes, and provided with a rich iconographic apparatus which I will examine in detail, the book is meant to guide the reader through a spiritual journey towards the acceptance of death. In Glissenti's dialogue, the city of Venice becomes a stage that, through images and words, summarises the features of the world as well as the inevitable fate of human life. Concerned with theatre not merely in metaphorical terms (in fact, it includes a critique of drama's place within the social fabric of the time), this peculiar work is a fit introduction to the actual stage on which the present investigation reaches its completion.

By bringing us back to the context of the Venetian hospitals from where this introduction began, Chapter 3 explores the other facet of Fabio Glissenti's production: a corpus of ten morality plays that the physician composed over the first two decades of the seventeenth century. The plays, largely based on narrative materials included in the *Discorsi morali*, were written for the female orphans based in the hospitals of Venice and were meant to be staged during Carnival. As such, they functioned as a moralised (and moralising) response to the variety of secular theatrical events that were held in the city at that time of the year. Inspired by the Latinate model of Jesuit school drama, Glissenti's plays aimed at the spiritual education of both performers and spectators by combining comic and serious components. Drawing on the medieval tradition of sacred drama, powerfully revived in Baroque Italy, the playwright combines stock characters and allegorical personifications, which are summoned to stage the inner conflicts of the individual as well as the fight between the spiritual and the earthly components of human life. As such, Glissenti's use of personified allegories bridges across spiritual practice and theatrical performance. At the same time, I posit that Glissenti's dramatic production is part of a consistent pedagogical project that, in line with the scope of the *Discorsi morali*, goes beyond the specific occasions on which the plays were actually staged. Indeed, such a project finds its ultimate outcome in forms of meditative reading that allow for the virtual staging of the plays in the 'theatre' of one's own conscience.

The convergence of performance and performativity is at the core of my conclusion, where I turn to yet another serendipitous connection that, in unexpected ways, sheds retrospective light on the allegorical moralities of early Seicento Venice. There I look at the 1987 revival of *La Morte innamorata* at the Accademia Nazionale d'Arte Drammatica in Rome. Directed by Luca Ronconi, the play was staged alongside Giovan Battista Andreini's comedy *Amor nello specchio* [Love in the Mirror] (1622). The two works could not be more different in nature and purpose: Glissenti's embodies the anxiety about salvation after death that was at the core of post-Tridentine Christian education; Andreini's celebrates the realm of the senses (as well as the confusion that may come through the senses) by exploring the risky business of same-sex attraction. Yet, as Ronconi's attempt to bring them together suggests, the two plays converge around the Baroque fascination with the possibilities entailed by theatrical fiction and its power to construct (and deconstruct) identities. The mirror, recurrent image of vanity in

Glissenti's morality plays, functions as a narcissistic source of love and an ambiguous instrument of knowledge in Andreini's comedy. Similarly, the theatre is a site that allows for the staging of both cautionary tales and uncannily appealing situations. Moving from the unusual pairing of *La morte innamorata* and *Amor nello specchio*, I propose to situate the experience of Counter-Reformation spiritual drama within a broader set of cultural — specifically theatrical — trends that expose the peculiar status of theatre in the period. Ultimately, I argue that allegorical drama, hanging in the balance between actual performance and meditative consumption through reading, offers itself as a discourse able to capture and control spiritual concerns as well as cultural and social anxieties. It is by displacing them on the stage, no matter whether real or imagined, that its performative quality is achieved.

CHAPTER 1

Bodiless Objects in Human Shape: Personification across Rhetoric and Drama

The full title of the 1613 edition of Cesare Ripa's *Iconologia* [Iconology] printed in Siena is a veritable precis of the visual culture of early modernity. A widely read handbook of iconology, Ripa's manual for image-making is, in the Sienese edition, marketed as an encyclopaedic work not only with regards to its subject matter, but also and most importantly with reference to its all-encompassing purpose. As per the title page, *Iconologia* provides descriptions of images of virtues, vices, affects, human passions, arts, disciplines, humours, natural elements, celestial bodies, all the parts of the world, and other infinite subjects. As such, the book promises to assist orators, preachers, poets, painters, sculptors, draftsmen, and scholars in inventing concepts and emblems ('concetti, emblemi, ed imprese'), in devising all sorts of nuptial, funeral, and triumphal 'apparati', and in the staging of dramatic poems ('per rappresentar poemi drammatici'). Ultimately, the instructions gathered by Ripa allow for the visual representation of whatever may be conceived by the human mind ('figurare co' suoi propri simboli ciò che può cadere in pensiero umano').[1] When compared to the title of the first edition of 1593, where *Iconologia* was simply presented as 'useful to poets, painters, and sculptors', the Sienese print widens the range of genres that Ripa's work is relevant to.[2] Alongside images described, spoken about, painted, and sculpted, room is made for images that are brought to life through theatre: in other words, images that, through the bodies of actors and performers (as well as through their clothing, attributes, and other props), acquire the status of veritable *imagines agentes* (literally, 'active images', or,

---

1   Cesare Ripa, *Iconologia di Cesare Ripa perugino cavaliere de' Santi Mauritio, e Lazzaro, nella quale si descrivono diverse imagini di virtù, vitij, affetti, passioni humane, arti, discipline, humori, elementi, corpi celesti, provincie d'Italia, fiumi, tutte le parti del mondo, ed altre infinite materie. Opera utile ad oratori, predicatori, poeti, pittori, scultori, disegnatori, e ad ogni studioso, per inventar concetti, emblemi, ed imprese, per divisare qualsivoglia apparato nuttiale, funerale, trionfale. Per rappresentar poemi drammatici, e per figurare co' suoi propii simboli ciò, che può cadere in pensiero humano* (Siena: Matteo Florimi, 1613), title page.
2   Cesare Ripa, *Iconologia overo descrittione dell'imagini universali cavate dall'antichità et da altri luoghi da Cesare Ripa Perugino. Opera non meno utile, che necessaria a poeti, pittori, et scultori, per rappresentare le virtù, vitij, affetti, et passioni humane* (Rome: Giovanni Gigliotti, 1593), title page.

as I will suggest, 'performative' ones). While not explicit in the original title, the theatrical dimension of Ripa's images is implicit since the author's first *Proemio*, where the importance of facial expression to the making of effective images (in fact, personifications) is indeed compared to the 'passions' conveyed by the faces of actors on stage ('come in teatro').[3]

By turning to this theatrical simile, Ripa captures one of the key issues at stake in the theories of images that early modern cultures inherited from classical antiquity: the idea that images are more effective when seized in motion or action. The concept is rooted in Greek and Latin rhetoric, specifically in the interrelated notions of *energeia*, *enargeia*, and *evidentia*. From Aristotle and Demetrius to Cicero, Quintilian, and the anonymous author of the treatise *On the Sublime*, these rhetorical devices were deemed crucial to the pursuit of vivid verbal communication, particularly through the use of tropes such as the so-called 'active metaphor'.[4] However, the most literal way of making a speech active and vivid is achieved through drama, that is, when the audience faces the representation of an ongoing action in which deeds and words coincide. Classical rhetoricians were very well aware that oratory, poetry, and drama met under the aegis of vividness and action. Turning to the modern lexicon of literary criticism and theory, I propose to identify such encounter with the performative moment.

If the variety of meanings and acceptations of the term 'performative' makes it a slippery one, which needs to be handled with care, it is precisely its slippery nature that makes it fruitful in the present discussion. Indeed, 'performative' as in 'relevant to performance' (i.e., relevant to an act of performance intentionally presented as such) and 'performative' as in 'related to the linguistic sense of performative act' are the two facets of the images that this study is concerned with.[5] These are the

---

3   Ripa, *Iconologia overo descrittione*, fol. [4★]ᵛ: 'Dispositione nella testa sarà la positura alta, o bassa, allegra, o malinconica, et diverse altre passioni, che si scuoprono, come in Teatro nell'apparenza della faccia dell'huomo' [When it comes to the head, disposition will consist in its being high, low, merry or melancholic, and various other affections, which are shown, as in the theatre, by the appearance of a given man's face].
4   For the notion of 'active metaphor', see Aristotle, *Rhetoric* 1411a 28; Demetr. *De eloc.* 81; more precisely on the notion of *evidentia* as it stems from Aristotle's rhetorical discussion in conjunction with the theory of metaphor, see Sara Newman, 'Aristotle's Notion of "Bringing-Before-the-Eyes": Its Contributions to Aristotelian and Contemporary Conceptualizations of Metaphor, Style, and Audience', *Rhetorica*, 20.1 (2002), 1–23; for an introduction to the concept of *evidentia* in classical rhetoric, see Alessandra Manieri, *L'immagine poetica nella teoria degli antichi: phantasia ed energeia* (Pisa: IEPI, 1998); and Stijn Bussels, *The Animated Image: Roman Theory on Naturalism, Vividness and Divine Power* (Leiden: Leiden University Press, 2012), pp. 57–82.
5   For the distinction between 'performative', 'performativity', and 'performance', see Andrew Parker and Eve Kosofsky Sedgwick, 'Introduction', in *Performativity and Performance*, ed. by Parker and Sedgwick, pp. 1–18; and, more recently — with a summary review of seminal contributions to the theories of performance and performativity such as John L. Austin, *How to Do Things with Words* (Cambridge, MA: Harvard University Press, 1962), Judith Butler, *Gender Trouble: Feminism and the Subversion of Identity* [1990] (New York: Routledge, 2007), Richard Bauman and Charles L. Briggs, 'Poetics and Performance as Critical Perspectives on Language and Social Life', *Annual Review of Anthropology*, 19 (1990), 59–88 (p. 65), and Eggington, *How the World Became a Stage* — see Jessica Goethals and Eugenio Refini, 'Genre-Bending in Early Modern Performative Culture', *The Italianist*, 40.3 (2020), 317–26 (pp. 319–20).

images, which, as suggested by works such as Ripa's *Iconologia*, result from processes of image-making that hang in the balance between the metaphorical and the literal. In Ripa's own words, such images 'embrace' all things human: both the things that are 'inside us' and those that are 'in close proximity to us', such as 'concepts', ensuing 'habits' and the 'actions' that stem from them. According to Ripa, whose argument is based on Aristotle's theory of language, concepts are all those things, which can be 'signified through words': these include emblems and devices, which convey positive or negative statements about the specific features of someone or something.[6] Yet, Ripa's main concern in *Iconologia* revolves around 'images' strictly speaking, whose epistemological and linguistic status is compared to that of 'definitions', and which are most conveniently expressed through the human shape:

> le quali appartengono al nostro discorso, per la conformità che hanno con le definitioni; le quali solo abbracciano le virtù ed i vitii, o tutte quelle cose che hanno convenienza con questi o con quelle, senza affermare, o negare alcuna cosa, e per essere o sole privationi o habiti puri, si esprimono con la figura humana convenientemente.[7]
>
> [They belong to discourse due to the conformity they have with definitions, which encompass virtues and vices, or all those things that are appropriate to either, without affirming or denying anything; since they are pure habits or lack [of given qualities], they can conveniently be expressed by the human figure.]

As a matter of fact, Ripa's concise discussion of concepts and images identifies one specific rhetorical and poetical tool — personification — as the primary option for bridging across the verbal and the visual, especially when it comes to the representation of notions that are normally, so to speak, shapeless. By translating concepts or habits into human figures provided with specific physical features and carefully chosen attributes, artists and poets have the possibility to make the invisible visible. These images are indeed performative in that their names, definitions, and functions coincide (i.e., they *do* what they *are*), but their performative status is enhanced when they are given actual life through an act of performance. In other words (and here I align with critiques of John L. Austin's theory of performativity such as William Egginton's) it is through the performance that the performative potential of the image is made literal and comes to the fore.[8]

The image-making process at the core of Ripa's *Iconologia* hinges upon two main

---

6   Ripa, *Iconologia*, fol. †3ᵛ: 'Il secondo modo delle Imagini abbraccia quelle cose, che sono nell'huomo medesimo, o che hanno gran vicinanza con esso, come i concetti, et gli habiti, che da' concetti ne nascono, con la frequenza di molte attioni particolari; et concetti dimandiamo senza più sottile investigatione, tutto quello, che può esser significato con le parole; il qual tutto vien commodamente in due parti diviso. L'una parte è che afferma, o nega qualche cosa d'alcuno; l'altra, che no' [The second kind of images encompasses those things, which are either inside man himself or very close to him, as is the case with concepts and habits, which stem from the concepts thanks to the reiteration of many specific actions. We call concepts, without subtler inquiry, all those things that can be signified through words, which may be conveniently divided in two parts: one affirms or denies something about anyone; the other does not].
7   Ibid.
8   Egginton, *How the World Became a Stage*, pp. 17–18.

preoccupations: first, the status of images vis-à-vis the mechanisms of knowledge and the intellectual dynamics that inform their production; second, the rhetorical concern with vividness and the ways in which it can be achieved. Crucial to both is the notion of visualisation that, as I recalled in my introduction, is key to theatricality: as much as theatre is concerned with showing and seeing, so is image-making (specifically, the personification process described by Ripa) concerned with translating intellectual content into visible shapes. The shift from the rhetorical notion of personification to its theatrical and dramatic uses is the focus of this chapter. I will review classical and early modern sources that bear witness to the productive tensions that inhabit discourses about the making of images through words and the paradoxical attempt to give back to words a truly visual dimension. I begin by surveying the intersections of verbal and visual dynamics in the handling of concepts and images as they were theorised by classical rhetoric, focusing in particular on their relevance to critical discussions of allegorical personification. By outlining the entanglements of rhetoric and drama in classical accounts of the figure, I then seek to identify the premises of the performative turn that triggered early modern uses of personified allegories across verbal and visual communication. Examples from works of rhetoric, poetics, artistic literature, and drama will help me lay out the mechanisms that facilitated the understanding of theatre as a space (at once real and metaphorical) suitable for the visualisation and consumption of subject matter that normally escapes the purview of the visible.

Image-Making and Allegory's Loophole

Ripa's notion that images are meant to represent 'whatever may be conceived by the human mind' builds on long-standing discussions of the processes through which images are produced and entails an array of questions. Is image-making bound to imitating what exists in reality, or does it include the possibility of creating effigies of non-existing things? How do the mechanisms of verbal and visual representation interact within the making of images? To what extent do rhetorical devices such as metaphor and allegory bridge between the verbal and the visual? These questions are particularly urgent when one considers the translation of concepts into images such as those surveyed by Ripa, which, in a way, manage to give a visual shape to things that normally fall outside eyesight's realm.

Despite Plato's scepticism about mimesis, whereby image-making is looked at as a weak form of knowledge that, together with belief (πίστις), pertains to the field of fallible opinion (δόξα), the Platonic discussion of images outlines a theoretical framework conducive to important developments in early modern culture. In fact, Plato's distinction between imitation of existing things ('icastic mimesis') and imitation of non-existing things ('phantastic mimesis') paves the way for the idea that, as Flavius Philostratus puts it, 'imagination' (φαντασία) is 'a more skilful artist than imitation (σοφωτέρα μιμήσεως δημιουργός), an idea that, as I will indicate, proved crucial to early modern discussions of image-making.[9] Yet, as Philostratus himself specifies, the opposition between imitation and imagination does not

---

9   Plat. *Soph.* 235d–236c; Phil. *Vita Apoll.* 6.19.2.

entail a radical detachment of the latter from reality, for imagination (φαντασία) is, according to the ancients, a combinatory faculty rather than one that creates images from scratch.[10] After all, Aristotle himself had been very clear on this point already: if imagination — a medium term between sense-perception (αἴσθησις) and thought (διάνοια) — is the process through which 'it is possible to call up mental pictures, as those do who employ images in arranging their ideas under a mnemonic system', those pictures are meant to result from knowledge acquired through sense perception.[11] Even if Aristotle's notion of imagination is not concerned with the visualisation of objects that are devoid of existence outside the human mind, the comparison between image-making and the art of memory hints at the fact that images can indeed be 'seen' when the physical eyes are closed, a feature of the making and consumption of images that is key to the case studies explored in this book.[12]

The interrelatedness of image-making, memory, and inner visualisation is further unpacked by Cicero in Book 2 of *De oratore*, where he dwells on the possibility of visualising (and reusing) what has been previously captured by sense perception:

> It has been sagaciously discerned by Simonides or else discovered by some other person, that the most complete pictures are formed in our minds of the things that have been conveyed to them and imprinted on them by the senses [*a sensu tradita atque impressa*], but that the keenest of all our senses is the sense of sight [*sensum videndi*], and that consequently perceptions received by the ears or by reflexion can be most easily retained in the mind if they are also conveyed to our minds by the mediation of the eyes.[13]

Following in Aristotle's footsteps, Cicero states that stimuli received through the senses are the ones that touch our soul more deeply, and that, among them, those acquired through eyesight are the most forceful ones.[14] At the same time, Cicero widens sight's purview to include the mental visualisation not only of things actually 'seen', but also of things 'heard' and, most important, of things 'thought':

> with the result that things not seen and not lying in the field of visual discernment [*res caecas et ab aspectus iudicio remotas*] are earmarked by a sort of outline and image and shape [*conformatio quaedam et imago et figura*] so that we keep hold of as it were by an act of sight [*intuendo*] things that we can scarcely embrace by an act of thought [*cogitando*].[15]

The mental image, which Cicero describes through the terms *conformatio*, *imago*, *figura*, is thus able to represent things which physical eyesight would not normally be able to grasp and which, unless they are converted into mental images, are hard for the intellect to seize. Cicero does not provide any specific example for this kind

---

10   Phil. *Vita Apoll.* 6.19.2: 'Imitation will create what it knows, but imagination will also create what it does not know, conceiving it with reference to the real' (trans. by Jones, p. 155).
11   Arist. *De an.* 3, 427b 20–21 (trans. by Hett, pp. 156–57); see, also, Arist. *De an.* 3, 428b 11–14: 'imagination seems to be some kind of movement, and not to occur apart from sensation, but only to men when perceiving, and in connection with what is perceptible' (trans. by Hett, pp. 160–61).
12   Arist. *De an.* 428a 10–16.
13   Cic. *De or.* 2.87.357 (trans. by Sutton and Rackham, p. 469).
14   Similar points made in Arist. *De an.* 429a 1–5; Hor. *Ars poet.* 180–81.
15   Cic. *De or.* 2.87.357 (trans. by Sutton and Rackham, p. 469).

of images; yet, by insisting that they be housed in relevant 'places' in order to be memorised and reused, he also mobilises the lexicon of mnemotechnics, recalling that images can only be imagined as corporeal and that bodies cannot be imagined without a physical space within which to place them ('corpus intellegi sine loco non potest').[16] Cicero's following point is of even more significance, for it opens the discussion up to the idea that, in order to be effective, images ought to be endowed with the kind of power that I earlier proposed to call 'performative': in Cicero's own words, such images must be lively (literally, *imagines agentes*), sharp, distinctive, quick and capable of penetrating the soul of the listener.[17]

The performative dimension of these images as well as their relevance to the kind of image-making that Ripa is concerned with, including personification, are better understood in light of the discussion of memorable images found in the anonymous *Rhetorica ad Herennium*:

> We ought, then, to set up images of a kind that can adhere longest in the memory. And we shall do so if we establish likenesses as striking as possible; if we set up images that are not many or vague [*non multas nec vagas*], but doing something [*sed aliquid agentes imagines*]; if we assign to them exceptional beauty or singular ugliness; if we dress some of them with crowns or purple cloaks, for example, so that the likeness may be more distinct to us; or if we somehow disfigure them, as by introducing one stained with blood or soiled with mud or smeared with red paint, so that its form is more striking, or by assigning certain comic effects to our images, for that, too, will ensure our remembering them more readily. The things we easily remember when they are real [*res veras*] we likewise remember without difficulty when they are figments [*easdem fictas*], if they have been carefully delineated [*diligenter notatas*].[18]

Here, the term *imago agens* is taken literally: 'imagines agentes' are those images that 'do something'. The present participle, 'agentes', entails a twofold meaning: first, images of this kind *do* something in that they are imagined as performing an action; second, they *do* something in that they affect the audience. As such, these images display the rhetorical quality of *energeia* [action] that, according to Aristotle and Demetrius, is deemed particularly suitable to effective metaphors (the aforementioned 'active metaphors').[19] While Cicero's discussion is primarily concerned with the theoretical correspondence between concepts, images, and words, the anonymous author of *Rhetorica ad Herennium* sheds light on the actual ways in which *imagines agentes* do their work. Key to the dynamic described in the passage are the specific features assigned to the images, including physical traits (which are supposed to convey given passions and emotions) and objects (which are meant to recall specific events or deeds).

The mechanism described is quite similar to the system of iconographic attributes

---

16   Cic. *De or.* 2.87.358: 'a material object without a locality is inconceivable' (trans. by Sutton and Rackham, p. 469).
17   Ibid.: 'one must employ [...] images that are effective and sharply outlined and distinctive [*imaginibus autem agentibus, acribus, insignitis*], with the capacity of encountering and speedily penetrating the mind [*percutere animum*]' (trans. by Sutton and Rackham, p. 471).
18   *Rhet. ad Her.*: 3.37 (trans. by Caplan).
19   Arist. *Rhet.* 1411a 28; Demetr. *De eloc.* 81.

that is at the core of Ripa's image-making and which is traditionally associated with personification, specifically when a concept, notion, or non-human object (be it real or imagined) is given human shape. Whereas tangible objects, which are perceived through the senses, are understood, described, and turned into images based on their material features, the same cannot be said of those objects that do not have a body.[20] As Cicero puts it in *Topica*, it is only when intellectual subject matter of this kind is given a visual shape that it can leave a mark on the mind:

> by things which do not exist I mean those which cannot be touched or pointed out [*quae tangi demonstrarive non possunt*], but can, for all that, be perceived by the mind and comprehended [*cerni tamen animo atque intellegi possunt*]; for example, you might define acquisition by long possession, guardianship, *gens*, agnation; of these things there is no body [*quarum rerum nullum subest corpus*], but a clear pattern and understanding impressed on the mind, and this I call a notion [*quaedam conformatio insignita et impressa intellegentia, quam notionem voco*]. In the course of argumentation this notion frequently requires definition.[21]

By being assigned a shape, immaterial and non-existing things can be thought of as images, hence as notions that, within the construction of an effective argument, may need to be turned into definitions. The convergence of image, notion, and definition outlines an intellectual process very similar to the one described by Ripa in the *Proemio* to his *Iconologia*. As such, it speaks to the interrelatedness of the verbal and the visual when it comes to handling concepts as if they were images. Indicative of this interrelatedness is the use of the word *conformatio*, the same term used by Cicero in *De oratore* and, as we will see shortly, in *Rhetorica ad Herennium*, to indicate personification. The word *conformatio* translates the Greek τύπωσις, a technical term from the Stoic lexicon that indicates the visual dimension of both impressions and notions. According to a Stoic fragment recalled by Tobias Reinhardt ('an impression is a printing in the soul'), visual representation produces images that leave a stamp on the soul, with the notion of *phantasia* proving key to discussions of the visual potential embedded in verbal communication.[22] From this point of view, a particularly instructive statement about the visual dimension of *phantasia* and its relevance to rhetorical and poetical vividness comes from the anonymous author of the treatise *On the Sublime*:

> Weight, grandeur, and urgency in writing are very largely produced, dear young friend, by the use of 'visualizations' [*phantasiai*]. That at least is what I call them; others call them 'image productions' [*eidolopoiiai*]. For the term *phantasia* is applied in general to an idea which enters the mind from any source and engenders speech, but the word has now come to be used predominantly of passages where, inspired by strong emotion, you seem to see what you describe and bring it vividly before the eyes of your audience.[23]

---

20 Cic. *Top.* 27: 'By things that exist I mean such as can be seen and touched [*ea ... quae cerni tangique possunt*]: for example, farm, house, wall, rain-water, slave, animal, furniture, food, etc.; sometimes you have to define objects of this class' (trans. by Hubbell, p. 399).
21 Ibid. (trans. by Hubbell, pp. 399–401).
22 Fr. 39A3 Long-Sedley, referenced in *Cicero's Topica*, ed. by Tobias Reinhardt (Oxford: Oxford University Press, 2003), p. 264.
23 Long. *De subl.* 15.1 (trans. by Fyfe and Russell, p. 215).

The term *phantasia*, which, in Aristotle, stood for the imagination process as a whole, is taken here as the product of that process, that is, the image itself. The word is thus connected with a given author's ability to bring the object of their speech in front of the audience's eyes (hence Fyfe's choice to translate it into 'visualisation'). The connection between *phantasia* and rhetorical vividness is made in even clearer terms by Quintilian, specifically in the oft-quoted passage from *Institutio oratoria* in which, focusing on the nexus between the production of emotions and the ability to visualise absent things, the rhetorician identifies *enargeia* (ἐvαργεία) as imagination's primary scope.[24] While Quintilian concentrates on the orator's ability to make absent things present 'secundum verum' (thus focusing on vivid verbal accounts of real things), the discussion in the treatise *On the Sublime* makes room for one further distinction that is of great importance to the theory of images: namely, the opposition between truthful and false images, where the latter are associated with the domain of poetical fiction. Regardless of pseudo-Longinus's implicit critique of a kind of oratory that makes excessive use of poetical devices, what matters to the present study is the rhetorician's attempt to outline a textual space — poetry — less constrained by verisimilitude than others. To a certain degree, such space allows for oddities and falsehood. However, far from granting total and unreasonable freedom to poets, pseudo-Longinus restricts the power of imagination by mobilising allegory. A veritable loophole, allegory is considered in its duplicitous nature. On the creator's side, it functions as an intellectual process, whereby given things are said, so to speak, in other words. On the audience's side, allegory is meant to stimulate the ability to decode the message and access the content hidden behind the fictional shape it has been given.[25]

The point is clarified in the treatise *On the Sublime* through the example of two poetical images discussed in the chapter devoted to 'concepts' (these are, in fact, allegorical personifications of abstract objects). The praiseworthy example of Homer's Eris [Discord] is compared to Hesiod's reproachable presentation of Achlys [Gloom]. According to the author, while Homer describes the devastating action of Eris by means of a grand if implausible image, Hesiod indulges in repugnant details that make the description of Achlys overtly grotesque.[26] As stressed by Carlo

---

24 Quint. *Inst. or.* 6.2.29–32: 'what the Greeks call *phantasiai* (let us call them "visions"), by which the images of absent things are presented to the mind in such a way that we seem actually to see them with our eyes and have them physically present to us. Some use the word *euphantasiōtos* of one who is exceptionally good at realistically imagining to himself things, words, and actions [...] The result will be *enargeia*, what Cicero calls *illustratio* and *evidentia*, a quality which makes us seem not so much to be talking about something as exhibiting it. Emotions will ensue just as if we were present at the event itself' (trans. by Russell, p. 61).
25 On the duplicitous nature of allegory, which has accompanied the entire literary history of the West, see Fletcher, *Allegory*; *Formen und Funktionen der Allegorie*, ed. by Walter Haug (Stuttgart: J. B. Metzlersche Verlagsbuchhandlung, 1979); Jon Whitman, *Allegory: The Dynamics of an Ancient and Medieval Technique* (Cambridge, MA: Harvard University Press, 1987); specifically focused on allegorical personification, James J. Paxson, *The Poetics of Personification* (Cambridge and New York: Cambridge University Press, 1994) and *Personification: Embodying Meaning and Emotion*, ed. by Bart Ramakers and Walter Melion (Leiden: Brill, 2016); for an overview of allegory from antiquity to modernity, see *The Cambridge Companion to Allegory*, ed. by Copeland and Struck.
26 Long. *De subl.* 9.4–5; the text refers to Hom. *Il.* 4.442–43; and Hes. *Scutum* 267; 'Quite unlike this is Hesiod's description of Gloom [...]: "Mucus from her nostrils was running." He has made the

Maria Mazzucchi, the term used for the personification of Achlys, εἴδωλον, relates to the word εἰδωλοποιία, already employed by pseudo-Longinus in the chapter on *phantasia* within the discussion of the process through which concepts are visualised. While the specifics of pseudo-Longinus's judgment of Homer and Hesiod go beyond the scope of the present study, what is of particular significance is the fact that these kinds of images need to be framed allegorically so as to justify their eccentricity. According to the rhetorician, they cannot be taken at face value, for they would break the laws of decorum.[27] Ultimately, the only way to conceive and consume personifications such as those evoked by Homer and Hesiod is through the filter of allegory.

A similar approach is found in Heraclitus's *Quaestiones Homericae* [Homeric Questions], which played a crucial role in early modern discussions of allegory, particularly in the aftermath of Konrad Gessner's 1544 Latin translation of the work.[28] Homer's poetical licences, which were deemed not only implausible but also sacrilegious by both Platonic and Epicurean philosophers, are examined systematically in *Quaestiones Homericae*. In his reading of the *Iliad* and the *Odyssey*, the author defends Homer by turning to allegorical interpretation. Particularly relevant are the remarks about the personification of abstract entities not assimilated to gods and goddesses. While Athena and Hermes, among others, can be taken as personifications of wisdom and reason, respectively, they are meant to exist and have anthropomorphic shape regardless of such identifications. The case of Hebe, Eris and the Prayers, to name a few, is different in that, before being included in the gallery of Olympian deities, they are — literally — 'youth', 'discord', 'the prayers'. It is in this capacity that they are discussed and interpreted in the work. As the author argues by referring to the same Homeric passage discussed by pseudo-Longinus, Homer has unveiled the very elements that constitute the allegorical representation of Eris:

> Homer has not used allegory covertly here, or in a way demanding subtle conjecture; indeed, he has paraded his account of her in plain terms: 'Small when she first arms, but later on | her head hits heaven as she walks on earth' [*Il.* 4.442–43]. In these lines, it is not a goddess to which Homer has given shape — one so utterly monstrous, capable of incredible changes and reversals of form, one moment cast down upon the ground, and the next reaching up to the infinite grandeur of the aether. Instead, he has used this allegory to portray vividly what always happens to quarrelsome people: strife begins with a trivial cause, but once roused it swells up into what is indeed a great evil.[29]

image not terrible, but repulsive' (trans. by Fyfe and Russell, p. 187).
27 Long. *De subl.* 9.7: 'they are utterly irreligious and breach the canons of propriety unless one takes them allegorically' (trans. by Fyfe and Russell, p. 189).
28 *Allegoriae in Homeri fabulas de diis* (Basel: Oporinus, 1544); on the reception of the *Quaestiones Homericae* within the broader Homeric tradition in the Renaissance, see Philip Ford, 'Conrad Gesner et le fabuleux manteau', *Bibliothèque d'Humanisme et Renaissance*, 47 (1985), 305–20; Filippomaria Pontani, 'From Budé to Zenodotus: Homeric Readings in the European Renaissance', *International Journal of the Classical Tradition*, 14.3–4 (2007), 375–430; Jessica L. Wolfe, 'Homer in Renaissance Europe (1488–1649)', in *The Cambridge Guide to Homer*, ed. by Corinne Ondine Pache (Cambridge: Cambridge University Press, 2020), pp. 490–504 (p. 493).
29 Heracl. *Quaest. Hom.* 29.4–7 (trans. by Russell, p. 55).

Even more interesting is the case of the Prayers. Whereas the personification of discord is informed by a highly metaphorical component that undermines its anthropomorphic characterisation, Homer's personification of prayers is based on the combination of eloquent physiognomic features: 'The Prayers are daughters of almighty Zeus; | lame they are and wrinkled and squinting in both eyes'.[30] The criticism by those who reprimand Homer for assigning the daughters of Zeus repugnant traits is rejected by means of an allegorical interpretation that revolves around the moral and human characterisation of the personification:

> However, what is actually portrayed in these lines is the appearance of suppliants. The conscience of a wrongdoer is always slow, and suppliants approach those whose help they beg with reluctance, measuring out their embarrassment step by step. Their gaze is not fearless either; they turn their eyes away and look back. Nor do the thoughts of suppliants set any blush of joy on their faces — they are pale and downcast, inviting pity at first glance.[31]

The personification of prayers thus coincides with the representation of the human type of the suppliant, identified through the physical features that express their attitude and behaviour. Homer 'is, as it were, a painter of human passions, attaching the names of gods allegorically to things that happen to us'.[32] Poetry is taken as a theatre where, thanks to the power of *phantasia*, the poet gives body and, occasionally, voice to human passions and emotions. Among the figures of speech classified and theorised within classical rhetoric, allegory and personification (or prosopopoeia, to stick to the Greek term) are key to such poetical theatre. By reviewing the ways in which the rhetorical tradition has conceived the relationship between the mental production of images and their representation through words, the next section will focus on personification as one of the poetical processes through which the verbal and the visual merge. By doing so, I will lay out the rhetorical premises of the early modern uses of personification in drama that will be at the core of the following parts of this study.

Across Thought and Speech: Personification in Classical Rhetoric

The examples discussed in the previous section indicate that ancient rhetoric identified personification as particularly suitable for the representation of concepts that do not normally entail a visual shape. In such a capacity, personification may facilitate both reasoning and communication. By visualising shapeless concepts, it performs a function that is similar to the kind of metaphor that rhetoricians label catachresis.[33] At the same time, by bridging across mediums and by translating concepts into something else (i.e., images), personification is tightly connected with the workings of allegory. If the performative potential embedded in the figure is easy to detect (once a concept — or anything else, for that matter — is given human

---

30 Hom. *Il.* 9.502–03.
31 Heracl. *Quaest. Hom.* 37.2–3 (trans. by Russell, p. 67).
32 Heracl. *Quaest. Hom.* 37.6 (trans. by Russell, p. 67).
33 'Improper use of words; application of a term to a thing which it does not properly denote; abuse or perversion of a trope or metaphor' (*Oxford English Dictionary*, s.v.).

shape, the possibility of seizing it in fictional motion is fairly straightforward), the actual place of personification within the figures of speech remains somewhat uncertain. Is it simply a way to say things differently, or is it a way to conceive things that would be otherwise difficult to process intellectually?[34] While any handbook-style distinction between speech and thought risks being artificial and simplistic, it is perhaps useful to reconsider personification through the traditional rhetorical categories that, over time, have been used to describe it. This will help us identify those features of the figure that, eventually, made it a flagship poetical tool of early modernity and one that proved particularly suitable for theatrical uses.

In order to handle the ambiguities that inform the rhetorical definition of personification, let us turn to the canonical definition of the figure by Pierre Fontanier (1765–1844), whose *Traité général des figures du discours* [General Treatise on the Figures of Speech] provides us with a synthesis of classical rhetoric filtered through the theoretical experience of both Renaissance classicism and modern neoclassicism. This transhistorical perspective will let us seize the permanence of the questions raised by personification's place among the figures. Fontanier distinguished between personification as a figure of speech and personification as a figure of thought. As a figure of speech, it is described as a trope spanning a few words:

> La Personnification consiste à faire d'un être inanimé, insensible, ou d'un être abstrait et purement idéal, une espèce d'être réel et physique, doué de sentiment et de vie, enfin ce qu'on appelle une personne; et cela, par simple façon de parler, ou par une fiction toute verbale, s'il faut le dire. Elle a lieu par métonymie, par synecdoque, ou par métaphore.[35]
>
> [Personification consists in giving inanimate and insensitive beings, or abstract and purely ideal ones, some sort of real and physical existence, provided with feelings and life, that is, what we call a person; this can be achieved either by means of a simple way of speaking, or through verbal fiction. It can be done through metonymy, synecdoche or metaphor.]

After listing a few examples of personifications that use metonymy, synecdoche, and metaphor, Fontanier narrows down the definition by explaining that the only personifications that should be considered as figures of speech are the 'quick' ones, those made incidentally, mere substitutes for more ordinary statements.[36] Such

---

34 On the rhetorical status of personification in classical rhetoric, see T. B. L. Webster, 'Personification as a Mode of Greek Thought', *Journal of the Warburg and Courtauld Institutes*, 17 (1954), 10–21; and, more recently, Harvey Alan Shapiro, *Personifications in Greek Art: The Representation of Abstract Concepts, 600–400 B.C.* (Zürich: Akanthus, 1993). For the long-standing implications of the figure across Western rhetoric and linguistics, see Ernst H. Gombrich, 'Personification', in *Classical Influences on European Culture, A.D. 500–1500*, ed. by Robert R. Bolgar (Cambridge: Cambridge University Press, 1971), pp. 247–57 (p. 248); Morton W. Bloomfield, 'A Grammatical Approach to Personification Allegory', *Modern Philology*, 60 (1963), 161–71; Paolo Valesio, 'Esquisse pour une étude des personnifications', *Lingua e stile*, 4 (1964), 1–21; Paxson, *The Poetics of Personification*.
35 Pierre Fontanier, *Les figures du discours* [1821–27], ed. by Gérard Genette (Paris: Flammarion, 1968), p. 111.
36 Fontanier, *Les figures du discours*, p. 113: 'les seules personnifications vraiment figures d'expression, ce sont ces personnifications courtes, rapides, qui ne se font qu'en passant, sur lesquelles

personifications are the ones that Aristotle refers to in his discussion of metaphor in Book 3 of *Rhetoric*, where he states that the πρὸ ὀμμάτων ποιεῖν [putting things before the eyes] can be achieved by giving life to inanimate objects: 'things are set before the eyes by words that signify activity', which can also be achieved by 'making use of metaphor to speak of inanimate things as if they were animate. It is to creating activity in all such cases that his popularity is due'.[37] Personification and metaphor thus merge, for instance in Aesion's description of Greece, which, personified and portrayed as screaming, is an example of inanimate entity brought to life.[38] As suggested by the Homeric examples gathered by Aristotle, metaphors of this kind create action: by evoking stimuli that, in real life, pertain to sense perception, they enter the mind of the audience with particular force.[39]

Of a totally different nature is, according to Fontanier, personification as the representation of abstract beings. Going beyond the strictly verbal features of the figures of speech, it pertains to the realm of the figures of thought, allegory in particular:

> Quant à ces personnifications si étendues et si marquées, par lesquelles on crée, on décrit, ou l'on caractérise un être allégorique et moral, avec une sorte d'intention de faire croire que cet être existe réellement; telles, par exemple que le Sommeil, la Famine et l'Envie, dans Ovide; que les Prières, dans l'*Iliade*; que la Chicane, le Rhin, la Piété, la Mollesse et son cortège, dans Boileau; que la Politique, la Discorde, le Fanatisme, l'Amour, et même les Vices, dans la *Henriade*: il faut, je crois, les rapporter à l'Allégorie, non pas dans les sens particulier et restreint auquel nous allons la réduire ici, mais dans son sens le plus étendu; il faut, dis-je, les ranger dans la classe des fictions ou inventions poétiques; et, si l'on veut absolument en faire des figures, c'est parmi les figures de pensées qu'il faut leur donner rang.[40]

> [A different domain is that of those broader personifications by means of which we create, describe, and characterise some allegorical and moral being, making the audience believe that such being truly exists. These are, for instance, Sleep, Famine, and Envy in Ovid; Prayers in the *Iliad*; Obstacle, the Rhine, Piety, Idleness, and its cortege in Boileau; Politics, Discord, Fanatism, Love, and the Vices in the *Henriade*: these are connected to allegory, not in the particular narrow meaning to which we are reducing it here, but in its wider sense. We must, in other words, place them in the group of fictions and poetical inventions; and if we wish to consider them as figures, it is among the figures of thought that we should place them.]

The French grammarian explains Ovid's personifications, as well as Homer's, Boileau's, and Voltaire's in terms of fiction: they are poetical inventions that fall

on n'appuie pas, et qui ne sont visiblement qu'une expression un peu plus recherchée, substituée à l'expression ordinaire' [The only personifications that are true figures of speech are the quick ones, made incidentally, on which one does not pause, and which are just a more refined form of expression in place of the ordinary one].
37   Arist. *Rhet.* 1411b 34–35.
38   Arist. *Rhet.* 1411a 28; as such, it corresponds to the metaphor that post-Aristotelian rhetoric would label 'active metaphor' (*kata enérgeian*): Demetr. *De eloc.* 81.
39   Arist. *Rhet.* 1412a 1–3.
40   Fontanier, *Les figures du discours*, pp. 113–14.

under the umbrella of allegory. They give body to abstract entities, making them the object of descriptions as well as active subjects within given narratives.

Fontanier's definition brings personification close to those figures of thought involving imagination, particularly prosopopoeia (*prosopopée*) and fabulation (*fabulation*). The first one, which Fontanier distinguishes from the broader meaning of personification, 'consiste à mettre en quelque sorte en scène, les absents, les morts, les êtres surnaturels, ou même les êtres inanimés; à les faire agir, parler, répondre [...] ou tout au moins à les prendre pour confidents, pour témoins, pour garants, pour accusateurs, pour vengeurs, pour juges, etc.'.[41] By turning to an explicitly theatrical metaphor ('mettre [...] en scène'), the statement stresses the dialogical dimension of the figure. Absent individuals, the dead, supernatural beings, and inanimate ones are conceived as actors who, literally brought on stage, move, speak, converse within a textual structure that summons them by providing them with both body and voice.

In this acceptation, prosopopoeia seems to exclude those personifications and fictional characters that Fontanier himself placed among the figures of thought. Room is made for them, though, within the field of what Fontanier calls *fabulation*, a broad figure that consists in considering the products of poetical imagination as if they were real: 'il n'y aurait qu'à ouvrir le premier poëte venu: on verrait les êtres fabuleux, les êtres moraux, allégoriques, se présenter en foule'.[42] After recalling once again allegorical personifications by Voltaire and Boileau, Fontanier highlights the vivifying power of poetical fiction, which is able to give body, soul, and spirit to all sorts of things. While the definition of prosopopoeia is, in Fontanier, rather narrow, that of *fabulation* (which ends up including what is usually labelled 'allegorical personification') is wide and makes it explicit that 'personification' and 'character' are tightly linked under the metaphorical aegis of drama: 'Mais par Fabulation, faut-il n'entendre qu'un personnage fictif donné par jeu d'esprit pour un personnage réel? Il me semble qu'il faut entendre encore tout ce qu'on raconte de ce personnage, toutes les actions qu'on lui attribue, et en général tout le rôle qu'on lui fait jouer'.[43]

Fontanier's tripartite distinction (*personification, prosopopée, fabulation*) stems from the attempt to handle a disparate rhetorical tradition whose terminology has been, over the centuries, far from stable. Before the advent of the Gallicism 'personification', used in Italy ('personificazione') since the late eighteenth century, the term that more precisely indicated the process of personification was indeed prosopopoeia (προσωποποιΐα).[44] The etymology is straightforward, for πρόσωπον

41 Fontanier, *Les figures du discours*, p. 404 ('[Prosopopoeia] consists, so to speak, in bringing on stage absent people, the dead, supernatural beings, or even inanimate ones; making them act, speak, respond [...] or at least taking them as confidants, witnesses, guarantors, accusers, avengers, judges, etc.').
42 Fontanier, *Les figures du discours*, p. 406 ('One just needs to open the first poet at hand to see a great number of imaginary beings, moral and allegorical ones').
43 Ibid. ('Is fabulation to be only understood as a fictional character introduced as a real personage? It seems to me that fabulations include all that is told about them, all the actions that are attributed to them, and, more generally, the roles that they are made to play').
44 See the entries 'Personificazione' and 'Prosopopea' in *Grande Dizionario della Lingua Italiana*, vol. XIII, p. 116, and vol. XIV, pp. 701–02; but also *Dizionario Etimologico Italiano*, s.v. (vol. IV, pp. 912,

ποιεῖν means 'to make a person'. However, the two terms that compose the word bear complex meanings. The verb ποιεῖν suggests a tangible kind of making, a veritable process of creation that, as in poetry (*poiesis*), prioritises the artisanal dimension of the creative act; πρόσωπον, as is the case with its Latin counterpart, *persona*, is a polysemous word: along with 'face' and 'aspect' (primarily referred to humans), the term can also be understood as 'figure', that is, a synonym of image. It can thus be the portrait of an ancestor (one might think of the Roman tradition of preserving and exhibiting the images of their forefathers), but also a theatrical mask, a character (or personage), and, more broadly, a person. Ultimately, prosopopoeia is the making (i.e., poetical creation) of a πρόσωπον, that is, a person in the various acceptations mentioned above, including that of fictional character in a literary work.

Classical rhetoric identifies prosopopoeia as a figure of thought that makes it possible for the orator to introduce a voice different from their own (e.g., the personification of the country, the ancestors, a historical figure, a hypothetical interlocutor, etc.) in order to increase the vividness of the speech and spur the audience's emotions. In the treatise *De elocutione*, Demetrius includes prosopopoeia among the figures of thought that contribute to the vehement style.[45] When a speech requires particular emotional strength, the orator can give voice to the dead or to inanimate things. By way of example, Demetrius quotes the ancestors' address to their descendants in Plato's *Menexenus*: here the orator 'does not speak in his own person but in that of their fathers'. The speaker leaves aside their *persona* in order to temporarily wear someone else's, as if they were wearing a mask. The advantage of this figure is significant: 'The personification makes the passage much more lively and forceful, or rather it really turns into a drama'.[46] The speech is made 'more active' (the adjective ἐνεργέστερα highlights the affinity between personification and *energeia*), hence more dramatic, a feature of the figure that will remain steadily present in rhetorical classifications till (and beyond) Fontanier. The idea that the orator is able to give voice to different 'persons' is, in fact, what brings prosopopoeia close to dialogism, a link that, as brilliantly indicated by Marc Fumaroli, exposes the rhetorical affinity of oratory and drama. Also, Demetrius stresses the interrelatedness of prosopopoeia and character, for personifications introduced within an oration (i.e., imagined interlocutors who play a role within the discourse of the orator) fulfil a function that is very similar to that of personages in a play.[47]

2866).
45 Demetr. *De eloc.* 265 (trans. by Innes, p. 499): 'Another figure of thought which may be used to produce force is the figure called prosopopoeia, for example "Imagine that your ancestors are rebuking you and speak such words, or imagine Greece, or your country in the form of a woman"'.
46 Demetr. *De eloc.* 266 (trans. by Innes, p. 499).
47 The fact that Demetrius's use of the adjective 'dramatic' connects directly to the field of drama (as in theatre) is appreciated by early modern translations of the treatise such as Stanislaus Ilovius's, which refers it to comedy (*Demetrii Phalerei De elocutione liber a Stanislao Ilovio Polono Latinitate donatus et annotationibus illustratus* (Basel: Johannes Oporinus, 1552), p. 163: 'Multo enim illustriora et graviora videntur, eo quod inducta est persona patrum, imo vero plane quandam comoediam referunt'), and Pietro Vettori's, which clarifies the meaning in his annotation to the text (Petri

For systematic definitions of the figure, though, one has to look at the Latin tradition, specifically *Rhetorica ad Herennium*. In order to provide the Greek prosopopoeia with a Latin equivalent, its anonymous author turns to the term *conformatio*, which I have already discussed as relevant to image-making. The Latin term entails a remarkable shift in meaning, for the sense of the verb *conformare* (to give something a shape) is significantly broader than the Greek πρόσωπον ποιεῖν: 'Personification [*conformatio*] consists in representing an absent person as present [*aliqua quae non adest persona confingitur quasi adsit*], or in making a mute thing or one lacking form [*informis*] articulate, and attributing to it a definite form [*forma*] and a language [*oratio*] or a certain behaviour [*actio*] appropriate to its character'.[48] *Conformatio* is thus about imagining an absent person as if they were present, or assigning speech, body, and convenient actions to an object that is normally silent or shapeless. The examples produced in the treatise are consistent with those found in Greek sources such as Demetrius's *De elocutione*: a city addressing its people, a dead politician speaking to his fellow citizens.[49] The orator may introduce a new *persona* giving voice to the dead and to inanimate things in order to increase the pathetic effect of the speech.[50] According to *Rhetorica ad Herennium*, cognate to *conformatio* are figures such as *effictio*, *notatio* and *sermocinatio*, which all aim at making the oration more vivid. *Effictio* is the art of portraying someone's physical aspect through words.[51] *Notatio* is the description of individuals based on the signs (*signa* or *notae*) that are peculiar to them.[52] Differently from *effictio* and *notatio*, both focused on third-person description, *sermocinatio* is the figure that assigns actual speech to the *persona* introduced within the orator's discourse, hence its affinity with prosopopoeia.[53]

These rhetorical devices are discussed by Cicero in Book 3 of *De oratore*, where he introduces the notion of 'personarum ficta inductio' (impersonation of people) among the figures of thought.[54] Very close to *notatio* as found in *Rhetorica ad Herennium*, the imitation of an individual's *mores* and life, either real ('in personis') or fictional ('sine illis'), is said to be of great appeal to the audience. Even more

Victorii, *Commentarii in librum Demetrii Phalerei De elocutione positis ante singulas declarationes Graecis vocibus auctoris, iisdemque ad verbum Latine expressis* (Florence: Bernardo Giunta, 1562), p. 230: 'multo enim evidentiora et graviora esse perspiciuntur vi personarum illarum: potius autem dramata fiunt', with the explanatory gloss: 'potius autem dramata, et instar fabularum scenicarum quippiam illo pacto efficitur').
48   *Rhet. ad Her.* 4.66 (trans. by Kaplan, p. 399). For a similar description, see Cic. *De or.* 2.87.357.
49   Ibid.
50   Ibid.: 'Personification may be applied to a variety of things, mute and inanimate. It is most useful in the divisions under Amplification and in Appeal to Pity' (trans. by Kaplan, p. 401).
51   *Rhet. ad Her.* 4.63: 'Portrayal consists in representing and depicting in words clearly enough for recognition the bodily form of some person' (trans. by Kaplan, p. 387).
52   Ibid.: 'Character Delineation consists in describing a person's character by the definite signs which, like distinctive marks, are attributes of that character' (trans. by Kaplan, p. 387).
53   Ibid.: 'Dialogue consists in assigning to some person language which as set forth conforms with his character' (trans. by Kaplan, p. 395).
54   Cic. *De or.* 3.53.204–5: 'imitation of manners and behaviour, either given in character or not, is a considerable ornament of style, and extremely effective in calming down an audience and often also in exciting it; impersonation of people, an extremely brilliant method of amplification' (trans. by Rackham, p. 163).

effective, however, is deemed the introduction of a person that, within the orator's speech, is given voice. The range of possibilities becomes wider in *Topica*, where Cicero's discussion of 'ficta exempla' includes the attribution of speech to silent objects.[55] In *De inventione*, Cicero explains that speech ('oratio') can be given to 'silent and inanimate things' ('mutas et expertes animi res'), a device which fosters the audience's enjoyment and emotional involvement.[56] Alongside the dead, prosopopoeia includes animals and inanimate beings (and, as such, it features prominently in the tradition of fables). The same rhetorical device is discussed by Cicero in both *Orator* and *De partitione oratoria*,[57] but it is *De inventione* that holds particular significance, for it places the figure within the discussion of *evidentia*, reasserting the pertinence of personification to verbal vividness.[58]

The use of prosopopoeia in genres other than oratory is floated by Rutilius Lupus in *Schemata lexeos*, a rhetorical handbook from the age of Tiberius that was widely read in the Renaissance. The first part of the figure's definition is canonical: 'Hoc fit, cum personas in rebus constituimus, quae sine personis sunt, aut eorum hominum, qui fuerunt, tamquam vivorum et praesentium actionem sermonemve deformamus'.[59] Before giving examples from oratory, Rutilius Lupus quotes a poetical fragment with moral undertones: 'Nam crudelitatis mater avaritiast, pater furor | Haec facinori iuncta odium parit; inde exitium nascitur'.[60] By turning metaphorically to the genealogical relationship between animals and their offspring in order to describe the derivation of a given attitude (cruelty) from two passions

---

55   Cic. *Top.* 45: 'Under this topic of similarity orators and philosophers have licence to cause dumb things to talk, to call on the dead to rise from the world below, to tell of something which could not possibly happen, in order to add force to an argument or lessen it' (trans. by Hubbell, p. 415).

56   Cic. *De inv.* 1.109: 'for example: if you should represent one as speaking to a horse, a house, or a garment, by which the mind of the audience who have loved something is greatly affected' (trans. by Hubbell, p. 161).

57   Cic. *Or.* 138: 'he will seem to consult the audience, and sometimes even with the opponent; he will portray the talk and ways of men; he will make mute objects speak' (trans. by Hubbell, pp. 411–13); Cic. *De part. or.* 16.55: 'Amplification of the facts is obtained from all the same topics from which were taken the statements made to secure credence; and very effective are accumulations of definitions [...] and also imaginary persons and even dumb objects must speak' (trans. by Rackham, p. 353). For the relationship between prosopopoeia and amplification see the aforementioned passages from *De or.* 3.53.204–5.

58   Cic. *De inv.* 1.107. However, Cicero is quite cautious about the use of prosopopoeia in oratory. In *Or.* 85, for instance, he warns against excessive use of the figure by recalling examples such as the prosopopoeia of a dead relative and that of the country addressing its own citizens; on the effects caused by the introduction of dead people, remarkable insight comes from *De or.* 1.57.245, where Cicero stresses the activeness and vividness of such device: 'and, if you had been appearing for the soldier, you would by your eloquence, in your usual way, have called up his father from the shades; you would have set him in sight of all; he would have embraced his son and tearfully committed him to the care of the Hundred Commissioners; I pledge my word he would have made every stone weep and wail' (trans. by Sutton and Rackham, p. 179).

59   Rut. Lup. *Schem. lex.* 2.6. ('This happens when we make a person out of something that is normally person-less or when we give action and speech to dead people as if they were alive and present').

60   Ibid. ('Avarice is cruelty's mother, furor is the father; together with crime, she gives birth to hatred; whence death rises'). The fragment is of difficult interpretation; see Rosa Maria D'Angelo, 'Rutilio Lupo 2,6: un tormentato esempio di prosopopea', *Museum Helveticum*, 62 (2005), 133–44.

of the soul (avarice and fury), the poetical fragment introduces a personification, with cruelty, avarice, and fury becoming Cruelty, Avarice, and Fury, respectively. The example is followed by a remark that stresses the significance of the device to poetical fiction: 'Hoc genere usi sunt poetae, qui fabulas scripserunt, in prologis. Nam humana figura produxerunt personas, quae in veritate artis et voluntatis sunt, non personae'.[61] According to Lupus, poets turn to personifications 'in prologis': the statement may refer to dramatic prologues, in which non-human things are given human shape as part of the fiction set up by the poet. Lupus does not share examples of prosopopoeia from dramatic prologues, but the relevance of his definition to the field of drama is suggested by Pietro Vettori in his 1562 commentary on the passage from Demetrius's *De elocutione* discussed above. The Florentine philologist notices that, while Demetrius overlooks the personification of abstract entities, Lupus's statement and the actual practice of playwrights such as Plautus (exemplified here through the prologue of the play *Trinummus*) fill the gap: 'cum aliquis inducit personam aliquam, quae nunquam fuerit [...] [Hoc] genere narrat Rutilius uti solere poetas in prologis: intelligit autem (ut puto) locum hunc Plauti in prologo Trinumi, qui loquentes una induxit Luxuriam, et inopiam, aliosque huic similes locos'.[62] As indicated by Vettori's remark, Lupus's *Schemata lexeos* seem to offer one of the earliest instances of the theoretical awareness of the link between prosopopoeia and drama, while also outlining the specific features of theatrical fiction, which need being assessed in their own terms.

Insightful remarks about the intersections of oratory and theatrical performance are found in Quintilian's *Institutio oratoria*. Quintilian first mentions prosopopoeia within the discussion of *lectio*, where he explains that the delivery of the figure does not need detaching too much from the regular pace and tone of the orator's speech. A simple inflection of the voice will do, so that the prosopopoeia will sound different from the words uttered in the orator's own person.[63] More information, though, is given in Book 3, where Quintilian devotes one entire chapter to both prosopopoeia and *suasoria* as rhetorical exercises crucial to the orator's training. While *suasoria* requires the orator to be able to seize the psychological attitude of the listeners so as to connect with them, the difficulty intrinsic to prosopopoeia relates to the construction of the character.[64] Whereas the orator keeps their own persona in the *suasoria*, they must wear someone else's persona — a mask — when delivering a prosopopoeia. In other words, they must appropriate the other persona's inner features and channel them through their own voice.

61 Rut. Lup. *Schem. lex* 2.6 ('This genre was used in prologues by those poets, who wrote fables. They introduced persons with human shape, who, in reality, are not persons').
62 Petri Victorii, *Commentarii in librum Demetrii Phalerei*, p. 230 ('When someone introduces a person, who never existed [...] Rutilius narrates that poets turned to this genre in prologues: I believe he refers to one passage by Plautus in the prologue of *Trinummus*, where Luxury and Poverty are introduced as speakers, and other similar places').
63 Quint. *Inst. or.* 1.8.3: 'Nor do I think that Prosopopoeiae, as some advice, should be pronounced in the manner of the comic stage, though there should be some inflection of the voice to distinguish them from passages in which the poet speaks in his own person' (trans. by Russell, vol. I, p. 201).
64 Quint. *Inst. or.* 3.8.49: 'This is why I regard *prosopopoeia* as far the most difficult exercise, because the difficulty of maintaining a character is added to the other problems of the *suasoria*' (trans. by Russell, vol. II, p. 139).

This kind of exercise is useful, Quintilian continues, beyond oratory, for instance to poets and historiographers.[65] In all these cases, the author must acquire the way of thinking of the persona, whom they aim to bring to life, so that *vox* and *imago* prove consistent with one another.[66] The issue addressed by Quintilian is the consistency of characters, a preoccupation central to both rhetoric and poetics, as indicated by famous statements such as those by Aristotle and Horace, and particularly important when it comes to introducing speeches in someone else's person.[67] The gallery of characters outlined by Quintilian recalls the characters of theatre:

> Declaimers of course must especially consider what best suits each character; for they rarely deliver their speeches as advocates, but generally as sons, parents, rich men, old men, the bad-tempered, the easy-going, misers, the superstitious, cowards or mockers; comic actors hardly have more roles to sustain in their performance than these men do in their speeches.[68]

Prosopopoeia hangs thus in the balance between the representation of a type (to be understood as in Theophrastus's *Characters*) and the impersonation of a real persona. Typology and individuation collide within a characterisation that is expected to be coherent and plausible.[69]

The pertinence of prosopopoeia to the dramatic arts is highlighted by Quintilian in Book 6, where he further explores the interconnection of oratory and drama. The use of prosopopoeia ('fictae alienarum personarum orationes') is recommended when the oration needs to raise the level of pathos in order to involve the audience emotionally. The reason behind it is one of the foundational principles of any kind of rhetorical device: 'the bare facts [*nudae res*] produce the effect; but when we pretend that the victims themselves are speaking, the emotional effect is drawn also from the persons [*ex personis quoque trahitur adfectus*]'.[70] While facts are effective by themselves, emotions are more strongly engendered in the audience when spokespersons are introduced in the speech. The distinction between subject matter and the way in which subject matter is delivered (in this case, the direct intervention of a given character) mobilises two modes (narrative and dramatic) that strike different chords in the audience. By looking at the issue from the standpoint of a judge in a trial (one could argue that the judge's position is similar to the spectator attending a theatrical performance), Quintilian explains that prosopopoeia gives one the impression not to be listening to a speaker lamenting someone else's misfortunes, but to be hearing the very voice and feelings of the individual who is suffering.[71]

65 Ibid.
66 Quint. *Inst. or.* 3.8.50: 'produce an image of those to whom he was lending his voice' (trans. by Russell, vol. II, p. 141), with reference to Cicero's ability to do that.
67 Quint. *Inst. or.* 3.8.51: 'A speech which is out of keeping with the speaker is just as bad as one which is out of keeping with the subject to which it ought to have been adapted' (trans. by Russell, vol. II, p. 141).
68 Quint. *Inst. or.* 3.8.51–52 (trans. by Russell, vol. II, p. 141).
69 Further remarks on prosopopoeia in Quint. *Inst. or.* 4.1.28; 4.2.103; 4.2.107.
70 Quint. *Inst. or.* 6.1.25 (trans. by Russell, vol. III, p. 31).
71 Quint. *Inst. or.* 6.1.26: 'The judge no longer thinks that he is listening to a lament for somebody else's troubles, but that he is hearing the feelings and the voice of the afflicted' (trans. by Russell, vol. III, p. 31).

BODILESS OBJECTS IN HUMAN SHAPE   37

Furthermore, Quintilian remarks that the audience's response is triggered not only by the words uttered, but also by the physical appearance of the plaintiff. Indeed, their silent face will move the bystanders to tears ('etiam mutus aspectus lacrimas movet'), according to a sympathetic mechanism that is also at work in drama. The reference to theatre is explicit:

> and, as their pleas would be more pitiful if only they could make them themselves, so to a certain extent the pleas become more effective by being as it were put into their mouths, just as the same voice and delivery of the stage actor [*ut scaenicis actoribus eadem vox eademque pronuntiatio*] produces a greater emotional impact [*plus ad movendos adfectus*] because he speaks behind a mask [*sub persona*].[72]

Words are all the more touching when uttered by the characters themselves, as is the case with actors ('scaenici actores'), who move the audience not because of their real identities, but in their capacity as characters ('sub persona').

The connection between oratory and drama is developed by Quintilian in the following paragraphs, where he focuses on the visual component of verbal communication. The audience's sympathy, in fact, is won over not only by means of words, but also through action ('Non solum autem dicendo, sed etiam faciendo').[73] Because of eyesight's forcefulness, it has become customary for those who are under trial to present themselves as suffering.[74] Furthermore, during the trial, objects are exhibited as vivid proofs of what happened: swords stained with blood, splinters of bones extracted from wounds, clothes soaked with blood, wounded bodies that, with a veritable *coup de théâtre*, are unveiled at the right moment in order to impress the audience.[75] These images — in fact, veritable props — are more eloquent than words: they play with the audience's emotions rather than with rational arguments, yet another way of increasing the speech's vividness that resonates with theatrical devices.[76] Within the oratorial context, though, according to Quintilian, visualisation should be kept to a minimum. He rejects, for instance, visual aids such as paintings representing the crime scene, for the orator should never renounce the vividness of his own verbal account. Indeed, only bad orators would find painted images ('muta effigies') more eloquent than their own speech.[77]

---

72   Ibid. (trans. by Russell, vol. III, p. 31).
73   Quint. *Inst. or.* 6.1.30.
74   Ibid.: 'Hence the practice of bringing the accused into court dirty and unkempt, and their children and parents with them' (trans. by Russell).
75   Ibid.
76   Quint. *Inst. or.* 6.1.31: 'These things commonly make an enormous impression, because they confront people's minds directly with the facts' (trans. by Russell, vol. III, p. 33). Quintilian recalls the striking effect produced in the audience by the sight of Caesar's toga stained with blood during the funeral. The exhibited object has the power to visually evoke the crime: 'This is how Caesar's toga, carried in his funeral, covered in blood, drove the Roman people to fury. It was known that he had been killed; his body lay on the bier; but it was the clothing, wet with blood, that made the image of the crime so vivid that Caesar seemed not to have been murdered, but to be being murdered there and then' (trans. by Russell, vol. III, p. 33).
77   Quint. *Inst. or.* 6.1.32: 'I would not however, for this reason, approve a practice of which I have read — and indeed have occasionally seen — of having a picture painted on a board or a

Quintilian goes back to the personification of abstract or inanimate beings in book 9, as part of his discussion of figures of thought. Prosopopoeia is described here as a rhetorical device that makes speech more vivid: 'Bolder, and needing (as Cicero puts it) stronger lungs, are Impersonations [*fictiones personarum*], or *prosōpopoiiai* as they are called in Greek. These both vary and animate a speech to a remarkable degree'.[78] The figure allows for a more effective presentation of someone else's thoughts, and gives the speech a dramatic twist, introducing various interlocutors in front of the audience's eyes. Needless to say, essential to a successful prosopopoeia is the consistency of a given character's words vis-à-vis their thoughts.[79] The figure can be used to introduce gods, the dead, cities and communities.[80] Rejecting a clear-cut distinction between prosopopoeia and *dialogoi* (which correspond to what *Rhetorica ad Herennium* called *sermocinatio*), Quintilian outlines a broad definition of prosopopoeia as imaginary speech assigned to a *persona*, no matter whether real or fictional.[81]

Among the objects that can be given a *persona*, abstract and inanimate ones deserve special attention: 'We also often invent Personifications [*formas quoque fingimus*], as Virgil invented Rumour, Prodicus — according to Xenophon's report — Pleasure and Virtue, and Ennius Death and Life, whom he represents in a Satire as debating with each other'.[82] Quintilian's examples capture three types of personifications that would prove extremely influential in the literature of medieval and modern Europe: (1) Virgil's Fame is a personification that acts as a character within a narrative; (2) Pleasure and Virtue, the opposite terms in the moral choice made emblematic by the image of Hercules at the crossroad, bring us into the context of philosophical literature, which may turn to poetical tools in order to convey its teachings; and lastly (3), the contest between Life and Death in Ennius opens up a window onto the wide tradition of allegorical conflicts that dramatise moral and spiritual dichotomies (the clearest instance being that of the psychomachia). The three examples go well beyond oratory, bearing witness to the productive role played by personifications in other literary genres.

The somewhat ambiguous status of personification vis-à-vis the construction of characters that one finds in Quintilian is also at work in Hermogenes' *Progymnasmata*, which, alongside later authors such as Aphthonius, Priscian, and Isidore of

---

canvas (*depictam in tabula sipariove imaginem*), depicting the horrible event of which the judge is to be reminded. What depths of incompetence must there be in a pleader who thinks a dumb image (*mutam illam effigiem*) will speak for him better than his own words!' (trans. by Russell, vol. III, p. 35).
78 Quint. *Inst. or.* 9.2.29 (trans. by Russell, vol. IV, p. 51).
79 Quint. *Inst. or.* 9.2.30: 'We use them (1) to display the inner thoughts of our opponents as though they were talking to themselves — but they are credible only if we imagine them saying what it is not absurd for them to have thought! –, (2) to introduce conversations between ourselves and others, or of others among themselves, in a credible manner, and (3) to provide appropriate characters for words of advice, reproach, complaint, praise, or pity' (trans. by Russell, vol. IV, p. 51).
80 Quint. *Inst. or.* 9.2.31.
81 Quint. *Inst. or.* 9.2.32: 'I follow the now established usage in calling them both by the same name, for we cannot of course imagine a speech except as the speech of a person (*sermo fingi non potest ut non personae sermo fingatur*)' (trans. by Russell, vol. IV, p. 51).
82 Quint. *Inst. or.* 9.2.36 (trans. by Russell, vol. IV, p. 53).

Seville, would be a model for many of the rhetorical handbooks produced in the Renaissance.[83] Hermogenes discusses prosopopoeia as a species of a broader figure, ethopoeia (ἠθοποιία). Within this context, the notion of πρόσωπον relates to that of ethos (ἦθος), which is essential to the making of characters. Aristotle himself identified ethos as one of the six components of tragedy and stressed its importance for the characterisation of personages: 'Character is that which reveals moral choice — that is, when otherwise unclear, what kinds of thing an agent chooses or rejects (which is why speeches in which there is nothing at all the speaker chooses or rejects contain no character)'.[84] Ethopoeia is thus the construction (literally, the making) of a character, and, as such, is included by Hermogenes in the exercises preparatory to rhetorical training: 'Ethopoeia is an imitation of the character of a person supposed to be speaking; for example, what words Andromache might say to Hector'.[85] Among the exercises, the composition of fictional speeches uttered by given characters in specific circumstances requires the orator to imagine words according to the character's ethos, so that the character proves consistent and plausible. By describing ethopoeia as the attribution of an individualising ethos to a *prosopon*, Hermogenes distinguishes it from prosopopoeia in the strict sense:

> It is called personification (*prosôpopoiía*) when we personify a thing, like Elenchus (Disproof) in Menander and as in Aristeides' speech where 'The Sea' addresses the Athenians. The difference is clear: in ethopoeia we imagine words for a real person, in prosopopoeia we imagine a non-existing person.[86]

As indicated by the examples listed by Hermogenes, the figure applies to both oratory (as in Aristeides) and drama (Disproof delivers the prologue in a play by Menander consistently with the same practice referenced by Rutilius Lupus).

Hermogenes' discussion includes the possibility of giving voice to the dead as well. What previous rhetoricians considered as a specific kind of prosopopoeia, is labelled by Hermogenes εἰδωλοποιία, consistently with the meaning of εἴδωλον (a lexical cluster similar to that of the Latin *simulachrum*): 'They say it is image-making (*eidolopoiía*) when we attribute words to the dead, as does Aristeides in *Against Plato on Behalf of the Four*; for there he has attributed words to Themistocles's companions'.[87] The chapter continues with a detailed typology of ethopoeia, which provides insightful remarks on the making of characters. These can be specific characters (e.g. Achilles speaking to Deidamia before his departure) or indefinite

---

83 Apht. *Progymn.* (ed. by Rabe) s.v. ethopooia; Prisc., *Inst. gram.* 12.18; Isid. *Etym.* 2.13.1–2. On the reception of the *progymnasmata* literature in Humanist and Renaissance culture, see D. R. Clark, 'The Rise and Fall of Progymnasmata in Sixteenth and Seventeenth Century Grammar Schools', *Speech Monographs*, 19 (1952), 159–263; and Manfred Hinz, *Die menschlichen und die göttlichen Mittel: Sieben Kommentare zu Baltasar Gracián* (Bonn: Romanistischer Verlag, 2002), pp. 114–203; 'Agudeza e Progymnasmata', in *I Gesuiti e la Ratio Studiorum*, ed. by Manfred Hinz, Roberto Righi and Danilo Zardin (Rome: Bulzoni, 2004), pp. 293–314 (on Hermogenes, pp. 295–96; on Aphthonius, pp. 296–97).
84 Arist. *Poet.* 1450b 9–11 (trans. by Halliwell, p. 53)
85 Herm. *Progymn.* 9.20.7–9 (trans. by Kennedy, p. 84).
86 Ibid.
87 Herm. *Progymn.* 9.20.14–18 (trans. by Kennedy, pp. 84–85).

ones (an unnamed father addressing his dear ones before leaving them). As far as its structure is concerned, ethopoeia can be simple (the character speaks to himself, as in a soliloquy) or composite (the character talks to some interlocutor). Building on Aristotle's discussion of characters, Hermogenes explains that they should be not only appropriate, but also consistent with both the external circumstances and themselves.[88] As noted by Michel Patillon, the acceptation of ethos that informs Hermogenes' notion of ethopoeia is broad, including both ethos understood as moral characterisation and pathos as the expression of temporary, often abrupt, emotions and feelings. It is through the interaction of these components that it is possible to articulate more or less individualised features.[89]

Hermogenes goes back to a wider notion of prosopopoeia in the treatise *De inventione*, where he uses the term according to Demetrius's εἰσαγωγή προσώπου, that is the temporary introduction of a character to whom the orator gives voice (the phrasing is a direct translation of Cicero's 'ficta personarum inductio').[90] In the chapter on the examination of facts, Hermogenes says that it is not advisable to overindulge in the use of prosopopoeia and that, whenever the figure is used, it is better to omit the *verbum loquendi* that would normally introduce it.[91] More interesting, though, are Hermogenes' references to prosopopoeia in the chapter devoted to the vivid description of an action.[92] Among the devices that the orator is recommended to turn to, especially when dealing with panegyric oratory, prosopopoeia stands out, for it does introduce multiple voices within the oratorial monologue.[93] Even if he does not use the lexicon of *evidentia*, Hermogenes confirms the double dimension of the figure at once with stressing its affinity with διατύπωσις: on the one hand, visual forcefulness; on the other, dramatic potential. These features were, as will be shown in the next section, key to the early modern reception of the figure, its theorisation, and poetical uses.[94]

---

88   Herm. *Progymn.* 9.21.6–9: 'Throughout the exercise you will preserve what is distinctive and appropriate to the persons imagined as speaking and to the occasions; for the speech of a young man differs from that of an old man, and that of one who rejoices from that of one who grieves' (trans. by Kennedy, p. 85). See Arist. *Rhet* 1389a ff.; and *Poet.* 1454a 16–36.
89   Herm. *Progymn.* 9.21.10–18.
90   Cic. *De or.* 3.53.205.
91   Herm. *De inv.* 3.10.
92   Herm. *De inv.* 3.15.
93   George A. Kennedy, *Invention and Method: Two Rhetorical Treatises from the Hermogenic Corpus* (Leiden: Brill, 2005), p. 129, stresses the proximity of Hermogenes' diatyposis and Quintilian's notion of *evidentia* as illustrated in *Inst. or.* 9.2.40.
94   The dialogical and dramatic dimension of prosopopoeia is addressed by Dionysius of Halicarnassus, who, speaking about Thucydides, establishes a direct connection between the introduction of new *personae* within the oration and the dialogue-like turn that the device gives to the speech: 'Thucydides begins by stating in his own person what each side said, but after maintaining this form of reported speech for only one exchange of argument, he dramatises the rest of the dialogue and makes the characters speak for themselves' (Dion Hal. *Thucyd.* 37, trans. by Usher, p. 575).

Personification in Early Modern Rhetoric and Poetics

Early modern discussions of personification are part of broader concerns with figures of thought. Rarely addressed on its own, the figure is often discussed in treatises of rhetoric and poetics, which rely primarily on *Rhetorica ad Herennium* and Quintilian's *Institutio oratoria* while also looking at more concise rhetorical compendia such those by Hermogenes and Aphthonius. Widely read and translated into both Latin and the European vernaculars, these works provided early modern theorists with handy classifications ready to be reused and adapted to their own literary traditions.[95] While personification did not stir the same amount of critical attention that fuelled early modern theories of metaphor, its theoretical proximity with tropes made it an important and somewhat ubiquitous field of rhetorical inquiry, as recently demonstrated by Blandine Perona.[96] Personification's affinity with metaphor, suggested by Aristotle and often referenced by Greek and Latin rhetoricians, had already been acknowledged in the Middle Ages by intellectuals such as Bede, whose *Liber de schematibus et tropis* paved the way for many of the later theoretical assessments of metaphor. By defining a trope ('tropica locutio') as the 'translation' of a term from its proper meaning into a non-proper one ('translata dictio a propria significatione ad non propriam'), either to fulfil a comparison or for aesthetic purposes ('similitudinem necessitatis aut ornatus gratia'), Bede outlined a broad notion of trope that allowed to understand personification as a metaphor. Among the four kinds of metaphor, in fact, he included the trope (literally, transfer) 'ab animali ad inanimale': namely, the attribution of features typical of animate beings to inanimate ones.[97]

Most definitions of personification (often labelled prosopopoeia) in Renaissance treatises of rhetoric and poetics tend to repeat statements from Greek and Latin sources without noticeable innovations. What is of particular interest to the present discussion is the attempt to replace examples from classical literature with examples taken from the vernacular literary tradition. By doing so, literary critics illustrate contemporary uses of the figure that go beyond the boundaries of oratory. In *Regole della lingua Fiorentina* (1552), for instance, Pier Francesco Giambullari (1495–1555) assimilates Cicero's prosopopoeia of Rome with Dante's supernatural characters, such as angels and demons. Other 'modern' examples made by Giambullari include the prosopopoeia of Justice, introduced by Dante himself in the canzone 'Tre

---

95 On the importance of Hermogenes to Renaissance literary criticism and theory, see Annabel M. Patterson, *Hermogenes and the Renaissance: Seven Ideas of Style* (Princeton, NJ: Princeton University Press, 1970); Herman Grosser, *La sottigliezza del disputare: teorie degli stili e teorie dei generi in età rinascimentale e nel Tasso* (Florence: La Nuova Italia, 1992).

96 Blandine Perona, *Prosopopée et 'persona' à la Renaissance* (Paris: Garnier, 2013); see, also, Véronique Montagne, 'La notion de prosopopée au XVIe siècle', *Seizième Siècle*, 4 (2008), 217–36.

97 Bed. *De schem. et trop.* 2.1.8–10. The example of 'translata dictio' given by Bede is an instance of metaphorical personification based on the analogical attribution of human features to an inanimate object: 'Non ad proprium id est quando mons dicitur habere caput et brachia et humeros et barbam' ('*Non ad proprium* is when it is said that a mountain has head, arms, humeri, and beard'); see the text of Bede's *De schematibus et tropis* in Beda, *Opera didascalica. 1. De orthographia; De arte metrica et de schematibus et tropis; De natura rerum*, ed. by C. W. Jones and C. B. Kendall, Corpus Christianorum, Series Latina, 123A (Turnhout: Brepols, 1975), pp. 59–171.

donne intorno al cor' [Three ladies around my heart], as well as the speaking goats in Luigi Alamanni's eclogues.[98] These diverse examples are followed by an explicit reference to the possibility of attributing language to things that are either inanimate or normally devoid of language ('attribuire il parlare alle cose inanimate o che non lo hanno'), a rhetorical device that overlaps with the address to inanimate interlocutors.[99] Similarly concise, and yet neater is the definition given by Gian Giorgio Trissino (1478–1550), who stresses the beauty ('vaghezza') of prosopopoeia by recalling a transhistorical canon of poets who used it: Homer, Virgil, Dante, and Petrarch.[100]

Giambullari and Trissino do not mention the theatrical use of personifications, which had been acknowledged by classical rhetoricians such as Lupus, Hermogenes, and Aphthonius.[101] In this respect, insightful remarks come from Julius Caesar Scaliger (1484–1558), whose posthumous *Poetices libri septem* (1561) stress the importance of distinguishing among uses of a given rhetorical device across different genres. Scaliger describes prosopopoeia as a double-sided figure: on the one hand ('ubi ficta persona introducitur') it corresponds to the introduction of poetical fictions such as Fame and Hunger in Virgil and Ovid, or the Furies, Rage,

---

98 Pier Francesco Giambullari, *Regole della lingua fiorentina*, ed. by Ilaria Bonomi (Florence: Accademia della Crusca, 1986), paragraph 367.

99 Ibid.: 'parlando ad esse cose senza anima; cosa familiarissima a' poeti nostri che parlano alle fonti, all'erbe, ed a' fiori; come Virgilio alla cenere di Troia' [speaking to soulless things; this is very common in our poets, who speak to springs, grass, and flowers; as does Virgil addressing Troy's ashes].

100 Gian Giorgio Trissino, *La quinta et la sesta divisione della Poetica* (Venice: Giovanni Bonadio, 1562), fol. 44^{r-v} (text quoted from *Trattati di poetica e retorica del Cinquecento*, ed. by Berbard Weinberg (Bari: Laterza, 1970–1974), vol. II, pp. 7–90 (pp. 84–85)): 'La prosopopeia [...] è una formazione di persone nuove alle quali si attribuiscono varii e diversi sermoni. E queste non solamente si fingono di uomini vivi, ma di morti, et ancora di angeli, e di dèi, e di cose inanimate come sono arbori, monti, città, e simili. E questa cosa usandola bene dà grandissima vaghezza ai poemi, di che ne è piena l'opera di Omero, e quella di Virgilio, e quella di Dante, e quella del Petrarca; il quale non solamente forma la persona della sua Laura già morta che li parla, ma ancora forma la persona di Amore che litiga con esso, e quella della Morte, e quella del Tempo, et altre. Alle quali si denno dare i propri e convenienti costumi' [Prosopopoeia [...] is the creation of newly invented persons to whom various attributes and speeches are assigned. This may be not only of living individuals, but also of the dead, and angels, gods, and inanimate things such as trees, mountains, cities, etc. Its use confers extreme beauty upon poetry; it is often found in Homer, Virgil, Dante, and Petrarch, who not only personifies his beloved Laura, who is already dead, and makes her speak to him, but he also personifies Love, who argues with him, as well as Death, Time, and others. To these personifications one must assign their specific and appropriate features]. For similar statements, see Alessandro Lionardi, *Dialogi della inventione poetica* (Venice: Plinio Pietrasanta, 1554), pp. 65–66; in *Trattati di poetica e retorica*, vol. II, pp. 213–92 (p. 273); Giason Denores, *Breve trattato dell'oratore* (Padua: Simone Galignani, 1574), fol. 26^r; in *Trattati di poetica e retorica*, vol. III, pp. 103–34 (p. 132); Camillo Pellegrino, *Il Carrafa, o vero della epica poesia* (Florence: Iacopo Sermartelli, 1584), p. 136; in *Trattati di poetica e retorica*, vol. III, pp. 309–44 (p. 316); Nicolò Rossi, *Discorsi intorno alla tragedia* (Vicenza: Giorgio Greco, 1590), fol. 34^v; in *Trattati di poetica e retorica*, vol. IV, pp. 61–139 (p. 99).

101 Particularly interesting, in this respect, is one of the glosses from Reinhard Lorich's commentary on Aphthonius's *Progymnasmata* found in the edition *Aphthonii Sophistae Progymnasmata partim a Rodolpho Agricola, partim a Ioanne Maria Cataneo latinitate donata* (Paris: Jean Mace, 1573), fol. 118^v, where Menander's Disproof is compared with Erasmus's Folly in the *Encomium Moriae*.

and Wrath as mentioned by Quintilian; on the other hand, prosopopoeia is taken as the verbal shaping of a given character. As specified by Scaliger, the first kind is not a simple figure, but 'pars argumenti poetici' [part of the poetical argument], which is particularly suitable for the theatrical stage ('in scaenis').[102] Unfortunately, the discussion of dramatic personifications that the author promised to provide at the end of the book was never completed. His attention to the matter remains nonetheless significant in a time period when the use of personifications in drama was steadily increasing.

Full awareness of the many ways in which prosopopoeia can be achieved is found in the *Arte poetica* (1563) by Antonio Sebastiani Minturno (1500–1574). The treatise offers one of the most exhaustive classifications of the figure, of which seven modes are identified:

1. 'dando voce a cose insensate o ad animali bruti';
2. 'dando forma alle cose che non l'hanno';
3. 'dimostrando i ragionamenti, e gli affetti espressi degli huomini';
4. 'introducendo ragionamenti di finte persone';
5. 'con parlar finto d'alcuna persona incerta';
6. 'con dimostrare senza la presenza della persona';
7. 'con parlare obliquo'.[103]

[1. giving voice to inanimate things or brute animals; 2. giving shape to things that do not have one; 3. showing the speeches and the passions expressed by men; 4. introducing speeches by fictional persons; 5. through the fictional speech of some unidentified person; 6. proving things in absence of the relevant person; 7. with indirect speech.]

Among the examples listed by Minturno, several come from Virgil and Petrarch, thus bearing witness to widespread use of the figure in both epic and lyric poetry (the choice not to provide examples from oratory is due to the treatise's focus on the poetical arts). The second 'mode' is the one that interests us here:

---

102 Jul. Caes. Scalig. *Poet.* 3.47, 422–24: 'Prosopopoeia vero duplex est. Primus modus, ubi ficta persona introducitur, ut Fama a Vergilio et Fames ab Ovidio. Haec non est figura, sed pars argumenti poetici. Hanc fictionem appellat Quintilianus ἰδεῶν, ut Dirarum et Irae et Furoris. Quales multae in Scaenis a nobis in fine huius libri declaratae sunt'; the text is quoted from Julius Caesar Scaliger, *Poetices libri septem*, ed. by L. Deitz and G. Vogt-Spira, 5 vols (Stuttgart: Fromman, 1993–2003). [Prosopopoeia is, in fact, two-pronged. The first kind is when a fictional person is introduced, as Fame in Virgil and Hunger in Ovid. This is not a figure, but a part of the poetical argument. Quintilian calls this fiction ἰδεῶν, as is the case with the Furies, Anger, and Furor. Many of this kind, which are used on stage, are illustrated at the end of this book]. The mention of Quintilian refers to *Inst. or.* 9.2.36.

103 Antonio Sebastiani Minturno, *L'arte poetica* (Venice: Giovanni Andrea Valvassori, 1564), pp. 393–95; to be compared with Minturno's abridged definition in the Latin treatise *De poeta* (Venice: Giordano Ziletti, 1559), p. 522: 'Conformatio. Age vero quam saepe eloquentia, quae muta sunt, inducuntur, ut Achillis equus ab Homero, Polydori cinis a Marone, amnes ab utroque formaque induuntur expertia figurae, ut famam Virgilius finxit, mortem, vitamque Ennius, famem, invidiamque Ovidius, opulentiam et paupertatem Aristophanes' [*Conformatio*. When things that are normally silent are introduced to speak, as Achilles' horse by Homer, Polydorus's ashes by Virgil, rivers by both of them; and when shape is given to things that are shapeless, as fame was feigned by Virgil, death and life by Ennius, hunger and envy by Ovid, abundance and poverty by Aristophanes].

> Diamo anco forma, e volto alle cose, che non hanno figura: sì come alla Fama Virgilio; alla Morte, e alla Vita Ennio; alla Fame, e all'Invidia Ovidio; alla Ricchezza, e alla Povertà Aristophane; alla Morte altresì, e alla Fama, ad Amore, al Tempo, alla Eloquenza, e alla Sapienza il Petrarca. Et io, alla Peste in una delle mie Selve Latine; e in un'altra al Piacere, e alla Vertù.[104]
>
> [We also give shape and face to things that are shapeless: as Virgil did with Fame; Ennius with Death and Life; Ovid with Hunger and Envy; Aristophanes with Richness and Poverty; but also Petrarch with Death, Fame, Love, Time, Eloquence, and Wisdom. And as I did myself with Plague in one of my Latin Silvae, and with Pleasure and Virtue in a different one.]

Minturno's typology is broad: alongside Virgil, Ovid, and Ennius — already mentioned by Quintilian — he refers to personifications in Petrarch's *Triumphi* as well as in his own *Selve*. The series includes one example from drama: the personifications of Poverty and Wealth from Aristophanes' comedy, *Plutus*. The first category is that of personifications appearing in narrative poetry, where it is the poet's duty to bring them to life by means of descriptions. The second includes instead personifications who take centre stage in a play and come to life through the body and voice of the actors. The distinction between these two categories, as highlighted by James Paxson, is crucial to the classification of the figure.[105] Minturno's definition is not devoid of some ambiguity: indeed, while it seizes upon the analogy between narrative and performative personifications, it does not unpack their formal divergences. Like Giambullari, Minturno includes within the same typology Petrarch's addresses to Envy and Death, in which the personifications are evoked as silent interlocutors. By doing so, his definition exposes the flexible grid within which the figure is theorised.

For a more articulate discussion of the use of prosopopoeia in the theatrical context, one must turn to the idiosyncratic exegesis of Aristotle's *Poetics* conducted by Lodovico Castelvetro (1505–1571). In the section of *Poetica d'Aristotele volgarizzata e sposta* (1570) devoted to the three kinds of imitation, the commentator dwells on the 'parlatori introdotti nella narrazione' (speakers introduced within the speech). Let us take a look at Aristotle's passage in Castelvetro's translation:

> Ora [segue] appresso la terza differenza di queste, [cioè delle rassomiglianze], la quale è come altri possa rassomigliare ciascuna maniera di queste [cioè delle differenze]. Perciochè aviene che alcuna volta si fa la rassomiglianza e con quelle medesime cose e di quelle medesime cose, o raccontando altri o divenendo un'altra cosa, secondo che fa Omero, o come [standosi] quello stesso e non tramutato, o [essendo] tutti i rassomiglianti come occupati in facende e operanti.[106]

---

104 Minturno, *L'arte poetica*, pp. 393–94.
105 Paxson, *The Poetics of Personification*, pp. 20–21.
106 Ludovico Castelvetro, *Poetica d'Aristotele vulgarizzata et sposta* (Vienna: Caspar Stainhofer, 1570); the text is quoted from the edition by W. Romani (Bari: Laterza, 1978–79), vol. I, p. 65; Aristotle's passage is *Poet.* 1448a 19–24: 'There is, beside these, a third distinction — in the mode of mimesis for these various objects. For in the same media one can represent the same objects by combining narrative with direct personation, as Homer does; or in an invariable narrative voice; or by direct enactment of all roles' (trans. by Halliwell, p. 35).

As per Castelvetro's reading of Aristotle, poetical imitation can be of three kinds: narrative (the poet never abandons his persona); dramatic (the characters are impersonated by actors); mixed (the poet tells the story, but may occasionally let the characters speak by themselves: as we have seen, this is one of the acceptations of prosopopoeia). As Castelvetro poignantly observes, Aristotle uses a gender-neutral phrasing ('sesso neutro') in the statement 'divenendo un'altra cosa [ἢ ἕτερόν τι γιγνόμενον]' because poets not only make men or women speak, but also other things ('ma altra cosa ancora'). Accordingly, there are various sorts of 'parlatori introdotti nella narrazione' [speakers introduced in the narration]. Beyond humans, gods, animals (both 'sensibili' and 'vegetabili'), and inanimate things ('cose insensate'), Castelvetro recalls the kind of personification that we are more directly concerned with here:

> quelle affezzioni o vizii o virtù dell'animo nostro che appresso la religione pagana non hanno deità personale né certo nascimento come hanno gli altri suoi iddii, come sono invidia, odio, perseveranza, castità, alle quali aggiungere si possono le condizioni e gli stati degli uomini, come ricchezza, povertà, gloria, infamia, nobiltà, viltà e simili; e di questa schiera sono ancora le città e le provinzie, le quali cose tutte si figurano in forma di donna o d'uomo e s'attribuisce loro la favella umana e sono stimate accostarsi alla natura divina.[107]

> [Those affections or vices or virtues of our soul, which in pagan religion have no individual deity nor clear birth, as is instead the case with the other gods — I am referring to envy, hatred, perseverance, chastity, to which one can add the conditions and statuses of men, such as richness, poverty, glory, infamy, nobility, cowardice, and similar; to this kind belong cities and provinces too; all of these are given the shape of women or men, as well as human speech, and are deemed nearing divine nature.]

Castelvetro's classification is remarkable in its exhaustiveness: he lists passions, vices, virtues, human conditions, cities, and lands, thus covering almost the entire repertory of things personifiable in terms that are indeed very close to the ones that we encountered in Cesare Ripa. He also identifies the two main features of personification (human shape and language) highlighting their similarity to the anthropomorphic representation of deities.[108] Castelvetro dwells on the ways in which poets ought to name their characters, and he offers some examples of 'prosopopee di cose senza anima e invisibili' (prosopopoeias of inanimate and invisible things) in both comedy (he refers to the same Aristophanic personifications mentioned by Minturno) and tragedy (these include Bia/Force and Kratos/Power in Aeschylus's *Prometheus Bound*).[109] Similarly to what happens with well-crafted metaphors, this kind of prosopopoeia pleases and amazes the audience thanks to its 'miraculous and unprecedented novelty' ('novità miraculosa e non usitata').[110]

The 'miraculous' flair of the figure is the object of thorough inquiry by

---

107 Castelvetro, *Poetica*, vol. I, pp. 73–74.
108 Castelvetro's list is very similar to the one found in the subtitle of Ripa's *Iconologia* mentioned at the outset of this chapter; see pp. 19–20.
109 Castelvetro, *Poetica*, vol. I, pp. 258, 260.
110 Castelvetro, *Poetica*, vol. I, p. 39.

Florentine scholar Francesco Bonciani (1552–1620) in the *Lezione della prosopopea* (1578), a veritable unicum in Renaissance literary criticism.[111] The author, who was a member of the Accademia degli Alterati and, later, of the Accademia Fiorentina, focuses on the notion of prosopopoeia as 'finzione di persone' (fiction of persons). Through his detailed examination, he provides useful insights into the theatrical use of personifications, specifically of abstract beings. As Bonciani says, the fictional shaping of characters is primarily concerned with two genres of things: those devoid of body ('incorporee') and those without soul ('le [cose] inanimate e i bruti'). The former can be given human shape ('finte in figura umana'), as it happens with Envy, represented as a slender and pale woman ('come l'invidia in forma di donna pallida e magra'). The latter can be made speak *as if* they were human ('favellare e discorrere come persone), as Homer did, for instance, with Achilles' horse ('il che fece Omero introducendo a parlare il caval di Achille'). Character, Bonciani continues, can be constructed by wearing someone else's persona ('vestendosi l'altrui persona') or through a third-person narrative, with no need for the author to 'transform' into someone else ('narrando egli stessi senza tramutarsi in altrui'). The first case is that of Aesop, who speaks in the person of the animals in his fables. The second is instead Dante's, who 'depicted' many celestial and infernal spirits in his poem ('nel suo divin poema molti spiriti celesti et infernali dipinse'), though it should be remembered that Dante himself made use of the first mode too, for example when, after describing Charon, he made him speak.[112] Regardless of the ways in which it is achieved, the 'finzione di persone' is a form of imitation that deals with things false and impossible ('false e impossibili'). As such, it is conducive to a potential contradiction (as well as to one of the questions that I posed at the outset of this chapter): how is it possible to imitate what is non-existent, unreal, and devoid of a visible form? After recalling that wonder, pleasure, and, as per Aristotle, knowledge may indeed be produced by depicting unreal things ('quello che non è stato o non può essere') through words ('col parlare'), Bonciani identifies the epistemological core of prosopopoeia:

> dovendo noi ragionare delle beate menti e delle sostanzie separate e di lor operazione, nol potemmo fare senza ricorrere a quelle voci che tali essenze ci manifestassono; ma elle son tanto remote da' sentimenti nostri e dal nostro intelletto che voci propie non abbiam saputo loro assegnare, onde siamo stati sforzati servirci di quelle che ne significano le nostre operazioni, le quali sono le più degne che noi conosciamo. Per questo attribuiamo a Dio lo 'ntendere, il volere, il ricordarsi, comeché queste cose sieno in lui d'altra guisa che negl'altri non sono.[113]

---

111 Francesco Bonciani, *Lezione della prosopopea* [Florence, Biblioteca Riccardiana, MS 2237, ff. 96–109], in *Trattati di poetica e retorica*, ed. by Weinberg, vol. III, pp. 237–53. For a biographical account of Bonciani, see Roberto Cantagalli, 'Francesco Bonciani', in *Dizionario Biografico degli Italiani*, 11 (1969), pp. 673–74; some aspects of the *Lezione* are discussed by Robert L. Montgomery, 'Allegory and the Incredible Fable: The Italian View from Dante to Tasso', *Proceedings of the Modern Language Association*, 81.1 (1966), 45–55; an overview of the *Lezione* is provided by Montagne, 'La Notion de prosopopée au XVIe siècle', pp. 226–36.
112 Bonciani, *Lezione*, p. 237.
113 Bonciani, *Lezione*, p. 239.

[Since we must speak about angelic minds, separate substances, and their operations, we will not be able to do it without turning to those words that such entities would eventually express to us; but those things are so far from our ability to perceive and understand, that we have not been able to assign them appropriate words; we were thus forced to use those words that describe our own operations, which are the worthiest we know of. For this reason, we attribute intellect, will, and memory to God, even if these qualities are, in him, different than they are in the others.]

The author applies explicitly to prosopopoeia the principle that informs catachresis.[114] Given that it is impossible to talk about supernatural entities such as 'beate menti' [angelic minds] and 'sostanzie separate' [separate substances], which fall beyond human knowledge, we need to attribute them the materiality that is peculiar to the way in which humans experience the world. The principle, upheld by Dante in Canto 4 of *Paradiso* where the poet justifies the anthropomorphic representation of both demons and angels, is the same as that adopted by early modern art theorists in order to legitimate the use of visual allegories such as the personifications of vices and virtues, a topic to which we shall return shortly.[115]

After identifying the origins of the figure, Bonciani defines it as an 'appropriate imitation of impossible things' ('imitazione di cose impossibili in maniera convenevole'). It can be achieved in narrative, dramatic, or mixed forms in order to produce knowledge, pleasure, or persuasion ('fatta nel modo narrativo semplice o misto o nel rappresentativo, a fine d'insegnare o dilettare o persuadere').[116] By leaving aside the fictional speeches of oratory, which (according to the same classification found in *Rhetorica ad Herennium* and Quintilian) he considers under the category of *sermocinatio*, Bonciani distinguishes four groups of *impossibilia* that prosopopoeia is concerned with: (1) anthropomorphic representation of gods, angels, and spirits, which, due to their incorporeal nature, would not be otherwise imaginable ('non ci potendo noi imaginare cosa che non sia corporea');[117] (2) anthropomorphic representation of abstract entities of various nature; (3) attribution of speech to animals and plants; and (4) attribution of speech to inanimate beings.[118] The second category is worth exploring in detail:

> La seconda maniera sono varie passioni et abiti dell'animo nostro come le virtù e l'arti e le scienze, e nella medesima schiera si posson riporre le città e le province

---

114 Heinrich Lausberg, *Handbook of Literary Rhetoric: A Foundation for Literary Study*, trans. by R. Dean Anderson (Leiden and Boston, MA: Brill, 1998), p. 254.
115 Dante, *Paradiso* 4.40–48: 'Così parlar conviensi a vostro ingegno, | però che solo da sensato apprende | ciò che fa poscia d'intelletto degno. | Per questo la scrittura condescende | a vostra facultate, *e piedi e mano* | *attribuisce a Dio*, et altro intende; | e Santa Chiesa *con aspetto umano* | Gabriel e Michel vi rappresenta, | e l'altro che Tobbia rifece sano', emphasis mine [Such signs are suited to your mind, since from | the senses only can it apprehend | what then becomes fit for the intellect. | And this is why the Bible condescends | to human powers, assigning feet and hands | to God, but meaning something else instead. | And Gabriel and Michael and the angel | who healed the eyes of Tobit are portrayed | by Holy Church with human visages] (trans. by Mandelbaum).
116 Bonciani, *Lezione*, p. 239.
117 Bonciani, *Lezione*, p. 240.
118 Bonciani, *Lezione*, p. 241.

finte tutte in forma umana et imitate come se corpo et anima ragionevole avessero; il che forse è nato perciò che i poeti, volendo discoprire per util nostro la natura di queste passioni, né potendo far ciò co' termini propii dell'arte [...] ce l'andarono insegnando sotto questi velami, i quali intanto le ci manifestano che poco più farebbono le proprie diffinizioni; anzi, la moltitudine rozza le comprenderà meglio di questa scorza coperte, che se avanti le si proponessero ignude. E questo ancora ad[i]viene perciò che le cose che son finte adoperare o son dipinte alla azione acconce, muovono più lo intelletto nostro.[119]

[The second kind includes various passions and habits of our soul, such as virtues, arts, and sciences; to this category belong cities and provinces too, represented under human shape as if they had body and rational soul. This was likely originated by the fact that poets, eager to unveil the nature of those passions to our benefit, but unable to do it with the tools of their art, taught them to us under those garments, which reveal them in a way not different from what the appropriate definitions would do. Rather, the rough multitude will better understand them covered by such bark than if they appeared stark naked. This happens because things that are feigned in action or suitable for action move our intellect more strongly.]

The anthropomorphic representation of passions and habits of the soul, vices, and virtues — the list is similar to Castelvetro's — is said to originate from the pedagogical scope of the poets, who have turned to the 'veil' of rhetorical figures in order to represent intellectual subject matter that would be otherwise impossible to depict.[120] Consistently with ideas common in early modern poetics, the poetical garment is deemed more effective than naked truth. In fact, as Bonciani explains it, the 'proper definitions of things' ('proprie diffinizioni') do not add anything to the meaning conveyed by poetical language.[121] Indeed, the populace ('moltitudine rozza') — the illiterate ones that, within Bonciani's argument, are meant to benefit from poetry's pedagogical scope — will acquire knowledge more easily when exposed to the 'bark' ('scorza') of poetry. If this is true of figures of speech in general, prosopopoeia's particular efficacy lies in the fact that things represented in motion touch the audience's soul stronger than static ones (Bonciani gathered this notion from Aristotle's and Demetrius's discussions of active metaphors).[122]

But how is it even possible to imitate things that fall beyond our understanding and perception? Moving from Aristotle's discussion of *phantasia* and Plato's distinction between 'icastic' and 'phantastic' mimesis, Bonciani attempts to solve the issue by turning to imagination as a combinatory process.[123] According to the mechanisms that I have described earlier as relevant to the antique notion of image-making, *phantasia* is meant to elaborate data acquired by the human mind

---

119 Bonciani, *Lezione*, pp. 240–41.
120 See Castelvetro, *Poetica*, vol. I, pp. 73–74.
121 The point is made by several interpreters of Aristotle's *Poetics* in the late Renaissace; among them, the most outspoken, yet balanced in his philological assessment of the sources, is possibly Alessandro Piccolomini, whose commentaries on Aristotle's *Rhetoric* and *Poetics* appeared in the 1560s and 1570s; see Eugenio Refini, *Per via d'annotationi: le glosse inedite di Alessandro Piccolomini all'Ars poetica di Orazio'* (Lucca: Pacini Fazzi, 2009), pp. 107–36.
122 Arist. *Rhet.* 1410b 35, 1411b 32 sff.; Demetr. *De eloc.* 81.
123 See Arist. *De an.* 427b 15–20; Plat. *Soph.* 235d–236c.

through sense perception. It does not create images from scratch; rather, it combines what is stored in one's memory. Images produced by *phantasia* may be unreal *per se* (in other words, they may represent objects that do not exist in reality), but they ought to be the result of the combination of bits and pieces that do exist in the real world. Chimeras, centaurs, and other monstrous creatures, which are not real, may be imagined and, as such, they may be imitated.[124] The process that informs the making of prosopopoeia follows the same dynamic:

> Somigliantemente procede la prosopopea la quale accoppia diverse nature, e togliendo dall'uomo la favella e 'l discorso, l'attribuisce al bruto, o vero prendendo la figura umana, la consegna a cosa che priva sia d'ogni forma visibile; né è però che queste cose separatamente non sieno, perciò che e la favella e 'l bruto e la forma umana e la virtù sono; non è già uno animale senza ragione che discorra, né è la virtù una donna; ma essendo conceduto alla fantasia l'immaginarle così, non ci vien già negato il dare ad intendere altrui sì fatte immaginazioni e per conseguenza imitarle.[125]

> [Prosopopoeia proceeds in a similar way: it combines different natures. Taking the ability to speak from man, it assigns it to the brute; it attributes human shape to things that are devoid of visible form. It is not that these things, taken separately, do not exist: human speech, the brute, human shape, and virtue do exist. What cannot exist is an irrational animal that speaks, or the fact that virtue is a woman. Yet, since fantasy is granted the power to imagine them as such, it is not denied to us to share such imagined things with others and to imitate them accordingly.]

Bonciani then discusses the three ways in which prosopopoeia can be used according to the tripartition that Aristotle outlines in his discussion of imitation.[126] For the narrative mode (both simple and mixed) the author mentions examples from Petrarch (the personifications of Italy and Love).[127] More articulate is the discussion of the dramatic mode, for which Bonciani goes back to Greek and Latin theatre:

---

124 Bonciani, *Lezione*, p. 242: 'Avendo noi varie cose conosciute, la fantasia nostra confonde talora le nature di esse, formandone una quanto al tutto diversa da tutte l'altre, ma simile nelle parti: e tali furono le chimere, i centauri e gl'altri mostri finti da' poeti' [Having known various things, our imagination occasionally blends some of them, giving shape to a new one, different from all others, yet similar when it comes to its parts: of this kind were chimeras, centaurs, and other monsters feigned by the poets]. To the same kind of images belong, in the field of the figurative arts, the 'capricci' (here called 'sogni', literally, dreams) and 'grottesche', understood by Bonciani as the product of fervid combinatory imagination: 'Onde noi veggiamo tutto giorno i nostri dipintori imitare con la loro arte le sirene, le sfingi e' cerberi; e per ventura la guisa di pittura da noi chiamata "grottesca" è della medesima maniera, non potendosi negare che ella ancora non imiti in qualche modo, comeché ella ritragga cose impossibili, come è l'accozzare insieme membra di diversi animali e congiungergli, se ben le viene, con foglie et altre parti d'alberi, come si vede; né guari da questa lontane son quelle pitture de' Fiamminghi che noi "sogni" addomandiamo' [Whence we see every day our painters imitating with their art sirens, sphynxes, and Cerberuses; accidentally, the kind of painting called *grottesca* is of the same sort; in fact, it cannot be denied that, in some way, it does imitate, even if it represents impossible things, putting together and combining limbs of different animals with leaves and other parts of trees, as can be seen; also, not far from this artform are those paintings by Flemish artists, which we call dreams].
125 Ibid.
126 See Arist. *Poet.* 1448a 19–24.
127 Bonciani refers to Petrarca, *Canzoniere*, 53.10–14; 151.9–12.

'Nel modo rappresentativo s'usò la medesima figura per gl'antichi per introdurre nelle lor tragedie quelle false deità, e Plauto se ne servì nella sua tragicomedia, e non dubitò ancora di rappresentare nel prologo del *Trinummo* la Lussuria e la Povertà'.[128] Not only does Bonciani's statement identifies the prologue as a textual space suitable for the staging of allegorical personifications (as we have seen in Lupus's and Scaliger's remarks on the same matter), but it also acknowledges Plautus as the canonical model for the use of personifications in early modern prologues. (While Greek rhetoricians such as Hermogenes and Aphthonius mentioned the example of Menander's personification of Disproof, the Greek playwright's text was hardly accessible to Renaissance readers, hence the priority acquired by Plautus in early modern discussions of allegorical personifications in drama.)[129]

As far as the 'moderns' are concerned, Bonciani outlines a heterogeneous picture:

> Al presente s'usa ciò in quegli spettacoli che noi propriamente chiamiamo 'rappresentazioni', come fu quella che in Santo Spirito si recitò più anni sono, nelle quali s'imita Iddio stesso e gli spiriti celesti, attribuendo loro forma e favellare umano. E questa maniera per ventura, comeché le maschere in se stesse abbiano avuto altra origine, ha dato forma alle nostre mascherate nelle quali si rappresentano varie e diverse cose incorporee in abito umano, come l'Ore e 'l Tempo e la Natura et altre, favellare per utile o diletto nostro, che tal facultà non hanno; [...] le quali finzioni non sono altro che una prosopopea nel modo rappresentativo.[130]
>
> [Nowadays this device is used in those spectacles that we appropriately call rappresentazioni, such as the one given in the church of Santo Spirito several years ago, in which God himself and the heavenly spirits are imitated by attributing them human shape and speech. Even if masks had a different origin, the same device has given shape to our *mascherate*, in which various and different bodiless things are represented under human shape, such as the Hours, Time, Nature, and others; these things, who do not have speaking abilities, are made speak for our benefit or pleasure. [...] These are but examples of prosopopoeia in the representative mode.]

Prosopopoeia is thus common to a variety of theatrical genres, all rooted deep in the Florentine tradition, which Bonciani was obviously familiar with. The sacred 'rappresentazioni' in which God and the angels are introduced and given a voice (a genre that remained steadily present in Florence from the time of Lorenzo il

---

128 Bonciani, *Lezione*, p. 243 ('In the representative mode the same figure was used by the ancients to introduce in their tragedies those false gods, and Plautus used it in his tragicomedy, and he did not hesitate to represent Wealth and Poverty in the prologue to *Trinummus*').
129 On the main features and developments of Renaissance dramatic prologues, see Emilio Goggio, 'The Prologue in the Commedie Erudite of the 16th Century', *Italica*, 18.3 (1941), 124–32; Nino Borsellino, 'Prologo', in *Enciclopedia dello Spettacolo* (Rome: Le Maschere, 1954–1968), vol. VIII, pp. 526–34; Alessandro Ronconi, 'Prologhi "plautini" e prologhi "terenziani" nella commedia italiana del '500', in *Il teatro classico italiano nel '500* (Rome: Accademia Nazionale dei Lincei, 1971), pp. 197–217; Donatella Riposio, *Nova comedia v'appresento: il prologo nella commedia del Cinquecento* (Turin: Tirrenia Stampatori, 1989); on the use of allegorical personifications in dramatic prologues, see Eugenio Refini, 'Prologhi figurati: appunti sull'uso della prosopopea nel prologo teatrale del Cinquecento', *Italianistica*, 35.3 (2006), 61–86.
130 Bonciani, *Lezione*, p. 243.

Magnifico to the Baroque era) share the city's stage with a typically mannerist genre, the *mascherata*.[131] Indeed, courtly festivals, usually held on the occasion of royal entries or princely weddings, offered the ideal context for the staging of grand spectacles with much room for the representation of 'many and diverse bodiless things in human shape' ('varie e diverse cose incorporee in abito umano').[132] The Hours, Time, Nature, and many other personifications triggered the audience's wonder. Their staging, usually meant to be filled with erudite meanings in the intention of the organisers, ended up charming the senses rather than speaking to the audience's intellect, thus paving the way for the performance of *meraviglia* [wonder] that was a flagship feature of late Renaissance and Baroque spectacle.[133]

Following the descriptive part of his *Lezione*, Bonciani moves onto some instructions on how to construct effective personifications. These suggest interesting parallels with other fields, particularly the figurative arts and the art of memory. Bonciani recommends that far-fetched personifications ('[che] tanto poco dell'essere partecipano') be avoided, for they would cross the boundaries of decorum and plausibility.[134] In its vagueness, the statement recalls what concurrent theories of metaphor said about the importance of avoiding implausible analogies

---

131 It is maybe worth recalling that Bonciani authored one *Discorso sopra le maschere*. While Weinberg (*Trattati di poetica e retorica*, vol. III, pp. 493–94) records it as found in Florence, Biblioteca Nazionale Centrale, MS Magl. IX.125, the text is indeed missing, and it has not been possible to locate it so far. On the tradition of the Florentine *sacre rappresentazioni*, see Nerida Newbigin, *Making a Play for God: The Sacre Rappresentazioni of Renaissance Florence* (Toronto: Centre for Renaissance and Reformation Studies, 2021).

132 On theatre and spectacle in Florence under the Medici, see *Le Temps revient: 'l tempo si rinuova. Feste e spettacoli nella Firenze di Lorenzo il Magnifico*, ed. by Paola Ventrone (Milan: Silvana editoriale, 1992); on the courtly festival of the late Renaissance, alongside the seminal study by Aby Warburg, 'The Theatrical Costumes for the Intermedi of 1589', in Aby Warburg, *The Renewal of Pagan Antiquity*, trans. by David Britt (Los Angeles: Getty Research Institute for the Research of Arts and Humanities, 1999), pp. 349–401, and Ludovico Zorzi's chapter on Florence in *Il teatro e la città: saggi sulla scena italiana* (Turin: Einaudi, 1977); but also Giovanna Gaeta Bertelà and Annamaria Petrioli Tofani, eds, *Feste e apparati medicei da Cosimo I a Cosimo II: mostra di Disegni e incisioni* (Florence: Leo S. Olshki editore, 1969); Nino Pirrotta, *Li due Orfei: da Poliziano a Monteverdi* (Turin: Einaudi, 1975); Anna Maria Testaverde Matteini, *L'officina delle nuvole: il teatro mediceo nel 1589 e gli Intermedi del Buontalenti nel Memoriale di Girolamo Seriacopi* (Milan: Edizioni Amici della Scala, 1991); Elvira Garbero Zorzi, *Teatro e spettacolo nella Firenze dei Medici: modelli dei luoghi teatrali* (Florence: Leo S. Olschki editore, 2001); Nina K. Treadwell, *Music and Wonder at the Medici Court: The 1589 Interludes for La Pellegrina* (Bloomington: Indiana University Press, 2008).

133 In this respect, insightful remarks remain those by Warburg on the *intermedi* given as part of the 1589 celebratory festivals held in Florence on the occasion of the wedding of Ferdinando de' Medici and Christine of Lorraine; see Warburg, 'The Theatrical Costumes' (p. 365): 'There is no doubt that Intermedio 1 afforded a brilliant and surprising spectacle; but whether it left the onlookers with any clear impression of the meaning of the characters, or of the connection between them, is another question altogether. The resources proper to the theater, those of words and action, were used hardly at all to characterize the mythological *concetti*. [...] The author, if he wanted to convey some sense of meaning and coherence to the spectator, was left with only one recourse: the path to the emotions, through the ear, was closed; but the path to the understanding, through the eye, remained open. The characterization must be conveyed through clear, symbolic visual signs, that would be familiar to the spectators as attributes of mythological beings. In the event, however, his excessive zeal in the pursuit of attributes led to some arbitrary and unnatural combinations'.

134 Bonciani, *Lezione*, p. 246.

in the making of tropes. The boundaries are difficult to set and, eventually, they are left to the poet's taste and sense of measure. The relevant example, Petrarch's personification of his own sighs in *Canzoniere* 117, is of great interest.[135] Petrarch personifies them in the narrative mode (he assigns them 'movimento umano parlandone in terza persona'), for it would have been inacceptable to describe them as if they really had human shape ('descriverli partitamente, quasi le membra avessero e l'abito umano').[136] As Bonciani points out, eyesight is too strict a judge, and does not allow for the artist's unbound freedom.

In a similar vein, the author outlines some specific instructions. By turning to Aristotle's recommendation on how to create characters, Bonciani argues that the personification of a given thing must be consistent with its nature ('quella forma e quell'abito se le deve attribuire che alla natura sua si confaccia').[137] Homer's Prayers and Dante's Fraud illustrate two different rhetorical strategies, one based on physiognomics and the other on metaphorical analogy:

> fingansi pertanto le preghiere zoppe e grinze e di lunghi manti coperte per la tardità e lunghezza del favellare ch'usa colui che priega; e la Froda che di nascosto s'ingegna di nuocere e mostra nell'apparenza di voler giovare, come la figurò Dante in que' versi: 'La faccia sua era facia d'uom giusto, | tanto benigna avea di fuor la pelle, | e d'un serpente tutto l'altro fusto. | Due branche avea pilose insin l'ascelle; | lo dosso e 'l petto et amendue le coste | dipinte avea di nodi e di rotelle'.[138]

> [Prayers should be pictured crippled and wrinkly and wearing long cloaks to signify the slowness and lengthiness of speech typical of those who pray; and Fraud, furtively attempting to harm while pretending to help, as Dante feigned it in those lines: 'The face he wore was that of a just man, | so gracious was his features' outer semblance; | and all his trunk, the body of a serpent; | he had two paws, with hair up to the armpits; | his back and chest as well as both his flanks | had been adorned with twining knots and circlets'.]

The characterisation of Prayers, which has its archetype in *Iliad*'s Book 9, is based on the idea that the traits of the suppliant (their being slow and demure in the way they talk) are assigned to the personification. It is not unlikely that Bonciani was familiar with the passage from *Quaestiones Homericae* that I have discussed above and which justified Homer's visual characterisation of Prayers by turning to allegory.[139]

Dante's Fraud, embodied by Gerion, the winged monster who carries the poet and Virgil to Malebolge, is an image of a different kind. While Prayers are personifications in the fullest sense of the word (i.e., bodiless things that are given anthropomorphic features), the shaping of Gerion is informed by the combinatory

---

135 Petrarch, *Canzoniere* 117.5-8: 'I miei sospiri più benigno calle | avrien per gire ove lor speme è viva; | or vanno sparsi e peur ciascuno arriva là dov'io 'l mando, ché sol un non falle' [then all my sighs would find a kinder road | to travel to that place where their hope lives; | now they go scattered, yet each one arrives | where I send him — there is not one that fails] (trans. by Musa).
136 Bonciani, *Lezione*, p. 246.
137 See Arist. *Poet.* 1454a 16-33.
138 Bonciani, *Lezione*, pp. 246-47; for Dante's allegory of Fraud, see *Inferno* 17.10-15 (trans. by Mandelbaum).
139 Heracl. *Quaest. Hom.* 37.2-3.

process that Bonciani described when talking about chimeras and centaurs. The poet creates an allegory by giving a composite body to an abstract concept: the head of a fair man, which stands for the false benevolence of fraudulent people, is added to the body of a serpent with leonine paws. Every detail in Gerion's figure stands for something else and requires readers to seize its meaning based on the moral code they share with the poet. Not only does the 'sozza imagine di froda' [filthy image of fraud] recall the many images of monsters typical of Christian iconography, but it also exposes its highly pedagogical function, which can be usefully compared to the tradition of images of memory, with specific attributes conveying specific meanings.[140]

Picking on Cicero's claim that corporeal images cannot exist without imagining a place to host them, Bonciani stresses that personifications should be given an appropriate space ('stanza'), that is, a *locus*. The affinity with mnemotechnics here becomes even more evident:

> Accade talora che a queste cose si attribuisce qualche stanza particolare e spezialmente da' poeti, e questa ancora si richiede convenevole alla condizion loro. Però gl'antichi, conoscendo il sonno amatore della notte e del silenzio, finsero il suo abituro in profondissime valli circondate di selve, dove raggio di sole non penetrasse già mai e lontano dalle abitate regioni. E Virgilio nell'entrata dell'inferno collocò que' mali a' quali più dolce stanza non si convenia, e molto più convenevolmente fu tal luogo alla Discordia assegnato, che non furo i conventi delle religiose persone, e massimamente a chi debbe aver per mira l'introdurre buon costumi.[141]

> [At times poets assign a particular location to those things, and such a location needs to be appropriate to their features. For this reason, the ancients, knowing that sleep is a lover of night and silence, depicted his lodging in deep valleys surrounded by woods, where no sunray ever entered, far from inhabited regions. And Virgil placed at the entrance of hell those evils which would not suit any sweeter location; that place was assigned to Discord much more conveniently than the convents of religious people, especially on the part of those who should aim at introducing honest behaviours.]

Good examples of convenient *loci* are the House of Sleep in Book 11 of Ovid's *Metamorphoses*, and the entrance of Hell, where Virgil aptly places those evils (the Vices) that would not fit anywhere else.[142] Conversely, Ariosto's depiction of Discord is deemed bad. The criticism targets the poet's satirical scope, specifically the idea of situating Discord and all other vices in churches and convents, a poetical trick that clashes with Bonciani's post-Tridentine perspective on the moral and pedagogical aim of poetry, where no room was made for anti-Catholic satire.[143]

140 On the didactic nature of the allegory mobilised by this interpretation of Gerion in relation to broader patterns in the pedagogical use of images, see Mary Carruthers, *The Book of Memory: A Study of Memory in Medieval Culture* (Cambridge: Cambridge University Press, 1990); eadem, *The Craft of Thought: Meditation, Rhetoric, and the Making of Images, 400–1200* (New York: Cambridge University Press, 1998); and Lina Bolzoni, *La rete delle immagini: predicazione in volgare dalle origini a Bernardino da Siena* (Turin: Einaudi, 2002).
141 Bonciani, *Lezione*, p. 247.
142 Ovid. *Met.* 11.592–649; Verg. *Aen.* 6.236 ff.
143 Ludovico Ariosto, *Orlando furioso* 14.76–84. Ariosto's treatment of allegorical personifications

Once the scene for such theatre of passions is set, the poet must proceed by assigning the 'finta persona' appropriate actions ('quell'azione che conforme le sia') and words ('parole ancora alla natura sua corrispondenti').[144] As regards actions, Bonciani gives only one example, a negative one, and once again from Ariosto: to his mind, it is inappropriate to introduce the Archangel Michael as 'poco diligente essecutore de' commandamenti divini' [negligent executor of God's will] and make him blush in shame ('arrossare per la vergogna').[145] Similarly, words will need to be consistent with the features of the 'finta persona': heavenly spirits cannot speak as demons do; likewise, beasts are expected to reveal their nature through their words (fraud in the fox, greed in the wolf, violence in the lion, etc.).[146]

Ultimately, Bonciani's *Lezione* brings the attention on prosopopoeia as a poetical device that, originally conceived as an oratorial tool, is prone to a variety of literary uses. By examining instances of the ways in which the figure may be used in lyric poetry, epic, and drama, the author outlines the widespread dissemination of the figure, confirming its status as central to the poetics of his own time. As such, Bonciani's survey of personification resonates with concurrent discussions of personified allegories in artistic literature, an area that, as the next section will suggest, has much in common with uses of the figure in dramatic contexts.

From the Verbal to the Visual: Personified Allegories as Images

The defence of personification based on its didactic potential resonates with similar arguments within the artistic literature that blossomed in the aftermath of the Council of Trent and which constituted the backbone of discourses about images and image-making throughout the late Renaissance and the Baroque era.[147] Allegorical images were indeed very frequent in both the secular and religious arts of the time. To give shape to what is shapeless ('[dar] forma a quello che non è'), as stated by Giovanni Andrea Gilio (d. 1584) in the dialogue *Degli errori e degli abusi de' pittori* [On the Errors and Abuses of Painters] (1564), consists in representing imaginary things ('cose favolose'), that is, objects devoid of tangible existence, the representation of which forces the boundaries of decorum and plausibility.[148] The notion of 'favoloso'

---

would deserve special attention: as evidenced by the examples of Silence and Discord, the poet tends to reverse (often comically) the most common assumptions associated with the allegorical code, with important repercussions on the overall agenda embedded in the poem.
144 Bonciani, *Lezione*, p. 247.
145 Ibid.; see Ariosto, *Orlando furioso* 27.35.1–4; for the fight between Michael and Discord, see *Orlando furioso* 27.38.1–2, which Bonciani quotes in full.
146 Bonciani, *Lezione*, p. 247.
147 In the aftermath of the seminal contribution by Rensselaer W. Lee, '*Ut pictura poesis*: The Humanistic Theory of Painting', *The Art Bulletin*, 22.4 (1940), 197–269, the bibliography on Renaissance theories of images and image-making has been growing steadily; for an overview of its main trends, see David Freedberg, *The Power of Images: Studies in the History and Theory of Response* (Chicago, IL: University of Chicago Press, 1989); John M. Steadman, 'Image-Making in the Verbal and Visual Arts: A Renaissance Obsession', *Huntington Library Quarterly*, 61.1 (1998), 53–80; and *Renaissance Theories of Vision*, ed. by John Shannon Hendrix and Charles H. Carman (Burlington, VT: Ashgate, 2010).
148 Giovanni Andrea Gilio, *Dialogo nel quale si ragiona degli errori e degli abusi de' pittori circa l'istorie*

[marvellous] includes all things that do not and cannot exist ('quello che non è e non può essere'): in other words, things that are not depictable, because they fall beyond sense perception.[149] The only way to give shape to intellectual content that is *per se* shapeless is to convey it through some form of support that may make it visible. Gilio mentions the personification of Fury in order to demonstrate how to create a personified allegory. Given that fury is a passion of the soul, one needs first to identify its characteristic features, and then give them shape through visual tropes:

> Le cose favolose, poi, si fingono dandosi forma a quello che non è: come l'istesso poeta finge il Furore, il quale altro non è che un moto d'animo acceso circa il cor de l'uomo per qualche ricevuta ingiuria, con appetito di vendetta; al quale, per essere irregolato e bestiale, fu dato forma d'uomo mostruosa più tosto che naturale, e per mostrar la quiete e la pace come a quello contrarie, lo finse legato con grosse catene di ferro, con le mani dietro, che siede sopra tutte le sorti de armi et istrumenti bellici, come cose appertenenti al furore, a l'ira et al desiderio de la vendetta. In compagnia del Furore sogliono andare l'Orrore, lo Spavento, la Discordia, la Guerra, l'Odio et altre cose tali, ridotte in forma umana, con le qualità appertenenti a ciascuna.[150]

> [As for fabulous things, they are imagined when a form is given to something that does not exist, as when the same poet imagines the figure of Fury. For this is nothing other than an emotion excited in a man's heart as a result of some injury received for which he wants revenge. Because of its unbridled and bestial quality, [Fury] was given the form of a monstrous rather than a natural man. In order to show he was the antithesis of peace and quiet, he was represented tied up with great iron chains, with his arms behind him and seated on different types of weapons and instruments of war; the kinds of things appropriate to fury, anger, and the desire for revenge. Along with Fury are often found Honor, Fear, Discord, War, Hate, and other such things converted into human form, each with its appropriate qualities.]

As Gilio reports, the creative process ('finzione') by means of which Honour and Virtue are given human shape ('dar forma humana a l'Onore et a la Virtù') was commonly used by the ancients, who made these personifications coincide with deities, and has been later appropriated and revived by Christian culture. Moving from examples found in classical literature, poets and artists have learnt how to give human shape to Religion, Faith, Hope, Charity, and the other theological virtues ('da questi esempi mossi, hanno imparato a dar forma umana a la Religione, a la Fede, a la Speranza, a la Carità et a l'altre virtù che, insieme con queste, vanno mescolatamente con le cose sacre e vertù teologiche si chiamano').[151] As indicated

---

(Camerino: Antonio Gioioso, 1564); the text is edited in *Trattati d'arte del Cinquecento tra Manierismo e Controriforma*, ed. by Paola Barocchi (Bari: Laterza, 1961), vol. II, pp. 3–115. For an English translation and introduction to the dialogue, see Giovanni Andrea Gilio, *Dialogue on the Errors and Abuses of Painters*, ed. by Michael Bury, Lucinda Byatt, and Carol M. Richardson, trans. by Michael Bury and Lucinda Byatt (Los Angeles: Getty Research Institute, 2018).

149 Gilio, *Dialogo*, p. 100.
150 Gilio, *Dialogo*, pp. 100–01. Gilio's description of Furor refers to Verg. *Aen.* 1.294–96; English trans. by Bury and Byatt, pp. 215–16.
151 Gilio, *Dialogo*, p. 102. For further details about the use of personifications (e.g., those of the Liberal Arts) in celebratory apparatuses, see p. 104: 'Penso che dagli antichi abbino i moderni

by Paola Barocchi, who has compared Gilio's passage with Johannes Molanus's *De picturis et imaginibus sacris* (1570), personifications are not conceived as mere images, but as ethical models endowed with a performative function: by making visible the *mores*, they urge the devout observer to adopt a Christian way of life.[152]

If Gilio and Molanus highlight the performative and disciplining power of the images (a topic that will interest us in the following parts of this book), an even more sophisticated approach, primarily concerned with the psychology and epistemology of image-making, is that of cardinal Gabriele Paleotti (1522–1597).[153] In Book 2 of his influential *Discorso intorno alle immagini sacre et profane* [Discourse on Sacred and Profane Images] (1582), Paleotti devotes two important chapters to the depictions of virtues and vices ('pitture delle virtù e dei vizii').[154] As Cristoforo Giarda would do thirty years later in his *Icones Symbolicae*, Paleotti dwells on the force with which images leave impressions on the audience's minds and inspire actions accordingly.[155] Within the context of his discussion, the cardinal endorses the platonic desire to 'see' virtue: 'chi potesse con gli occhi rimirare la faccia della virtù et onestà, si accenderebbe di meraviglioso desiderio di quella' [whoever had a chance to see

---

imparato l'uso di dar forma di donne a le virtù che liberali si chiamano, come la Geometria, la Filosofia, l'Astrologia, la Musica, la Rettorica, la Grammatica, l'Aritmetica, aggiungendovi anche la Teologia. E queste oggi si pongono per il più ne le piramidi e pili che si fanno ai prencipi et ai gentiluomini morti, che 'l mondo per famosi, per eccellenti e per grandi celebra' [I think that the ancients taught the moderns the practice of giving female form to the virtues that are called liberal, like Geometry, Philosophy, Astrology, Music, Rhetoric, Grammar, Arithmetic, not to mention Theology. And today these are most frequently placed on pyramids and tombs erected to dead princes and to gentlemen whom the world celebrates for their fame, excellence, and greatness] (trans. by Bury and Byatt, p. 222). On Gilio's contribution to concurrent debates in art theory, see Stefano Pierguidi, *'Dare forma humana a l'Honore et a la Virtù': Giovanni Guerra (1544–1618) e la fortuna delle figure allegoriche da Mantegna all'Iconologia di Cesare Ripa* (Rome: Bulzoni, 2008).

152 Barocchi, *Trattati d'arte*, vol. II, p. 609. See the passage referred to by Barocchi in Johannes Molanus, *De picturis et imaginibus sacris, liber unus: tractans de vitandis circa eas abusibus, et de ea earundem significationibus* (Leuven: Hieronymus Welleus, 1570), f. 98ᵛ, which provides a set of interesting examples: 'picturae, quae non solum imagines exprimunt, sed simul mores nostros formant, aut ad virtutem instigant. Hae enim ethicae dici merentur, et medium locum occupant inter prophanas et sacras' [pictures that not only express images, but shape our mores too, or spur us to virtue. These deserve to be called ethical, and occupy a medium place between secular and sacred images]. Greek and Latin examples mentioned by Molanus include Justice, Discord, Harmony, Love, and Envy.

153 Luigi Scorrano, 'Gabriele Paleotti e il catechismo dei pittori "teologi mutoli"', *Studi rinascimentali*, 3 (2005), 113–27; Vincenzo Caputo, 'Gli abusi dei pittori e la norma dei trattatisti: Giovanni Andrea Gilio e Gabriele Paleotti', *Studi rinascimentali*, 6 (2008), 99–110; Paolo Prodi, 'Introduction', in Gabriele Paleotti, *Discourse on Sacred and Profane Images*, trans. by William McCuaig (Los Angeles: Getty Research Institute, 2012), pp. 1–42.

154 Gabriele Paleotti, *Discorso intorno alle imagini sacre et profane* (Bologna: Alessandro Benacci, 1582); the text is edited in Barocchi, *Trattati d'arte*, vol. II, pp. 119–503) For the two chapters that I am discussing here, see pp. 452–61: 2.43, 'Delle pitture delle virtù e dei vizii, e della molta difficoltà in poterle rappresentare' [On pictures of the virtues and vices and the great difficulty in representing these]; 2.44, 'Alcuni avvertimenti per rappresentare le imagini delle virtù e vizii' [A few guidelines for representing images of the vices and virtues], and the English translation in Paleotti, *Discourse*, pp. 280–86.

155 On Giarda, whom I mentioned in the introduction to this volume, see p. 15.

the face of virtue with their eyes, would be ignited by marvellous desire of her].[156] Unfortunately, Paleotti continues, the quality of the images produced by both ancients and moderns is poor.[157] Since virtues and vices can only be conceived in terms of genre (virtue and vice broadly meant) and species (particular virtues and vices), their depiction proves very difficult. As intellectual operations ('operazioni dell'intelletto') that can be conceived only in abstract terms ('si intendono solamente in astratto'), it is not possible to perceive them through the senses ('non potiamo noi così vestirle che le facciamo venire obietto del senso, né possiamo sottoporre agli occhi del corpo quello ch'è proprio della mente').[158] Attempts made by artists have proved ineffective, for they have been informed by two opposite mistakes. First, Paleotti criticises the conceit-laden depictions produced by artists, who, wishing to shy away from 'vulgar' things ('partirsi dale cose volgari'), aimed to express virtue through noble and refined inventions ('con alti concetti e squisite invenzioni').[159] Second, he criticises the common practice of representing virtues as women: by drawing the audience's attention towards the physical beauty of the female body, it distracts them from morality and religion.[160]

Turning to pragmatic recommendations, Paleotti acknowledges that personification is the only rhetorical device able to accomplish the visual representation of virtue. The process is the same that informs the representation of other things

---

156 Paleotti, *Discorso*, p. 453; see Plat. *Phaedr.* 250d; Paleotti recalls Cicero's rephrasing of Plato's statement as well (Cic. *De off.* 1.5: 'Facies honesti si oculis cerneretur, mirabiles amores excitaret sui').
157 Paleotti, *Discorso*, p. 453: 'non si vedono disegni antichi né moderni, che in parte alcuna agguaglino la grandezza et eccellenza loro [della virtù e dell'onestà], perché, da certe poche imagini in poi, molto ordinarie e trite, della Giustizia, Fortezza, Temperanza o simili, la schiera gloriosa di tante altre virtù resta come derelitta, parendo quasi smarrita la strada di rappresentarle, vedendosi che rari oggi si mettono o più tosto riescono in questa impresa' [we see neither ancient nor modern designs that in any way equal the greatness and excellence of the virtues. Apart from a few ordinary and trite images of Justice, Fortitude, Temperance, and the like, the glorious rank of so many other virtues is left, so to speak, derelict; it almost seems as if the path to their representation has been lost, so rare are those who attempt, or rather who succeed, in this enterprise] (trans. by McCuaig, p. 281).
158 Paleotti, *Discorso*, p. 456: 'We are unable to dress them in such a way that they become objects of the senses, nor can we set before corporeal eyes that which is proper to the mind' (trans. by McCuaig, p. 283).
159 Ibid.: 'questi hanno partorito opera tanto oscura et intricata, che senza l'aiuto appresso d'alcun valente filosofo o teologo non se ne può cavare i piedi, e resta il concetto loro incomprensibile' [these have given birth to works so obscure and intricate that, without some expert philosopher or theologian standing by, you cannot make head or tail out of it, and their concept remains incomprehensible] (trans. by McCuaig).
160 Ibid.: 'quegli che, volendo farle conoscere al popolo, le hanno figurate, come volgarmente si usa, in forma di donna con gli abiti et insegne che le si danno; il che viene tanto ad abbassare et avilire la grandezza loro, che perdono tutta la dignità e splendore della virtù, talché, dive dovriano queste imagini rapir l'animo per meraviglia et infiammarlo d'ardore di bontade, rendono più tosto negligente il pensiero, parendoli rimirare cosa comune e triviale, come sono le donne che si veggono ogni giorno' [those who wished to make the virtues known to the people and have shown them, as the vulgar practice is, in the form of a woman with whatever dress and attributes they give her. This is to abase and vilify their greatness to the point that they lose all dignity and splendor of virtue, and these images, which were meant to ravish the mind with marvel and inflame it with ardor for goodness, instead render thought negligent, for it seems to itself to be gazing upon something trivial and common, no different from the women one sees everyday] (trans. by McCuaig).

intelligible, yet invisible, things that do exist, but cannot be seized through the senses ('le altre cose intelligibili et invisibili, che hanno veramente il loro essere reale, ma non però sottoposto al senso': this is the case, for instance, of the anthropomorphic depiction of angels). The mechanism is, in principle, straightforward: one should identify the essence ('sostanza') of the vice or virtue that needs to be pictured, and give it an appropriate shape. After providing a few basic instructions (shininess suits virtue, filthiness suits vice, etc.), Paleotti recommends that image-makers follow the example of renown authors who have talked about such matters and look at their descriptions, so that the paintbrush will achieve what those writers accomplished by means of the pen ('autori gravi et approvati, che di queste cose hanno ragionato, e vedere come da quelli sono state descritte, valendosi del modo, in dipingerle col pennello, che quelli con la penna hanno tenuto').[161] Within a first list of examples, which includes authors as diverse as Church Fathers and Lucian, Paleotti gives special attention to John Chrysostom's depiction of Avarice, which he quotes in full. The author continues by recalling other poets, pagan and Christian, who should be taken as models in the making of personifications, for they have produced materials useful to the scope ('materia non volgare a questo effetto'). These include Ovid, Lucan, Silius Italicus, Claudian, Prudentius and, more recently, Battista Mantovano.[162] However, Paleotti does not hide some scepticism about the very concept of personification. Indeed, by suggesting that abstract notions may be more poignantly represented through real characters who have embodied them (for instance, saints the likes of George and Christopher), Paleotti touches upon the tension between personification and character that has been running across the history of the figure for centuries.[163]

161 Paleotti, *Discorso*, pp. 458–59.
162 Paleotti, *Discorso*, pp. 459–60: 'sì come della umiltà e della fucata bellezza appresso il Nazianzeno; dell'iracondia et invidia appresso il Nisseno; dell'avarizia appresso S. Basilio; della eloquenza e della calunnia appresso Luciano; della giustizia, della discordia, della emulazione, del silenzio e di molte altre appresso altri autori, che ne hanno parlato giudiziosamente e molto a proposito per poter fare un ritratto de' detti loro e rappresentarlo al popolo: sì come Tertulliano dipinge la imagine della pazienza nella orazione dove raccomanda questa virtù a tutti i buoni; e parimente S. Crisostomo descrive diligentemente l'avarizia e le sue parti [...] Potrassi parimente da alcuni poeti cristiani e gentili scieglere materia non volgare a questo effetto; poi che con l'ingegno suo hanno mirabilmente espresse alcune cose, sì come, presso Prudenzio, della fede et idolatria, della castità e libidine, e di molte altre virtù e vizii; presso il Carmelitano, dei sette vizii capitali; presso Ovidio, della invidia e sua casa; presso Lucano, del lusso e della parsimonia; presso Silio Italico, della virtù e della voluptà; e presso Claudiano, della eternità; e così presso molti altri' [Examples would include humility and artificially enhanced beauty in Nazianzenus; wrath and envy in Nyssenus; avarice in Saint Basil; eloquence and calumny in Lucian; and justice, discord, emulation, silence, and many other virtues and vices in other authors who have spoken judiciously and very much to the point. The artist must make a portrait of their words and represent it to the people. Tertullian, for example, depicts the image of patience in the oration in which he commends this virtue to all good people; likewise, Saint Chrysostom diligently describes avarice and its parts [...] It is also possible to find dignified material for this purpose in a few of the Christian and pagan poets because they have used their talent to express some things admirably. There are passages on faith and idolatry, chastity and libidinousness, and many other virtues and vices in Prudentius; on the seven capital vices in the Carmelite; on envy and its house in Ovid; on luxury and parsimony in Lucan; on virtue and voluptuousness in Silius Italicus; on eternity in Claudian; and so forth in many other poets] (trans. by McCuaig, pp. 285–86).
163 Paleotti, *Discorso*, pp. 460–61.

The cautious recommendations of the cardinal tackle the difficulties intrinsic to the use of personifications in the figurative arts. In this regard, it is worth noticing that the sources indicated by Paleotti are strictly textual, and not visual. Accordingly, at the end of the chapter 'Avertimenti per rappresentare le imagini delle virtù e vizii' [Instructions on the representation of images of virtues and vices], Paleotti privileges the verbal and explanatory component of personification by recommending that the painting be integrated by words:

> E sopra tutto, per maggiore distinzione e chiarezza, lodaressimo assai alcuno breve e significante motto, che venisse a dar anima e vita alla imagine; poi che, essendo formata di cose forsi non molto note, viene a restare come corpo morto, se non è vivificato da alcune parole o dal luogo dello autore approvato, come di sopra in altro proposito si è discorso.[164]
>
> [Above all, for greater distinctness and clarity, we strongly recommend some brief and telling phrase that adds soul and life to the image because it may be derived from sources that are not well known and risks remaining a dead body, so to speak, unless it is vivified by some words or by the source text from the approved author; this has been discussed above.]

It is, in the end, the verbal text that, according to Paleotti, is able to bring an image to life. In a similar fashion, Cesare Ripa would return on the usefulness of combining words and images, specifically in his discussion of the enlivening function of the motto, which, by capturing the 'soul' of the figure, achieves the fullest scope of personification. The slippery interaction of the visual and the verbal seized by authors as different as Gilio, Paleotti, and Ripa, among others, is what made the use of allegorical personifications particularly suitable for the performance of spiritual and devotional practices, whereby performance hangs, once again, in the balance between its literal, pragmatic, meaning and the metaphorical framework of its theatrical use. If, according to mnemotechnics, it is by placing *imagines agentes* into specific *loci* that they fulfil their performative potential, theatre proves a particularly productive site — indeed, the stage functions as a *locus* — for the visualisation of impactful images.

From the Visual to the Theatrical: Personified Allegories on Stage

As suggested by works of literary criticism and artistic theory such as those by Bonciani, Gilio, and Paleotti, personification is a particularly effective tool when it comes to the staging — be it real or imagined, described or painted — of the theatre of virtues, vices, and various human affections that populates the poetical and visual culture of early modernity. Accordingly, theatrical uses of allegorical personifications, which the Renaissance inherited from classical antiquity and the Middle Ages, remained steadily present throughout the early modern period, when the multifaceted world of theatre offered many opportunities for personified allegories to be brought on stage. If courtly festivals such as those held on the occasion of royal entries and princely weddings tended to privilege the visual dimension of the spectacle, conceived as a wonder to be admired, other forms of

---

164 Paleotti, *Discorso*, p. 461 (trans. by McCuaig, p. 286).

theatre (religious and school drama in the first place) focused on the persuasive power of words, particularly their ability to make things (even abstract things) visible. Towards the end of the timeframe taken into account by the present study, the point was made clearly by Emanuele Tesauro (1592–1675) in his *Cannocchiale aristotelico* [Aristotelian Telescope] (1670), which includes prosopopoeia among the 'pathetic figures' ('figure patetiche') meant to 'express the movements of the soul' ('forme esprimenti alcun movimento dell'animo').[165] Adopting a markedly Aristotelian epistemology, Tesauro gathers together the figures that make it possible to represent 'non existing objects' ('obietti non esistenti'). Among them, priority is given to prosopopoeia, the most 'miraculous one', capable of giving a voice to what is normally silent ('figura infra tutte l'altre miracolosa, che dona a' mutoli la favella').[166] As the author explains it, pathetic figures are peculiar to the 'histrionic art': by making the speech 'pathetic', they make it somewhat 'tragic and theatrical' ('rendono la oration patetica, et consequentemente alquanto tragica e teatrale'). This is the feature that, based on Aristotle's discussion in Book 3 of *Rhetoric*, distinguishes the 'hypocritical' style ('hipocritico, cioè simulato') from the 'historical' ('historico'): whereas the latter, by means of 'clear' words, represents concepts and ideas as if they were 'dead' on 'dead pages' ('rappresenta mortamente il concetto nelle morte pagine, con un dir piano e schietto'), the former, animated by pathetic figures, is capable of imprinting not only words and concepts into the ears and minds of the audience, but also the speaker's soul into the soul of the listener.[167] The 'living' speech afforded by the hypocritical style is thus the kind of speech that leaves a trace on whoever is listening. As such, it can manipulate, reform, and, if needed, regulate the audience.

Tesauro's provenance from the ranks of the Jesuit order points towards a crucial feature of his training: namely, the idea of a rhetorical and poetical system that hinges upon the creative and gnoseological power of language.[168] Indeed, Tesauro's

---

165 Emanuele Tesauro, *Il cannocchiale aristotelico, o sia idea dell'arguta et ingeniosa elocutione che serve a tutta l'arte oratoria, lapidaria et simbolica esaminata co' principii del divino Aristotele* (Turin: Bartolomeo Zavatta, 1670), p. 212.
166 Tesauro, *Il cannocchiale*, p. 220.
167 Tesauro, *Il cannocchiale*, pp. 209–10: 'agitato da queste forme patetiche et contentiose, imprime non sol le parole nell'orecchio o il concetto nella mente, ma l'animo di chi parla nell'animo di chi ascolta'.
168 Claudio Scarpati and Eraldo Bellini, *Il vero e il falso dei poeti: Tasso, Tesauro, Pallavicino, Muratori* (Milan: Vita e Pensiero, 1990), pp. 35–72; Malvina Fiorani, 'Aristotelismo e innovazione barocca nel concetto di ingegno del Cannocchiale aristotelico di Tesauro', *Studi secenteschi*, 46 (2005), 91–129; Alessandro Benassi, 'Lo "scherzevole inganno": figure ingegnose e argutezza nel "Cannocchiale aristotelico" di Emanuele Tesauro', *Studi secenteschi*, 47 (2006), 9–55; Monica Bisi, 'Visione e invenzione: la conoscenza attraverso la metafora nel Cannocchiale aristotelico', *Studi secenteschi*, 47 (2006), 57–87. On Tesauro's relationship with the Jesuit tradition, see Gianfranco Damiano, 'Il Collegio gesuitico di Brera: festa, teatro e drammaturgia tra XVI e XVII sec.', in *La scena della Gloria: drammaturgia e spettacolo a Milano in età spagnola*, ed. by Annamaria Cascetta and Roberta Carpani (Milan: Vita e Pensiero, 1995), pp. 473–506; Roberta Carpani, 'Hermenegildus/Ermegildo: la tragedia cristiana nell'opera di Emanuele Tesauro', *Comunicazioni sociali*, 19.2 (1997), 181–220; Giovanna Zanlonghi, *Teatri di formazione: actio, parola e immagine nella scena gesuitica del Sei-Settecento a Milano* (Milan: Vita e Pensiero, 2002).

remarks on the 'hypocritical' style are consistent with the role played by language and, more precisely, by oratorial speech within the educational programmes of Jesuit pedagogy. As indicated by Marc Fumaroli, drama and oratory are tightly connected within the cultural mission pursued by Jesuit education, which addressed not only members of the order, but also laymen, who, often destined to public careers and social prestige, were expected to be able to navigate the world's stage.[169]

The Jesuit model spread widely across Europe in the sixteenth and seventeenth centuries. The French classical drama of the *grand siècle* appropriated it by reshaping the allegorical code typical of confessional theatre into the representation of customs (*mœurs*) and psychologically complex characters. Differently from what happens in England, Germany, and Spain, France tends to limit the use of personified abstractions in drama. This is largely due to the poetics of verisimilitude that informs the classicist turn of French culture during the seventeenth century, with playwrights privileging the staging of moral conflicts through real characters rather than by turning to personifications.[170] The dichotomy between character and personification, which is at a work in other national traditions as well, exposes different strategies to tackle moral themes and the very function of drama. Within the anti-realistic perspective of the allegorical code, as Calderón de la Barca argued in theoretical statements about his own works, the scope is not the construction of characters, but the representation of ideas.[171] Paraphrasing the Spanish playwright, Chris Rauseo has talked about 'sermons imagés': not 'imaginary speeches', but 'speeches made of images'. The allegorical use of personifications allows for the staging of those moral concepts and theological truths that, remediated through images, bring to life the 'great theatre of the world' of which Calderón's plays are one of the most eloquent examples.

Studies such as Rauseo's, which focus on the interconnected, yet distinct notions of 'character' and 'personification' in seventeenth-century drama, have usually overlooked the Italian corpus. The distinction, however, provides a useful framework for the study of theatre (confessional in particular) in Italy too. As a matter of fact, the phenomenon has ramifications beyond the Jesuit case, which has been looked at on multiple occasions. Jesuit drama is only the most visible and celebrated example of broader developments that spanned across geographical contexts and, most importantly, across languages. Alongside Latin school drama, which has received the bigger share of the scholarly attention, vernacular forms of confessional

---

169 Marc Fumaroli, *L'Âge de l'éloquence: rhétorique et "res literaria" de la Renaissance au seuil de l'époque Classique* (Geneva: Droz, 1980); idem, *Héros et Orateurs: rhétorique et dramaturgie cornéliennes* (Geneva: Droz, 1990).

170 Chris Rauseo, *Mœurs et Maximes: personnification, représentation et moralisation théâtrales, du "Gran teatro del mundo" au "Malade imaginaire"* (Heidelberg: Universitätsverlag C. Winter, 1998), p. 10, 16.

171 Pedro Calderón de la Barca, *La segunda sposa y triunfar muriendo*, in *Obras completas* (Madrid: Aguilar, 1991), vol. III, p. 427: the playwright speaks about the use of allegorical personifications in his own sacred dramatic production as 'Sermones | puestos en verso, en idea | representable, cuestiones | de la Sacra Teología | que no alcanzan mi razones | a explicar ni comprender' [Sermons made into verse, into representable ideas, questions of sacred theology, which my intellect is not enough to explain nor understand]; for insightful remarks on this particular feature of Calderón's allegory, see Rauseo, p. 23.

Fig. 1.1. Andreini, *L'Adamo* (1617), title page.

theatre existed and made significant contributions to the unfolding of Christian education throughout the late Renaissance and the Baroque period.

Rooted in the allegorical tradition of medieval theatre, which was only apparently put in the shade by the Renaissance rediscovery of classical drama, spiritual and morality plays acquired an ambiguous status between the end of the sixteenth and the beginning of the seventeenth centuries. Because of their educational scope and their cultural proximity to catechetic and devotional literature, they were challenging the boundaries between the actual practice of drama (as an activity that takes place on stage) and meditative reading (be it individual or collective). As we will see in Chapter 3, the dramatic production of Fabio Glissenti inhabits comfortably this ambiguity, within which the 'theatre of the world' merge with the 'theatre of the soul'. Before turning to Glissenti, though, it is important to assess the complex relationship between these two 'theatres' (the world and the soul) by considering a few texts that, in different ways, bear witness to their osmotic interplay. Within the large corpus of spiritual and morality plays produced in the decades around 1600, it is worth turning to works that explicitly address the double-sided nature of drama, giving special attention to the visual dynamics entailed by the inner staging of the plays themselves.

Whoever happens to leaf through the first printed edition of the sacred drama *L'Adamo* [Adam] by Giovan Battista Andreini (1576–1654), published in Milan in 1613, notices that the book is rather peculiar when compared to the average prints of dramatic works of the time.[172] The text of the play is, in fact, provided with a rich series of images: starting from the titlepage [Fig. 1.1], engravings illustrate the action scene after scene.[173]

The first illustration, which follows the list of characters, is meant to integrate the stage direction about the setting of the play: 'la scena si finge nel terrestre paradiso' [the set pretends to be the earthly paradise] [Fig. 1.2].[174] The language of the statement, with the term *scena* [scene, set] accompanied by the verb *fingere* [to feign or pretend], is consistent with the picture, where the garden of Eden is indeed depicted as a theatrical stage (and not simply as a garden): in front of the perspectival backdrop, the observer can easily recognise the wooden boards of the proscenium where actors are expected to be playing.

The image does not represent Eden, but a theatrical stage on which Eden is, so to speak, recreated. The scene, empty in this first instalment, is filled with characters in the following illustrations: after an image that, corresponding to the play's prologue, depicts singing angels with musical instruments, the other illustrations bring the various characters on the stage of Eden [Figs 1.3, 1.4].

---

172 Giovan Battista Andreini, *L'Adamo sacra rapresentatione* (Milan: Girolamo Bordone, 1613; 2nd edn 1617); for a modern edition, see the one by Alessandro Ruffino (Trento: La finestra, 2007).
173 The illustrations provided here come from the 1617 edition of the play which, except from a few details in the title page, follows the first one.
174 Andreini, *L'Adamo*, fol. [c4]^v.

Ciascuna delle Scene porta in fronte vna figura efprimente al viuo gli affetti, e le cofe che fi contengono in effa. Il gentilifsimo Signor Carlo Antonio Procaccino, che gentilmente procaccia appunto à fe ftesso con la cortefia, e con la Virtù la via dell'immortalità; fece le figure, & honorò doppiamente l'Autore co'l fuo Ritratto, eternando fe fteffo, fe non l'Opera, che poco merita, & vccidendo la Morte con lo ftrale finifsimo del fuo pennello.

Fig. 1.2. Andreini, *L'Adamo* (1617), fol. [c4]ᵛ.

123

ATTO QVINTO
SCENA PRIMA.
Carne, Adamo.   32

E forza haurà da vn cor di selue alpestra
  Amoroso focil, esca d'inganno
Di trar fauilla ardente
Onde s'accenda inestinguibil foco

                              Hoggi

Peccatum originale quod in primo homine fuit actiue, in nobis autè passiue, vt inquit vgo de S. Victore lib 1. de sacram. cap. 26.

FIG. 1.3. Andreini, *L'Adamo* (1617), p. 123.

DELL'ADAMO. 149
SCENA QVINTA.
Eua, Mondo.

Serai più *Eua* dolente, e mesta,
  Le tue luci inalzar del Sole al raggio?
  Nò nò, tù ne se' indegna, e ben lo scorgi,
Che già fiso il mirasti,
E quell'aureo fulgòr tù vagheggiasti;
Ed hor s'osi mirarlo
Il suo raggio t'abbaglia, anzi ti sembra,
Che doppo hauer il suo splendor sofferto,
T'habbia gli occhi coperto
                              D'vn

FIG. 1.4. Andreini, *L'Adamo* (1617), p. 149.

An iconographic apparatus of this kind, running throughout the text and built specifically for it, is very rare in the context of early modern prints of dramatic works, usually marketed as small-format volumes devoid of illustrations.[175] More usual were illustrated frontispieces decorated with images that would highlight some features of the work; in most cases, however, even those images, often reused from other prints, tended to be generic rather than specific. An absolute rarity, and hence the exceptional status of Andreini's *L'Adamo*, is the visual representation of a play *as* a performance. When theatrical stages appear in illustrated editions of dramatic works, they are either generic perspectival scenes or, more frequently, images meant to record the specifics of a given spectacle, a typology of illustrated book conceived for the luxury market with celebratory scopes.[176]

In order to understand what is at stake in the print of Andreini's *L'Adamo*, one has to turn to the paratextual materials that accompany the play. The caption below the first illustration explains that each scene opens with a picture that 'expresses in vivid manner' the 'affections and actions' to be found in the scene itself ('ciascuna delle scene porta in fronte una figura esprimente al vivo gli affetti, e le cose che si contengono in essa').[177] While the images offer precious evidence of the stage techniques of the time, as thoroughly indicated by Davide Daolmi's detailed analysis of the print of *L'Adamo*, their scope goes beyond the desire to document a given staging of the play.[178] Rather, they aim to represent actions and affections as if they were in front of the reader's eyes: in other words, they make the text visible, thus transforming the book itself into a theatre. The fact that *L'Adamo*, regardless of the highly theatrical features of Andreini's writing, which lends itself naturally to the performance, is a book to be read and seen in the first place, is suggested by the playwright himself in the dedication letter to the queen of France, Maria de' Medici. Within a refined eulogy entirely played around the idea of the specular relationship between author, reader, sovereign, and subject, Andreini begs the queen to spend some time with the book so as to contemplate the wonders of God ('trattenersi nel mio libro contemplando le meraviglie di Dio, e i suoi parti divini'), where the Italian phrasing, 'trattenersi nel mio libro' [to dwell *in* my book] implies a spatial metaphor that highlights the meditative component of the work.[179]

The sacred drama is conceived by the author as an exercise of contemplation and the printed edition is thought of as an aid for the devout reader: building on what they see in the images, they will be able to visualise the action within their inner stage. It is Andreini himself who, remembering the genesis of the work in the preface to the 'benevolent reader', encourages a reading of this kind. Tired of

---

175 Luciano Mariti, *Commedia ridicolosa: comici di professione, dilettanti, editoria teatrale nel Seicento. Storia e testi* (Rome: Bulzoni, 1978), pp. xl–lxx.
176 See, for instance, the examples recorded in Stefano Mazzoni, *Atlante iconografico: spazi e forme dello spettacolo in Occidente dal mondo antico a Wagner* (Pisa: Titivillus, 2003), pp. 159–226 (with bibliographical references, pp. 13–46).
177 Andreini, *L'Adamo*, fol. [c4]^v.
178 Davide Daolmi, *Le origini dell'opera a Milano (1598–1649)* (Turnhout: Brepols, 1998), pp. 131–33, 481–93.
179 Andreini, *L'Adamo*, fol. [a3]$^{r-v}$.

concentrating the physical eye on earthly matters ('stanco d'haver con l'occhio della fronte troppo fiso rimirate queste terrene cose'), the author has elevated the 'inner eye' ('occhio interiore') towards divine things. Amazed by God's greatness and kindness, he has gone through a mystical experience that he is now attempting to reproduce through the sacred drama:

> tutto internato in questi divini affetti, mi sentii rapire a me stesso, e trapportare da dolce violenza là nel Terrestre Paradiso, ove pur di veder mi parea l'Huomo primiero Adamo, fattura cara di Dio, amico de gli Angeli, herede del Cielo, familiar delle Stelle, compendio delle cose create, ornamento del tutto, miracolo della Natura, Imperador de gli animali, unico albergatore dell'universo, e fruitore di tante meraviglie e grandezze.[180]

> [Entirely plunged into such divine affections, I felt I was taken away from myself and transported by some sweet force to the Earthly Paradise, where I seemed to see the first Man, Adam, beloved creature of God, friend of the Angels, heir of the Heavens, kin to the stars, compendium of all creatures, ornament of all things, miracle of Nature, emperor of the animals, sole host of the universe, and beneficiary of many wonders and great things.]

The poet, willing to use his art to serve God, has thus decided to bring to the light of the world ('dare alla luce del mondo') what was previously in the deepest recesses of his mind ('tenebre della mente'): namely, his mystic vision, an object that escapes regular speech as well as other forms of representation.[181] Trusting the reader's benevolence, Andreini dwells on a component of the play which needs some kind of justification so as to prevent criticism: the choice to give human shape ('forma humana') to the temptations (World, Flesh, the Devil, the Serpent) that harassed Adam and Eve in the Garden of Eden. Andreini explains it in these terms:

> si fa questo, perché le cose sieno più intese dall'intelletto con que' mezi che a' sensi s'aspettano: posciaché in altra guisa come le tante tentazioni, che in un punto sostennero Adamo ed Eva, furono nell'interno della lor mente, così non ben capir lo spettator le poteva. [...] e pur farà di mestieri per esprimere quegli interni contrasti, meditar qualche cosa per di fuori rappresentarli.[182]

> [This is done so that things may be understood by the intellect with those means that pertain to the senses: otherwise, the spectator would not be able to comprehend the many temptations which Adam and Eve had to face, for these were all internal to their minds. [...] likewise, in order to express those internal conflicts, it will be necessary to imagine a way to represent them externally.]

The anthropomorphic representation of abstract entities (Andreini introduces Hunger, Strain, Desperation, Death, and Vainglory, as well as the Seven Sins) is based on the predisposition of the human intellect to better grasp what is acquired through sense perception. Since temptations are inner affections of the human mind, the only way to make them visible to the audience is to give them body and voice. Turning to the commonplace comparison between painting and poetry, Andreini

---

180 Andreini, L'Adamo, fols [a4]ᵛ–b[1]ʳ.
181 Andreini, L'Adamo, fol. b[1]ʳ.
182 Andreini, L'Adamo, fol. b2ʳ.

claims the right of the poet (who is a 'pittore parlante', literally, a 'speaking painter') to represent those inner conflicts through images and speech ('rappresentare quegli interni contrasti per mezo d'immagini e voci pur tutte humane').[183] Accordingly, he makes the contemplative scope of *L'Adamo* explicit by defining the play a 'theatro dell'anima' [theatre of the soul] that should leave a mark on the reader's soul:

> Rimira dunque, Lettor benigno, più la sostanza che l'accidente, per così dire, contemplando nell'Opera il fine di portar nel Theatro dell'Anima la miseria, e il pianto d'Adamo, e farne spettatore il tuo cuore, per alzarlo da queste bassezze, alle grandezze del Cielo, co 'l mezo della Virtù, e dell'aiuto di Dio.[184]

> [Observe, benevolent reader, more the substance than the accident, so to speak, contemplating in this work the purpose to bring into the theatre of the soul the misery and tears of Adam; and to make your heart a spectator, so as to lift it from this wretchedness to the greatness of the Heavens through Virtue and God's help.]

In his preface to the reader, Andreini touches upon an issue that was at once crucial and highly controversial in the poetical and rhetorical debates of the time, monopolised as they were by the question of likelihood and plausibility in the subject matter of poetry. In fact, even if occasionally legitimised by the rhetorical tradition, the possibility to give a shape (most commonly a human one) and a voice to abstract entities raises several problems in terms of poetical credibility.

Agostino Manni (1547–1612), the author of the libretto of the *Rappresentatione di Anima et Corpo* [Representation of Soul and Body], set to music by composer Emilio de' Cavalieri (1550–1602) in Rome in 1600, felt the need to address the issue explicitly.[185] The prologue of the *Rappresentatione* stages a dialogue between two young men, whose eloquent names, Avveduto and Prudenzio, unveil their allegorical connotation, referring to wisdom and prudence, respectively. After listing various definitions of 'mortal life', mostly employing oxymoron, paradox, and other conceits, the two interlocutors agree that humans should reject the senses while privileging the goods of the soul, so as to guarantee their access to heaven. The ensuing *Rappresentatione di Anima et Corpo* is introduced by Avveduto and Prudenzio as the tangible visualisation of such important truth. Someone took it upon themselves to bring it before our eyes ('alcuni s'hanno preso per carico di

---

183 Ibid.; but see the whole passage for better contextualisation of the argument: 'Ma se al Pittore, Poeta muto, è permesso con caratteri di colore l'esprimere l'antichità di Dio in persona d'huomo tutto canuto, e dimostrare in bianca Colomba la purità dello Spirito, e figurare i divini messaggi, che sono gli Angeli, in persona di giovenni alati: perché non è permesso al Poeta, Pittor parlante, portar nella tela del Theatro altro huomo, altra donna ch'Adamo et Eva, e rappresentare quegli interni contrasti per mezo d'immagini e voci pur tutte humane?' [But if the painter, who is a mute poet, is allowed to express with colours the antiquity of God through the figure of a white-haired man, to visualise the purity of the Holy Spirit through a white dove, and to represent the divine messengers, that is, the angels, as winged youths; why is it not permitted to the poet, who is a speaking painter, to bring on the theatre's stage men and women other than Adam and Eve, and represent those internal conflicts by means of entirely human figures and words?].
184 Ibid.
185 Agostino Manni, *Rappresentatione di anima et corpo nuovamente posta in musica dal sig. Emilio del Cavaliere per recitar cantando* (Rome: Niccolò Muzi, 1600).

mettercela inanzi a gli occhi'), as Prudenzio affirms by turning to the rhetorical commonplace of *evidentia*. 'In this place', he continues, 'there will be represented a living and wonderful example that will show our conclusions to be true' ('ci verrà rappresentato un vivo e stupendo esempio, che mostrerà esser vero, quanto abbiamo concluso').[186] The *exemplum* brought to the spectators (who, in this case, will be listeners in the first place) does not stage real characters, but allegorical personifications: Soul, Body, Pleasure, Time, World, Intellect, Good Counsel, Mundane Life. Advocating for the rhetorical efficacy of a practice common in spiritual and moral drama around 1600, Manni's prologue justifies it in terms that are similar to the ones that inform Andreini's sacred play:

> E si vedranno venire inanzi le cose istesse, le quali sotto figura di persone umane apparendo, mentre con le nuove e strane immagini dilettaranno, nell'istesso tempo serviranno per una idea, dove ciascuno mirando puotrà formarsene un ritratto nel core, nel quale riconosca chiaramente, che questa vita, questo mondo, queste terrene grandezze sono veramente polvere, fumo ed ombra: e finalmente poi che non ci è altro di fermo, né di grande che la virtù, la grazia di dio, e 'l regno eterno del cielo.[187]

> [and the same things will be seen to happen as is shown figuratively as human people, while with new and strange images they will delight, at the same time will serve as an idea in which each one will be able to see and form a picture in the heart, in which he will clearly recognise that this Life, this World, these earthly grandeurs are truly dust, smoke and shadow: and finally that there is nothing else that is firm or great but virtue, the grace of God, and the eternal Kingdom of Heaven.]

Things themselves ('le cose istesse'), that is, abstract notions, are made appear on stage under human shape ('sotto figura di persone umane'). Personifications please the attendees because they bring unusual images in front of the audience's eyes. At the same time, they perform a didactic function because they let the audience interact directly with the 'idea'. The spectator can thus acquire the idea and make it their own by visualising it in their heart ('formarsene un ritratto nel core'), a process that would be much more difficult without the aid of image-making.[188]

The inner staging of a morality play can be stimulated by an iconographic aid such as the series of illustrations found in Andreini's *L'Adamo*, but it can also be triggered by the attendance at an actual performance (this is the case, for instance, of Manni and Cavalieri's *Rappresentatione*, which, based on the interaction of words and music, can hardly prescind from the concrete staging of the play). On other occasions, the effort entailed by the visualisation process is entirely entrusted to the reading audience. The principle behind it, though, is the same. A case in point

---

186 Manni, *Rappresentatione*, prologue.
187 Ibid.
188 On the relevance of allegorical personifications to the poetics that inform Manni and Cavalieri's *Rappresentatione*, see Silvia Casolari, 'Allegorie nella *Rappresentatione di anima et di corpo* (1600): testo e immagine', *Rivista Italiana di Musicologia*, 33.1 (1998), 7–40; Murray C. Bradshaw, 'Salvation, Right Thinking, and Cavalieri's *Rappresentatione di anima, et di corpo* (1600)', *Musica Disciplina*, 52 (1998–2002), 233–50.

is offered by the address to the readers that opens the *Rappresentatione spirituale dell'Anima e del Corpo* [Spiritual Representation of Soul and Body] by Buonaventura de Venere, a Franciscan friar based in the Tuscan hermitage of Castigloncello del Trinoro.[189] The 'azione scenica', printed in Rome in 1608, abstains from mixing real characters and personifications, and turns entirely to the world of 'persone imaginate':[190]

> Avverti, che in quest'opera fatta solo ad edificatione de' devoti, il nome di Rappresentatione Spirituale vuol dir solo introduttione di Persone imaginate, che vengono rappresentate separatamente, ancorché non siano veramente separate; come Anima, Corpo, Ragione, Senso, Amor proprio, Carne, e gli altri che s'introducono, è ragionamento ad uso di persone ordinarie, come se ciascuna d'esse fosse persona da per sé, e similmente i Demonii, e i Vitii introdotti parlano contra le Virtù, e in dispregio de' buoni, non perché il detto loro sia verità; ma per introdurre questi Vitii e Demonii con la mala proprietà loro.[191]

> [Be aware that in this work, solely composed for the edification of devotees, the term 'Spiritual Representation' simply means introduction of imagined persons. These are represented as separate entities even if they are not actually separate, such as Soul, Body, Reason, Sense, Self-regard, Flesh, and the others that are introduced; it is a conversation among ordinary people, as if each of them were a self-standing person; similarly, Demons and Vices speak against Virtue and in contempt of the good ones, not because their speech is real, but in order to introduce these Vices and Demons with their own evil features.]

Bonaventura feels the need to specify that 'persone imaginate' [imagined persons] are introduced in the play 'separatamente' [separately], that is, as if they were separate from one another, while in reality they are not 'veramente separate' [actually separate]: Soul, Sense, Reason and the others brought on stage do not exist autonomously and the choice to make them speak and converse as if they were human beings (in other words, as if each of them were an individual) is due to the didactic and devotional scope of the text. According to the medieval traditions of psychomachiae and *contrasti*, the play stages the conflict between man's material and spiritual components, which are summoned to interact with one another as if they were the actual characters of a drama. The artificial nature of the personifications makes the audience concentrate on the distinctive traits of such components, facilitating the acquisition of a moral code markedly oriented towards Christian discipline. Similarly, vices and demons are given human shape so as to make their evil attitude ('mala proprietà loro') stand out. Bonaventura's preface tackles the same

---

189 Bonaventura de Venere, *Rappresentatione spirituale dell'anima, et del corpo, con alcune laudi, et altre ottave, fatte dal Pellegrino Romito* (Rome: Guglielmo Facciotti, 1608); the edition that I have used is the one printed in Rome and Perugia: Bartoli e Lorenzi, 1644.
190 The list of interlocutors is instructive: 'Angelo, Anima, Corpo, Morte, Ragione, Senso, Amor proprio, Superbia, Vanità, Ipocrisia, Diletto, Pazienza, Grazia, Mondo, Carne, Vanagloria, Peccato'. The only two characters that do not fit the allegorical status of the others are Satan and one rather curious Lucone, 'demonio capitano', literally, 'demon captain', who relates to the braggarts of the *commedia dell'arte* tradition.
191 Bonaventura de Venere, *Rappresentatione*, fol. 5.

concerns that, perhaps more sophisticatedly, were also at the core of Andreini's reflection on the representation of objects that normally escape human discourse. While devoid of lavish illustrations, Bonaventura's *Rappresentatione* is also built on the idea of an inner theatre in which to give visible shape to spiritual exercises. The 1644 reprint of the play, however, includes a foldable illustration worthy of attention: it represents the hermitage of San Francesco del Sasso di Castiglioncello del Trinoro, where the author was based [Fig. 1.5]. The image has a meditative scope: not only does it depict the temptations of Saint Francis, accurately described in the caption, but it also recalls Buonaventura's own stay in the same location. In a way, the experience of Saint Francis is revived through the identification of the friars with him.[192]

My reference to the tradition of the spiritual exercises, powerfully revamped by Ignatius of Loyola and a flagship component of Jesuit culture, is not meant to suggest mere analogies. There are, in fact, many examples of the ways in which spiritual and confessional drama gradually acquired modes, features, and scopes peculiar to the practice of Christian meditation, especially in the forms laid out by Loyola.[193] The theatrical dimension of the *Spiritual Exercises* has been often highlighted by scholars in relation to both the late-Renaissance blossoming of Jesuit drama[194] and concurrent literary and poetical experiences that identify the soul as their ultimate stage, be the soul conceived as the subject of a given contemplative action or the *locus* within which such contemplative action takes place.[195]

In this respect, an instructive example comes, once again, from the Franciscan ranks: I am referring to the preface that opens the spiritual tragedy *Il mortorio di Christo* [The Passion of Christ] by Bonaventura Morone da Taranto (1557–1621),

192 The foldable illustration is inserted between fols A2 and A3.
193 The *Spiritual exercises* first appeared in Latin: Ignatius of Loyola, *Exercitia spiritualia* (Rome: Antonio Blado, 1548); they were translated into Italian by the Jesuit, Giovanni Battista Peruschi: *Esercitii spirituali* (Rome: Collegio Romano, [1555]). For an overview of the various prints of the text, see the critical edition *Exercitia spiritualia. Textuum antiquissimorum nova editio*, ed. by José Calveras s.i. and Cándido de Dalmases s.i. (Rome: Istituto Storico della Società di Gesù, 1969; Peruschi's translation is included, pp. 646–720). Particularly useful because of the annotations is the edition *Esercizi spirituali*, ed. by Giuseppe De Gennaro s.i., in Ignatius of Loyola, *Gli scritti*, ed. by Mario Gioia (Turin: UTET, 1977), pp. 65–184. For a discussion of those aspects of the Jesuit tradition that are more directly relevant to the present study, see Pierre-Antoine Fabre, *Ignace de Loyola. Le Lieu de l'image: le problème de la composition de lieu dans les pratiques spirituelles et artistiques jésuites de la seconde moitié du XVIe siècle* (Paris: Vrin — EHESS, 1992); François Marty, *Sentir et goûter: les sens dans les 'Exercices spirituels' de saint Ignace* (Paris: Les Éditions du cerf, 2005); on Jesuit pedagogy, see *I Gesuiti e la Ratio Studiorum*, ed. by Hinz, Righi and Zardin.
194 On Jesuit drama, see *I gesuiti e i primordi del teatro barocco in Europa*, ed. by Maria Chiabò and Federico Doglio (Viterbo: Centro studi sul teatro medioevale e rinascimentale, 1995); but also Bruna Filippi, '"...Accompagnare il diletto d'un ragionevole trattenimento con l'utile di qualche giovevole ammaestramento...": il teatro dei gesuiti a Roma nel XVII secolo', *Teatro e storia*, 9 (1994), 91–128; Bernadette Majorana, 'Governo del corpo, governo dell'anima: attori e spettatori nel teatro italiano del XVII secolo', in *Disciplina dell'anima, disciplina del corpo e disciplina della società tra medioevo ed età moderna*, ed. by Paolo Prodi (Bologna: il Mulino, 1994), pp. 437–90; Zanlonghi, *Teatri di formazione*.
195 Bologna, 'Esercizi di memoria'; of relevance to the discussion of poetics inspired by the Jesuit notion of spiritual exercise is Pasquale Guaragnella, *Gli occhi della mente: stili del Seicento italiano* (Bari: Palomar, 1997), pp. 123–82.

BODILESS OBJECTS IN HUMAN SHAPE 73

FIG. 1.5. Bonaventura de Venere, *Rappresentatione spirituale dell'anima e del corpo* (1644), foldable illustration between fols A2 and A3.

printed in Venice in 1615.¹⁹⁶ Even in this case, the play, which was published without illustrations, is conceived as a meditation aid rather than as a text to be actually staged.¹⁹⁷ The prefatory letter addressed to the Franciscan friars of San Niccolò is a veritable *accessus* to the 'funebre scena' [funeral scene]: the author, pre-empting possible criticism, explains the reasons behind his poetical inventions and provides the readers with instructions to adopt such inventions in their own meditations.¹⁹⁸ Morone explains that there are various ways to meditate on Christ's death: this can be done through wonder, gratefulness, imitation, compunction, compassion, or even joy ('o per via di meraviglia, o di ringratiamento, o d'imitatione, o di compuntione, o di compassione, o d'allegrezza ancora').¹⁹⁹ All these options imply the mental elaboration of images that, thanks to their vividness, are able to trigger the true devotion of the heart ('sempre ponno formarsi nell'intelletto, o nell'imaginativa del divoto contemplante alcune specie, et imagini, che rappresentino più al vivo i misteri, che s'hanno da meditare, e destino più agevolmente la divotione del cuore').²⁰⁰

When one compares statements of this kind with the instructions given by Ignatius of Loyola in the first prelude to the first spiritual exercise, the 'composition by seeing the place', the affinity of their theoretical premises stands out. One of Ignatius's examples is the very Passion of Christ:

> Il primo preambolo è la compositione del luogo, per la quale se deve notare che in ciascuna meditatione, overo contemplatione de cosa corporea, siccome de Christo, deveremo fingendo representare come fosse cosa vera, secondo una certa visione imaginativa, un loco corporeo che ripresenti quel che contemplamo, come un tempio overo monte, nel quale ritroviamo Iesù Christo overo la Vergine Maria, et altre cose le quali apertengono all'argumento della nostra contemplatione.²⁰¹

---

196 Bonaventura Morone, *Il mortorio di Christo, tragedia spirituale* (Venice: Sebastiano Combi, 1615), fols †5ʳ–[†9]ʳ.
197 Eloquent are the statements of the author in the dedication of the work to the Virgin Mary: '[...] né ho havuto mai pensiero, che questo mio divoto trattenimento uscisse a vista de gli huomini, o che facesse di sé superba mostra in qualche famoso Teatro d'Italia; ma che alcuni miei Religiosi, che con affettuosi prieghi me n'hanno molte volte richiesto, havessero nelle loro meditationi alcuni incentivi, per li quali con maggior sentimento ruminassero le vostre più lagrimevoli sventure, et honorassero con più decevole apparecchio l'essequie del morto figlio' (Morone, *Il mortorio*, fols †2ᵛ–†3ʳ) [I have never imagined that this devout entertainment would be seen by others, or that it would make proud appearance in some famous theatre of Italy; I conceived it to give to some of my religious brothers, who asked for it several times with affectionate prayers, some stimulus in their meditations, through which they could ruminate your tearful miseries with stronger affection and honor the exequies of your son with more convenient apparatus]; the contemplative dimension of the work in conjunction with the embodiment of the spiritual experience is stressed further in the conclusion (fol. †3ᵛ).
198 Morone, *Il mortorio*, fol. †5ʳ⁻ᵛ.
199 Morone, *Il mortorio*, fol. †5ᵛ.
200 Ibid.
201 Loyola, *Esercizi spirituali* [henceforth *ES*], 47; in order to highlight lexical similarities, here and below I refer to the 1555 Peruschi translation, which I quote from the critical edition by Calveras and De Dalmases; for an insightful discussion of this passage, see Fabre, *Ignace de Loyola: Le Lieu de l'image*, pp. 28–38.

[The First Prelude is the composition of the place, through which it is to be noted that in any meditation or contemplation of a corporeal thing, such as Christ, we will need to represent, according to a certain imaginative vision, a corporeal place depicting what we are contemplating, such as a temple or a mountain, where we find Jesus Christ or the Virgin Mary, and the other things that pertain to the subject of our contemplation.]

The experience proposed by Morone to the readers of *Il mortorio di Christo* is very similar to the one outlined by Ignatius when he recommends that the mental image be built starting by setting the 'place'. It is the inner vision of the crucifix that Ignatius encourages his own readers to seek, in the form of a mental conversation with Christ.[202] As regards the actual process of internal visualisation, Ignatius does not provide details: once the place and the object of the vision are defined, it will be necessary to enrich them with all the 'other things' that pertain to the topic of our contemplation ('argomento della nostra contemplatione'). The creative effort embedded in the mental elaboration of images is expected to be significant and is entrusted to the imagination of the devout Christian who is willing to commit to the spiritual exercise.[203]

As suggested by Morone in the preface to his play, the 'species' ('specie') and 'images' ('imagini') aimed at stirring the devotion of the heart may be based on the Scriptures. However, they can also build on what the Scriptures have been silent about, details and additions that do not alter the truth of the sacred narrative, but enrich it ('non alterano la verità dell'historia, ma l'arricchiscono') and contribute to moving the soul of the listeners ('movere, e destare maggior affetto spirituale ne gli animi de gli uditori').[204] This is what Augustine, Anselm and Bonaventure did in their own meditations. If such device is granted to authors of 'history' ('historia'), then it should be all the more viable in the context of drama. The 'tragic style' ('stile tragico'), as Morone puts it, allows the author to integrate and develop the plot without altering its essence. The Franciscan, who privileges the mystic and contemplative dimension of the work over the poetical one, makes his intention explicit through an evocative musical metaphor:

> Havendo io dunque scritto con stile tragico il Mortorio di Christo, ho voluto adornare l'attione con alcune divote speculationi, più tosto da contemplativo che da poeta, facendo sopra il tenore dell'historia un accordato contrapunto, non di favole, o di menzogne, ma d'inventioni piene di sentimenti mistici,

---

202 Loyola, ES, 54: 'Il colloquio se farrà voltandosi a Giesù Christo, imaginandosi haverlo avanti gl'occhi crocifisso, considerando quel che ha fatto per te e quel che vol fare; e considera quel che tu l'hai retribuito per tanti beneficii et amore da lui ricevuto, e che doveresti retribuirli per l'advenire, raggionando con sua maestà, come un servo con il signore, overo un amico con l'altro amico, domandando perdono, overo chiedendo conseglio, overo aiuto' [The colloquy will be performed by turning to Jesus Christ, imagining to have him on the cross in front of our eyes, considering what he has done for you and what he is willing to do; and consider how you have rewarded him for the many gifts and love you received from him, and that you should reward him in the future, speaking to his majesty, as a servant to his lord, or as a friend to a friend, asking forgiveness or advice or help].
203 Of particular interest are De Gennaro's remarks in his annotated edition of the *Spiritual exercises*, p. 107.
204 Morone, *Il mortorio*, fol. †5ᵛ.

che illustrino la scena, appaghino i curiosi, movino a divotione i semplici, e spieghino con maggior pompa i ritratti della Bontà, e della Pietà di Dio.[205]

[Having written the Passion of Christ in tragic style, I wished to decorate the action with some devout speculations, more as a contemplative than as a poet, crafting around the tenor of the plot a harmonious counterpoint, not made of fables or lies, but of inventions filled with mystical meanings that illustrate the scene, satisfy the curious audience, move the common people to devotion, and disclose the portraits of God's benevolence and piety with greater splendor.]

Additions to the plot — that is, the account of Christ's death as narrated by the Gospels — are labelled 'devout speculations', which the reader shall acquire, digest, and revive within their own mind. The boundaries between the theatrical stage and the theatre of the soul are thin: the 'inventions full of mystic senses' are in fact expected to enlighten the stage by making more visible, evident, and, in a way, tangible, the portrayals of God's goodness and pity.

Among the poetical licences granted to drama, the use of personifications is paramount. As with Andreini's *L'Adamo*, Morone's *Il mortorio* stages human characters (the Virgin, Judas, etc.) alongside allegorical ones (Justice, Mercy, Peace, Desperation, Death). Before justifying the use of personifications, the author has something interesting to say about the ghost of Adam, who is summoned to deliver the play's prologue: 'Ho introdotto per far il prologo l'ombra d'Adamo, cioè lo spirito vestito di corpo fantastico, come sovente sogliono comparire e gli Angioli, e l'anime de' defonti'.[206] Adam's ghost, as is the case with angels and the souls of the dead, is conceived as a 'corpo fantastico', an imagined body that is meant to house the immaterial soul of the character. The statement, oxymoronic and potentially paradoxical, pairs the materiality of the body and the immateriality of the images produced by the imagination. The process of image-making identified by Morone is the same that informs the personification of abstract entities. Accordingly, spiritual drama becomes a space within which imagined bodies can be given a shape and activate forms of meditation and contemplation.

Ignatius himself, in completing the instructions for the first exercise, considers the possibility of meditating on non-physical objects, and provides us with insightful remarks that shed light on the context that we are examining:

Ma se la cosa la quale non ha corpo, come il considerare alli peccati, dedicata hora alla contemplatione, sta nascostamente, potrà essere de tal sorte la compositione del luogo, come se vedessimo per imaginatione l'anima nostra essere in questo corpo corruttibile come inclusa in una prigione, et noi medesimi essere in questa valle de miseria come sbanditi dalla nostra patria, habitando fra li brutissimi animali.[207]

---

205 Morone, *Il mortorio*, fol. †6ʳ.
206 Ibid. ('I have introduced Adam's ghost to deliver the prologue, that is, a spirit clothed in an imagined body, as often are made appear both the angels and the souls of the dead.').
207 Loyola, *ES*, 47; the Latin text makes even more explicit the distinction between soul and body as the two main components of human life: 'compositio erit videre oculo imaginationis animam corpori corruptibili tamquam carceri inclusam, et totum compositum ex anima et corpore in hac valle miseriae, inter bruta animalia exul'.

[But if the contemplation is about a thing that has no body, as is the case with considering one's sins, the composition of the place will be to imagine our soul in this corruptible body as secluded in a prison, and ourselves being in this valley of misery as if we were banned from our land, living with the most brute animals.]

The point is about 'seeing' both soul and body with the eyes of the mind, according to a separation of the components of human life that, since the Middle Ages, had dramatic potential, and which fuelled early modern spiritual drama (a case in point being that of Glissenti's morality plays, as I will show in Chapter 3). As poignantly observed by Giuseppe De Gennaro, this second kind of contemplation is not properly 'visual' because it focuses on bodiless objects. The Latin text of the *Spiritual Exercises* states it clearly, for the 'contemplatio visibilis' [visible contemplation] of the crucifix is discussed in opposition to the 'contemplatio invisibilis' [invisible contemplation] of the sins.[208] While in the first case the object of the contemplation has both a body and a real place to be housed in, the second mobilises metaphorical bodies and spaces similar to those of allegorical drama.[209]

With regards to personified abstractions such as Mercy, Justice, Peace, and Death, Morone finds another legitimation in the Scriptures. The 'friendly contest' ('amichevole contesa') between Justice and Mercy, a principle that informs the opposite destinies of Christ and Judas, veritable *leitmotiv* of the play, is based on a passage from the letter to the Romans. The reconciliation fostered by the intervention of Peace alludes instead to a famous verse from the *Psalms* duly referenced by the author ('misericordia, et veritas obviaverunt sibi; iustitia, et pax osculatae sunt').[210] The use of allegorical personifications responds here to the need for unveiling the moral teachings of the story by giving them a body and by making them act as characters fully involved in the action.

It goes without saying that this kind of spiritual drama does not seek any effect of realism. Morone, thoughtful exegete of his own work, is outspoken about it. What he is bringing on stage (Adam's ghost, personifications, angels, and demons) belongs to a sort of reality that is not tangible. He explains that these various things, which have been made visible through the play, had never been seen by human eyes before, for they happened invisibly ('se ben queste cose non si viddero da gli occhi de gli huomini, accadero nondimeno invisibilmente').[211] Devout readers, who are supposed to bring the sacred drama on the stage of their mind, will be able to contemplate 'imagined bodies' in action and meditate upon their meaning. Spiritual drama thus becomes a mystic theatre that makes it possible for the audience to fully identify with the subject of the play. Particularly eloquent, in this respect, the closing remarks of Morone's preface, entirely built on the analogy between the contemplation of the tragic scene on the part of the Franciscan friars and the ecstatic

---

208 Loyola, *ES*, 47.
209 See De Gennaro, *ad loc.* (p. 107), who stresses the similarity between Ignatius's instructions about metaphorical spaces and the symbolic visualisation typical of Calderón de la Barca's *Autos sacramentales*.
210 Psalms, 84. 11 ('Mercy and truth have met each other: justice and peace have kissed').
211 Morone, *Il mortorio*, fol. [†7]^v.

contemplation of the crucifix by Francis of Assisi, who was so deeply focused on Christ's body that he somatised his pain and wounds:

> Vedete dunque, Rever. Padri, come con tante devote inventioni non s'è tolta, né aggiunta cosa alcuna al vero, ma solamente adornato il Mortorio con sentimenti mistici, dalli quali potrete cavar fuori molte divote meditationi, per accendere maggiormente il vostro spirito all'amor del Crocifisso, e farvi veri imitatori, e figli del vostro Serafico Padre, che non sapea distaccarsi dalle piaghe del suo Signore, tanto che al fine se l'impresse nel suo proprio corpo a quel modo, che la donna gravida vogliosa di qualche cibo, imprime indelebilmente la cosa bramata nelle tenere membra del fanciullo.[212]

> [You see, reverend fathers, that with these many devout inventions nothing has been taken away from, or added, to the truth; the Passion of Christ has just been adorned with mystical meanings, from which you will be able to draw many devout meditations to ignite your spirit in the love of the Crucifix and make yourselves true imitators and sons of your seraphic father, who could not detach from the wounds of his Lord; therefore, he eventually got them impressed in his own body as a pregnant woman desirous of some food impresses the desired thing indelibly on the tender limbs of the baby.]

The mystic and contemplative component acquires central importance in texts that are meant to be consumed through meditative reading. Their affinity with spiritual practices of meditation such as Ignatius's *Exercises* is even more evident when no visual aid is offered to the reader. As Corrado Bologna observes, Loyola's exercises are basically devoid of images: 'aseptic in their insistence on the interior rebirth of the image that reconstructs the external world', they preserve their 'imaginative chastity' from the 'proteiform spiral of transmutation'.[213] Ultimately, the scope is not really about seeing through the eyes of the mind what is not usually visible to the physical eyes. The production of mental images does not need to be mimetic; rather, it has to stem from deep meditation and comprehension of the object of the contemplation, no matter whether real or intellectual. A fitting parallel within the tradition of spiritual drama comes from another play about the biblical fall of the ancestors, the *Scena tragica d'Adamo e d'Eva* by Troilo Lancetta, published in Venice in 1644. In the preface to the readers, the author states that the setting ('apparato') is mystic because it is the product of a vision in which the visual component is superseded by the deep meanings that the vision itself conceals.[214] Following Moses' instructions, which he allegedly received in a dream, the playwright wishes to represent Adam's tragedy in order to encourage the audience to examine their conscience and follow the path of salvation. The call for self-examination does not find any aid in depictions of Adam and Eve such as those found in Andreini's *L'Adamo*. Rather, the meditation is supported by a diagram [Fig. 1.6] that, by reducing the characters involved in the play to the basic functions of human interiority, leads the reader towards the comprehension of both God and oneself.[215]

---

212 Morone, *Il mortorio*, fols [†8]^v–[†9]^r.
213 Bologna, *Esercizi di memoria*, p. 218.
214 Troilo Lancetta, *La scena tragica d'Adamo e d'Eva, estratta dalli primi tre capi della sacra Genesi, et ridotta a significato morale* (Venice: Giovanni Guerigli, 1644), fol. ★2^v.
215 Lancetta, *La scena tragica d'Adamo e d'Eva*, fol. ★4^v.

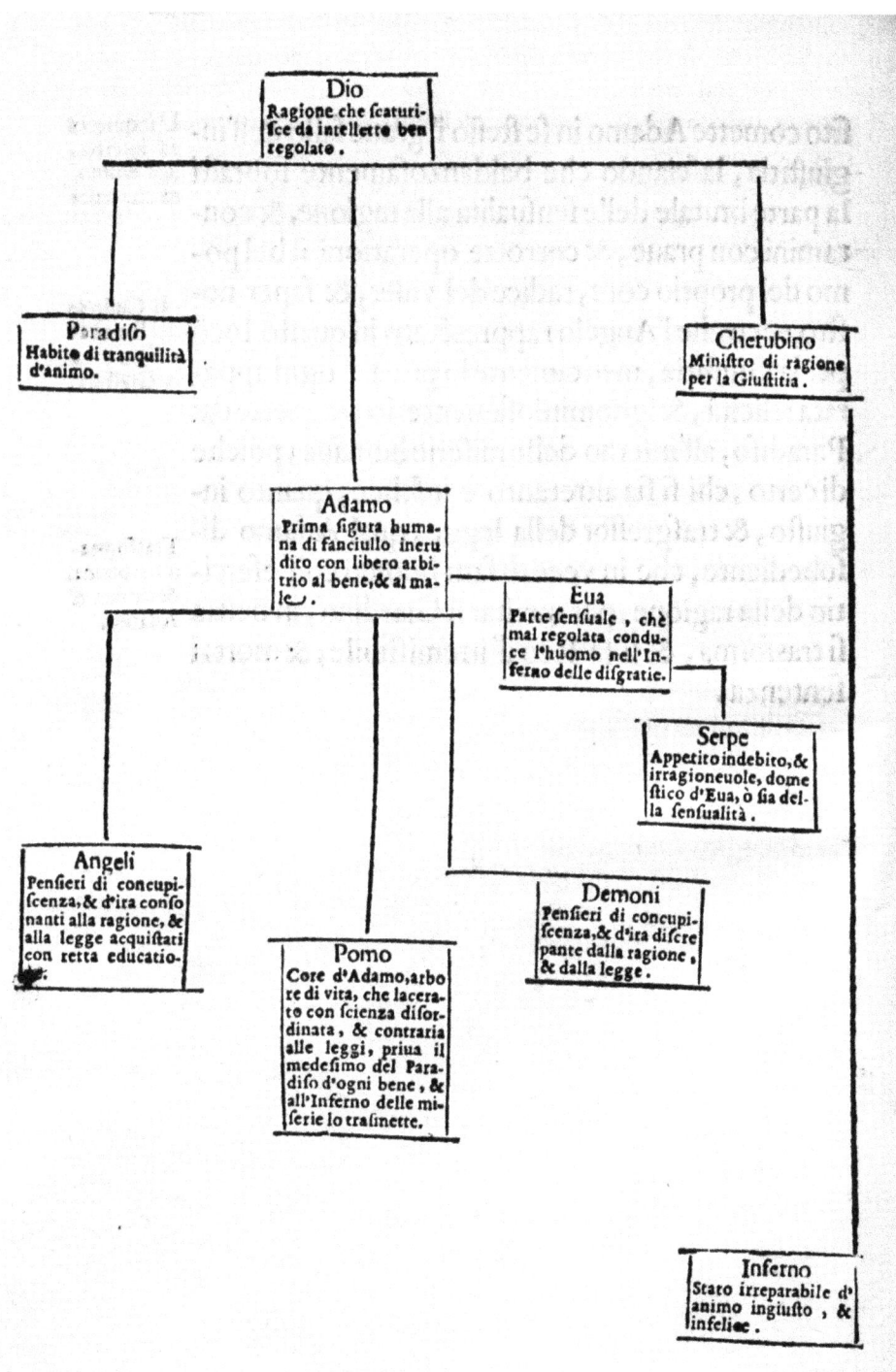

FIG. 1.6. Lancetta, *La scena tragica d'Adamo e d'Eva* (1644), fol. *4ᵛ.

'Contemplate', 'consider yourself': the instructions that Lancetta addresses to the reader confirm the correspondence between stage and soul that informs the profound cultural, poetical, and ideological structures of confessional drama. As Chapters 2 and 3 will demonstrate, such correspondence comes to the fore when the tradition of spiritual and confessional drama is looked at as intertwined with concurrent uses of theatrical metaphors and personified allegories in textual products that, nominally non-dramatic, did intersect the complex realm of performance and performativity.

CHAPTER 2

The Tragedy of Human Life: *Ars Moriendi* and *Theatrum Mundi* in Fabio Glissenti's *Discorsi morali* (1596)

Ranging from rhetorical treatises to sacred dramas, the examples discussed in the previous chapter indicate that the entanglements of allegorical theatre and spiritual practice in early modern Italy were extremely heterogeneous. While more extensive reviews of the relevant corpus, yet to be undertaken, will hopefully allow for more cogent assessments of the phenomenon in the future, in-depth explorations of specific case studies are, for now, the most useful way to approach the topic. As anticipated in my introduction, Chapters 2 and 3 of this book aim to offer a contribution to the study of allegorical drama in the early Seicento by looking at the writings of Fabio Glissenti, whose morality plays were written for the benefit of the spiritual education of the female orphans housed in the hospitals of Venice. As with any selection of case studies, the group of works analysed and discussed here does not allow for broad generalisations. However, given the fortunate circumstances of their transmission and thanks to concurrent historical evidence, these works let us draw a picture of the ways in which allegorical drama, doctrinal concerns, and spiritual practices merged in the educational context of the Venetian hospitals in the early seventeenth century.

As will be shown, the works of Glissenti share many of the features that inform early modern allegorical drama more widely. At the same time, they are characterised by a certain degree of eccentricity, which make them an ideal testbed for reconsidering a phenomenon that remains, to date, largely unexplored. Studied alongside the author's major work — the philosophical dialogue entitled *Discorsi morali contra il dispiacer del morire* [Moral Discourses against the Sorrow Caused by Death] (1596) — Glissenti's plays provide us with a rare opportunity to grasp the extent to which drama was used as an educational tool in the complex and mutable context of Counter-Reformation Italy. At the same time, they allow us to identify cultural motifs that were at the core of the Baroque imagination more broadly.[1]

---

1   For a recent assessment of dynamics of innovation and hybridisation in Counter-Reformation Italy see *Innovation in the Italian Counter-Reformation*, ed. by Shannon McHugh and Anna Wainwright (Newark: University of Delaware Press, 2020), particularly Amedeo Quondam's foreword (pp. xi–xxxii), the editors' introduction (pp. 1–12) and Virginia Cox, 'Re-Thinking Counter-Reformation Literature' (pp. 15–55).

Chapter 2 focuses on the professional and intellectual profile of the author, Fabio Glissenti, before turning to the analysis of the *Discorsi morali*. Virtually neglected by scholarship (the only significant exceptions being George McClure's illuminating contribution on the *artes* and the *ars moriendi* in Renaissance Venice, and, more recently, Luca Piantoni's study of the iconographic apparatus of the book), the *Discorsi morali* will be examined here as one instructive example of the ways in which theatrical metaphors provided early modern culture with a powerful filter through which to look at, represent, and, to some extent, discipline human life.[2] By reading the *Discorsi* as a philosophical dialogue conceived and organised according to theatrical structures, I will suggest that Glissenti's attempt to represent life and death *sub specie theatri* is part of a twofold project. On the one hand, the *theatrum mundi* metaphor provides him with a pedagogically effective device for the staging of moral and spiritual teachings. On the other, the notion that the world is a stage onto which the play of human life unfolds paves the way for the merger of 'performance' and 'performative' that, as I will indicate in Chapter 3, is at the core of Glissenti's morality plays. Particularly instructive in this regard are the ways in which theatre and drama are discussed in the *Discorsi morali* both as metaphors and as actual forms of entertainment. By looking at these competing perspectives on theatre, my analysis of Glissenti's philosophical dialogue is also meant to identify theatricality, a flagship feature of Baroque culture, as key to the forms of spiritual practice that the author promotes, including the meditation on death (that is, the *Discorsi morali*'s main concern) and the examination of conscience (that is, one of the recurring themes of Glissenti's morality plays).

Physician, Philosopher, Playwright

Biographical information on Fabio Glissenti is scant, as is the critical bibliography on his works. With few exceptions, scholars have neglected Glissenti, likely due to his rather hybrid profile. A medical doctor who wrote morality plays alongside a voluminous treatise of moral philosophy, Glissenti, as many 'irregulars' of early modernity, does not fit the disciplinary grid along the lines of which scholarship tends to be organised. Basic information about his life was gathered in the relevant

---

2   George McClure, 'The "Artes" and the "Ars moriendi" in Late Renaissance Venice: The Professions in Fabio Glissenti's *Discorsi morali contra il dispiacer del morire, detto Athanatophilia* (1596)', *Renaissance Quarterly*, 51.1 (1998), 92–127; and, by the same author, *The Culture of Profession in Late Renaissance Italy* (Toronto: University of Toronto Press, 2004), pp. 177–202; see, also, Luca Piantoni, 'Morte a Venezia: l'"Athanatophilia" di Fabio Glissenti, 1596', in *Visibile teologia: il libro sacro figurato in Italia tra Cinque e Seicento*, ed. by Erminia Ardissino and Elisabetta Selmi (Alessandria: Edizioni dell'Orso, 2012), pp. 221–50. Preliminary remarks on some of the aspects addressed in the present study are to be found in Eugenio Refini, '"Quasi una tragedia delle attioni humane": le tragique entre allégorie et édification morale dans l'œuvre de Fabio Glissenti (1542–1615)', *Cahiers d'études italiennes*, 19 (2014), 185–98; 'The Courtier and the Philosopher's Stone: Dialogue and Conflict in Fabio Glissenti's *Discorsi morali*', in *Forms of Conflict and Rivalries in Renaissance Europe*, ed. by David A. Lines, Marc Laureys, and Jill Kraye (Bonn: Bonn University Press, 2015), pp. 207–22; and 'Reforming Drama: Theater as Spiritual Practice in the Works of Fabio Glissenti', in *Innovation in the Italian Counter-Reformation*, ed. by McHugh and Wainwright, pp. 169–89.

entry of the *Dizionario biografico degli italiani*, and has not been expanded by the most recent monograph that studied Glissenti in some detail, George McClure's *The Culture of Profession in Late Renaissance Italy*, which offers, to date, the most extensive study of the doctor's major work, the *Discorsi morali*.[3] Glissenti was born in Vestone di Valle Sabbia, near Brescia, around 1542. His father, Antonio (1512–76), was a physician himself, and a figure of interest in his own terms. Working at the service of Count Paride of Lodrone, Antonio was the author of texts about medical hygiene with a focus on plague, a constant threat in early modern Europe.[4] The *Trattato del regimento del vivere* [Treatise on Life Regime], published in Venice in 1576, is part of a public debate that involved another physician, the Veronese doctor Annibale Raimondo.[5] Plague is also at the core of the *Oratione divotissima nella liberatione del male contagioso di Venetia* [A Most Devout Oration on the Liberation of Venice from the Contagious Disease], likely published in the same period (1576–77).[6] Another Antonio, likely a cousin (1540–1602), was instead the author of works on irrigation, as indicated by the *Risposta* [Response] and the following *Replica* [Reply] to cartographer Cristoforo Sorte's *Modo d'irrigare la campagna di Verona e d'introdur più navigationi per lo corpo del felicissimo Stato di Venetia* [On the Way of Irrigating Verona's Countryside and Introducing Several Water Passages through the Blessed Territory of Venice], both printed in 1594.[7] The remarkable status acquired by the family is

3   Anna Laura Saso, 'Fabio Glissenti', in *Dizionario Biografico degli Italiani*, 57 (2001), pp. 406–08; McClure, *The Culture of Profession*, pp. 177–202. Previous scholarship on Glissenti, specifically focused on biographical information and overviews of his production with bibliographical details about the editions of his works, includes: Girolamo Ghilini, *Teatro d'huomini letterati* (Venice: Guerigli, 1647), vol. II, p. 74; Leonardo Cozzando, *Libraria bresciana* (Brescia: Giovanni Maria Rizzardi, 1694), pp. 78–79; Vincenzo Peroni, *Biblioteca bresciana* (Brescia: Nicolò Bettoni, 1818), vol. II, pp. 127–29; Bartolomeo Gamba, *Delle novelle italiane in prosa, bibliografia* (Florence: All'insegna di Dante, 1835), p. 182; Giovanni Papanti, *Catalogo dei novellieri italiani in prosa* (Livorno: Francesco Vigo, 1871), pp. 179–80; Giambattista Passano, *I novellieri italiani in prosa. Parte I* (Turin: Stamperia Reale, 1878), pp. 366–71; Ferdinando Neri, 'Le moralità di Fabio Glissenti', in *Scritti vari di erudizione e di critica in onore di Rodolfo Renier*, ed. by Arturo Graf (Turin: Bocca, 1912), pp. 187–96; Ugo Vaglia, 'Fabio Glissenti e la sua opera letteraria', *Memorie dell'Ateneo di Salò*, 16 (1952–54), 143–51; idem, *L'arte del ferro in Valle Sabbia e la famiglia Glisenti* (Brescia: Geroldi, 1959), pp. 34–45, 67–74.
4   Antonio's work at the service of the Count of Lodrone is mentioned by Fabio in one of the dedication letters included in *DM*, fol. V2r.
5   Antonio Glissenti, *Trattato del regimento del vivere, et delle altre cose che deveno usare gli huomini per preservarsi sani nelli tempi pestilenti. Continuato alla cognitione delle cause che producono la peste* (Venice: Rutilio e Camillo Borgominieri, 1576); idem, *Il summario delle cause che dispongono i corpi de gli huomini a patire la corrottione pestilente del presente anno 1576. Quelle che producono la peste, quelle che gli prestano aiuto, & fauore nel aggrandirla, & quelle che la fanno parere piu crudele* (n.p.: n.pub., 1576). The reply to Annibale Raimondo's *Apologia intorno alcuni amorevoli avisi mandateli, et per la risolutione di varii, et diversi dubii. Indirizzata a tutti quelli che si dilettarano di leggerla, overo di udirla leggere* (Venice: Domenico Nicolini da Sabbio, 1576) is in Antonio Glissenti, *Risposta fatta per il sumario delle cause pestilenti alla apologia dell'eccell. m. Anibal Raimondo veronese* (n.p.: n.pub., 1576).
6   Antonio Glissenti, *Oratione divotissima per ringratiare il nostro Signore Iddio, nella liberatione del male contagioso di Venetia* (n.p.: n.pub., 1576).
7   Cristoforo Sorte, *Modo d'irrigare la campagna di Verona e d'introdur più nauigationi per lo corpo del felicissimo Stato di Venetia trovato* (Verona, Girolamo Discepolo, 1593); Antonio Glissenti, *Risposta al modo d'irrigare la campagna di Verona* (Venice: n.pub., 1594); *Replica in proposito della risposta de m. Christoforo Sorte* (Venice: n.pub., 1594). On the confusion between the two Antonios, see <https://

also suggested by the fact that Antonio was invited to deliver a panegyric to the Venetian doge, Sebastiano Venier, in 1577.[8] The variety of interests that characterised both Antonios, as well as their tight links with Venice, are witnessed by other works: the *Dialogo del Gobbo da Rialto et Marocco dalle pipone da le colonne di S. Marco*, a *pasquinata* about a comet appeared over Venice featuring two famous Venetian *statue parlanti* [speaking statues]; and, closer to the moral preoccupations that would be at the centre of Fabio's literary works, *L'assoluta conclusione dell'humana libertà* [The Ultimate Argument about Human Freedom], which focuses on the notion of Free Will while also dismantling common assumptions about fortune and inclination.[9]

Fabio followed in his father's footsteps: after studying medicine in Padua alongside his brother Cornelio, he worked as a physician in Venice, where he lived with both Cornelio and their sister, Glissentia, who, as I will show, played an important role in the dissemination of her brother's works.[10] Fabio's philosophical training in Padua left important traces in his production, including an erudite set of Latin commentaries on works by Aristotle, Porphyry, and Gilbert of Poitiers, which he published in Venice in 1593–94. The voluminous folio gathers notes that, according to Fabio's preface to the readers, he accumulated over the years when reading in Padua under Jacopo Zabarella and Bernardino Petrella. Making the most of a relatively quiet summer, Glissenti put together 'per methodicas divisiones' (supported by a number of diagrams) his 'brevissima commentaria' on Porphyry's *Liber de praedicabilibus*, Gilbert's *Sex principia* and, above all, Aristotle's works of logic, the *Praedicamenta, De interpretatione, Analytica priora et posteriora*.[11]

A significant part of Glissenti's publications falls on the side of his medical profession. In 1596, Venetian printer Domenico Farri published Glissenti's major vernacular work, the *Discorsi morali contra il dispiacer del morire detto Athanatophilia*.[12] The book — over 1200 pages — is one of the most interesting products of late sixteenth-century Venetian typography. A five-day dialogue that takes place in Venice, it includes a final section entitled *Brevissimo trattato nel qual si discorre moralmente qual sia la pietra di filosofi* [A Brief Moral Treatise on the Nature of the Philosopher's Stone], which is, in fact, one of the several textual layers that constitute the complex framework of the book.[13] The work was apparently well received, as suggested by the fact that it was reprinted by Bartolomeo Alberti in 1600 and republished in an epitomised version by Angelo Veniero in 1605 under the

www.digitaldisci.it/glisenti-glissenti-antonio-detto-il-magro/> [accessed 23 November 2022].
8   Antonio Glissenti, *Elogio per il serenissimo principe dell'illustrissima republica Venetiana, il signor Sebastian Veniero* (Venice: n.pub., 1577).
9   Antonio Glissenti, *Dialogo del Gobbo da Rialto, et Marocco dalle pipone dalle colonne di S. Marco, sopra la cometa alli giorni passati apparsa su nel cielo* (Venice: n.pub., 1577); *L'assoluta conclusione dell'humana libertà* (Venice: Giovanni Antonio Rampazzetto, 1597).
10   On the professional success and personal wealth of Glissenti, see early information in Ghilini, *Teatro d'huomini letterati*, vol. II, p. 74.
11   Fabio Glissenti, *In quinque praedicabilia Porphyrij. In sex principia Gilberti Porretani. In Praedicamenta Aristotelis. In perihermenias Aristotelis. In priora, et posteriora Aristotelis. Per methodicas Divisiones brevissima commentaria* (Venice: Giovan Battista Ciotti, 1594). See Peroni, *Biblioteca bresciana*, vol. II, pp. 127–29.
12   I have consulted the copy at Florence, Biblioteca Nazionale Centrale, Pal. 7.7.5.7.
13   For a discussion of the treatise on the philosopher's stone that concludes the *Discorsi*, see Refini, 'The Courtier and the Philosopher's Stone'.

eloquent title *Theatro de' viventi e trionfo della morte* [Theatre of Men and Triumph of Death].[14]

Similar concerns with moral education and, more precisely, with the importance of meditating on death as a way of preparing for the salvation of the soul, are at the core of the ten *favole morali* [moral fables] published by Glissenti from 1606 onwards: *La Ragione sprezzata* [Reason Scorned] (1606), *L'Andrio cioè l'huomo virile* [Andrio, or the Strong Man] (1607), *Il bacio della Giustizia e della Pace* [The Kiss of Justice and Peace] (1607), *Il Diligente overo il Sollecito* [The Diligent, or the Solicitous man] (1608), *La Morte innamorata* [Smitten Death] (1608), *L'Androtoo* (1616), *La giusta Morte* [Fair Death] (1617), *Lo Spensierato fatto Pensoroso* [The Cheerful made Thoughtful] (1617), *Il mercato overo la fiera della vita humana* [The Market, or the Fair of Human Life] (1620), *La Sarcodinamia cioè la possanza della Carne* [Sarcodinamia, or the Power of the Flesh] (1620). These morality plays, which I will discuss in Chapter 3, were written to be performed by the female orphans based at the hospitals of Venice. According to the paratextual materials included in some of the printed editions, backed by evidence that I found in previously unpublished documents, Glissenti's commitment as a playwright pertained to the Ospedale degli Incurabili and the Ospedale di San Giovanni e Paolo, also known as Ospedale dei Derelitti or Ospedaletto. Some of the prints were released by Giovanni Alberti, but, starting with the posthumous publication of *L'Androtoo* (1616), it was the printer Marco Ginammi who took the lead in the dissemination of Glissenti's plays. As suggested by a series of reprints promoted in the 1630s by Ginammi's son, Bartolomeo, who carried on his father's focus on moral and devotional literature, Glissenti's plays retained a steady place in the book market, being advertised as particularly suitable for female readers, both lay and religious.[15]

Finally, *L'horribile e spaventevole inferno* [The Horrific and Frightful Hell], published in 1617 by Marco Ginammi, develops some of the topics and materials already covered by the *Discorsi morali* with the aim of providing preachers, and readers more broadly, with a set of reusable *exempla* focused on the punishments suffered in hell by the souls of sinners.[16]

The literary and scientific production of Glissenti is mentioned by Giovanni Stringa's continuation of Francesco Sansovino's *Venetia città nobilissima*.[17] More

---

14   Fabio Glissenti, *Discorsi morali contra il dispiacer del morire detto Athanatophilia* (Venice: Bartolomeo Alberti, 1600): this edition omits the dedication letters included in the original one; Angelo Veniero, *Teatro de' viventi e trionfo della morte diviso in due parti raccolte da i Discorsi morali dell'eccellentiss. Sig. Fabio Glissenti, dove si ragiona e discorre con molto profitto della salute di tutta la somma della morale, e Christiana filosofia, che insegna il bene et il virtuoso vivere, e come si possa e sappia santamente morire* (Venice: Fioravante Prati, 1605).

15   On the publishing activities of the Ginammi, see Maria Napoli, *L'impresa del libro nell'Italia del Seicento. La bottega di Marco Ginammi* (Naples: Guida, 1990), pp. 107–10.

16   Fabio Glissenti, *L'Horribile e spaventeuole inferno, dove si discorre della poca consideration che si ha d'intorno alle tremende pene di lui* (Venice: Marco Ginammi, 1617). Saso, 'Fabio Glissenti', p. 407, attributes to Glissenti two works published by Ginammi, *La ninfa guerriera* (1624) and *Gli effetti d'amore* (1626), that were, in fact, by different authors (Agostino Lampugnani and Lorenzo Longo, respectively; for *La ninfa guerriera*, the mistaken attribution is first found in Napoli, *L'impresa del libro*, p. 109).

17   McClure, *The Culture of Profession*, p. 178; Francesco Sansovino, *Venetia città nobilissima, et*

informative, though, is the reference made to Glissenti in the dedication letter of Giacomo Franco's *Habiti delle donne venetiane* [Dresses of Venetian Women].[18] The choice to address the work, which gathers drawings of dresses of Venetian women ('diversi habiti di donne venetiane'), to Glissenti is apparently due to the dedicatee's expertise in the figurative arts: 'subito mi cadé in mente la V.S. perché so quanto la si diletta di Pittura, Scoltura e Disegno, diletto invero d'animo nobilissimo' [I immediately thought of your lordship, for I know how much you enjoy painting, sculpture and the art of drawing, a pleasure that fits the noblest soul]. It is likely that Franco had in mind Glissenti's *Discorsi morali*, whose iconographic apparatus is, as we will see, not simply decorative in nature, but essential to the very conception of the work.

The *Discorsi morali* caused their author some problems with the Inquisition. As evidenced by a document from 1596, the censors asked Glissenti to expurgate a few passages from the book, but the author did not comply, and was eventually fined, alongside the printer Domenico Farri. The fact that the issue was settled with the payment of a penalty suggests that the doctrinal concerns of the censors did not involve any major theological issue. After all, the *Discorsi morali* showcase an eminently orthodox content, though one might argue that the author's handling of notions such as Divine Grace could leave some room for ambiguity.[19]

As regards the timing of Glissenti's death, two documents (a letter by his brother, Cornelio, and Bartolomeo Ginammi's dedication of the play *L'Androtoo*) let us situate it in September 1615.[20]

Setting the Stage for the Dialogue

Glissenti's major work, *Discorsi morali contra il dispiacer del morire*, is hard to label. The alternative title, *Athanatophilia*, is an erudite Hellenism that refers to the main topic of the work: namely, the invitation to appreciate death's role in human life in order to gain the salvation of the soul. (Literally, the Greek-sounding coinage plays with the double meaning 'love of immortality' *vs.* 'love of death', depending on whether the first letter, *a*, is considered part of *athanaton* or as alpha privative that reverses the sense of the word.) The Italian term 'discorsi' is itself quite vague: frequently used in titles of early modern works, it may refer to a variety of genres and sub-genres. The adjective 'morali' narrows the field in the direction of moral literature, inviting comparisons with works as diverse as Girolamo Naselli's Italian translation of Montaigne's *Essays*, published in 1590 under the title *Discorsi morali, politici et militari* [Moral, Political, and Military Discourses], a work of wide impact in the

---

singolare (Venice: Stefano Curti, 1663), p. 637.
18 Giacomo Franco, *Habiti delle donne venetiane* (n.d.: n.pub., n.d.); see the facsimile edition ed. by Lina Urban (Venice: Centro internazionale della grafica, 1990); on Franco, see Carlo Pasero, 'Giacomo Franco, editore, incisore e calcografo nei secoli XVI e XVII', *La Bibliofilia*, 37 (1935), 332–45; Christopher Witcombe, *Copyright in the Renaissance: Prints and the Privilegio in Sixteenth-century Venice and Rome* (Leiden and Boston: Brill, 2004), p. 128.
19 Giuliano Pesenti, 'Libri censurati a Venezia nei secoli XVI–XVII', *La Bibliofilia*, 58 (1956), 15–30 (p. 26).
20 Saso, 'Fabio Glissenti', p. 407.

moral literature of the period.²¹ Closer to Glissenti's own concerns are works such as Paolo Regio's *Discorsi intorno le virtù morali* [Discourses on Moral Virtues], Panfilo Fenario's *Discorsi sopra i cinque sentimenti* [Discourses on the Five Senses] and, in part, Cesare Rao's *Invettive, orationi e discorsi* [Invectives, Orations, and Discourses].²² Moral preoccupations are explored in different ways in these various works. Yet, features common to all of them are the 'discursive' attitude (be it developed in the form of dialogues or essay) and the gradual shift of morals towards Christian morality understood as the practice of Christian virtues.

The idea of 'discourse' as a form of oral communication is, in the case of Glissenti's *Discorsi morali*, conveyed through the dialogical form, which is also the feature upon which hinges the theatrical undertone of the work. Over five days, two main interlocutors — the Philosopher ('il Filosofo') and the Courtier ('il Cortigiano') — talk to each other while also engaging further characters in their conversations. The background to their dialogue is Venice, a location that is not merely ornamental, but crucial to the construction of the work. The spatial and narrative framework of the *Discorsi morali* is, in fact, what enables the unfolding of the dialogue: Venice is not just a static setting, but a walkable location that, evoked through its architecture, provides the protagonists with a space that is meant to mirror the broader configuration of the world.²³

---

21   Michel De Montaigne, *Discorsi morali, politici, et militari ... Tradotti dal sig. Girolamo Naselli dalla lingua francese nell'italiana* (Ferrara: Bendetto Mammarello, 1590). On the widespread circulation of 'moral' literature in the period, see Amedeo Quondam, *Forma del vivere: l'etica del gentiluomo e i moralisti italiani* (Bologna: il Mulino, 2010).

22   Paolo Regio, *Discorsi intorno le virtù morali ove con sentenze, et esempi di detti, et fatti degli antichi da diversi illustri autori raccolti, si tratta della giustizia, prudenza, temperanza, et fortezza. Con molti avertimenti utili così per la vita humana, come per il governo de' i prencipi, et delle repubbliche* (Naples: Orazio Salviani, 1576); Panfilo Fenario, *Discorsi sopra i cinque sentimenti; ne i quali si dimostrano le varie lor potenze, et effetti, e fin dove per lor mezo arriva l'intelletto humano. Con un trattato del medesimo delle virtù morali, dove con brevità si dichiara quale sia il vero loro fine* (Venice: Giovan Battista Somasco, 1587); Cesare Rao, *Invettive, orationi, et discorsi fatte sopra diverse materie, et a diversi personaggi dove si riprendono molti vitii, et s'essortano le persone all'esercitio delle virtù morali, et alle scienze, et arti liberali* (Venice: Damiano Zenaro, 1587).

23   Day 1 is set entirely in Piazza San Marco; more properly 'itinerant' are the dialogues of the other *giornate*. The actual journey of the protagonists through the city can be followed in detail thanks to precise topographic references. Day 2: Piazza San Marco, docks (fol. 69^r), bridge (fol. 69^v), Castello, 'ponte della Tana lungo l'Arzanà' (fol. 78^r), San Zaccaria (fol. 86^v), 'Piazzetta del Palagio del Principe' (fol. 100^v), 'Traghetto della Pescheria', Dogana in front of Giudecca (fol. 113^r), Dogana-Pescheria (fol. 135^v), on a gondola down the Grand Canal (fol. 138^v), dock at Fondamenta di S. Croce (fol. 143^v), the Philosopher's house (fol. 144^r). Day 3: Piazza San Marco, Mercerie (fol. 161^v), Prisons (fol. 186^r), courtyard of the Ducal Palazzo (fol. 196^v), the invalid's abode (fol. 207^v), Santa Maria Formosa (fol. 215^v), San Francesco della Vigna (fols 225^r, 233^v), fondamenta facing the islands of the lagoon (fol. 236^v), bridge facing the direction of Murano (fol. 239^r), SS. Giovanni e Paolo (fol. 245^{r-v}), on a boat (fol. 294^{r-v}), towards Santa Chiara (fol. 294^v), back home (fol. 315^v). Day 4: towards Santa Chiara and Santa Maria Maggiore (fol. 319^v), Santa Maria Maggiore and Tempio del Carmine (fol. 325^v), 'Speziaria dei Due Angeli presso il Carmine' (fol. 328^r), towards campo Santa Margherita (fol. 336^r), San Barnaba towards the 'traghetto' for San Vitale (fol. 338^v), Piazza Santo Stefano, house of an actress ('la Recitante') (fol. 339^r), Carmine (fol. 424^v), Santa Maria Maggiore and fondamenta (fol. 427^r), the Philosopher's house (fol. 429^r). Day 5: the house of one sick philosopher (fol. 446^r), towards San Marco (fol. 497^{r-v}), 'Dogana di mare' (fol. 499^v), towards San Sebastiano (fol. 525^v), towards San

The long subtitle on the title page of the Farri edition offers further information about the topic at the centre of the *Discorsi morali*, 'ne' quali si discorre quanto ragionevolmente si dovrebbe desiderare la Morte, e come naturalmente la si vada fuggendo' [in which it is argued that, according to reason, Death should be desired, whereas it is naturally rejected]. The *Discorsi* are thus introduced as dialogues on death in the first place, the moral tradition merging with that of the *ars moriendi* [art of dying well]. As observed by McClure, Glissenti's work is much indebted to the many works on the topic published throughout the fifteenth and sixteenth centuries.[24] Since the appearance of Jean Gerson's *De scientia mortis*, a number of *artes moriendi* filled the European book market, with medieval *topoi* such as the *Totentanz* [dance of Death] and the triumph of Death being revived throughout the Renaissance and revamped even more powerfully during the Baroque age.[25] Glissenti's aim is to teach the readers how to defeat the fear of death by acknowledging that death is not evil, but the gateway to a better life freed from earthly struggles. Key to the process are contempt for vanity and a focus on spiritual preoccupations, which, within the *Discorsi morali*, have their proactive mouthpiece in the Philosopher.

One of the tools used by the Philosopher to persuade the Courtier and the other interlocutors is a series of thirty *novelle*, which are introduced as moral *exempla* throughout the five days of the dialogue. As stated in the frontispiece, the work includes 'trenta vaghi et utili ragionamenti, come tante piacevoli novelle interposti, cavati da gli abusi del presente viver mondano' [thirty beautiful and useful *ragionamenti*, inserted as pleasant *novelle*, extracted from the current errors of mundane life]. The dialogue functions as a framework that gathers allegorical narratives populated by allegorical characters (Death, Reason, Opinion, Discourse, Time, Nature, etc.) who are meant to stage the ubiquitous conflict between Man and his sensual components. (I am intentionally using the theatrical metaphor here, not only because of the dialogical format of most *novelle*, but also because, as we will see, some of them were direct sources for the plots of Glissenti's morality plays.)

However, within the fiction of the dialogue, the Philosopher's attempt to convince the Courtier that death is desirable does not lead to the intended outcome: at the end of their Venetian tour, the Courtier's opinion is unchanged, and he continues to reject the very idea of accepting death and preparing for it. The last word is given to the Philosopher: anticipating the Courtier's reaction, he had promised a gift in case his attempt failing. The gift is no other than the 'curioso trattato della pietra de' filosofi' [curious treatise on the philosopher's stone], which

---

Niccolò (fol. 531^r), San Niccolò, Santa Marta, Santa Maria Maggiore (fol. 540^v), the Philosopher's house (fol. 563^v), the Courtier's house (fol. 565^v).
24 McClure, *The Culture of Profession*, pp. 178–79.
25 See the classical studies on the topic by Leonard P. Kurtz, *The Dance of Death and the Macabre Spirit in European Literature* (New York: Columbia University, 1934); Alberto Tenenti, *La Vie et la Mort à travers l'art du XVe siècle* (Paris: Cahiers des Annales, 1952); idem, *Il senso della morte e l'amore della vita nel Rinascimento (Francia e Italia)* (Turin: Einaudi, 1957). On the Protestant reshaping of the *ars moriendi* tradition, see Austra Reinis, *Reforming the Art of Dying: The 'ars moriendi' in the German Reformation (1519–1528)* (Aldershot: Ashgate, 2007).

was mentioned in the title of the book as a sort of appendix to the *Discorsi morali*. The *Trattato*, which brings together the various layers of the framework, rewrites the trope of the philosopher's stone by identifying it with man's choice to consider God as the ultimate focus of human life.[26] As its various components demonstrate, Glissenti's work is a hybrid: an *ars moriendi* in the form of a dialogue that includes novelle and closes with a book-in-the-book evoked within the narrative as a gift from one character to another and offered by the author to the reader (whose own 'role', in a way, is meant to coincide with that of the incredulous Courtier).

Before declaring that the *Discorsi morali* are dedicated to Fabio's sister, Glissentia, the title page mentions another important component of the work: the iconographic apparatus. The *Discorsi* are in fact advertised as 'adornati di bellissime figure, a' loro luoghi appropriate' [decorated by most beautiful illustrations aptly placed in conjunction with specific passages]. All the chapters open with woodcuts that visualise the main topic of the book, the meditation on death. More than one hundred illustrations are used throughout the work in order to make the dialogue visible to the reader, according to the rhetorical principle of *evidentia* that is key to the conception of the book, and which, as I have demonstrated in Chapter 1, is integral to the long life of the *theatrum mundi* trope. While many of the illustrations appear more than once within the book, their scope goes beyond mere decoration. They visualise the 'theatre of human life' that Glissenti represents through the image of Venice, with the city functioning as the stage for a deadly dance that involves all humans, whether they like it or not.

A Little Bit of Everything

The reasons behind the writing of the *Discorsi morali* are declared by Glissenti in the dedication letter of the work addressed to his sister, Glissentia, dated from Venice, 18 June 1596.[27] The letter turns to commonplaces of the genre, starting with a customary declaration of modesty: Glissenti promised his sister a book that would alleviate the physical distance between them by letting her converse with him ('in cui leggendo vi paresse come di ragionar meco, sì che con minor travaglio poteste sofferire questa mia lontananza').[28] Two difficulties have made the completion of the work hard: the language and the topic. Claiming a lack of expertise in vernacular literary writing, and fearing the comparison between his work and those of professional literary authors, Glissenti found it impossible to proceed, he says.[29]

---

26 The *Trattato* has been reprinted in a facsimile edition: Fabio Glissenti, *Breve trattato nel quale moralmente si discorre qual sia la pietra di filosofi* (Brescia: F.lli Gerolli, 1987); for a discussion of the *Trattato* vis-à-vis the broader framework of *Discorsi morali*, see Refini, 'The Courtier and the Philosopher's Stone'.
27 *DM*, fols a2^r–a4^v.
28 *DM*, fol. a2^r.
29 *DM*, fol. a2^v: 'dovendomi io scrivere volgarmente, in lingua, della quale non feci mai altra professione, che per intender altrui, et esser inteso, come è apunto la natìa nostra; e vedendo che tutti quei che volgarmente scrivono fanno scelta delle più belle parole, e s'affaticano con ogni suo potere di Toscanamente favellare, son restato in questo all'impossibile di potervi cosa alcuna attendere' [Since I had to write in the vernacular, that is in a language that I have never used, if not for understanding

As far as subject matter is concerned, the female gender of his addressee prevented him from turning to his own professional knowledge (medicine) and discouraged him from tackling other topics not suitable for women. Eventually, he thought about matters of devotion and spirituality ('scrivere qualche cosa di divotione'), topics that would be fitting both for virtuous women and anyone who cares about God.[30] But even this project was then left aside because of the many writings already available on such subjects.[31] However, Glissentia's insistence made him decide to go ahead and write a little bit of everything ('scrivere di ogni cosa un poco'). The statement is of importance, for it witnesses the encyclopaedic ambition that informs the *Discorsi morali*. Accordingly, another feature of the work that surfaces in the dedication letter is the fact that Glissenti proceeded as a compiler, accumulating materials rather than inventing them. He compares himself to a poor man who, devoid of riches, shares with his friends a little salad ('insalatuzza') made of herbs and flowers from his garden, valuable not because of its quality, but because of the affection put into it:

> Così parimente io povero di bella lingua, d'inventione e di soggetto, ma desideroso di compiacervi, son entrato nel sterile horticello dell'ingegno mio, e fra le cose altrove lette, et le imaginate da me son ito tanto raccogliendo hor quinci una favola, come un'herba, e quinci un'autorità, e moralità, che finalmente ho ridotto insieme questo libretto, come una insalatuzza per presentarvelo.[32]

> [Equally devoid of beautiful language, invention and subject matter, but eager to please you, I entered the sterile garden of my mind, and, among the things read elsewhere and those I imagined myself, I have been gathering here a fable, as if it were some greens, there an authority and a morality, which eventually I collected into this booklet, presenting it as a little salad.]

The 'insalatuzza' recalls the salad mentioned by Montaigne in the opening of the chapter 'On Names' in Book 1 of the *Essays*, though Glissenti had more likely in mind the preamble of Paolo Giovio's *Dialogo dell'imprese militari e amorose*, in which the author compares the pleasant and occasional nature of his work to a 'tasty salad' ('saporita insalatuccia').[33] In Glissenti's letter to his sister, the image of the salad is

---

others and being understood, as is our mother tongue; and seeing that all those who write in the vernacular choose the most beautiful words and endeavour to write in Tuscan as best as they can, I have not been able to accomplish anything].

30   *DM*, fols a2^v–a3^r.
31   *DM*, fol. a3^r: 'Ma considerando poi, che non mancano in tal soggetto tanti, e tanti libri, scritti da celebri Autori, e massime da huomini santi, che possono a pieno sodisfare ogni divota, e curiosa mente, io mi rissolsi al tutto di non farne altro' [Realising that there is no shortage of books on this topic written by famous authors, and especially by honourable ones, that fully satisfy any devout and curious intellect, I decided not to do more of that].
32   *DM*, fol. a3^v.
33   Michel De Montaigne, *Essays. Livre premier*, ed. by Jean Céard (Paris: Le Livre de poche, 2002), pp. 495–96: 'Quelque diversité d'herbes qu'il y ait, tout s'enveloppe sous le nom de salade. De même, sous la considération des noms, je m'en vais faire ici une galimafrée de divers articles' [What variety of herbs soever are shufed together in the dish, yet the whole mass is swallowed up under one name of a sallet. In like manner, under the consideration of names, I will make a hodge-podge of divers articles] (trans. by Cotton). Paolo Giovio, *Dialogo dell'imprese militari e amorose*, ed. by Maria Luisa Doglio (Rome: Bulzoni, 1978), p. 33: 'essendomi riuscito questo picciol trattato assai piacevole e

meant to tone down the gravitas of the work, which is far from being a 'booklet' ('libretto'). As a matter of fact, the variety of its ingredients (novelle, dialogues, *exempla*) is not put together randomly; quite the opposite, the claim to 'write a little bit of everything' entails the attempt to use the *meditatio mortis* as the main thread around which to forge a broader picture of the world:

> Leggete adunque quest'opera, che di cosa che reale, e veramente è per tale riuscire, ragiona e discorre: che annuntia cosa, che ad ogn'uno (non eccettuando alcuno) ha da accadere una fiata, e però non meno a gli altri, che a voi, et a me appartiene, e parla: che finalmente discorre di cose diverse, di morire, di vivere, di guerre, d'amore, di bellezze, di favole, d'istorie, d'opinioni, di verità, et d'altre curiose novità, tutte cose conformi all'universale saper vostro.[34]
>
> [Read this work, which speaks about a topic that is true and that will prove true: it announces what will happen to all of us, no one excluded; for this reason, it speaks and relates to both you and myself no less than to any other person: eventually, it talks about various things, such as death, life, wars, love, beauties, fables, histories, opinions, truth, and other curious novelties, all convenient to your universal knowledge.]

The main topic — death — allows the author to discuss a variety of issues relevant to human life, including those that he initially found unsuitable for a female reader, as well as 'other curious novelties' aimed at raising the audience's interest. The work can thus be read in different ways and at multiple levels: Glissentia, alongside all readers, will receive pleasant entertainment from the *Discorsi morali* while also being given the opportunity to commit to a more profound reading that may grasp the 'senso interiore della lettera' [inner sense of the text], that is, the acquisition of moral conduct in accordance with Christian doctrine ('per apprendere ad essercitarvi bene in questa vita, conforme e politica e civile donna, a buona e vera Christiana').[35] A note to the readers, added at the end of the index of chapters, refers explicitly to the complementarity of dealing with two dimensions (the human and the divine) at once, while insisting on the non-literary nature of the work and its practical focus:

giocondo e non poco grave per l'altezza e varietà de' soggetti, mi sono assicurato di mandarvelo, pensando che vi possa esser opportuno passatempo in così fastidiosa stagione; e in ciò ho imitato il vostro semplice ortolano, che spesse volte sopra la vostra tavola, ricca di varie e preziose vivande, s'arrischia di presentare un panierino de' suoi freschi fiori di ramerino e di borana per servire a uno intermesso d'una saporita insalatuccia. Ha questo trattato molta similitudine con la diversità di detti fiori, ameni e gratissimi al gusto' [Given that this little treatise proved pleasant and amusing, yet quite serious in the nobility and variety of the topics, I made sure to send it to you, thinking that it might be a convenient pastime during such an annoying season; in doing so, I just imitated your gardener, who often dares to bring to your table, rich in various and precious food, a small basket of his fresh rosemary flowers and borage to be served as a tasty salad between courses. This treatise resembles the variety of such flowers, beautiful and pleasing to the taste]. In a similar vein, the image was used by Masuccio Salernitano, *Il Novellino*, ed. by Alfredo Mauro (Bari: Laterza, 1940), p. 288, in the opening of novella 36: 'ho avuto recorso a le non saporose erbecciole del mio incolto iardini, de quale composta la presente insalatuccia, a te, fiume de eloquenzia, la mando' [I made use of the tasteless herbs which spring from my ill-cultivated garden, out of which I have compounded the medley salad I now send to you, river of eloquence as you are] (trans. by Waters).

34   *DM*, fol. a4^{r-v}.
35   *DM*, fol. a4^{v}.

> Io non scrivo nuova scienza, né meno faccio professione di bella volgar lingua; né cosa alcuna curiosa di sublimi ingegni vo dimostrando; eccetto che una certa pratica di ben vivere, e di ben morire. Perciò in stile basso conforme al mio sapere, et in lingua nostrana, come meglio ho saputo l'intention mia son andato spiegando, per farmi meglio intendere da chi mi mosse a scrivere.[36]
>
> [I do not write about new knowledge, nor do I showcase beautiful vernacular language; I do not demonstrate any curious achievement of sublime minds; I only write about a certain practice of living well and dying well. I have been explaining my intention in humble style, appropriate to my knowledge, in our mother tongue, as best as I could, so as to make myself better understood by the one who asked me to write.]

Further details about the work's structure and scope come from the 'Argomento' that precedes Book 1.[37] It functions as a methodological preamble to the *Discorsi morali* and provides the readers with a set of instructions that helps them navigate the book under the aegis of the metaphor of the *theatrum mundi*. In approaching the unpleasant topic of death, Glissenti declares that he is doing what a good doctor would do in order to administer some medicine to a patient: fearing that they may refuse it because of its bitterness, the doctor would mix the medicine with something sweet, so as to make it easier to ingest ('volendo porgere allo infermo salutifera medicina, dubitando che per l'amarezza non la pigli, vi mescola alcune cose dolci, et al gusto soavi, per farnelo volonteroso, o meno ritroso nel pigliarla').[38] The Lucretian metaphor is particularly pertinent because of Glissenti's actual profession: as a physician usually concerned with physical health, he turns here to spiritual care. In order to make the *Discorsi* more palatable and compensate for his own lack of eloquence ('poca facondia'), he has included several pleasant things and poetical quotations from famous poets ('cose piacevoli e curiose, e parimente molti versi di famosi e conosciuti poeti').[39] The *Discorsi* are indeed rich in references to philosophical and poetical *auctoritates*, quotations from the Bible, and proverbs meant to support the arguments upheld by the interlocutors. Numerous rubrics in the margins help readers identify the sources of Glissenti's quotations: Petrarch is possibly the most frequently quoted poet, but other references include Dante, Boiardo, Ariosto, and Tasso, as well as classical authors such as Homer, Virgil, and Horace.

When it comes to the structure of the work, the division of the dialogue into five days evokes the five-act division typical of plays. Glissenti's explanation triggers the most explicit theatrical allusion in the work:

> Fu parimente il mio pensiero di rapresentarvi innanzi agli occhi come una tragedia delle attioni humane, le quali il più delle volte vanno terminando in fine mesto, e miserabile; con pensiero che si apparasse dal canto nostro a

---

36 *DM*, fol. a11^v.
37 *DM*, fols A[1]^r–A2^v.
38 *DM*, fol. A[1]^r.
39 Ibid. On the Lucretian metaphor and its widespread circulation in early modern culture, see Valentina Prosperi, *Di soavi licor gli orli del vaso: la fortuna di Lucrezio dall'Umanesimo alla Controriforma* (Rome: Aragno, 2004).

ritirarle in una comedia, il cui fine riesca lieto e pien di gioia. Per tanto ho diviso questa operetta in cinque dialoghi, o cinque giornate, come in cinqu'atti di tragedia, co' quali andiamo componendo nella vita nostra tutto il progresso di lei, dimostrando le passioni, e gli accidenti, ch'ogn'or l'accompagnano.[40]

[It was likewise my intention to represent in front of your eyes the tragedy of human actions, which most often end badly and miserably; my scope in doing this was to turn it into a comedy, whose end may prove cheerful and full of joy. I have thus divided this small work into five dialogues, or five days, as in the five acts of a tragedy, through which, in our life, we represent its progress, showing the passions and the accidents that accompany it throughout.]

In keeping with the rhetorical principle of *evidentia*, Glissenti wished to bring the 'tragedy of human actions' before the audience's eyes. Thanks to the conspicuous iconographic apparatus, the rhetorical device is pursued in a very literal way. The drama staged in the book and made visible through the images printed on the pages is tragic because most human actions end badly. However, the book is meant to make the readers work intensely on themselves and take action so as to transform their own tragedies into comedies. As such, the five days of the *Discorsi morali* correspond to the five acts of a tragedy that stages the passions and events of human life.

The theatrical framework employed complements a fundamentally sensualist vision of the human kind. Within it, the five acts correspond to the five senses ('sentimenti') that coordinate human actions ('le attioni del viver nostro'). Men and women tend to follow the senses rather than reason, which is described by Glissenti as the only guide that would be able to lead them to redemption and salvation.[41] The *Discorsi morali* thus outline a sensorial progress that, beginning with eyesight, reaches touch by going through taste, hearing, and smell. By reviewing the main features of each sense, the author illustrates the analogy that exists between each of them and the five parts of the book.[42]

The first dialogue, in which Reason seems to prevail over Sense, corresponds to eyesight, the noblest among the senses due to its minimal involvement with the materiality of sense perception. Somewhat removed from the physical experience of feeling, reason imitates the mechanisms of eyesight.[43] Eyesight is also described

---

40 *DM*, fol. A[1]ʳ.
41 Ibid.: 'E sono questi cinqu'atti o dialoghi corrispondenti a cinque nostri sentimenti, co' quali andiamo regolando le attioni del viver nostro, attratti per lo più da gli appetiti loro, sovente aiutati dal senso comune, e talhora, ma di rado, guidati dalla Ragione' [These five acts or dialogues correspond to our five senses, by means of which we regulate the actions of our life, mostly following their appetites, often helped by common sense, and occasionally, but seldom, guided by Reason].
42 For a similar organisation of moral subject matter, see Fenario, *Discorsi sopra i cinque sentimenti*; but it is also worth recalling the importance that the senses hold within the experience of meditation outlined by Ignatius of Loyola, with which, as I will suggest, Glissenti's spiritual project had much in common. On the place of the senses in Ignatius's *Spiritual exercises*, see Marty, *Sentir et goûter*.
43 *DM*, fol. A[1]ᵛ: 'in cui ragionandosi, e discorrendo più secondo la ragione, che secondo il senso, viene ad un certo modo la cognitione, che si ha per via di ragione, ad imitare l'instromento della vista; il qual opera e conosce le cose visibili con spiritale operatione, quasi lontana dal sentire' [In which, discussing and arguing according to reason more than to sense, the cognition obtained through reason comes to imitate the instrument of sight, which operates and knows the visible things

as the sense that is most effective at moving the affections of the audience, and it is likely due to such a feature that the *Discorsi morali* assign great importance to the representation of the narrative through both words and images. Taste, which settles for savouring tasty food without caring for reason, nature, or law ('cose gustose, senza osservanza di ragione, di natura, o di legge'), does not wait for proofs from the other senses: accordingly, the characters that the Philosopher and the Courtier encounter in the second dialogue feel satiated by the earthly and very tangible pleasures of life. They do not wish to reach better understanding ('intenderne più oltra') and do not enquire about the real purpose that makes life 'savoury' and pleasant ('fine per cui la vita sia fatta gustevole e grata').[44] Hearing is described as an ambiguous sense: it makes wide room for deception, because the transmission of sound through the air is conducive to misunderstandings ('in questa attione facilmente si può ingannare, pigliando bene spesso un suono per un altro'); yet hearing is the sense by means of which humans learn from one another, acquire knowledge, and are taught how to handle reason. The third dialogue thus introduces a set of characters who, while certainly inclined to deception and mistake, make use of judgment ('persone più essercitate, e giudiciose') and are aware of the fact that sense perception does not provide immediate access to truth, but only to opinions and appearances.[45] The fourth dialogue corresponds to smell, a most deceitful sense, which, based on vapours and odours that contaminate the air, does not provide access to the source that causes them ('la sostanza della cosa'). The protagonist of this dialogue is a professional actress ('la recitante'), who embodies the superficiality associated with smell: while upholding an apparently wise opinion, she does not care for actual knowledge, and is unable to go beyond the appearance ('non penetrando nella sostanza della verità, ma così superficialmente contentandosi d'haverne tal opinione').[46] The descent through the senses staged by Glissenti reaches its conclusion in the fifth dialogue, which is compared to the sense of touch. Intrinsically concerned with the experience of the material world, hence quite far from the detachment of eyesight, touch is the sense that allows men and women to assess the reality of things. At the core of this dialogue is the figure of a scientist ('letterato e professore di scienze') who, through his faith and the example of his own death, makes the audience see truth first hand, that is, the fact that human actions are constantly misled by sense perception.[47]

through a kind of spirit-based operation, quite removed from feeling].
44   Ibid. In the second dialogue, the Philosopher and the Courtier begin their stroll through Venice and meet with many individuals that represent the city's professional world, primarily of humble extraction, including a vintner, a warden, a butcher, a pedlar, a gypsy woman, a servant, and a gondolier.
45   Ibid. During day 3, the Philosopher and the Courtier encounter several artisans who occupy a slightly higher step on the social ladder when compared to the characters met in the previous book. Of particular importance, and somewhat different from the conversations held with the others, are the exchanges with a prisoner and a gravely ill man.
46   Ibid.
47   *DM*, fols A[1]^v–A2^r: 'col lume della fede, e con l'essempio della sua morte viene a scoprire la verità, facendoci toccar con mano quanto nelle attioni nostre, e ne gli alti sentimenti ci troviamo ingannati' [through the light of faith and the example of his death, he reveals the truth, making us

After outlining the analogies between the five senses and the five parts of the book, Glissenti goes back to the theatrical metaphor and unpacks it in detail. By turning to the Aristotelian distinction of the tragic plot in peripeteia, catastrophe, and anagnorisis, he provides a tripartite account of the 'tragedy of human actions' and identifies its main actors as 'Uomo' [Man], 'Ragione' [Reason], and 'Senso' [Sense]:

> Che sì come nella Tragedia si trovano propositioni facili, varie attioni, e fine doloroso — come che nel primo atto si propongano i pensieri, le deliberationi, et i fatti d'huomini illustri e persone di grado; nel secondo si vadino disponendo varie attioni secondo la diversità de i pareri; nel terzo accommodando le già disposte alle proposte fatte; nel quarto rivoltando sossopra ogni cosa, tutte le cose fatte si rendono sospette; e nel quinto con iscoprimento d'infelicità si terminano e conchiudono fini differenti da i proposti –; così io volendo rapresentare questa Tragedia della vita humana, presi soggetto da questo illustre principe de gli animali; e suppongo che l'Huomo stia con gravità a sedere, come dispensator e giudice della sua vita e delle sue attioni, ascoltando quei due Angeli buono e cattivo, che lo vanno consigliando: overo (come dicono i Naturali) la Ragione, e il Senso.[48]

> [As in a tragedy one finds easy propositions, various actions, and a sorrowful end — in the first act, thoughts, decisions, and facts of illustrious men and people of high rank are introduced; in the second, various actions are set in motion based on different opinions; in the third, the proposed plans are accommodated to those that have been achieved; in the fourth, by reversing everything, all deeds accomplished are made suspicious; and in the fifth, when the sad outcome is revealed, a conclusion different from the expected one is reached — likewise, eager to represent this tragedy of human life, I took my subject from this illustrious prince of the animate beings. And I imagine Man seated solemnly, as the judge of his own life and actions, listening to the two Angels, good and evil, who advise him: or, as the natural philosophers say, Reason and Sense.]

Man, according to a commonplace of medieval allegory that had been made popular by the psychomachia tradition and *contrasti*, hangs in the balance between Good (salvation) and Evil (damnation). Reason and Sense, allegorical characters that appear frequently both in Glissenti's novelle and in his morality plays, are caught in the constant fight over the control of Man's soul. Entrusted with Free Will, Man has the burden of deciding which path to follow. Given these premises, the author divides the 'tragedy of human life' into five dialogues.

The first dialogue is entitled 'Filologo' ('amator di ragione') for it stages Reason's attempt to show Man what path to pursue in order to live according to virtue and making good use of his intellectual resources, which distinguish him from the beasts.[49] Despite the opportunity laid out for him by Reason, Man is seduced by

---

realise how we are deceived in our actions and feelings].
48 *DM*, fol. A2^r; on the structure of tragedy, see Arist. *Poet*. 1450a 32–35.
49 *DM*, fol. A2^r; Reason is described as follows: 'Reina delle potenze dell'anima, va [...] proponendo all'huomo il fine per lo qual egli è nato, la vita che deve tenere, li travagli che deve passare, e la eccellenza delle virtù e della futura vita; acciocché a questa aspirando viva da huomo

the appetites and pleasant promises made by Sense: the second dialogue (dedicated to one female member of the aristocratic Donà family) is thus entitled 'Estisifilo', which literally translates into 'lover of the senses'.[50] Undecided whether to follow the 'vivid reasons' advanced by the Good Angel ('le ragioni vive propostegli dall'Angelo buono') or the tempting promises made by the Evil Angel ('le promesse de' godimenti presenti offertegli dall'Angelo cattivo'), Man does not know what to do: eventually, due to human nature's inclination towards the senses, he resolves to follow them ('finalmente egli appigliandosi al peggio, come che la natura in lui sia inclinata al male più che al bene, si rissolve volontariamente d'adherir a' sensi, compiacendosi ne i godimenti, e diletti loro'). Far from functioning as a justification, the inclination towards the senses makes Man's choice even more reproachable. The third dialogue, entitled 'Eleutteron' (dedicated to Count Sebastiano Paride of Lodrone), focuses in fact on Man's Free Will, which is solely responsible for such bad decision ('Libero Arbitrio, o libero volere, col quale egli si dà in preda ai sensi').[51] Once Man turns his back to Reason, his mind is obfuscated by a form of false belief — opinion — which has nothing to do with truth, and which eventually brings him far from the true knowledge of things.[52] As Glissenti argues, it is very hard for men to shy away from their opinions, and this is why the fourth dialogue, which focuses on the fallacy of beliefs, is entitled 'Doxacolutho' [follower of opinion] (dedicated to Camilla Soranzo, 'podestaressa' of Crema). Man's mistake will only be revealed in the fifth dialogue, 'Alithinoo' [truth finder] (dedicated to the Bishop of Brescia, Marino Zorzi). The passage that illustrates this part of the *Discorsi morali* is of great interest, in that it outlines a dynamic that will later be at the core of Glissenti's morality plays:

> Formato che si ha l'Huomo questa opinion nel capo, cioè che il viver mondano, il seguitar i sensi, e dilettarsi in quelli, con procacciarsi felicità mondane, sia il meglio che far possi, vive baldanzosamente in questo suo pensiero, e vi fa tal habito, che poco cura qual si voglia ragione in contrario sia detta: et in questa sua falsa opinione così trascuratamente vive, che fin che non sopragiunge la morte, non s'avvede del suo grand'errore, alla cui giunta poi scoprendosi la verità, che stava nascosta sotto la tela dell'opinione, macchiata dalle lusinghe de' sensi, e vedendosi ad un tratto privo e spogliato di quanto s'havea persuaso, tardi viene a provare, che la opinione in cui havea fondato le sue speranze è riuscita falsa; e che quella ragione cui prima non volle ubidire, consigliava il giusto e honesto; e che quei sensi, che lo allettarono, gli persuasero il male; e

ragionevole, e non da bruto animale, sovrastando alle cupidità de' sensi, et operando virtuosamente' [Queen of the powers of the soul, Reason [...] outlines to man the scope to which he was born, the life he must conduct, the troubles he must go through, and the excellence of the virtues and of the future life, so that, seeking this life, he may live as a reasonable man, and not as a brute animal, dominating the greed of the sense and behaving virtuously].
50 Ibid.: 'in questo s'introduce certa consuetudine humana appresa dall'uso de' sensi, senza articoli, od argomenti efficaci dal suo canto' [in this [book] it is introduced a certain human habit, acquired through the senses, that is, without any solid argument on its side].
51 DM, fol. A2^{r-v}.
52 Ibid.: 'opinione [...] una particolar credenza o prosontione de gli huomini e delle cose, senza vero fondamento di ragione' [opinion [...] [is a] particular belief or assumption of men and things, with no real foundation based on reason].

che egli, poi che se gli accostò volontariamente, ne viene meritamente ad esser deluso.⁵³

[Once Man has formed such an opinion in his mind — namely, that mundane life, following the senses and taking pleasure from them, together with procuring earthly happiness, are the best things one can do — he lives merrily with this belief and gets used to it, disregarding whatever reason might be opposed to it. He so carelessly lives in this false opinion that he does not see his mistake until death's arrival. When death comes and the truth — which was hidden by the cloth of opinion stained by the flatteries of the senses — is revealed, and man sees himself deprived of all that he was persuaded about, he realises that the belief on which he based his hopes was untrue; and that reason, which he initially did not want to obey, gave him right and honest advice; and that the senses, which lured him, persuaded him to misbehave; and that, having followed them voluntarily, he deserves to be disappointed.]

Man's amendment arrives too late: when Death tears out the 'fabric of opinion' ('tela dell'opinione') and exposes the vanity of mundane matters, true redemption is not possible anymore and Man is doomed to the flames of hell. This, as we will see in Chapter 3, is exactly what happens in *La Ragione sprezzata*, a play, based on narrative materials extracted from the novelle included in the *Discorsi morali*, that revolves around the bad advice that Man receives from his servants, the Senses.⁵⁴

The main characters of the tragedy of human life are Reason, Sense, Free Will, Opinion, and Truth. Its tragic progress relies in the sequence of 'nobile principio' [noble beginning], 'festevole mezzo' [joyful middle] and 'infelice compimento e fine' [unhappy achievement and end]. In order to turn it into comedy, one should stick to the 'nobile principio' and, abhorring the 'festevole mezzo', achieve a happy ending ('fine lieto e gioioso').⁵⁵ The rejection of the 'festevole mezzo' is the core of Glissenti's moral teachings, and one that would inform his morality plays as well.

Making Death Visible

As mentioned in the title page, the *Discorsi morali* are enriched by a series of illustrations that are meant to accompany specific passages of the text ('adornati di bellissime figure, a' loro luoghi appropriate'). If the reference to the quality of the images is clearly part of the advertising effort pursued by the frontispiece, the indication that these images are relevant to specific places should be taken seriously. Differently from illustrated books that privilege the ornamental function of images, the *Discorsi morali* showcase a complex iconographic apparatus that is integral to the narrative and must be understood as part of an active conversation with the text itself.⁵⁶ As is frequently the case with voluminous publications of this kind, the same

---

53 Ibid.
54 See Chapter 3, pp. 138–39, 147–52, 166–83.
55 *DM*, fol. A2ᵛ.
56 Phrasings such as 'figure a' loro luoghi appropriate' are fairly common in sixteenth-century illustrated books. One could recall, for instance, the widely read *Della imitatione di Christo, e del disprezzo del mondo* (Venice: Altobello Salicato, 1580, with numerous reprints), a text that Glissenti was likely familiar with; its long subtitle specifies that the illustrations ('figure') are not placed

illustrations are used more than once: yet, with a corpus of 117 unique woodcuts, the author and publisher manage to create a product that stands out within the tradition of the *artes moriendi* and, more broadly, among early modern illustrated books.

Consistently with the main topic of the work, the title page is decorated with a device — a tree over three hills, a rising sun, and the Latin motto 'occulto gliscit' — in a frame made of skeletons [Fig. 2.1]. The motto refers to the sun, but it also conceals a reference to the author's surname, Glissenti. The pun is revealed on the frontispiece's *verso*, where the same frame surrounds the author's portrait and the motto 'aperte degliscit' [Fig. 2.2], which alludes to the inevitable decline of life, a sound introduction to the volume.[57]

The illustrations to the *Discorsi morali* can then be divided into two main groups. A first set of images illustrates the journey of the Philosopher and the Courtier through Venice, thus visualising the main narrative of the work. A second set is instead concerned with the illustration of what is told within the dialogue, including the novelle narrated by the Philosopher. Each chapter of the book opens with an image associated with the chapter's title, according to a repetitive layout that is characterised by death-inspired decorative frames. The woodcuts focus predominantly on the two protagonists and their walks through the city, which is evoked in some detail. The images that are meant to illustrate the novelle turn instead to other figures, and shy away from the Venetian focus of the first set, with some of them depicting the moral of the story rather than the narrative itself.[58]

Constant throughout the book is the presence of Death: represented by skeletons, Death appears in the illustrations, often holding emblematic objects such as the scale and the hourglass. Many of these illustrations draw on a famous series of woodcuts based on drawings by Hans Holbein (d. 1543), reprinted many times across Europe since their first appearance in a Lyonnais edition of 1538, *Les Simulachres et historiées faces de la mort, autant élégamment pourtraictes que artificiellement imaginées* [The simulacres and illustrated faces of death, elegantly portrayed as much as artfully imagined].[59] Holbein's woodcuts circulated in Italy thanks to the 1545 Valgrisi edition under the title *Simolachri, historie e figure de la morte* [Simulacres, stories, and figures of death].[60] Also known as Holbein's *Totentanz*, the series was cut by engraver Hans Lützelberger, whose activity is documented in Basel between 1522 and 1526. While a precise date for the production of the woodcuts remains unknown, they were likely to have been cut before Holbein's first stay in England (1526–28) and certainly

randomly ('a' suoi luoghi appropriate').
57   The double device is used again at the opening of the following dialogues as well as in the title page of the *Breve trattato sulla pietra filosofale*.
58   On this specific feature of Glissenti's work, see Piantoni, 'Morte a Venezia'.
59   *Les Simulachres et historiées faces de la mort, autant élégamment pourtraictes que artificiellement imaginées* (Lyon: Trechsel, 1538). The Lyonnais print is available in the facsimile edition by Henry Green, *Les Simulachres et historiées faces de la mort, commonly called The Dance of death* (Manchester: A. Brothers, 1869), which includes a still useful outline of the work in relation to both Holbein's career and the *ars moriendi* tradition. See also Kurtz, *The Dance of Death*, pp. 195–96.
60   *Simolachri, historie, e figure de la morte* (Venice: Vincenzo Valgrisi, 1545); see Kurtz, *The Dance of Death*, pp. 196–97.

DISCORSI MORALI
DELL'ECCELLENTE
S. Fabio Gliſſenti.
CONTRA IL DISPIACER DEL MORIRE,
Detto Athanatophilia.

Diuiſi in cinque Dialoghi, occorſi in cinque giornate.

Ne'quali ſi diſcorre quanto ragioneuolmente ſi dourebbe deſiderar la Morte;
E come naturalmente la ſi uada fuggendo.

Con trenta vaghi, & vtili Ragionamenti, come tante piaceuoli Nouelle
interpoſti; cauati da gli abuſi del preſente viuer mondano;
Et vn molto curioſo Trattato della Pietra de'Filoſofi.

Adornati di belliſſime Figure, a' loro luoghi appropriate.

Alla molto Mag. Mad. Gliſſentia Gliſſenti.

CON PRIVILEGIO.

IN VENETIA, Appreſſo Domenico Farri. M. D. XCVI.

FIG. 2.1. Glissenti, *Discorsi morali* (1596), title page.

FIG. 2.2. Glissenti, *Discorsi morali* (1596), title page's *verso*.

before Lützelberger's death in 1526. As indicated by Oskar Bätschmann and Pascal Griener, the Trechsel edition of the *Simulachres* printed in Lyon in 1538 includes 41 woodcuts by Lützelberger based on Holbein's drawings, but ten more were added in later editions.[61] The series opens with four images covering Genesis and the ejection of Adam and Eve from the Garden of Eden. Death appears for the first time in the third image, which depicts the progenitors' departure from the garden. The fifth woodcut stages a musical ensemble of skeletons with a Renaissance city in the background, thus marking the shift from the biblical past to the urban present of human history. Starting with the sixth woodcut, the reader/observer is shown all the members of society grappling with Death: churchmen and nuns, lay men and women, aristocrats and bourgeois, all doomed by the looming presence of Death. In most cases, she dissimulates her appearance, being only visible to the reader; elsewhere, the artists turn to the trope of the dance of Death by representing men and women caught in the lively ball that brings them to their last hour. The book is conceived as a mirror of human life that makes it possible for the reader to visualise the otherwise invisible presence of Death.[62]

The same scope is at the core of Glissenti's work and, more precisely, is one of the overarching themes that hold the structure of the *Discorsi morali*. His book reuses several among the Holbein woodcuts that circulated in Italy through the Valgrisi edition and its reprints.[63] The series is enriched by other images that fit the specifics of Glissenti's narrative and which were made for the book: these are the illustrations that depict the conversations between the Philosopher, the Courtier, and the other characters they encounter during their Venetian wanderings. The image that opens the first chapter of the first dialogue has, consistently with the text, a proemial function. It represents a man and a woman at the sides of a macabre coat of arms with a skull depicted on it, an image that belongs to the iconographic type that Walter Benjamin labelled 'Death's Head'.[64] It is the illustration at the beginning of the second chapter that brings the reader *in medias res* by picturing the occasion of the dialogue ('l'occasione del dialogo'), namely, the encounter of the Philosopher, accompanied by a skeleton, and the richly dressed Courtier [Fig. 2.3].[65] While made to suit Glissenti's text, the image — specifically, the characterisation of the Philosopher — draws on Holbein's depiction of the Prince [Fig. 2.4].[66]

---

61 Oskar Bätschmann and Pascal Griener, *Hans Holbein* (Princeton, NJ: Princeton University Press, 1997), pp. 56–60.
62 Ibid., p. 59: 'neither the intended victims nor the bystanders are aware of his presence. The dialogue between Man and Death as it is staged in the traditional Totentanz has here been modified. The image is instead intended for the reader and the beholder, who must reckon with the unexpected irruption of Death into their everyday life'.
63 Twenty-four woodcuts based on Holbein (through the Valgrisi edition) are reused in Glissenti's book; five are remade, but they clearly replicate the originals (see Kurtz, *The Dance of Death*, p. 197).
64 Walter Benjamin, *The Origin of German Tragic Drama* [1925], trans. by John Osborne (London and New York: Verso, 2003); on the circulation of emblems such as the Death's Head in early modern culture, see Monica Calabritto and Peter Daly, eds, *Emblems of Death in the Early Modern Period* (Geneva: Droz, 2014).
65 DM, fol. 5^r.
66 *Les Simulachres et historiées faces de la mort*, c. Dii^v; this very woodcut does appear in the *Discorsi*

Fig. 2.3. Glissenti, *Discorsi morali* (1596), fol. 5ʳ.

In the initial section of the work, which introduces the theme of the dialogue, the narrative itself proceeds rather slowly. Accordingly, the relevant images illustrate the philosophical scope of the text (that is, the Philosopher's invitation to meditate on death) more than the actions of the characters. Instructive, in this respect, is the woodcut that accompanies chapter 2, 'Che 'l più eccellente studio è la contemplatione della Morte, e qual frutto si cavi da questo nobile essercitio' [The most useful activity is the contemplation of Death, and the benefits that come with it]. The contemplation of death is visualised through an image that, differently from the previous one, shies away from any form of realism, turning instead to a visual code that is truly emblematic in nature. A woman, posing in what is a gesture traditionally associated with melancholy, meditates over a skeleton lying before her. The geometrical perspective in the background enhances the somewhat abstract context of the picture, while also marking the theatrical dimension of the *locus* in which the meditation is supposed to be taking place [Fig. 2.5]. The *memento mori* outlined in the text is translated literally into an image that merges long-standing concerns with the theme of *vanitas* and a visual language that finds fecund ground in the burgeoning culture of the Baroque.[67]

morali (fol. 57ᵛ).
[67] Similarly, chapter 4 in the first dialogue, 'Che per la salute dell'anima è molto necessario lo studio della Morte, il quale se si trovassimo infervorati nella fede ci farebbe nascer desiderio di morire' [That for the salvation of the soul the contemplation of death is necessary, which, were we filled with faith, would make us wish to die], opens with the image of a hermit in a cave meditating over a candlestick and a skull (*DM*, fol. 10ʳ).

Princeps induetur mœrore. Et
quiescere faciam superbiā po
tentium.
    EZECHIE.   VII

Vien, prince, auec moy, & delaisse
Honneurs mondains tost finissantz.
Seule suis qui, certes, abaisse
L'orgueil & pompe des puissantz.

FIG. 2.4. *Les simulachres et faces historiées de la mort* (1538), fol. Dii^v.

104 The Tragedy of Human Life

Fig. 2.5. Glissenti, *Discorsi morali* (1596), fol. 7ʳ.

Fig. 2.6. Glissenti, *Discorsi morali* (1596), fol. 22ᵛ.

FIG. 2.7. Glissenti, *Discorsi morali* (1596), fol. 43ᵛ.

The two protagonists of the dialogue take centre stage again in the woodcut that opens chapter 9, this time against a backdrop that would look familiar to anyone acquainted with Venice's topography: the portico in the background is clearly evocative of the architecture of Piazza San Marco [Fig. 2.6].[68] The actual conversation between the two characters is also depicted in chapter 16, where the Philosopher and the Courtier sit next to a column, a detail that suggests a context similar to the one featured in the previous illustration [Fig. 2.7].

Reconvening the following day, the two begin a veritable tour of the city, which can be followed in detail. The second and third dialogues are particularly rich in illustrations that represent landmarks of Venice — San Marco [Fig. 2.8], the traghetto della Dogana [Fig. 2.9], Rialto [Fig. 2.10] — as well as the encounters with the other interlocutors.

While in certain cases the Venetian setting is easily recognisable, as in the encounter with the servant [Fig. 2.11], the urban context is, in others, less specific [Fig. 2.12].[69] The island of Murano (or, possibly, the island of San Michele, where Venice's cemetery is located) appears as the background of a conversation that takes place on the Fondamenta Nuove [Fig. 2.13].[70]

Slightly different are the illustrations in dialogues four and five, which focus on

---

[68] The encounter of the two old friends under the colonnade of Piazza San Marco is narrated in Glissenti *DM*, fol. 5ʳ⁻ᵛ.
[69] *DM*, fol. 127ʳ (encounter with the servant); fol. 79ʳ (encounter with the pedlar); fol. 87ᵛ (encounter with the warden).
[70] *DM*, fol. 245ᵛ.

106 THE TRAGEDY OF HUMAN LIFE

FIG. 2.8. Glissenti, *Discorsi morali* (1596), fol. 107^r.

FIG. 2.9. Glissenti, *Discorsi morali* (1596), fol. 135^v.

FIG. 2.10. Glissenti, *Discorsi morali* (1596), fol. 138ᵛ.

FIG. 2.11. Glissenti, *Discorsi morali* (1596), fol. 127ʳ.

Fig. 2.12. Glissenti, *Discorsi morali* (1596), fol. 87^v.

Fig. 2.13. Glissenti, *Discorsi morali* (1596), fol. 245^r.

Fig. 2.14. Glissenti, *Discorsi morali* (1596), fol. 339ʳ.

the encounters with the actress [Figs 2.14–2.15][71] and the dying scientist [Fig. 2.16],[72] respectively, turning the attention from the urban space to the private context of households. The shift is consistent with a gradual increase of the argumentative tone, which is less concerned with the portrayal of the urban society and more focused on the philosophical implications of the conversations among the characters.

Different dynamics are at stake in the images that accompany the novelle. Rather than visualising the stories, they tend to unpack the allegorical and moral teachings that the novelle themselves are supposed to convey. This is the context in which there is more frequent reuse of the Holbein woodcuts: thanks to their universal claim, they provide a particularly fitting commentary on the novelle, which do not stage the individual destiny of specific characters, but aim at outlining the collective tragedy of human life. The way in which these images are supposed to interact with the text is fairly intuitive. One can think of novelle 4 and 5 in chapters 6 and 12 of the first dialogue, both devoted to Man's fight against the senses.[73] In the first case,

71 DM, fols 339ʳ, 341ʳ.
72 DM, fol. 446ᵛ.
73 See, respectively, DM, 2.6: 'Persuade il Senso la Volontà sua padrona a credere all'Epicuro, il qual metteva la somma felicità ne i piaceri. E come consentendo ella per questo ne fu condannata all'inferno insieme con lui' [Sense persuades his mistress, Lady Will, to believe Epicurus, who placed the greatest happiness in pleasure. Having agreed, she is condemned to hell together with him]; and 2.12: 'Contendono la Ragion et il Senso intorno al governo dell'Huomo; et egli appigliandosi al Senso promette, divenuto che sia vecchio, darsi alla Ragione. Ma in quella etade, per l'uso contratto col Senso, non si sa emendare, come s'havea promesso' [Reason and Sense argue about the government of Man; having decided to follow Sense, he promises to turn to Reason once he gets old. Yet, at that age, due to his acquaintance with Sense, he is not able to amend himself, as he promised].

Fig. 2.15. Glissenti, *Discorsi morali* (1596), fol. 341ʳ.

Fig. 2.16. Glissenti, *Discorsi morali* (1596), fol. 446ᵛ.

FIG. 2.17. Glissenti, *Discorsi morali* (1596), fol. 77ᵛ.

FIG. 2.18. Glissenti, *Discorsi morali* (1596), fol. 99ʳ.

the novella ends with a dialogue between Epicurus and Intellect: the philosopher rejects the path of virtue and is condemned to hell. In the second, Man meets the same destiny because he has not followed Reason's advice. Both stories are sealed by the same depiction of the entrance of hell. In the first one, the image is paired with an illustration that evokes Intellect's reprimand [Fig. 2.17]; in the second, the image is accompanied by another one in which Man, now old, is caught in a dialogue with Reason [Fig. 2.18].

Consistently with the obsessive reiteration of the same argument throughout the work, the repetitive use of images functions as a visual aid that aims to make the message stick with the reader while also giving visible shape to something — death — which is, *per se*, shapeless. The attempt to give a body to bodiless and inanimate things, whose rhetorical status I have discussed in Chapter 1, was key to the iconographic archetype of Glissenti's illustrations: the French edition of the *Simulachres et faces historiées de la Mort*. In the preface to the abbess of the Convent of Saint Pierre in Lyon (incidentally, a female addressee), the author pre-empts an objection about the visual representability of death, which tackles the very issue of visualising what is normally invisible to the physical eyes:

> Quelle figure de Mort peult estre par vivant representée? [...] Il est bien vray que l'invisible ne se peult par chose visible proprement representer: mais tout ainsi que par les choses crées & visibles, comme est dit en l'epistre aux Romains, on peult veoir & contempler l'invisible Dieu & incrée.[74]
>
> [Which image of death may be represented as living? [...] It is true that what is invisible cannot be conveniently pictured through visible things: but it is also true that through visible and created things, as the epistle to the Romans says, we can see and contemplate God invisible and uncreated.]

The difficulty of visualising the invisible is solved by means of a reference to Paul's epistle to the Romans.[75] Similarly to what happens with God, whose presence is visible through the creation, Death can be seen through the traces left by her passage:

> Pareillement par les choses, lesquelles la Mort a faict irrevocables passaiges, c'est ascavoir par les corps es sepulchres cadaverisez & descharnez sus leurs monumentz, on peult extraire quelques simulachres de Mort (simulachres les dis ie vrayment, pour ce que simulachre vient de simuler, & faindre ce qui n'est point).[76]
>
> [Similarly, from those things through which Death has made its final passages, such as the corpses, defleshed and made cadavers in their sepulchres, we can extract some simulacres of Death — indeed I say simulacres, for a simulacre simulates and feigns what is not there at all.]

74 *Simulachres et faces historiées de la mort*, fol. Aiii^r.
75 Romans 1.19–20: 'quia quod notum est Dei manifestum est in illis Deus enim illis manifestavit; invisibilia enim ipsius a creatura mundi per ea quae facta sunt intellecta conspiciuntur sempiterna quoque eius virtus et divinitas ut sint inexcusabiles' [since what may be known about God is plain to them, because God has made it plain to them. For since the creation of the world God's invisible qualities — his eternal power and divine nature — have been clearly seen, being understood from what has been made, so that people are without excuse] (*New International Version*).
76 *Simulachres et faces historiées de la mort*, fol. Aiii^r.

As was the case with *eidolopoiia* in the ancient rhetorical tradition, the simulacrum is the representation of what is not there. If the human shape is the most immediate option when one needs to visualise vices, virtues, and affections of the soul, the most effective way to represent Death will also be to do it through the human body (in fact, through the corpse). The primary scope of such visualisation is, once again, the pursuit of *evidentia*: indeed, no verbal description will be able to match the vivid representation of death afforded by the image of a dead body or a skeleton.[77] The function of these images (as is the case with personified allegories in spiritual drama) is contemplative in the first place: by looking at the simulacra of death and by keeping them firmly in one's memory (hence, in one's heart) the good Christian will know how to better discipline their life in order to save their soul.[78]

Fabio Glissenti tackles similar questions in the introductory chapter of the first dialogue of the *Discorsi morali*. While explaining the reasons behind the traditional depiction of death (represented as either a skeleton or a corpse), he dwells on the difficulty of visualising something that all can easily conceive in their minds, but which comes to fruition only through its effects:

> Et anchor che non si habbia saputo fin qui isprimere da alcuno così bene la natura, od effigie della Morte, che se ne habbia potuto havere quella conoscenza che si vorrebbe (come che né anco i Pittori, quando quella vogliono figurare sanno come dipingerla, ma in vece di lei vanno delineando alcune ossa congiunte insieme, che per esser elleno state l'ordinamento di un corpo humano già vivo, per la corrottione di poi spogliate della carne, sono piuttosto effetto, e cose, che segue dopo la morte, che la morte stessa) non è però alcuno che goffo che sia, che nella sua imaginatione non si rapresenti una cosa la più brutta, la più spaventosa, et la più horribile, che si possi pensar al mondo; anzi va tant'oltre questo suo pensiero, che talhora ricercato, che riveli, ciò ch'intenda per la morte, non sa ritrovare cosa, con cui servendosi di similitudine venghi a scoprirla.[79]
>
> [We have not been able to express the nature and effigy of Death in such a way that would allow to achieve the desired knowledge of it. Not even painters

---

77 Ibid.: 'Et pourtant qu'on n'a peu trouver chose plus approchante a la similitude de la Mort, que la personne morte, on a d'icelle effigié simulachres, & faces de Mort, pour en noz pensées imprimer la memoire de Mort plus au vif, que ne pourroient toutes les rhetoriques descriptions des orateurs' [Since we have not been able to find a thing closer to the resemblance of Death than a dead person, we have pictured simulacres and faces of Death based on it, so as to impress in our mind the memory of Death more vividly than any rhetorical description of orators would do].
78 The author of the preface talks about the 'simulachres' as 'tresutile, & contemplative literature' (very useful and contemplative literature) addressed, as the images painted and sculpted in churches, to illiterate bystanders in the first place (*Simulachres et faces historiées de la mort*, fol. Aiii^v). The kind of fruition imagined for the *Simulachres* — one that is very similar to Glissenti's own scope — is made explicit in the conclusion of the preface, where the reading of the book (and the contemplation of its images) is recommended to the nuns of the convent overseen by the abbess to whom the volume is dedicated: 'Parquoy, Madame, prendrez en bonne part ce triste, mais salubre present: & persuaderez a voz devotes religieuses le tenir non seulement en leurs petites cellules, ou dortouers, mais au cabinet de leur memoire, ainsi que le conseille sainct Hierosme' [For this reason, milady, you will gladly accept this sad, but useful gift: and you will persuade your devout religious sisters to keep it not only in their small cells or dorms, but also in the cabinet of their memory, as Saint Jerome recommends it] (*Simulachres et faces historiées de la mort*, fol. Aiiii^v).
79 *DM*, fol. 3^v.

know how to depict Death when they want to represent it: thus they draw a few bones put together, which, once the structure of a living body, but now corrupted and defleshed, are the result of death rather than death herself; yet there is no one, not even a fool, who in their mind would picture a thing that is more ugly, fearful, and horrible to imagine in the world; rather, they go far beyond this thought, and they are not able to find a thing that may be used to unveil death by means of similitude.]

Since not even philosophers have been able to find a way to picture her, the only way to talk about death is to take it for granted that, albeit difficult to grasp in her essence, everybody knows what she is. That said, the visualisation of death as a skeleton or corpse remains the most effective *memento* of her presence and proves a useful device to promote meditation and, possibly, repentance.

Venice, Theatre of the World

Key to Glissenti's project is the attempt to situate the meditation on death within the urban context of Venice. In order to grasp the theatrical significance of such choice, it is worth returning to one of the most intriguing documents relevant to Glissenti's biography: the dedication letter addressed to him by Giacomo Franco in the undated print of *Habiti delle donne venetiane*.[80] The engraver is proud to show the physician 'the drawing of the marvellous city of Venice represented as a spherical map' ('il disegno della meravigliosa città di Venetia in forma sferica'), which decorates the frontispiece of the book [Fig. 2.19]. The city, seen from above, is given a spherical shape, as if it were a globe.

The curious artefact joins a long cartographic tradition that, over the centuries, had produced many maps of Venice, mostly for celebratory purposes. The immediate scope of Franco's map, though, is to represent the Republic as a figure of the globe, with the engraving presented as a 'reliable portrait of the world' ('vero ritratto del Mondo').[81] Venice, according to Franco's phrasing, looks like 'the whole earthly globe' ('tutto l'orbe della terra'): indeed, whoever observes the map is able to see both the Arctic and the Antarctic poles, as well as the East and the West, and all the other parts of the earth, surrounded by water, so that one has the impression of looking at the continent encircled by the ocean.[82] As the globe is divided into two main parts (Europe, Africa, and Asia on the one hand; the Americas on the other), so Venice consists of a main body and the Giudecca, which, alongside the minor islands, recalls the new world ('risembra il nuovo mondo'). By looking at Franco's spherical map, the observer has a chance to see that the whole of Venice is

---

80   Franco, *Habiti delle donne venetiane*, p. [27].
81   On maps of Venice, see Giocondo Cassini, *Piante e vedute prospettiche di Venezia, 1479–1855* (Venice: Istituto federale delle Casse di Risparmio delle Venezie, 1971); Franco's spherical map is reproduced there, pp. 69–70 (with a detailed description).
82   Franco, *Habiti delle donne venetiane*, p. [27]: 'chi ben mira detto disegno, scuopre in un alzare di ciglia il Polo Artico, et l'Antartico insieme; ove si vede anco il Levante, et Ponente, con tutte le altre parti ch'in esso Mondo concorrono, circondata parimenti dall'Acqua in maniera che ben pare il continente tutto circondato dal gran mar Oceano'.

FIG. 2.19. Franco, *Habiti delle donne venetiane*, title page.

indeed similar to the globe ('vedrà il tutto corrispondere alla vera similitudine del Mappamondo'). As Franco explains it, the image is not detailed enough to show all the neighbourhoods ('contrade') of the city, that are as innumerable as the regions of the world ('provincie del mondo'), but he promises that he will soon craft a larger drawing capable of representing the correspondence between Venice and the entire 'worldly machine' ('tutta la machina mondiale').

It is not easy to spot the reason why Franco dedicated the *Habiti delle donne venetiane* to Glissenti. As recalled above, Franco refers to Glissenti's expertise in the figurative arts ('so quanto la si diletta di Pittura, Scoltura, et Disegno, diletto invero d'animo nobilissimo'), but there may be something more behind the dedication. Despite obvious differences, Franco's is an exploration of Venetian customs as much as Glissenti's *Discorsi* provide an account of Venice's arts and professions, and both works rely heavily on illustrations. One detail, though, looks even more cogent than these similarities: namely, the fact that both authors use the metaphor of the world-as-machine ('machina mondiale'), which, in the literary tradition, is tightly related to that of the *theatrum mundi*. As such, the two metaphors appear intertwined in the *Discorsi morali*, which describe Venice as a mundane scene. The centrality of the Piazza San Marco, emblem of the city, in Glissenti's work is made explicit since it stands at the very beginning of the book. The Philosopher and the Courtier meet under the loggia of the Ducal Palace after the Courtier's many years of absence from Venice. The place where they meet is described as the usual location for those aristocratic and literate men who wish to entertain each other by discussing about the many things of the world ('diverse cose del mondo').[83] Further attention to the Piazza is given by the narrator at the beginning of the second day, when he joins a group of people debating about various topics, including the opportunity to build a 'perpetual fountain' ('fontana perpetua') at the centre of the piazza itself [Fig. 2.20]:

> Il giorno seguente, desiderosi d'intender il rimanente del ragionamento della Morte, venimmo per tempo alle consuete loggie del palagio, accompagnati da gran curiosità di sapere, a che si fosse risolluto il parer del Cortigiano. Ma la voglia nostra anticipò la di lui venuta: per lo che passeggiando noi fra tanto per quella nobilissima piazza, di diverse cose ragionando (e forsi leggiermente diverse cose secondo l'opinione nostra interpretando). Perché chi lodava la bella prospettiva della piazza dalle due colonne fin all'Horologio; chi biasimava l'antica architettura della facciata della Chiesa di San Marco; chi proponeva che sarebbe stato bene far un foro presso le Beccarie corrispondente a quello delle colonne, acciò che la Zecca restasse in isola [...] facendosi piazza fino alla

---

83   *DM*, fol. 5^{r-v}: 'In questa famosissima e serenissima città di Venetia, pochi giorni fa si ritrovò un Filosofo molto illustre [...] Questi per lo più si ritirava nella piazza di San Marco, dove sotto le logie del palazo del Prencipe si sogliono ridurre molti, spetialmente huomini nobili, e letterati a discorrere di diverse cose del mondo. E non sì tosto era veduto da quelli, che circondatolo d'ogn'intorno pendevano dalla bocca di lui, come da famoso Oracolo ad udirlo intenti. Insegnava egli, riprendeva, essortava, e non sparmiava qual si voglia occasione per giovar altrui' [A few days ago, an illustrious Philosopher happened to be in this famous and most serene city of Venice [...] He spent most of his time in the piazza of Saint Mark, where, under the loggias of the Prince's Palace, many men usually come, especially noble and literate, to discuss various matters of the world. As soon as they spotted him, he was surrounded by many who listened to him very carefully, as one does with a famous oracle. He taught, reprimanded, urged, and did not spare any chance to benefit others].

DELL' ATHANATOPHILIA,
ouero, che à nessuno piace il morire,

Dialogo Secondo.
ESTISIPHILO,
ouero Amante del Senso.

Interlocutori il Filosofo, il Cortigiano, vn Vastagio, vn Portator de vino. Vn Mendicante, vn Macellaio, vn Castaldo, vna Cingara, vn Scruitore, & vn Gondoliere.

Si mostra un modo curioso di far una fontana perpetua nella piazza di San Marco.   Capitolo Primo.

L giorno seguente, desiderosi d'intender il rimanente del ragionamento della Morte, uenimmo per tépo alle consuete loggie del palagio, accompagnati da grã curiosità di sapere, a che si fosse rissoluto il parer del Cortigiano. Ma la uoglia nostra anticipò la di lui uenuta: per lo che passeggiando noi frà tanto per quella
                                                                    nobi-

FIG. 2.20. Glissenti, *Discorsi morali* (1596), fol. 58^v.

> Pescaria; e chi lodava sommamente le statue antiche, i cavalli famosissimi di Fidia, posti sopra la porta della Chiesa (i quali per esser senza freno dinotano la libertà di questa patria), e chi le statue moderne, riposte sopra la Libraria; et altri dicevano doversi fabricare la facciata del palagio del gran Conseglio, simile all'architettura contraposta delle fabriche nuove. Non mancarano anco chi si vantavano di poter far una fontana perpetua nel mezo della piazza per sopremo ornamento di questa Città.[84]

> [The following day, eager to hear the rest of the conversation about Death, we came early to the usual loggias of the palace, very curious to know how the Courtier's opinion developed. But our desire hastened his arrival: we were wandering through that most noble piazza, discussing various matters (and possibly interpreting different things somewhat light-heartedly according to our own opinions); some praised the beautiful perspective of the piazza from the two columns up to the clock; others criticised the ancient architecture of the façade of Saint Mark; some argued that it would be good to dig a hole at the Beccarie corresponding to that of the columns, so that the Zecca [the mint] would remain isolated [...], making a piazza till the Pescaria; others praised highly the ancient statues, the famous horses by Phidias at the top of the Church (which, being without bits, stand for the liberty of this land); some praised the modern statues at the top of the Library; others said that the façade of the Great Counsel's palace should be made similar to the architecture of the new buildings on the opposite side of the piazza. There were even some who bragged about the possibility of building a perpetual fountain at the centre of the piazza as the supreme ornament of this city.]

The narrator explains the project in detail, dwelling on both its technology and allegorical decoration. A grandiose example of Venetian artistry, the fountain is imagined as an eloquent testimony to Venice's greatness.[85]

The arrival of the Courtier interrupts the digression on the fountain, moving the attention towards the Ducal Palace and its ornaments. Waiting for the Philosopher, the Courtier admires the sculpted capitals on the columns in the loggia ('quegli intagli di mezo rilevo posti ne i capitelli e ne gli archi delle colonne del palagio').[86] Once the Philosopher joins him, the Courtier states his admiration for those ancient sculptures and their meaning (they are defined 'antiche' and 'sententiose', where the latter term refers to the *sententia* conveyed by the sculptures, that is, the philosophical — mostly moral — value of their teachings). The Philosopher agrees that their meaning is indeed worthy of consideration, but he adds that his attention leans elsewhere. However, his apparently cursory remark paves the way for a digression that is extremely significant when considered in the light of the 'world-as-machine' metaphor exploited by Franco in the *Habiti delle donne venetiane*:

> non v'era in quel palazzo colonna, base, capitello, arco, pietra o trave che non fosse con somma maestria et intelligenza ivi stata riposta. Le quali cose tutte formavano così bel theatro, così ricca e sontuosa casa, che per esplicare la sua grandezza non trovava cosa a cui assomigliare la potesse meglio che a tutta la sfera del mondo.[87]

---

84   DM, fols 58^v–59^r.
85   DM, fol. 60^r.
86   DM, fol. 60^{r-v}.
87   DM, fol. 60^v.

[In that palace, there was no column, base, capital, arch, stone or beam that was not put there with excellent craftsmanship and knowledge. They all formed such a beautiful theatre, such a rich and sumptuous household, that the only way to explain its greatness was to compare it to the whole sphere of the world.]

At the core of the Piazza San Marco and the heart of the city, the Ducal Palace is itself compared to the globe ('la sfera del mondo') by means of an explicitly theatrical metaphor ('così bel theatro'). Asked by his interlocutors to unpack the simile, the Philosopher introduces a digression that occupies the entire following chapter, entitled 'Bella similitudine del Palazzo di San Marco comparato alla gran sfera del Mondo' [Beautiful simile of the Palace of Saint Mark compared to the globe].[88] The Philosopher begins by outlining the broader structure of the world, including the earth and the heavens:

> Voi sapete tutti che questo vago theatro del mondo è composto di Cieli, secondo l'opinione de' Filosofi, incorrottibili, e d'elementi i quali gli uni con gli altri e gli altri da gli uni si generano e corrompono. In questo d'incorrottibile, e corrottibile formato mondo vi sono due stanze principali, conformi alli habitatori loro; l'una è ne' Cieli, o sopra i Cieli, dove stanno gli immortali et impassibili beati; l'altra è nell'elemento della Terra, dove habitano gli infelici mortali.[89]

> [You all know that this beautiful theatre of the world is made of incorruptible heavens, according to the philosophers' opinion, and of elements, which are generated and corrupted with one another. In this world made of corruptible and incorruptible substances, there are two main lodgings, appropriate to their inhabitants: one is in or above the Heavens, where the immortal and imperturbable blessed spirits reside; the other is in the element of earth, where the unhappy mortals live.]

The metaphor of the *theatrum mundi* proves much more than a commonplace. Indeed, it informs the very structure of the *Discorsi morali* and, more broadly, Glissenti's entire production. The partition of the 'theatre of the world' into two domains, the heavens and the earth, finds a precise correspondence with the structure of the palace. The top floor ('il più alto appartamento') is the seat of the prince, a place rich in decorations and luxurious things that he shares with senators and ministers: it is similar to the heavens, from where God, lord of the universe, governs the world. The administration of the Republic is thus celebrated as the mirror of divine justice. The other part of the Palazzo (that is, the other part of the world) is constituted by the lower floors, where ordinary people mind their various businesses based on either their natural inclination or habit ('secondo la natural inclinatione e genio, o secondo cert'habito contratto'). Accordingly, this second section of the palace ('secondo appartamento del palagio') is used by the officials who deal with common people's affairs ('offici e magistrati i quali hanno cura delle attioni particolari de gli huomini').[90] This is the realm of opinion, mutability of beliefs and of the many passions and affections of human life. The negative vision of the narrator is conveyed by the image of a society in which falsehood prevails

---

88   DM, fol. 61[r].
89   Ibid.
90   Ibid.

and humans tend to harm one another, with much room made for disputations and trials.[91] The ground floor ('il terreno appartamento del palagio') corresponds to the ground-level area of the world ('la stanza terrena del mondo più verso il centro'), which is compared to Purgatory, where the souls of the sinners who have repented endure their punishments looking forward to be eventually saved. Similarly, the corresponding part of the palace is where prisoners do their time. The descent towards the recesses of the world then reaches Limbo and Hell. Limbo is mirrored, in the palace, by the basement ('sotterranea stanza'), where prisoners who got a life sentence reside with no hope to see daylight again ('i confinati nelle Prigion Forti, tutta la vita loro sententiati in oscurissime tenebre, senza speranza di poterne uscire'). Hell corresponds to the so-called 'Camerotti', where those who have been sentenced to death wait for their execution ('ne i quali sono riposti quei miseri che aspettano la mortal sentenza').[92] The analogy between the world and the palace is precise, but what seemed to be a purely celebratory statement, reveals more sombre implications:

> Il mondo nell'esterno appare bello, promette bene e cuopre con false mostre li suoi inganni. Il palagio meraviglioso per l'architettura, per l'ampie sale, per le statue, per li colossi invita con larghe scale a rimirarlo: ma non si può però ben conoscere se lungamente non vi si prattica. Il mondo è un giuoco di Fortuna, una gabbia di matti, un trattenimento da sciocchi, et una rete da invogliere gli incauti. Il palazzo un giuoco a trappola, uno scrigno d'astutie, un vorace lupo delle facultadi, un perdimento di cervello, et un rivolgimento delle volontà humane. In somma si ritrova così favorita la Serenissima Città di Venetia di questo mondo picciolo, quanto la Natura del mondo grande.[93]

> [Seen from outside, the world looks beautiful; it looks promising and hides its deceptions behind false appearances. The palace, marvellous for its architecture, large rooms, statues, colossi and grand staircases invites us to admire it: yet, it is not possible to know it well unless one experiences it for a long time. The world is a game of Fortune, a cage of fools, an entertainment for idiots, a net that catches imprudent people. The palace is a trap, a box of tricks, a wolf eager to devour man's faculties; it makes one lose their mind and reverse their will. In sum, the most serene city of Venice is provided with this small world as Nature is provided with the great one out there.]

In the eternal conflict between truth and appearance, the 'small world' of the Palazzo is the exact double of the 'greater world': both seduce with their beauties, while proving insidious and difficult to navigate without the right amount of knowledge and experience. The 'theatre of the world', in this acceptation, is thus the domain of vanity, in which it is hard not to lose the thread of reason.

The theatrical metaphor finds yet another variation in the image of the 'gioco di Fortuna' [Fortune's game], a commonplace that, from Boccaccio and Petrarch,

---

91 *DM*, fol. 61^{r-v}.
92 *DM*, fol. 62^{r}. Glissenti turns to the same simile on the occasion of the encounter of the Courtier and the Philosopher with a convict sentenced to death (fol. 193^{v}).
93 Ibid. Incidentally, the images of the 'mondo piccolo' and 'mondo grande' will come back in the play *L'Androtoo*.

runs across the philosophical reflection of humanists such as Leon Battista Alberti and is powerfully revived in the sixteenth century, when its political undertones come to the fore. Fortune's game, responsible for both sudden successes and quick declines, had been at the core of Antonio Fileremo Fregoso's *Dialogo di Fortuna* [Dialogue on Fortune], which circulated widely in the first half of the Cinquecento, when optimistic views of Virtue's power over Fortune began to be challenged systematically.[94] One might think of Baldassar Castiglione's instructive statement in the *Libro del Cortegiano* [Book of the Courtier], where Gaspare Pallavicino turns to the metaphor of the game to recall that Fortune is indeed responsible for the various fates of men.[95] While this is not the place for an examination of the ways in which the metaphor of Fortune's game spread across early modern culture, it will be nonetheless useful to remind a few instances that speak to its relevance to the moral reflection that is also at the core of Glissenti's narrative. Alongside many occurrences in Tasso's writings, it is Lodovico Guicciardini's use of the metaphor in the *Ore di ricreazione* [Hours of Recreation] (1568) that provides us with a key to understanding Glissenti's own variation on the trope: 'Aristotile domandato che cosa fusse l'uomo, rispose: "Esempio d'imbecillità, preda del tempo, giuoco della fortuna, imagine della inconstanza, suggetto della invidia, stoffo della calamità mondana, il rimanente collora e flemma"'.[96] If the world is the stage on which the game of Fortune unfolds, man is its protagonist. The productive ramifications of this theatrical understanding of the wheel of Fortune are witnessed by dramatic works such as Guido Casoni's comedy *Il giuoco di Fortuna* [Fortune's Game], a work that bears several similarities with Glissenti's plays.[97]

However, Fortune is not the only ruler of the world, which, as Tommaso Campanella puts it, can be also described as a 'cage of lunatics' ('gabbia di matti').[98] Reminiscent of Erasmus's parodic treatment of Folly, the image used by

---

94 For an overview of this broad theme, see *Il tema della fortuna nella letteratura francese e italiana del Rinascimento* (Florence: Leo S. Olschki, 1990). For Fregoso's influential work, see Antonio Fileremo Fregoso, *Opere*, ed. by Giuliano Dilemmi (Bologna: Commissione per i testi di lingua, 1976), pp. 87–128.
95 Baldassar Castiglione, *Il libro del Cortegiano*, ed. by Walter Barberis (Turin: Einaudi, 1998), 1.15, p. 42: 'delle diversità nostre e gradi d'altezza e di bassezza credo io che siano molte altre cause: tra le quali estimo la fortuna esser precipua, perché in tutte le cose mondane la veggiamo dominare e quasi pigliarsi a gioco d'alzar spesso fin al cielo chi par a lei senza merito alcuno, e sepellir nell'abisso i più degni d'esser esaltati' [the various gradations of elevation and lowliness that exist among us have many other causes. The first and foremost is Fortune, who rules everything that happens in the world, and often appears to amuse herself by exalting whoever she pleases, regardless of merit, or hurling down those worthiest of being raised up] (trans. by Bull).
96 Lodovico Guicciardini, *L'ore di ricreazione*, ed. by Anne-Marie Van Passen (Rome: Bulzoni, 1990), n°403, p. 195 ('Aristotle, asked about man's essence, replied: "An example of stupidity, prey of time, Fortune's game, image of instability, subject of envy, victim of mundane calamities, the rest anger and stolidity"').
97 Guido Casoni, *Il giuoco di fortuna* (Venice: Tommaso Baglioni, 1622). As Guaragnella, *Gli occhi della mente*, p. 135, puts it, Casoni's play is a typically 'literary' comedy informed by an exquisitely theatrical idea of literature influenced by the art of memory.
98 Tommaso Campanella, *Le poesie*, ed. by Francesco Giancotti (Turin: Einaudi, 1998), madrigale 2 (*inc.* 'Cosa stupenda ha fatto il Senno Eterno' [The Eternal intelligence has created a stupendous thing], ll. 11: 'Gabbia de' matti è 'l mondo' [The world is a cage of fools].

Campanella offers a lens through which to look at encyclopaedic renderings of the trope that seize upon the exquisitely baroque taste for accumulation that Glissenti himself shares: Tomaso Garzoni's *L'hospidale de' pazzi incurabili* [The Hospital of Incurable Madness], *Il theatro de' vari e diversi cervelli mondani* [Theatre of the Various and Diverse Mundane Brains] as well as *La piazza universale di tutte le professioni del mondo* [The Universal Piazza of All the Professions of the World] come readily to mind.[99] The insidious nature of the worldly stage is further enhanced by the other definitions used by Glissenti: 'trattenimento di sciocchi' [entertainment of simpletons] and 'rete da invogliare gli incauti' [a web that lures the imprudent].

The dangers of the world correspond to the insidious nature of the palace: the game is not only playful, but risky ('giuoco a trappola'); the riches found in the palace are not without tricks ('scrigno d'astutie'); the pervasive presence of Folly, understood as man's wilful refusal to follow Reason, and Fortune's inevitable ambushes are captured by the other definitions — 'perdimento di cervello' [loss of mind] and 'rivolgimento delle volontà umane' [reversal of human will] — which turn to a kind of lexicon that, as I will show in Chapter 3, is particularly relevant to Glissenti's moralities. The 'machina mondiale', to stick to Franco's phrasing, is thus mirrored by Venice, and more precisely by the Ducal Palace. The celebratory purpose of Franco's dedication informs Glissenti's *Discorsi* as well, where the comparison between the Palazzo and the world conveys praise for the magnanimous and fair government of the Doge. Yet, consistently with the work's moral framework, the author unveils the other side of the globe, the one where appearances tend to prevail over truth; the one, which requires men and women to learn how to avoid falling prey to evil.[100]

As suggested by this brief overview, Glissenti turns to images and tropes that had been part of the literary and philosophical tradition for a long time. While some of the references that I have indicated are simply meant to outline the intellectual backdrop against which the author situates his own work, examples such as Franco's help us depict an exquisitely Venetian framework for the very conception of Glissenti's *Discorsi morali*. Being a compiler, if imaginative, rather than the original creator of poetical devices, the physician displays an impressive familiarity with a literary tradition that includes the classics (ancient and modern) as well as popular works that tend to be overlooked by modern scholarship. A case in point is that of a very peculiar text that seems to have provided Glissenti with the inspiration for the tripartite description of the Palazzo Ducale: the *Opera nuova in versi volgare, intitulata Specchio de la Giustitia. Nel quale se dimostra lo Inferno, il Purgatorio, et il Paradiso del*

---

99 The affinity between Glissenti's *Discorsi morali* and Garzoni's encyclopaedic works is stressed by McClure, *The Culture of Profession*. See also Tomaso Garzoni, *La piazza universal di tutte le professioni del mondo*, ed. by Paolo Cherchi and Beatrice Collina (Turin: Einaudi, 1996). More specifically focused on the topic of folly, are Tomaso Garzoni, *L'ospidale de' pazzi incurabili*, ed. by Stefano Barelli (Rome and Padua: Antenore, 2004); and *Theatro de' vari e diversi cervelli mondani* (Venice: Paolo Zanfretti, 1583).

100 The ambivalence of the image is also at the core of the play *Il bacio della Giustizia e della Pace*, Glissenti's only drama that, set in Venice, turns to allegory as a way to celebrate the enlightened government of the Republic.

Mondo [New Work in Vernacular Verse, Entitled Mirror of Justice, in which the World's Hell, Purgatory, and Heavens are Illustrated], published in Venice in 1539 by the rather mysterious 'Z.M.', likely the polymath Giovanni Manenti.[101] The work, which belongs to the genre of the *stampe popolari* that Venice was particularly famous for, especially in the early sixteenth century, is of great interest for reasons that will be immediately clear.[102] A poem organised in three books (for a total of fourteen 'capitoli'), the *Specchio de la Giustitia* is clearly inspired by the model of Dante's *Divine Comedy*, not only in terms of prosody (the poetry is made of *terzine*), but also, and most important, in terms of subject matter. The work, as detailed in the brief prose preamble, covers a number of 'examples' of justice ('perfettissimi essempii et documenti') aimed at facilitating the self-emendation of those who have misbehaved ('acciò che li cattivi et scelerati habbiano causa di emendarsi'). By doing so, the work demonstrates what the 'Inferno', 'Purgatorio' and 'Paradiso' of the world look like ('per li quali si dimostra qual sia lo Inferno, il Purgatorio, et il Paradiso del Mondo'). If the subdivision entails an all too obvious allusion to Dante's three *cantiche*, what interests us here is the fact that the three locations are made to correspond to the three areas of Venice's Palazzo Ducale concerned with the Venetian administration of justice. Differently from what we find in Glissenti's own description of the Palazzo, the author of the *Specchio de la Giustitia* proceeds from the lower areas to the upper floors, thus outlining a sort of progression from the harshness of the punishments to the celebration of those (i.e., the Doge in the first place, surrounded by the various officials of the Republic) who are responsible for the administration of Justice. According to such a structure, the first book addresses the 'good and holy justice that is administered in the city of Venice' and focuses on the Palace's prisons, which are called 'Inferno del Mondo'. (Incidentally, these are the same 'camerotti' mentioned by Glissenti as the harshest area of the prisons.) Book 2 dwells instead on the 'civic and criminal officials and authorities' directly concerned with the management of justice through trials and litigations, hence the appellation 'Purgatorio del Mondo', which stresses the tensions and conflicts that characterise this part of the Palazzo. In the third book, eventually, the author turns to the beautiful decorations that adorn the 'Sala del Gran Consiglio di sopra', that is, the most important room in the Palace, where the Doge and the highest officials of Venice reside, a veritable summa of Justice, Virtue, Prudence, Peace, Love, and Civic Union, fittingly called 'Paradiso del Mondo'.

The relevance of the *Specchio della Giustitia* to Glissenti's *Discorsi morali* is evident. What makes it even more significant is the fact that the *Specchio* entails a visual component that further resonates with Glissenti's later project. The book opens with an overtly Venetian depiction of the personification of Justice surrounded not

---

101 Giovanni Manenti, *Opera nuova in versi volgare, intitulata Specchio de la Giustitia. Nel quale se dimostra lo Inferno, il Purgatorio, et il Paradiso del Mondo* (Venice: Giovanni Antonio Nicolini da Sabbio, 1539); on this rather peculiar work, see Dante Pattini, 'Un percorso dantesco all'interno del Palazzo Ducale di Venezia: lo Specchio de la Giustitia di Giovanni Manenti (1539)', *Studi veneziani*, 61 (2010), 109–56.
102 See Rosa Salzberg, *Ephemeral City: Cheap Print and Urban Culture in Renaissance Venice* (Manchester: Manchester University Press, 2014).

only by two lions, but also by a group of male figures evocative of the officials of the Republic [Fig. 2.21].

Each of the three books is then introduced by a woodcut that aims to summarise the subject matter of the section: a prisoner *alla gogna* for the Inferno; an image of the Palazzo Ducale itself for the Purgatorio, possibly a reminder of the very urban and human context of litigation [Fig. 2.22]; and an image of Saint Mark for the Paradiso, an iconographic choice that combines the spiritual dimension of the ascent towards Justice and the Venetian context of the work.

Converting (through) Drama

If Venice is the stage upon which the dialogues between the Philosopher and the Courtier unfold, the theatrical flair of the urban space in the *Discorsi morali* is not only conveyed through the structural function that the *theatrum mundi* metaphor holds within the economy of the work. In Glissenti's lifetime and throughout the modern history of Venice, theatre was integral to the social and cultural fabric of the city. Secular forms of theatre such as the *commedia dell'arte* and the various genres involved in the inception of musical theatre held the main share of the theatrical business.[103] Yet, as suggested by the liveliness of theatrical activities in confessional spaces such as convents and hospitals, alternatives to the overwhelming success of secular drama were pursued with energy and, in some cases, rather successfully. It is within the tension between the fortunes of secular theatre and the educational agendas of spiritually inflected contexts that, as I will show in Chapter 3, Glissenti's own commitment as a playwright should be looked at. Before turning to his morality plays, though, it is worth dwelling on another aspect of the theatricality that informs the *Discorsi morali*, which will provide us with a useful pathway to Glissenti's work as a playwright: namely, the author's preoccupation with the idea that the risky business of secular theatre may indeed be reformed and made conducive to experiences of spiritual enhancement for both performers and their audiences.

As a matter of fact, Glissenti's reflection on drama goes beyond the use of theatrical metaphors in the *Discorsi*. This is suggested by an articulate discussion that, in day 4 of the dialogue, echoes contemporary debates on the morality of theatre.[104] As recalled earlier, the book 'Filodoxo' (that is, the lover of opinion), focuses on the philosopher's critique of the natural inclination of men and women to base their choices on beliefs rather than on truth and solid facts. Central to day 4 is the encounter between the philosopher, the courtier, and a professional actress,

---

103 For an overview of the multifaceted theatrical life of Venice, see the chapter on Venice in Zorzi, *Il teatro e la città*; and Raimondo Guarino, *Teatro e mutamenti: Rinascimento e spettacolo a Venezia* (Bologna: il Mulino, 1995).
104 Ferdinando Taviani, *La commedia dell'arte e la società barocca*, vol. I: *La fascinazione del teatro* (Rome: Bulzoni, 1991), and Ferruccio Marotti and Giovanna Romei, *La commedia dell'arte e la società barocca*, vol. II: *La professione dell'attore* (Rome: Bulzoni, 1991). For a more detailed discussion of this section of *Discorsi morali*, see Refini, 'Reforming Drama'.

OPERA NVOVA IN VERSI VOLGARE, INTITVLATA SPECCHIO DE LA GIVSTITIA.

Nel quale se dimostra lo Inferno, il Purgatorio, et il Paradiso del Mondo.

Con Gratia et Priuilegio de lo Illustriss. Do. di Venetia. Che niuno possi quella in primer, ne uender, sotto le pene che in esso priuilegio se contiene. MDXXXIX.

FIG. 2.21. Manenti, *Opera nuova* (1539), title page

PVRGATORIO

Capitolo Settimo Interlocutorio, il qual tratta de partirsi da cercar tutte le Pregion de lo Illustrissimo Do. Veneto, ne le qual per Giustitia sono posti li Malfattori, et quelle se assimigliano a luochi Infernali del Mõdo, & hora andar a cercar con la guida di vno eccellente & pratico aduocato tutti li Offity Criminali & Ciuili del suo Palazzo, iquali per fraude, pertinacia, & malignita de Litiganti, se chiama in questa Opera esser il Purgatorio del Mondo. Et prima si tratta del Criminal, cioè de l'Offitio di Clarissimi Signori Auogadori di Comun, Dignissimi Signori di Notte, & Signori Sindici, & de le principal autorita & ordini de quelli, & buona & santa Giustitia che a tutti fanno indifferentemente.

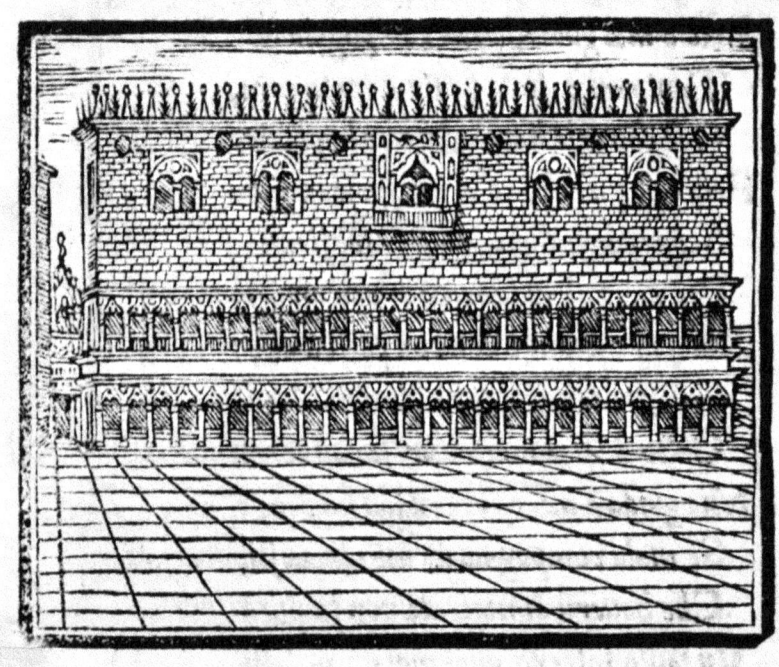

FIG. 2.22. Manenti, *Opera nuova* (1539), fol. D[1]ᵛ

simply referred to as 'la recitante'.¹⁰⁵ Their conversation sheds light on Glissenti's ideas on theatre and on the agenda behind the author's own morality plays.

The woman is described as a renowned actress, famous for her performances in genres as diverse as tragedy, comedy, and the pastoral, as well as for an international career that has given her a chance to travel across many countries ('è ita vagando per tutto il Mondo') and learn multiple languages ('è peritissima di diverse lingue').¹⁰⁶ While unnamed, the actress recalls the many divas celebrated throughout Europe for their acting and singing skills (names such as those of Isabella Andreini and Margherita Costa come readily to mind). In particular, the ability to be at ease with different genres was perceived as a mark of excellence. As we shall see, this protean quality is one of the issues addressed by Glissenti in his criticism of drama. The woman represents a professional category that was the target of numerous attacks in Counter-Reformation Italy, above all by the Church (an instructive case in point being that of Carlo Borromeo's statements against theatre's immorality).¹⁰⁷ In line with this vision, theatre and Christian morality are described by Glissenti as poles apart. Actors are singled out as simulators, liars, creators of appearances, and instigators of bad behaviours. However, even if the author does not conceal his negative opinion of the actress (labelled a 'donna vana', a vain woman), he acknowledges her debating skills. In fact, she is aware of being part of a profession that has shied away from the classical idea of theatre as an educational and moral tool.

The somewhat ambiguous position of the actress vis-à-vis concurrent developments in the show business emerges through her critique of buffoonery, which does feature a nostalgic attitude towards the times when literate men used to attend theatrical performances. Endorsing a kind of discourse that, as recently indicated by Jessica Goethals, was key to discussions of comic theatre in the Baroque period, the actress reports that buffoons have gained prominence and corrupted their audiences, thus making cultivated men consider theatre a debased form of entertainment.¹⁰⁸ Despite her awareness of the issue, she must admit that, in order to remain in the business, actors need to chase the audience's taste, with theatre's traditional function, *docere*, being replaced by *delectare*. The crisis of drama goes along with the decline of truth, a topic dear to Glissenti's pedagogical project, as shown in

---

105 *DM*, fols 339ʳ–421ᵛ (Book 4, Chapters 7–26).
106 *DM*, fol. 338ᵛ.
107 The primary source on Carlo Borromeo's criticism of theatre remains Giovanni Battista Castiglione, *Sentimenti di S. Carlo Borromeo intorno agli spettacoli* (Bergamo: Lancellotti, 1759); for a discussion of Borromeo's opinion on theatre, see Taviani, *La fascinazione del teatro*; as well as the editor's annotations in Nicolò Barbieri, *La Supplica: Discorso famigliare a quelli che trattano de' comici*, ed. by Ferdinando Taviani (Bologna: Cue Press, 2015), 38–40.
108 *DM*, fol. 340ʳ: 'il corrotto costume dell'Italia ha usato di introdurre nelle scene certi buffoni, i quali non servono ad altro che a mover riso' [The corrupted mores of Italy has introduced certain buffoons on stage, who only serve to trigger laughter]; 'gli huomini letterati che soleano essere i primi, tengono al presente per cosa infame il venire ad udirci' [the literate men, who used to be the first to attend, now find it hideous to come and see us]; on debates about comedy and buffoonery in the decades around 1600, see Jessica Goethals, 'Worth Its Salt: Margherita Costa's Ridiculous Defence of Buffoonery', *The Italianist*, 40.3 (2020), 362–81.

particular by the morality play *La Ragione sprezzata*, which I will discuss in Chapter 3. As the actress herself puts it, 'those who wish to instruct others, must tell the truth and admonish their interlocutors', a kind of preoccupation that is normally associated with preaching. Actors, who need to make money from their profession, must instead entertain their audience without caring for the educational function that used to be at the core of classical theatre: 'Truth fosters remorse and self-examination [il rimordimento della conscienza], which make men uncomfortable. For this reason, men hate those who, by means of their words, aim to produce such effects'.[109] The actress's review of the human kind is ruthless: only a few men are eager to improve themselves and willing to be admonished and led towards virtue. Most men, prisoners of their false opinions, reject good advice and do not mind receiving their adulators' praise. Responding to the philosopher's objection, according to which it is the audience that should accommodate to the actors and not the actors to the audience, the actress admits that the contrary is true: 'fa mestieri che noi ci accommodiamo al popolo, se ne vogliamo riuscire, altrimente non ne riceveressimo né utile, né lode'.[110]

The ideas of theatre upheld by the philosopher and the actress could not be more different. Reinterpreting the classical and humanist tradition through the lens of Christian doctrine, the philosopher considers drama as an educational tool: by means of exempla, spectators are taught how to conduct themselves and reject the sins that would lead them to damnation. The ethical dimension of classical theatre is thus made subservient to the disciplining function of Christian drama, according to the theatrical model that, as I recalled in Chapter 1, is also at the core of contemporaneous practices of meditation. The actress focuses instead on pleasure as the only scope of her profession, for any other preoccupation would make her unsuccessful.[111]

The philosopher identifies falsehood as another negative aspect of drama, a judgment that allows for a subtle and revelatory objection on the part of the actress. When aimed at pleasing the audience, acting is undoubtedly mendacious; yet, its scope can be restored thanks to its potentially moral content. Asked about the benefit that comes from lying, the woman maintains that lies are beneficial when they teach what is good, 'covering moral examples by means of the veil of falsehood'.[112] Consistent with ideas of poetical fictions discussed in late Renaissance

---

109 *DM*, fol. 340[r-v].
110 *DM*, fol. 340[v]: 'We actors must accommodate to the populace if we want to be successful, otherwise we will gain neither profit nor praise'.
111 *DM*, fol. 341[v]: 'al presente il fine che noi habbiamo è solo per dilettare. E quinci avviene, che quelle Comedie, o Tragedie, ove non entrano buffoni, che facciano smascellar dalle risa, sono dal popolo universalmente poco stimate; come che egli sia così svogliato di moralità, che da queste ne riceva più maninconia, che diletto. E se nel fine da gli antichi usato, cioè nell'ammaestrare, pungere, e riprendere, volessimo noi stare, se non da pochissimi saremmo uditi, et a pochissimi piacerebbono le nostre inventioni' [Nowadays our only purpose is entertainment. Comedies or tragedies without risible buffoons are thus generally despised by the audience; people are so careless about morality that they receive nuisance rather than pleasure from similar plays. If we actors wanted to stick to the purpose of drama according to the ancients — namely to instruct, sting, and scold — we would only be heard by very few and even fewer would appreciate our performances].
112 *DM*, fol. 342[v]. For a discussion of Renaissance debates on poetic fiction in its relation to truth

Italy, the statement conceals the awareness of a benefit that, far from being truly moral, is mere distraction, hence a debased form of entertainment. The opinion of the philosopher is final, with actors being considered as makers of frivolous fiction, which, combined with slapsticks and clownish words, is simply meant to please and amuse the silly populace.[113]

Eventually, the philosopher's criticism bears some spiritual fruit. Spurred by the remorse of conscience, the woman asks the philosopher to expand on what he has just said. He thus outlines a more constructive argument that illustrates the metaphor of the *theatrum mundi*. By doing so, he invites the actress to reflect on her profession:

> FILOSOFO   Quantunque poco io vaglia nel dar buon consiglio altrui, nondimeno direi che consideraste una fiata da dovero quello che tante, e tante volte in scena dovete haver rapresentato.
> RECITANTE   E che è cotesto?
> FILOSOFO   Questo, che il Mondo è una scena, et i Recitanti siamo noi mortali tutti, i quali con vari habiti, con differenti portamenti, con gesti, e con parole conformi alle opinioni nostre, andiamo rapresentando ogn'uno la nostra parte in questa Scena del Mondo, facendo chi da padrone, chi da servo, chi da savio, chi da pazzo, chi da innamorato, e chi da vecchio. E sì come nelle scene vostre alcuni di voi fanno meglio la parte loro de gli altri; così in questa scena del mondo alcuno si porta meglio dell'altro, alcuni peggio, et altri così male, che n'acquistano vergogna e danno.[114]
>
> [PHILOSOPHER   Even if I am not good at advising others, I would like you to carefully consider what you have oftentimes represented on stage.
> ACTRESS   What is that?
> PHILOSOPHER   The fact that the world is a stage and that we mortals are actors: every day, with different habits, behaviours, gestures, and words concordant to our opinions, we perform our respective roles on the scene of the world: the master, the servant, the fool, the wise man, the lover, the elderly. As happens on your stage, where some actors perform their roles better than others, likewise, on this worldly scene, some people behave better than others, and some conduct themselves so badly that they obtain shame and damnation.]

The catalogue of characters (masters, servants, wise men, lovers, old men) alludes to the tradition of ancient comedy revived by humanism.[115] Yet the more profound analogy between world and stage is not due to characters who embody the real mores of men and women. Taking the metaphor literally and, to some extent, speaking the same language of the actress, the philosopher implies that all the world is a stage because, as happens with actors, the performances of men and women

---

and falsehood, see Bernard Weinberg, *A History of Literary Criticism in the Italian Renaissance* (Chicago, IL: University of Chicago Press, 1961); and, more precisely focused on the late sixteenth-century debate that involved poets such as Torquato Tasso, see Scarpati and Bellini, *Il vero e il falso dei poeti*.
113   *DM*, fol. 343^v.
114   *DM*, fol. 344^v.
115   See the canonical outline of this phenomenon in studies such as Antonio Stäuble, *La commedia umanistica del Quattrocento* (Florence: Istituto Nazionale di Studi sul Rinascimento, 1968); and Mario Baratto, *La commedia del Cinquecento: aspetti e problemi* (Vicenza: Neri Pozza, 1977).

can be of either good or bad quality. From this standpoint, shame does not come from the characters' morality (or lack thereof), but from the bad outcome of one's performance. However, two crucial differences exist between the terms of the simile:

> V'è solo questa differenza tra le vostre e quelle del mondo, che in quelle voi recitate talhor Comedie, Tragedie, Pastorali, Egloghe, Tragicomedie, e nuovamente Tragisatiricomiche, e Comisatiritragiche e, finite che l'havete, ritornate, deposti che havete gli habiti, nella vostra primiera forma. Ma in queste solo una sorte di rapresentationi vi si recitano, che sono le Tragedie, le quali tutte comminciansi con allegrezza, e grandezza apparente, ma tutte finiscono in dolore e morte; perché tutti, recitata c'habbiamo la nostra parte, se ne moriamo.[116]

> [There is only one difference between your stage and the world's: on your stage, you play comedies, tragedies, pastorals, eclogues, tragicomedies and, lately, tragic-satiric-comic and comic-satiric-tragic plays, and, once you are done with your performance, you remove your costumes and go back to your real persona. On the world's stage, instead, only one genre of drama is performed, tragedy: it always begins in happiness and apparent wealth, but it ends in sorrow and death, for we all die after playing our part.]

Glissenti's irony about the hybridisation of dramatic genres ties into the idea that, while actors perform different roles in different kinds of plays, men and women are allowed to only play in tragedies. In fact, human life (as already argued in the preface to the *Discorsi morali*) is but a tragedy. Differently from actors, who regain their identity after the show and can do better in future performances, men and women have only one chance to perform, without any possibility of repeating it.[117] Glissenti appropriates an argument that the humanist tradition had exploited within the debate on the nature and greatness of man, within which — as witnessed by authors such as Pico della Mirandola and Giovan Battista Gelli — the trope of the world as a stage was taken literally. Men and women acting in the tragedy of human life do not have further chances to do it better. Their one and only performance is what determines their fate after death. The actress, realising the divergence between the stage and the real world, seizes upon the unpleasantness of the simile, which, in fact, does not leave much space for compromise. According to the Philosopher, the woman should withdraw from her profession and focus on the role that she is expected to play on the world's stage, the only one that may secure her spiritual salvation.[118] The only audience she should be caring about is that of

---

116 *DM*, fol. 344[v].
117 Ibid.: 'E non possiamo [...] ritornar a recitare la seconda fiata. Onde se malamente si havremo portato la prima, non possiamo la seconda fiata racquistarsi l'honore perduto, come voi nelle vostre far potete. Nelle quali più, e più volte reiterando le attioni, potete nella seconda, o la terza rapresentatione correggere, e sodisfare a gli errori della prima' [We cannot [...] go back on stage and perform a second time. If we conducted ourselves badly the first time, we cannot regain our lost honour the second time, as you instead can do in your performances, where, the second or third time, you can amend and make up for the mistakes of the first].
118 *DM*, fol. 344[v]: 'tralasciando queste vostre stolte scene, cominciate da dovero a pensar di dover rapresentar bene la parte, che vi tocca a recitare nella scena del mondo; acciò che ne possiate,

the angels. (Here Glissenti makes explicit another component of the trope of the *theatrum mundi*: the idea that, as an actor, man performs his role in front of God, the highest spectator and judge of the performance.)[119]

Sticking to the metaphor, the philosopher recommends that the actress engage in a process of self-moralisation based on the contemplation of death. More broadly (and this is paramount to the author's attempt to reform drama) the philosopher calls for a moralisation of the actors' profession:

> Et acciò che a questi, e non a quelli voi arrechiate allegrezza, lasciando cotesta vostra infame professione, datevi ad una representatione di vita buona e santa, a gli honesti costumi, et alle attioni virtuose, aspettando di cuore la Morte, dopo la quale possiate ricever l'honore, degno premio in Cielo, a chi si havrà portato degnamente in questa scena. E parimente, acciò che habbiate occasione con che portarvi bene, studiate questa Morte che vi aspetta; a questa attendete, et in questa fissate gli occhi; che come in specchio lucidissimo mirarete qual progresso e qual parte dovete recitare in questa vita.[120]

> [In order to please the angels and not the demons, you should quit your ignoble profession and devote yourself to the representation of a good and holy life, to honest customs and virtuous deeds. By waiting for death with good cheer, you will afterwards be able to receive the honourable and heavenly prize that is assigned to those who conduct themselves well on this earthly stage. Furthermore, in order to help you behave well, contemplate Death, which awaits you: meditate upon it, fix your eyes on it; by doing so, as in a shiny mirror, you will see which progress and which part you need to perform in this life.]

The 'rapresentatione di vita buona e santa' [representation of a good and holy life] evokes the features of educational theatre that became so important in the aftermath of the Council of Trent, and which Glissenti himself pursued in his morality plays.[121]

The philosopher's opinion on acting is clear, and is a negative one. However, his judgment about the act of impersonating a role is articulate, making room

---

facendola bene, riportarne quel honore che in premio de' buoni portamenti stassi apparecchiato in Cielo' [neglecting these foolish stage of yours, begin to think seriously that you should perform well the part that is assigned to you on the stage of the world; by performing it appropriately, you will obtain the reward that, in Heaven, awaits good behaviours].

119 *DM*, fols 344ᵛ–45ʳ: 'Ricordatevi che havete a morire, et apparecchiatevi a far buona vita, per ricever anco una buona morte. Che queste vostre ridiculose scene, sì come non apportano al popolazzo ignorante altro, che un pazzo trattenimento et un vano diletto, così nella scena del mondo, se voi vi portarete male, darete diletto a gli spiriti infernali, i quali sono gli auditori, che si burlano e ridono d'allegrezza per la cattiva rapresentatione che fa alcuno di sua vita; sì come per lo contrario rallegransi gli Angeli, quando veggono alcuno a diportarsi bene nella scena mondana' [Remember that you will die and prepare to conduct a good life in order to have a good death. Also, remember that, as this risible stage does not bring to the ignorant populace other than foolish entertainment and vain pleasure, so you will only entertain the demons of hell if you will misbehave on the stage of the world. In fact, those demons who attend the performance of mortals are delighted by bad impersonations that people make of their own lives; on the contrary, angels rejoice when they see someone behaving well on the world's stage].

120 Ibid., fol. 345ʳ.

121 For the notion of educational theatre ('teatro di formazione') as it was outlined in the Jesuit context, see Zanlonghi, *Teatri di formazione*.

for the possibility of a moral reform of drama. The main problem with acting is that a skilful actor is one who is able to feign and simulate, both actions that are normally at odds with the notion of virtue. When the actress performs the role of the prostitute Thais in Terence's *Eunuchus*, for instance, a 'good' performance requires the woman to give a credible portrayal of the character, which, given the immorality of the character, is a bad example for the audience. But the argument, from the actress's point of view, can be reversed, for the staging of evil characters does not necessarily aim to stimulate the audience's emulation. On the contrary, its scope is to warn the audience against those sorts of people in everyday life.[122] Furthermore, even assuming that the impersonation of an immoral character is a vicious action, the actress wonders what happens when unquestionably virtuous characters are brought on stage. Examples may range from Lucretia and Cornelia to Artemisia, Rhodopis, Hippo, and Antigone, all well known to both classical and early modern tragedy ('una casta Lucretia, una eloquente Cornelia, una fidele Arthemisia, una continente Sofronia, una rissentita Rodope, una pudicissima Ippo, overo una religiosa Antigone'). In order to be even more convincing, the actress also makes the case of female saints in sacred drama ('una Santa del Cielo, come si usa in qualche rappresentatione').[123] The reference is interesting because, by bringing religious theatre into the discussion, it bears witness to the range of possibilities that professional actors dealt with. While a modern readership tends to separate fields in terms of opposition (e.g., comic *vs.* tragic, sacred *vs.* secular), things were different at the time of those actors who would easily cross the boundaries between genres and dramatic forms. The philosopher, however, does not believe that secular theatre can be turned into something moral, the primary obstacle being the very nature of virtue. Since virtue is 'a disposition of the soul aimed at what is good in both actions and thoughts under the guidance of reason', it definitely consists in 'performing good operations and not just in mimicking them'.[124] By turning to the art of perspective illusion, the philosopher leads the actress through an argument that, while rejecting any connection between virtue and acting, leaves some space open to the idea of a theatre with educational purposes. The philosopher observes that there is no equivalence between a perspectival painting, which depicts a landscape, and a real landscape; likewise, the actor, who, by performing virtuous actions onstage, spurs the audience to act virtuously, is not necessarily virtuous himself.[125] For sure, the representation of good actions is good when considered

---

122 *DM*, fol. 362^r.
123 *DM*, fol. 362^v.
124 *DM*, fol. 362^v: 'una propria dispositione e facoltà dell'animo in atto et in pensiero volta al bene, sotto il governo della ragione'; 'operare e veramente essercitare operationi virtuose, et non a rappresentarle'.
125 *DM*, fols 362^v–63^r: 'FILOSOFO Direste voi che una vaga prospettiva fatta per mano di eccellente pittore, che rappresentasse un bel giardino, fosse giardino veramente? RECITANTE Direi che è tanto ben fatta, che pare propriamente un giardino. FILOSOFO Tale è il rappresentare la conditione altrui; il che non è virtù realmente, ma pare virtù. Hor quello che è virtù non è egli virtù sempre, e non alcuna volta pare virtù, non essendo virtù? RECITANTE Già l'ho detto. FILOSOFO Se il rappresentare fosse virtù, sarebbe sempre virtù. RECITANTE Che cosa sarà egli quello che non è virtù e non è ancora vitio, quando si rappresentano cose buone? FILOSOFO Sarà un essempio, uno incitamento

per se, but when considered in relation to the performer, impersonation is an act of vanity. Accordingly, if the actress who impersonates the role of a virtuous woman or a saint is not virtuous herself, the potentially virtuous function of acting fails. The dialogue discloses the moral fault of the woman's profession and reveals the only kind of theatre acceptable within the limits of Christian morality:

> FILOSOFO   Siete per caso voi tale, quale rappresentate altrui in quella maniera c'habbiamo detto, di quelle famose donne, o Sante del Cielo, delle quali rappresentate la vita?
> RECITANTE   Oh, io non mi trovo di quella essemplar lor vita.
> FILOSOFO   Il mostrare quello che non siete, non è egli il mostrar di falso e male?
> RECITANTE   Io non mostro per mostrar me, ma rappresento la persona altrui, per mostrarla.
> FILOSOFO   Rappresentando la persona altrui, fatelo voi per imitarla, et per sforzarvi di non partirvi in tutto il tempo di vostra vita da così nobile essempio, o pur lo fate per compiacerne altrui?
> RECITANTE   A quello io non attendo, ma solo a dilettare altri in quella parte, ch'io rappresento.[126]
>
> [PHILOSOPHER   When you impersonate someone else in the way we just discussed, are you by any chance one and the same as those famous women or holy saints whose life you represent?
> ACTRESS   Oh, no, I do not live that exemplary life.
> PHILOSOPHER   So, to exhibit what you are, isn't it the same as exhibiting falsehood and evil?
> ACTRESS   I do not exhibit myself; rather, I represent someone else's persona, in order to exhibit it.
> PHILOSOPHER   By representing someone else, do you do it to imitate them and force yourself to never depart from that noble example in your life, or do you do it just to entertain others?
> ACTRESS I do not do it; my only purpose is to please others by impersonating that given role.]

Through his questions, the philosopher sketches a model of drama that is educational for both audience and actors. Indeed, the impersonation of a virtuous character or

---

alla virtù, sì come il rappresentare una Taide sarà uno incitamento al vitio. RECITANTE Hor lodato Iddio, quello che incita a virtù non farà egli più tosto bene, che male? FILOSOFO Sarà più tosto bene considerato in se stesso, ma considerato il soggetto, da cui vien rappresentato sarà vanità, e più tosto male' [PHILOSOPHER Would you argue that a beautiful perspective made by a skilful painter to represent a delightful garden is, in fact, a garden? ACTRESS I would say that it is so well done that it looks exactly like a garden. PHILOSOPHER The same can thus be said about impersonating someone else's condition: it is not real virtue, but it looks like virtue. Now, virtue, isn't it always virtue? Or is virtue even what looks like virtue without being, in fact, virtue? ACTRESS I said it. PHILOSOPHER Then, if representation were virtue, it would always be virtue. ACTRESS What is that, which is neither virtue nor vice, when good deeds are represented? PHILOSOPHER It is an exemplum, an exhortation to virtue, as is the representation of, say, Thais an exhortation to vice. ACTRESS But, for God's sake, what spurs to virtue, isn't it good rather than evil? PHILOSOPHER It is indeed something good when considered per se; but if we consider the individual who is representing [the exemplum], then it is vain and evil].
126 Ibid., fol. 363^r.

a saint is a virtuous action only when it coincides with the acquisition of the same moral habit on the part of the performers. Once again, preaching offers a fitting analogy, for both preachers and actors are entitled to push their audiences to good behaviours only if they are good themselves. Horace's notion that the poet's feelings should correspond to the effects produced in the audience is thus reshaped into a moral requirement that applies to theatrical performance.

The situation suggested by Glissenti recalls the theatrical model installed by the Jesuits, a model that, as I will show in Chapter 3, the author adopted in his own plays. The female orphans of the Venetian hospitals for whom Glissenti composed his *favole morali* were in fact meant to interiorise the moral teachings conveyed by the plays. Drama, banned as immoral when it deals with pure fiction and entertainment, can thus been converted into an instrument of moral and spiritual discipline targeting the conscience of the performer, a didactic experience in which players are required not simply to 'represent' an action but to truly 'perform' it. In the same vein, when the play is read instead of being performed, readers are invited to internalise it and have it performed on the stage of their conscience. The philosopher's criticism of buffoons and actors is thus part of a wider reflection that condemns the mundane stage as a theatre of deceiving appearances. Glissenti's polemic against theatre, which apparently implies a rigorous condemnation of drama in all its forms, is, in fact, backed up by the promotion of educational practices based on the convergence between the act of representing and the moral content of what is represented. While the theatrical reform endorsed by Glissenti's mouthpiece in the *Discorsi morali* would fit a number of spiritual and confessional dramatic works produced in the late Renaissance and Baroque period, instructive evidence of the ways in which such a programme could be put into practice comes from the author's own experience as a playwright. As Chapter 3 will demonstrate, it is by looking at Glissenti's morality plays in the light of the *Discorsi morali* that the various facets of the physician's literary production reveal their preoccupation with a notion of theatricality that is not simply focused on issues of 'representation', but primarily concerned with the proactive — one could say 'performative' — dimension of drama.

CHAPTER 3

Anatomy of the Soul: Morality Plays as Spiritual Exercises in Early Seicento Venice

The reform of drama promoted by the Philosopher in his dialogue with the Actress in the *Discorsi morali* captures preoccupations that were key to ongoing debates about the morality of theatre. Indeed, the critical lexicon mobilised by the Philosopher in his critique of drama resonates with the vast corpus of writings on the subject that, from Carlo and Federico Borromeo to Giovanni Domenico Ottonelli, marked the ambiguous ways in which the hyper-theatrical culture of the Counter Reformation negotiated the potentially dangerous charms of theatre.[1] However, if Glissenti's reprimand of secular drama outspokenly targets specific genres such as the *commedia dell'arte*, the virtuous theatre he hints at is less obvious to pin down.

Interestingly enough, useful clues come from within the *Discorsi morali* themselves, specifically from a passage in day 3 where Glissenti mentions a theatrical work by Giovanni Battista Leoni (1542–1613), the 'tragicomedia spirituale' [spiritual tragicomedy] *La conversione del peccatore a Dio* [The Sinner's Conversion to God], first printed in Venice in 1591.[2] The reference is cursory and concerned with a specific feature of the play's plot.[3] Yet, the praise of Leoni's work speaks to Glissenti's penchant for spiritual allegory and provides us with insight into his conception of virtuous drama more broadly. In Leoni's play, the prologue (delivered by the

---

1 Castiglione, *Sentimenti di S. Carlo Borromeo*; Giovanni Domenico Ottonelli, *Della christiana moderatione del theatro*, 5 vols (Florence: Luca Franceschini and Alessandro Logi, 1648–52); on both Borromeo and Ottonelli, as well as on the debates triggered by their statements on theatre, see Taviani, *La fascinazione del teatro*; Claudio Bernardi, 'Censura e promozione del teatro nella Controriforma', in *Storia del teatro moderno e contemporaneo*, I: *La nascita del teatro moderno Cinquecento–Seicento*, ed. by Roberto Alonge and Guido Davico Bonino (Turin: Einaudi, 2000), pp. 1023–42; Carla Maria Bino, '"Lo Spiritual Teatro" e la "Sacra Scena": una prima indagine negli scritti di Federico Borromeo', *Studia Borromaica*, 20 (2002), 263–82; Michael Zampelli, '"Lascivi spettacoli": Jesuits and Theatre (from the Underside)', in *The Jesuits*, II: *Cultures, Sciences and the Arts, 1540–1773*, ed. by John William O'Malley et al. (Toronto: University of Toronto Press, 2006), pp. 550–71.
2 Giovanni Battista Leoni, *La conversione del peccatore a Dio, tragicomedia spirituale* (Venice: Francesco de' Franceschi, 1591), reprinted various times (1591, 1592, 1613). On Leoni, with full bibliography of his works, see Dennis E. Rhodes, *Giovanni Battista Leoni, diplomatico e poligrafo* (Manziana: Vecchiarelli, 2013).
3 *DM*, fol. 160^r.

personification of Truth) declares that true pleasure does not come from 'l'amor del Senso' [love of Sense], but from 'l'amor dell'Intelletto' [love of Intellect]. In a similar vein, Truth argues that the 'piacer interno | che ne l'oggetto suo gode la mente' [the internal pleasure that the mind receives from its own object] is sweeter than the external one that comes from physical love.[4] Framing the spiritual and moral content of the play in terms of genre, Truth explains that the work is not about comedy's silly facts or tragedy's dreadful deeds: spectators will learn how to avoid the deceits of 'senso rubelle' [disobedient sense], 'mondo traditor' [treacherous world], and 'rio peccato' [guilty sin] at once with admiring the victory of the 'magnanimo eroe' [magnanimous hero] over all of them.[5] The hero mentioned in the prologue is no other than Man himself, 'l'Huomo', here called Andro, caught in an allegorical interaction (one could call it a psychomachia) with a set of characters who, in fact, are personifications with names issuing from Greek etymologies: from 'Fisia' [Nature] to 'Icomeno' [World], from 'Zoi' [Human life] to 'Fronimo' [Intellect] and 'Idonèo' [Sense], among others, the dramatisation of the fight between body and soul is meant to provide the audience with an *exemplum* to learn from, while also exposing, the inner — invisible — working of human life.[6]

La conversione del peccatore a Dio is not the only instance of spiritual play that would fit the Philosopher's dramatic reform outlined in the *Discorsi morali*. However, the relevance of Leoni's work to Glissenti's theatrical concerns comes to the fore when one considers that its features resonate not only with the critique of theatre in the *Discorsi*, but also and most important with Glissenti's own commitment as a playwright, which he pursued in conjunction with his professional duties in the hospitals of Venice. In this respect, another play by Leoni, *La falsa riputatione della Fortuna* [The False Reputation of Fortune], first printed in 1596, proves particularly instructive, starting with the generic label chosen by the author, 'favola morale'.[7] The term 'favola morale' was seldom used to describe a dramatic work: Leoni's seems to be the earliest example of this use, followed a few years later by Glissenti's own plays, which were presented and marketed as 'favole morali'. If the term speaks to the fact that the play is more suitable for reading than for actual performance (a quality that, to some extent, we will find in Glissenti's plays as well), the printed edition reveals that *La falsa riputatione della Fortuna* was actually performed. As recalled by the preface, the play was 'recitata dagli Academici Generosi del Seminario Patriarcale di Venezia' [performed by the Generous Academics of the Patriarchal Seminary of Venice]. This piece of information evokes an educational context that, even if reserved to male students with sophisticated training, can be compared to the context of Glissenti's dramatic production.[8] Alongside the

---

4   Leoni, *La conversione*, fol. A4^v.
5   Leoni, *La conversione*, fol. [A5]^r.
6   See the full list of characters in Leoni, *La conversione*, fol. A3^r.
7   Giovanni Battista Leoni, *La falsa riputatione della fortuna favola morale* (Venice: Giovan Battista Ciotti, 1596), reprinted various times (1598, 1601, 1606).
8   Reference to the performance at the Seminario is made on the title page of the work. Theatrical activities at the Seminario are also worthy of investigation, as suggested by another anonymous spiritual play, *David penitente*, which was given at the same institution, and which is preserved by the

common adoption of a purely allegorical code for the dramatisation and staging of spiritual fights, the context in which Leoni's work was performed (the Patriarchal Seminary) makes it the most immediate model for Glissenti's plays. At the same time, the physician gives the model a very personal twist, not only pursuing, through the plays, a veritable Christian reform of drama, but also making them integral to the wider educational project begun with the *Discorsi morali*.

If the metaphor of the *theatrum mundi*, as I have shown in Chapter 2, holds a structural function in the *Discorsi*, the trope is returned to its literal meaning in Glissenti's ten *favole morali*, published between 1606 and 1620. In most of them, the World ('il Mondo') is both a character *and* the location where the action unfolds. Accordingly (and very much in line with the tradition of medieval allegory that authors such as Leoni had been drawing on), Man ('l'Huomo') is the protagonist of the plays as well as the point of convergence of *theatrum mundi* and *theatrum animae*. The two terms — the world and the soul — represent the opposite poles of the universe that Glissenti brings to life in his plays: the World is the space of earthly matters, the scene upon which Man plays his role and lives his life, the realm of Sense, Opinion, and Flesh; the Soul, which also appears as both a character and a setting, represents the spiritual preoccupations that Man ought to nurture in order to achieve salvation after death. A variety of characters move between these two extremes, including both personified allegories of Man's intellectual functions, which are supposed to guide his behaviours, and the external factors that affect Man's choices. A crucial role within this universe is that of Free Will, which, according to the same philosophical and theological premises of the *Discorsi morali*, is introduced as the ultimate decision-maker in all human affairs, constantly challenged by Inclination, that is, Man's bent for things earthly.

Hanging in the balance between Free Will and Inclination, Man is the protagonist of a psychomachia that is given dramatic shape through a process that I propose to describe as a metaphorical dissection. Human psychology and physiology are, so to speak, anatomised. In other words, they are deconstructed into their components, which are made to interact on stage as if they were real characters. Playing with the correspondence between a given character's name and their functions, the playwright turns to allegorical personification as an effective tool to make visible the invisible. At the same time, by having personifications perform the roles embedded in their names (Reason reasons, Sense feels, etc.), Glissenti triggers a short circuit between their performativity and the performative context of the plays, be it conveyed through actual staging or meditative reading. Ultimately, I argue, this short circuit between the work of allegory and its theatrical framework is what enables the reshaping of drama into spiritual practice. To this purpose, after outlining the context in which Glissenti's plays were originally conceived and consumed, I will illustrate their salient features, giving special attention to matters of poetics, themes, and the ways in which the *favole morali* interacted with concurrent developments in spiritual and devotional literature.

---

same miscellaneous codex (Venice, Biblioteca Nazionale Marciana, Ital. IX.316) that witnesses the manuscript copy of Glissenti's *La Morte innamorata*, which I will discuss below, pp. 139–41.

School Drama in the Venetian *ospedali* and Beyond

A better understanding of Glissenti's dramatic production is possible when one looks at its destination. Despite the lack of archival documentation, the context in which the *favole morali* were first produced and the dynamics of their circulation can be partially reconstructed from the numerous printed editions of the plays and manuscript copies of two of them (*La Morte innamorata* and *L'Andrio*). As indicated by the paratextual materials included in some of the prints, Glissenti's plays were originally conceived as pedagogical entertainments for the female orphans (*putte*) based at the *ospedali* of Venice, which, as is well known, functioned not only as hospitals but also as orphanages.[9] By situating Glissenti's dramatic works within the context of the *ospedali* and, more precisely, within their educational framework, it is possible to shed light on the pedagogical use of drama in the Venetian orphanages, a topic that remains, to date, virtually unexplored. While more detailed studies, including further archival research, will be needed for a thorough assessment of the phenomenon, the evidence gathered around the case of Glissenti's *favole morali* is instructive of the status acquired by allegorical drama in the early Seicento and its relation to the ever-growing production and consumption of texts of spiritual practice.[10]

The earliest indication that Glissenti's morality plays were performed comes from the paratext of the first one to be published, *La Ragione sprezzata* (1606). In the dedication letter to the Duchess of Mantua, Eleonora de' Medici, the author recalls a Venetian performance of the play delivered by 'some young women' ('ad opera di alcune virginelle qui in Venetia'), with simple sets and in a place that would not normally be associated with this kind of activities ('ancorché povere di scena, d'apparato e di luogo conveniente').[11] The dedication letter, by invoking a vague memory of the performance, is instrumental to inviting the Duchess to promote similar events in her own court.[12] More precise details about the original

9   Bibliography on the Venetian hospitals is, unsurprisingly, very rich. See, at least, Franca Semi, *Gli ospizi di Venezia* (Venice: Edizioni Helvetia, 1983); and *Nel regno dei poveri: arte e storia dei grandi ospedali veneziani in età moderna, 1474–1797*, ed. by Bernard Aikema and Dulcia Meijers (Venice: Arsenale editrice, 1989). More broadly, on the health care system in Venice during the early modern period, see Brian Pullan, *Rich and Poor in Renaissance Venice: The Social Institutions of a Catholic State, to 1620* (Oxford: Blackwell, 1971); and a few chapters in *Storia di Venezia*, 14 vols (Rome: Istituto della Enciclopedia Italiana, 1991–2002): Dennis Romano, 'L'assistenza e la beneficenza', vol. v, pp. 355–406; Luciano Bonuzzi, 'Medicina e sanità', vol. v, pp. 407–40; Massimo Costantini, 'Le strutture dell'ospitalità', vol. v, pp. 881–912; Giovanni Scarabello, 'Le strutture assistenziali', vol. vi, pp. 863–74.
10   More work needs to be done, specifically in Venice's Archivio delle Istituzioni di Ricovero e di Educazione (I.R.E.), which has been closed to the public for several years including the period of time when research for this book was beeing conducted; see Giuseppe Ellero, *L'archivio IRE: inventari dei fondi antichi degli ospedali e luoghi pii di Venezia* (Venice: I.R.E., 1987).
11   Fabio Glissenti, *La Ragione sprezzata, favola tragica morale* (Serravalle: Marco Claseri, 1606), fol. [A4]^r.
12   *La Ragione sprezzata*, fols [A4]$^{r-v}$: '[...] non curandomi del primo effetto, ma del seguito profitto, mandandola alle stampe a V. Altezza l'ho voluto offerire; sicuro, che a lei non manca né sapere, né potere di farla nel decoro conveniente a beneficio del prossimo interamente rappresentare' [[...] unconcerned about its first effect, but caring about the ensuing benefit, I wished to offer it to your

production of the play are included in the preface to the readers ('Alli lettori'), which, as we will see, is also key to the definition of Glissenti's poetics. The text explains that the *favola* was composed during Carnival as a gift for the 'girls' of the Hospital of San Giovanni e Paolo, who would perform it, 'as usual', as part of their 'recreational activities' ('con animo di consignarla [...] a certe dongelle dell'Hospitale di San Giovanni e Paulo, che fra loro la recitassero, come usano di fare in tempo di ricreatione'), a statement that gives a proper identity to the unspecified 'virginelle' mentioned in the dedication to Eleonora.[13] Glissenti then reports that the play performed at the Hospital of San Giovanni e Paolo, also known as Derelitti or Ospedaletto, proved extremely successful, in spite of being given in a shortened version:

> essendo ella nello spatio di giorni vinti stata recitata almeno otto fiate, quantunque in più luoghi [...] abbreviata, ha nondimeno così piacciuto a quelli che l'hanno udita la prima fiata, che (dove io la stimai novella da raccontarsi a feminelle) non se ne sono contentati se non l'hanno udita la seconda, la terza, e la quarta volta; e se tutto l'anno fosse stata recitata, per il numeroso concorso senza dubbio havrebbe havuto sempre concitata udienza.[14]

> [As it has been represented at least eight times over twenty days, though shortened, it has so much pleased those who saw it the first time that, while I considered it just a novella to be told to girls, they were not satisfied till they saw it a second, third, and fourth time; were the play to be represented all year long, due to the numerous audience, it would always be met with excitement.]

The fact that the occasion was not an isolated one is confirmed by further evidence. A staging of *L'Andrio* (1607) involving the 'girls of the Incurabili' is mentioned by the humanist Giovan Giunio Parisio in the dedication of Glissenti's play to Bartolomeo Buontempelli del Calice, a beloved friend of the author's and a philanthropist who donated abundantly to the Venetian hospitals.[15] Proofs that *Il Diligente* and *La Morte*

---

highness by having it printed, as I am aware that you do not lack knowledge or the ability to have it conveniently staged to the benefit of others].

13   *La Ragione sprezzata*, fol. A6^r.
14   *La Ragione sprezzata*, fol. A6^v.
15   Fabio Glissenti, *L'Andrio cioè l'huomo virile favola morale* (Venice: Giovanni Alberti, 1607), fol. A3^v; the reference to the original destination of the play is relevant to the celebration of the dedicatee's humility and charitable philanthropy: 'essend'ella stata dettata a studio dall'autore in stile così dimesso, e humile, per accommodarlo al genio et capacità delle recitanti, che doveano essere le figliuole dell'Hospital de gl'Incurabili, a chi più si conveniva di voi? che tanto aborrite le pompe, che sembrate l'humiltà istessa, poi che facendo tesser così superbi panni d'argento, e d'oro, per vestir Regi, e Imperatori, ve n'andate voi coperta di pura e schietta lana?' [Having been composed by the author in humble and demure style so as to fit the mind and ability of the actresses, who were meant to be the daughters of the Hospital of the Incurabili, who would be more suitable a dedicatee than yourself? you, who abhor celebrations and resemble humility itself; who make superb garments in silver and gold for kings and emperors, while going around covered with pure and simple wool]. Buontempelli is celebrated in similar terms in the preface of *Il Diligente*, which is also dedicated to him. On Buontempelli, see Ugo Tucci, 'Bontempelli (Bontempello) dal Calice (Calese) Bartolomeo', in *Dizionario Biografico degli Italiani*, 12 (1970), pp. 426–27. As mentioned above, *L'Andrio* is one of the two plays for which manuscript copies exist (Venice, Biblioteca Nazionale Marciana, MS Ital. IX.316, pp. 89–184).

innamorata, both printed in 1608, were performed at the Derelitti come instead from an unusually rich set of interrelated documents that deserve special attention. Not only do these materials tell us that the plays were staged, but they also indicate that the productions included music and singing. These documents thus suggest that the practice of school drama in the Venetian hospitals was, at this particular juncture, already connected to the burgeoning role of music as a substantial part of the life of the *putte* and their soon-to-be flagship endeavour.[16]

One performance of *La Morte innamorata* (1608) is mentioned in the dedication of the play to the English ambassador, Sir Henry Wotton, whose stay in Venice I recalled in my introduction. The playwright's niece, Elisabetta Serenella Glissenti, who penned the epistle and dated it from Venice, 1st March 1608, mentions that Wotton attended and enjoyed the play, thus stressing the correspondence between the dedicatee's virtuous nature and the morality of the work ('un'opera virtuosa, e morale non sarebbe piaciuta se non ad uno virtuosissimo, e moralissimo Signore').[17] More precise information about the performance history of *La Morte innamorata* emerges from a manuscript copy of the play, now in the Biblioteca Marciana, and from the 1608 printed edition of the *Rime spirituali et morali* by the Venetian poet Giacomo Castellano.[18] These materials are of interest for various reasons: first, the manuscript provides a wealth of details about the individuals involved in the production of *La Morte innamorata* at the Derelitti; second, it bears witness to a complex process of textual revision (the manuscript version of the play is significantly different from the printed one, with changes, additions, and erasures that let us follow adjustments likely made ahead of the performance, most of which did not even make it into the print); third, both the manuscript and Castellano's *Rime* confirm that the staging at the Derelitti included music, with other artists involved in the production. The latter feature is not surprising, given that musical activities (singing, in particular) are recorded in the hospitals of Venice as early as in the 1570s. Yet, this piece of information contributes to a more articulate picture of the recreational life of the hospitals in a phase of their history for which the documentation remains scant. While the place of music in the history of the hospitals is fairly well documented and has been the object of thorough study (though most substantially for later periods), the case of Glissenti's *La Morte innamorata* suggests that school drama should be considered as one of the factors that fuelled the musical ferment which the Venetian hospitals would soon be renown for.

---

16 For an overview of music's place in the hospitals of Venice, see Giuseppe Ellero, 'Origini e sviluppo storico della musica nei quattro grandi ospedali di Venezia', *Nuova Rivista Musicale Italiana*, 13.1 (1979), 160–67; M. V. Constable, 'The Venetian 'figlie del coro': Their Environment and Achievement', *Music & Letters*, 63.3 (1982), 181–212; Pier Giuseppe Gilio, *L'attività musicale negli ospedali di Venezia nel Settecento: quadro storico e materiali documentari* (Florence: Leo S. Olschki, 2006); on the specific case of the Ospedaletto, see *Arte e musica all'Ospedaletto: schede d'archivio sull'attività musicale degli ospedali dei Derelitti e dei Mendicanti di Venezia (sec. XVI–XVIII)* (Venice: Stamperia di Venezia, 1978).
17 Glissenti, *La Morte innamorata*, fol. A2^r.
18 The manuscript copy of *La Morte innamorata* is in Venice, Biblioteca Nazionale Marciana, MS Ital. IX.316, fols 1^r–87^r; see also Giacomo Castellano, *Rime spirituali et morali* (Venice: Evangelista Deuchino and Giovan Battista Pulciani, 1608).

According to the manuscript copy, which is part of a miscellaneous collection of plays in the Marciana, MS Ital. IX.316 (including, though by a different hand, the text of *L'Andrio*), *La Morte innamorata* was staged at the Hospital of San Giovanni e Paolo in 1607 ('L'anno 1607 in Venetia. Fu recitata la presente favola morale composta dall'eccellente signor Fabio Glisenti dalle Figlie di SS. Gio: Paulo').[19] Even more interesting is the fact that the manuscript includes a list of the 'figlie' [daughters] of the hospital, who performed the play. Unsurprisingly, it is difficult to pin down the identities behind the names. The list suggests a rather diverse pool of performers: alongside orphans, whose family names (e.g. Sanudo, Foscarini) bear weak echoes of their provenance, others — for whom only the given names are recorded — were likely foundlings. On the same page, details about the musical components of the play are reported as well: the choruses between the acts were set to 'beautiful music' by Giovanni Bassano and the madrigals (such as the one that opens the play) were by poet Giacomo Castellano, who is said to be residing at the Lippomanni household at the Ponte de Noal.[20]

If the names of the performers offer a glimpse into the actual people who brought Glissenti's play to life, those of Bassano and Castellano let us situate the production of the play within the broader cultural commitments that the Ospedale dei Derelitti was concerned with in the early years of the seventeenth century. Composer Giovanni Bassano (1558–1617) was a key figure in the musical life of Venice in the period.[21] As a musician, he had been involved with the instrumental ensembles of the Basilica of Saint Mark since the 1570s, and was later appointed as the Basilica's director of instrumental music in 1601. As a composer, he produced church music as well as secular pieces that enjoyed a successful reception beyond Italy. It is within this context that we should place his collaboration with the Ospedale dei Derelitti, of which Bassano became the second known music teacher, in 1612 (the first one being Baldassarre Donati, who had died in 1604).[22] Bassano's role in the production of *La Morte innamorata* suggests that, even before his official appointment, he was already involved in the musical and theatrical activities of the hospital. Whereas the music composed for the choruses seems to be lost, the extant production by Bassano let us appreciate the kind of polyphony that would have resounded on the occasion of the staging. Furthermore, it is likely that the composer was also responsible for the setting of other parts of the work that, as suggested by their prosodic shape, seem to have required music. These include the aforementioned madrigals by Giacomo Castellano, which illuminate another component of the play not recorded in the printed edition of *La Morte innamorata*: namely, the fact that the

---

19   Venice, Biblioteca Nazionale Marciana, MS Ital. IX.316, fol. 2^r.
20   Ibid.: 'Li chori furono di bellissima musica composti dal S.r Giovanni Bassan. Li madrigali et [cerca] furono fatti dal s.r Giacomo Castellan sta in ca' Lippamanno al ponte di Noal.'
21   Fabio Fano, 'Bassano, Giovanni', *Dizionario Biografica degli Italiani*, 7 (1970), pp. 112–13; David Lasocki and Roger Prior, *The Bassanos: Venetian musicians and instrument makers in England, 1531–1665* (Brookfield, VT: Ashgate, 1995), p. 254; Rodolfo Baroncini and Marco Di Pasquale, *Monteverdi a San Marco. Venezia 1613–1643* (Lucca: LIM, 2020), pp. 211–15, 247–48.
22   *Arte e musica all'Ospedaletto*, ed. by Scarpa, p. 43; *Nel regno dei poveri*, ed. by Aikema and Mejiers, p. 99.

staging was the result of a collaboration, with introductory and concluding pieces penned by an author other than the playwright. Incidentally, the 1608 print of Castellano's *Rime* indicates that the poet was involved not only with the production of *La Morte innamorata*, but also with that of *Il Diligente*, for which he wrote similar liminal pieces.[23] (Given their significance to the poetical and spiritual scope of the performances, I will address these pieces shortly in my discussion of Glissenti's poetics.)

As indicated by the documents that I have reviewed so far, some of Glissenti's *favole morali* were performed at the Incurabili and Derelitti, which, since the mid-sixteenth century had been increasing their commitment to the care of orphans, female in particular.[24] The idea that healthcare should go hand in hand with the cultivation of spiritual well-being, especially when it came to foundlings and orphans, had been strongly promoted by the so-called Compagnie del Divino Amore [Oratories of Divine Love].[25] Alongside the educational activities fostered by the Schools of Christian Doctrine, which expanded their outreach significantly in the aftermath of the Council of Trent, the Compagnie del Divino Amore insisted on the importance of instructing children in the catechism and basic literacy.[26] In a similar vein, religious orders and congregations such as the Jesuits, Somaschians, Barnabites, and Theatines held major roles in the development of pedagogical programmes that opened the doors of the Venetian hospitals to rhetoric and drama.

The importance of the Jesuits in Venice, at least until the *interdetto* of 1606, cannot be overstated: both Ignatius of Loyola and Francis Xavier had ties with the Incurabili and Derelitti, where they pursued their apostolate while also committing to providing assistance.[27] Several traces of their significance to Venetian culture are found in Glissenti's works: the plays adapt some of the features of Jesuit rhetoric while also appropriating the disciplining scope of the spiritual practices revamped by Ignatius (we will see that the founder of the Jesuits is explicitly mentioned in the play *L'Androtoo*). Also crucial to the educational programmes of both Derelitti

---

23 Castellano, *Rime*, fols B3v–B4v; for a contextualisation of Castellano's poetry within the patronage connected to the hospitals of Venice, see Rodolfo Baroncini, 'Gli Ospedali, la nuova pietas e la committenza musicale cittadinesca a Venezia (1590–1620): i casi di Bartolomeo Bontempelli dal Calice e di Camillo Rubini', in *Atti del Congresso internazionale di musica sacra in occasione del centenario di fondazione del PIMS: Roma, 26 maggio–1 giugno 2011*, ed. by Antonio Addamiano and Francesco Luisi (Vatican City: Libreria Editrice Vaticana, 2013), pp. 569–85.
24 M. V. Constable, 'The Education of the Venetian Orphans from the Sixteenth to the Eighteenth Century: An Expression of Guillaume Postel's Judgement of Venice as a Public Welfare State', in *Postello, Venezia e il suo mondo*, ed. by Marion Leathers Kuntz (Florence: Leo S. Olschki, 1988), pp. 179–202.
25 Pullan, *Rich and Poor*, pp. 231–38.
26 Christopher Carlsmith, *A Renaissance Education: Schooling in Bergamo and the Venetian Republic, 1500–1650* (Toronto: University of Toronto Press, 2010), p. 143–56.
27 Semi, *Gli ospizi di Venezia*, pp. 120, 273. More broadly, on the activities of Jesuits and Somaschians in Venice, see Maurizio Sangalli, *Cultura, politica e religione nella Repubblica di Venezia tra Cinque e Seicento: Gesuiti e Somaschi a Venezia* (Venice: Istituto Veneto di Scienze, Lettere ed Arti, 1999). On Loyola and Xavier in Venice, see Pullan, *Rich and Poor*, pp. 264–66; see also Giuseppe Ellero, 'Guillaume Postel e l'ospedale dei Derelitti (1547–1549)', in *Postello, Venezia e il suo mondo*, ed. by Kuntz, pp. 137–62.

and Incurabili was Girolamo Miani (1486–1537), founding father of the Somaschian congregation, whose role in the education of foundlings and orphans was key to several northern Italian cities, Bergamo in particular, before spreading across the peninsula.[28] If the commitment of the Jesuits to the spiritual life of those who resided in the hospitals included the staging of *tableaux vivants*, Miani had been promoting mnemonic exercises in the form of dialogues with catechetic functions, which were a first step towards more articulate forms of dramatic engagement.[29] Similarly, the Barnabites and the Theatines gave special attention to the education of foundlings and orphans, often turning to rhetorical devices that aimed at the combination of moral teachings, doctrinal instruction, and spiritual practices such as confession, meditation, examination of conscience, and penitence.[30]

As indicated by Brian Pullan, despite the inevitable tensions that informed the interaction of the numerous stakeholders involved in the Venetian healthcare system, the educational priority given to the teaching of Christian doctrine in the hospitals proved successful across the board. Particularly eloquent are, from this point of view, the *Ordini et capitoli* [Rules and statutes] of the Compagnia dell'Oratorio at the Incurabili.[31] Gathered by the Theatine Giovanni Paolo da Como and published in 1568, they refer to the 'schole de Putti [...] nelle quali s'insegna la dottrina Christiana a' figliuoli il giorno della Festa doppo il disinare' [schools for the boys in which Christian doctrine is taught on Sundays after the main meal]. The educational model outlined by Giovanni Paolo da Como hinges upon a few basic principles, which, as we will see, are the same that inform the plays composed by Glissenti for the female orphans of Venice's hospitals. The overarching recommendation that the *putti* focus their attention on the needs of the soul rather than on those of the body aims to foster 'sober and submissive conduct'.[32] In order to enforce such attitude, the *Ordini et capitoli* prioritise practices such as the 'interrogatorio' [interrogation] and the 'catechismo' [catechism], both based on the careful reading of the 'libro della dottrina' [the book of doctrine], which the boys were expected

---

28   On Miani, see *San Girolamo Miani nel V Centenario della nascita*, ed. by Gionvanni Scarabello (Venice: Studium Cattolico Veneziano, 1986), in particular the essay by Giuseppe Ellero, 'San Girolamo Miani e i Somaschi all'Ospedale dei Derelitti' (pp. 39–54); and Giovanni Bonacina, *Origine della congregazione dei Padri Somaschi: la compagnia pretridentina di San Girolamo Miani elevata ad ordine religioso* (Rome: Curia Generale Padri Somaschi, 2009); on the specific contribution of Miani and the Somaschians to the Venetian hospitals, see Pullan, *Rich and Poor*, pp. 257–63; on Miani in Bergamo, see Carlsmith, *A Renaissance Education*, pp. 177–213. More generally on the early development of the Somaschian congregation, see Marco Tentorio, *Saggio storico sullo sviluppo dell'ordine Somasco dal 1569 al 1650* (Rome: Archivio Storico Padri Somaschi, 2011).

29   Evidence of such practice, which has several features in common with that of Jesuit school drama, comes from the Roman hospital of the Incurabili; see Brian Pullan, 'La nuova filantropia nella Venezia cinquecentesca', in *Nel regno dei poveri*, ed. by Aikema and Mejiers, pp. 19–34 (p. 32); and Giuseppe Ellero, 'Personaggi e momenti di vita', in *Nel regno dei poveri*, ed. by Aikema and Mejiers, pp. 109–20 (p. 111).

30   Pullan, *Rich and Poor*, pp. 382–83.

31   Pullan, *Rich and Poor*, p. 402; see Giovanni Paolo da Como, *Ordini et capitoli della Compagnia dell'Oratorio il quale è nell'Hospitale de gli Incurabili in Venetia, circa il governo delle Schole de Putti, che sono in detta città* (Venice: Gabriel Giolito de' Ferrari, 1568).

32   *Ordini et capitoli*, p. 12; Pullan, *Rich and Poor*, p. 403.

to memorise.³³ Similarly, confession was deemed key to the spiritual training of the students, which would eventually lead to the appropriation of good habits and the practice of Christian life.³⁴

Other sources suggest that similar, though possibly stricter, educational patterns applied to the spiritual training of girls. Useful evidence comes from the *Constitutioni et regole* [Constitutions and rules] of the Zitelle, a religious shelter founded in 1559 by the Jesuit father, Benedetto Palmi. In spite of the later date of their publication (1701), the *Regole* outline a system that had been in place since the foundation of the institution, thus providing us with a useful element of comparison. Instruction in devotion, humility, obedience, purity, chastity, and in the examination of conscience was at the core of a six-year course that included 'disputations in Christian doctrine at Carnival time', '*tableaux vivants* depicting sacred subjects', as well as 'singing or versifying hymns'.³⁵ All in all, the organisation of female communities inside the hospitals recalled that of convents, especially in terms of education, with strict rules disciplining the lives of the orphans.³⁶

As far as the Derelitti is concerned, the regulations 'pertinenti al buon governo delle fie' [relevant to the good education of the girls] for the period 1549–75 found in Venice's Archivio di Stato tell a story made of systematic prohibitions and limitations in matters of clothing, attire, belongings, and interaction with the other *putte*.³⁷ The 'ordini' do not go into the specifics of recreational activities, which, as we know from later regulations, were very limited too.³⁸ The importance of reading skills, for instance, is only mentioned in relation to devotional practices, which did include singing. Whereas there is no explicit mention of activities such as the staging of plays until later, we know that performances of vocal music were already part of the endeavours pursued by the *putte* as early as in the 1570s. According to an oft-quoted document from April 1575, gifts and donations came to the Derelitti from patrons, who enjoyed the musical performances of the girls.³⁹ As is well known, this would become a famous feature of the Venetian hospitals throughout the Baroque age, reaching its peak in Antonio Vivaldi's lifetime.

While a significant amount of scholarly work exists on the musical activities of the hospitals and their role within the education of the orphans, almost nothing is known about the use of drama as part of the pedagogical agenda of those institutions, especially for the decades around 1600.⁴⁰ From this point of view, Glissenti's *favole*

---

33   *Ordini et capitoli*, pp. 25, 43.
34   *Ordini et capitoli*, pp. 38, 43.
35   Pullan, *Rich and Poor*, p. 389; see *Constitutioni et Regole della Casa delle Cittelle di Venezia* (Venice: Girolamo Albrizzi, 1701), pp. 49–55.
36   Ellero, 'Personaggi e momenti di vita', pp. 114–17.
37   Venice, Archivio di Stato, Ospedali e luoghi pii, Busta 910, folder 2, fols 1r–3r ('Coppia tratta dal libro delle parte et ordini dell'Hospedal d S. Zuan e Polo pertinenti al buon governo delle fie').
38   See, for instance, the 'Ordini per il buon governo della Casa delle Figliole, riformati per l'anno 1667' sampled in *Arte e musica all'Ospedaletto*, pp. 141–53 (pp. 147–49).
39   *Arte e musica all'Ospedaletto*, p. 50 (4 April 1575).
40   Cf. Denis Arnold, 'L'attività musicale', in *Nel regno dei poveri*, ed. by Aikema and Mejiers, pp. 99–108; more specifically focused on music at the Ospedaletto are *Arte e musica all'Ospedaletto*; and Giuseppe Ellero and Silvia Lunardon, *Guida all'Ospedaletto: itinerario storico, artistico e musicale della*

morali provide us with unique insight into a phenomenon that, primarily due to poor documentation, has escaped the attention of theatre studies. Indeed, differently from Latin school drama, the many facets of confessional theatre in the vernacular are still awaiting thorough investigations. Notable exceptions include Elissa Weaver's seminal study of convent theatre in Florence and Nerida Newbigin's groundbreaking work on sacred drama.[41] Convent theatre in Venice has also been the object of important studies such as those by Mary Laven, Christine Scippa Bhasin, and Jonathan Glixon.[42] However, without downplaying the similarities between convents and orphanages, the two contexts were significantly different. For one thing, only some of the 'daughters' of the hospitals would eventually become nuns. For most of them, moral discipline was not aimed at living in the cloister, but at navigating the many dangers of the secular world. Accordingly, as much as they focused on the rejection of earthly concerns in favour of spiritual preoccupations, Glissenti's morality plays tackled topics directly relevant to the handling of secular life, thus appealing, once printed, to broad audiences.

Easily turned into texts to be read and meditated upon, the *favole morali* joined the ever-growing devotional literature that flooded the book market in the age of the Counter-Reformation. It is largely through print that they circulated beyond the occasions on which they were performed. The fact is not surprising since, in many respects, these plays look more suitable for reading than for the stage: despite numerous moments in which they follow the trends of secular drama, including slapstick typical of the *commedia dell'arte*, they are characterised by lengthy sections that would undoubtedly prove rather tedious in performance (something the author himself implicitly acknowledged when *La Ragione sprezzata* was staged in a shortened version). After all, one should not forget that most of the plays were drawing on the novelle (or 'ragionamenti') that Glissenti included in the *Discorsi morali*, of which they preserved their quintessentially narrative features.[43]

Prints of the plays provide us with information on the kind of readership they were addressing beyond the performance as well. Those published between 1606 and 1616 (*La Ragione sprezzata, L'Andrio, Il bacio della Giustitia e della Pace, Il Diligente, La Morte innamorata* and *L'Androtoo*) are introduced by paratextual materials directly connected with the author. Glissenti dedicates *La Ragione sprezzata* to the Duchess

---

Chiesa e Ospedale dei Derelitti (Venice: I.R.E., 2005).
41   Elissa Weaver, *Convent Theatre in Early Modern Italy: Spiritual Fun and Learning for Women* (Cambridge: Cambridge University Press, 2007), especially the chapters 'Renaissance Culture in Italian Convents, 1450–1650', pp. 9–48; 'The Convent Theatre Tradition', pp. 49–95; and, even more relevant to the present study, 'Beyond Tuscany', pp. 216–37; Newbigin, *Making a Play for God*.
42   Mary Laven, *Virgins of Venice: Broken Vows and Cloistered Lives in the Renaissance Convent* (London: Viking, 2002), pp. 132–37; Jonathan E. Glixon, *Mirrors of Heaven or Worldly Theaters? Venetian Nunneries and Their Music* (Oxford: Oxford University Press, 2017), pp. 251–65. See, also, Christine Scippa Bhasin, 'Nuns on Stage in Counter-Reformation Venice (1570–1750)' (unpublished PhD dissertation, Northwestern University, 2012); and 'Prostitutes, Nuns, Actresses: Breaking the Convent Wall in Seventeenth-Century Venice', *Theatre Journal*, 66.1 (2014), 19–35; Charlotte Cover Moy, 'The Enclosed Renaissance: Intellectual and Spiritual Learning in Early Modern Venetian Convents' (unpublished PhD dissertation, Northwestern University, 2018).
43   The point is made, more broadly about this genre of works, by Glixon, *Mirrors of Heaven*, p. 265.

of Mantua, whereas *Il bacio della Giustitia e della Pace* is dedicated to Contarina Leoni with explicit mention of the female readership targeted by the author: 'Eccovi Clarissima Signora la Novelluccia, per le vostre fanciulle da me promessa' [Here, milady, is the little novella that I promised for your girls].[44] When dedicatory letters and notes to the readers are not written by Glissenti himself, they are penned by family members or friends. *L'Andrio* and *Il Diligente* are dedicated to Bartolomeo Buontempelli, with dedicatory letters by Giovan Giunio Parisio and Glissenti's sister, Glissentia, respectively; *La Morte innamorata*, as recalled above, is dedicated to Henry Wotton by Glissenti's niece, Elisabetta; *L'Androtoo* bears a dedication by Bartolomeo Ginammi to Marino Zane, in which the author's recent passing is mentioned. The four *favole* printed after Glissenti's death feature dedicatory letters by the publishers, Marco and Bartolomeo Ginammi, addressing individuals not directly related to the playwright: Bernardo Giordani, guardian of San Francesco della Vigna (*La giusta Morte*); Pietro Contarini (*Lo Spensierato*); Ottavio Rivarola (*Il mercato overo la fiera della vita humana*); and one Giovanni Stanauser (*La Sarcodinamia*).

The fact that Ginammi, a publisher specialising in devotional literature, decided to reprint most of the plays in the 1630s indicates that they enjoyed a remarkable success in the book market.[45] Omitting the references to family and friends found in the editions printed during Glissenti's lifetime, Ginammi addresses a kind of readership that, while different from the one originally conceived by the author, shares with it a markedly gendered identity. The 1634 edition of *L'Andrio* is instructive in this regard. The booklet is issued with a dedication to Sister Maria Perpetua da Camoro, 'monaca professa' in the Venetian monastery of San Zaccaria. The short epistle stresses, perhaps for advertisement's sake, the extraordinary success of Glissenti's works:

> L'opere del Signor Fabio Glissenti si sono rese ammirabili all'universale, inserendo la dottrina col diletto, e la moralità con le piacevolezze. Le stampe, gareggiando con le scene, l'hanno portate infinite volte alla luce sempre con applausi. Ma crescendo il desiderio di così degna lettura, ne sono mancate le coppie [*sic*], ed in particolare della presente, intitolata *l'Andrio*, ch'io consagro al merito di Vostra Signoria Illustrissima e Madre Reverendissima.[46]

> [The works of Fabio Glissenti have been admired by all, for they unite knowledge and pleasure, morality and pleasantness. In competition with the stage, prints have brought them to light several times, always with applause. Yet, due to growing desire for this worthy reading, copies have been scarcely available, especially of the present play, entitled *L'Andrio*, which I dedicate to your illustrious ladyship and most reverend mother.]

---

44   Fabio Glissenti, *Il bacio della Giustitia e della Pace. Favola morale* (Venice: Giovanni Alberti, 1607), fol. [A2]^r. In the dedication letter, the addressee and 'all other noblewomen' ('tutte l'altre Gentildonne') are identified as the most suitable audience for the subject matter of the work.

45   Napoli, *L'impresa del libro*, pp. 58–68; see Napoli's remark (p. 62) about the affinity between Glissenti's plays and those by Vincenzo Piccino, the author of sacred dramas printed by Ginammi. As Napoli explains, these works were viable for both recitation and reading, with productive intersections of educational and recreational scopes.

46   Fabio Glissenti, *L'Andrio cioè l'huomo virile, favola morale* (Venice: Tommaso Ginammi, 1634), fol. A2^r.

In a similar vein, the edition of *Lo Spensierato* from the same year is dedicated to Sister Maria Francesca Coccina, 'monaca professa' in the monastery of San Rocco and Santa Margherita. The epistle identifies religious women as the ideal reading public for the text, and justifies the reprint by mentioning the high demand for the work, which was apparently not available on the market any more. Nuns are said to be demanding such work because of the 'morality' that informs it and the 'pleasure' that comes with it ('per la moralità et per il dilettevole che in essa si ritrova').[47] The remark that the subject matter of the play is consistent with its religious concerns ('s'accompagna con i suoi religiosi pensieri') indicates a consumption of the text that shies away from the actual occasion of the performance. The play thus invites forms of individual meditative reading and 'inner' staging which scholarly narratives of early modern theatre associate with the notion of 'closet drama', a notion that entails reading experiences similar to the ones surveyed in my discussion of the works of Andreini, Romito Pellegrino, and Bonaventura Morone.[48]

The Poetics and Performance of Purgation

The moral dimension of Glissenti's *favole* is central to the playwright's poetics, which I propose to describe as a poetics of reform through purgation. Alongside the dialogue between the Philosopher and the Actress in the *Discorsi morali*, which can be read as a declaration of poetics paving the way for Glissenti's direct experience with drama, the idea that theatre should be conducive to moral and doctrinal improvement returns in other texts that help us assess the author's claim. These include some of Glissenti's most outspoken statements as well as a diverse set of paratextual materials. Penned by others, these paratexts shed light on the scope of the *favole morali* both within the context of the performance and within the practice of individual reading that, eventually, constituted their main channel of circulation.

Particularly useful for outlining Glissenti's poetics are the dedication letter of *La Ragione sprezzata* to Eleonora de' Medici and the note to the readers that introduces the same play. By presenting his 'morale operetta' [little moral work] to the Duchess of Mantua, Glissenti highlights the primary inspiration of the text: the phrasing stresses the moral import implied by the term 'favola', with the adjective 'morale' referring to the play's ability to affect the morality of both performers and audience. Within the celebratory framework of the dedication to Eleonora, who is praised for her moral profile and exemplary spiritual life ('vita molto spirituale e per Christiana religione molto essemplare'), the author alludes to the benefits that the consumption of the play would bring to those in the court who wish to conduct themselves according to Christian doctrine ('comune utilità di chi brama viver spiritualmente e da huomo da bene, conforme').[49]

---

47   Fabio Glissenti, *Lo Spensierato fatto pensoroso, favola morale* (Venice: Giovanni Antonio Ginammi, 1634), c. A2r–v.
48   See the examples discussed in Chapter 1, pp. 63–78; on the notion of closet drama and its evolution, see *Closet Drama: History, Theory, Form*, ed. by Catherine Burroughs (London: Routledge, 2018).
49   *La Ragione sprezzata*, fols A3v–[A4]r.

The allusion to the 'utilità' pursued by the play dovetails with the note to the readers, which opens under the aegis of radical modesty. The play is presented as faulty in terms of both composition and style ('difettosa, così nella compositione, o vogliamo dire inventione, come nella stessa arte poetica'), for the art of poetry requires good verses, beautifully chosen words, convenient examples and similes, plausible metaphors, and all those ornaments that win the audience over by stirring emotions and passions.[50] Not only does the author acknowledge his lack of poetical expertise, but he also claims that his 'invention' ('invenzione') intentionally eschews poetical norms. The reader is warned that the doctor-turned-playwright has taken several liberties, including the handling of the plot, which, contravening the unity of action and leaving aside any attempt to realism, follows the entire course of human life, from the protagonist's youth to his old age.[51] Stressing once again his unfamiliarity with the business of poetry, Glissenti pre-empts some of the criticisms that the play might raise.[52] Accordingly, he explains that the work is but a Carnival divertissement, not meant for publication.[53] It is only due to the printer's insistence following the unexpected success of the performance at the Derelitti that Glissenti has eventually agreed to publish the play. His main ambition, though, remains that of bringing some utility to his audience, as evidenced by his remarks on the effects produced by the staging:

> che habbia dilettato et apportato piacere a gli uditori, l'isperienza l'ha dimostrato, et il testimonio di quelli, che l'hanno udita ne rende indubitata fede; che sia stata utile, è cosa chiara, che quell'Hospitale per questa Rappresentatione ne ha havuto, in più volte più di due mila ducati in dono da i pietosi uditori.[54]
>
> [that the play pleased the audience was demonstrated by the actual experience of it and proved beyond doubt by the testimony of those who attended; it

---

50 *La Ragione sprezzata*, fols A5^{r-v}: 'la sonorità de i versi', 'vaghe e leggiadre parole', 'essempi o similitudini proprie', 'traslati probabili verisimili', 'rapire a forza gli animi di chi leggono alla credenza, alla commiseratione, all'allegrezza, et altre così fatte passioni'.
51 *La Ragione sprezzata*, fol. A5^v: 'Io in vero confesso, che questa mia rappresentatione ha tutti i sudetti, e molti altri mancamenti; poiché è fatta contra le regole di chi ha insegnato il modello di così fatte cose, e quanto all'attione rappresentata nella lunghezza della vita dell'huomo, e quanto all'altre circostanze, che vi si richiedono' [I acknowledge that this play has all the aforementioned faults, and many others, for it is composed against the rules established by those who have set the model for this kind of works: this applies both to the action represented through the length of man's life and to the other features required by the genre].
52 Ibid.: 'io non faccio professione di Poesia (essendo io occupato in altro più tedioso essercitio) come che mai non habbia studiato tal arte Poetica, o che meno per natura io me le trovi inchinato, poiché in verità confesso non haver mai a' miei giorni composto un tal sonetto, non che saputo render ragione di quello' [I am not a professional poet, as I am busy with another, more tedious commitment; I have never studied the art of poetry and am less than inclined to it by nature, for I admit that I have never composed a sonnet nor have I been able to explain one].
53 *La Ragione sprezzata*, fol. A6^r: 'questa favola me la posi a scriver un carnovale, per solo passatempo, come sogliono far tal'hora alcuni, che ritrovandosi a balli, quantunque non habbiano appresa l'arte del ballare, tuttavia o per diporto, o invitati si levano a danzare' [I endeavoured to write this fable during carnival, as a pastime, as do those who, happening to be at a ball, even if they do not know the art of dance, they nonetheless join the ball either for pleasure or because they are invited to].
54 Ibid.

is also evident that it has been useful, since the hospital, thanks to this play, received more than two thousand ducats from the pitiful audience over several performances.]

Without diminishing the utility of the money cashed in by the hospital, there is another kind of utility that Glissenti highlights, more concerned with spiritual rather than with material earnings:

> Ma parlando di quella utilità che deve essere propria di simili favole, che è del *purgar gli animi da i vitii et invitarli alla virtù*, certamente che utilissima è riuscita: poi che ha spaventato di sì fatta maniera molti, et altri posti in sì fatta *consideratione de i fatti loro*, che quello, che non hanno fatto molte e frequentate persuasioni di eloquenti Predicatori, et le rigide ammonitioni di Prelati, ha fatto la presente rappresentatione, col *porli innanti a gli occhi l'essempio* del fine loro; che mossi più dall'essempio che dalle parole, si sono rissoluti a *confessarsi*, e *chiamarsi in colpa* di molti eccessi loro, che per più anni se n'erano passati prima senza alcuna *consideratione, o rissentimento delle sue colpe*.[55]

> [Speaking of the usefulness that fits similar fables, that is, *purging the souls from vice and spurring them to virtue*, it certainly proved most useful: indeed, this play frightened many and led others to *consider their own actions*; as such, it accomplished what many and well-attended sermons by preachers and strict reprimands by priests were not able to; it has done so by *bringing the example of their own fate in front of their eyes*; moved by the example more than by words, the audience — who for many years lived without *considering or regretting their sins* — resolved to *confess* and *acknowledge the guilt* caused by their many excesses.]

This passage offers invaluable insight into Glissenti's poetics: according to a strictly Christianised interpretation of Aristotle's *catharsis*, the play is said to be useful because it produces the purgation of the soul from the vices.[56] (Incidentally, the Aristotelian flair of the statement resonates with the intermingling of pleasure, fear, and dread mentioned in the manuscript copy of *La Morte innamorata*, where the successful reception of the performance is indeed measured in terms of the emotional work triggered in the audience).[57]

By aiming to purge the souls of the attendees of their sins and push them towards virtue, this kind of play proves consistent with the reform of drama outlined by Glissenti in the *Discorsi morali*. More broadly it fits the idea of guiding the audience through processes of self-cleansing, which both the *favole morali* and the *Discorsi* share with other forms of spiritual and devotional literature in the period. In that respect, three features of the situation described by Glissenti in the preface to *La Ragione sprezzata* are particularly illuminating. First, the acknowledgment that theatrical performances may be more effective than the homilies and sermons of preachers and priests. Second, the idea that what actually moves the audience is

---

55 *La Ragione sprezzata*, fols A7^{r-v}, emphasis mine.
56 Arist. *Poet.* 1449b 24–29.
57 Venice, Biblioteca Nazionale Marciana, MS Ital. IX.316, fol. 2^r: 'Fu recitata la presente favola morale [...] con applauso grandissimo di tutta la città, ancor che il fine d'essa sia mesto, et apportasse pavura et terrore a molti' [The present moral fable was represented [...] with great applause of the entire city, in spite of its sad ending and the fear and terror it brought to many].

the vivid representation of *exempla*. Third, the practices of self-examination and confession that, promoted by the play, lead to repentance and, eventually, to the soul's salvation. Glissenti argues that, thanks to the play, people who had been spiritually negligent were brought back onto the path of virtue. Differently from the secular performances criticised in the *Discorsi*, solely focused on light-hearted entertainment, the *favole morali* are meant to have a profound impact on the audience's conscience. From this point of view, the lexicon mobilised by Glissenti is very eloquent and deserves special attention, for, as I will show, it returns in a dramatised form in the plays themselves.

If confession ('confessarsi'), acknowledgment of faults ('chiamarsi in colpa') and remorse ('rissentimento delle sue colpe') evoke the language of catechism and Christian doctrine in the aftermath of Trent, another term used by Glissenti, 'consideratione' (specifically, in the phrasing 'consideratione de i fatti loro', consideration of their actions), recalls a current of spiritual literature which drew on the medieval notion of *consideratio*, as outlined by Bernard of Clairvaux in his treatise *On Consideration* (c. 1150).[58] Bernard's discussion of the term, which sets the investigative nature of consideration against the permanence afforded by contemplation, includes remarks on cognate practices such as self-examination and the consideration of things invisible. Revamped in conjunction with the religious reforms of the sixteenth century, this tradition contributed to (and merged with) the broader revival of spiritual practices such as those promoted by Loyola's *Exercises*. The very notion of *consideratio*, however, was key not only to the Jesuit model of spiritual exercise, but also to the broad tradition of spiritual literature initiated by texts such as the treatise *De Imitatione Christi* [The Imitation of Christ].[59] Widely read, translated into most vernacular languages, and regularly reprinted throughout the sixteenth and seventeenth centuries, this book reached an audience broader than the one targeted by Loyola. Less erudite and sophisticated in terms of spiritual training, the average profile of readers of *De Imitatione Christi* was likely very similar to that of the audience addressed by Glissenti. Furthermore, the playwright's concern with moral and spiritual reform resonates with many of the works that, in the footsteps of Clairvaux and *De Imitatione Christi*, focused on practices of consideration, self-examination, repentance, and conversion. Among these numerous works, it is worth recalling those by the Spanish theologian, Luis de Granada (1504–1588), which were translated into Italian (as well as into other languages) and circulated throughout the sixteenth and seventeenth centuries. As I will suggest in my discussion of Glissenti's plays, works such as Granada's *Specchio della vita humana* [Mirror of Human Life] and *Devotissime meditationi* [Most Devout Meditations], which focus on contemplation, *contemptus mundi*, and penitence, also feature rhetorical devices that, alongside those showcased by the Ignatian exercises, seem to have influenced the playwright's dramatisation of spiritual fights.[60]

58 Bernard of Clairvaux, *On Consideration*, trans. by George Lewis (Oxford: Clarendon, 1908).
59 For an overview of the broad circulation of *De imitatione Christi*, which has been attributed to authors as diverse as Thomas à Kempis and Jean de Gerson, see Maximilian Von Habsburg, *Catholic and Protestant Translations of the Imitatio Christi, 1425–1650: From Late Medieval Classic to Early Modern Bestseller* (London: Routledge, 2011).
60 Luis de Granada, *Specchio della vita humana, nel quale si contiene il libro della contemplatione, et il*

As the paratext of *La Ragione sprezzata* indicates, the consistency of Glissenti's moral agenda hinges upon the idea that the pursuit of virtue and its performance should be conceived as one and the same; in fact, it is the convergence of the two that triggers the disciplining function of drama. Evidence that such an agenda was key to the performances held at the hospitals of Venice comes from the documents relevant to the staging of *La Morte innamorata* and *Il Diligente* at the Derelitti. As I recalled above, the manuscript of *La Morte innamorata* and the print of Giacomo Castellano's *Rime* tell us that the plays were framed by spiritual madrigals explicitly crafted for the occasion. These poems, which were not included in the printed editions of the *favole morali*, constituted what I suggest to call the 'paratext of the performance'. In other words, as my brief discussion will demonstrate, their function is comparable to that of the liminal pieces that introduce the plays in the printed editions, a substantial difference being their focus on the performance. The introductory madrigals were meant to be performed 'nel calar della tenda' [when the curtains were lifted], thus providing moral introductions to the plays as well as overviews of the plots. Let us have a look at the one that introduces *La Morte innamorata*:

> Caggiano homai le tenebrose tende
> e di pomposa scena
> il superbo apparato a noi si mostri.
> Mirino gl'occhi nostri
> del Mondo le grandezze,
> dell'Huomo l'allegrezze;
> mentre funesta, e altera,
> horrida, infausta, e fera
> vien, ch'ogn'intorno altrui terror apporte,
> fintasi amante, l'inimica Morte.[61]

[May the dark curtains fall down and the beautiful setting of the sumptuous scene be revealed to us; may our eyes observe the great things of the World and the joys of Man, while Death arrives, frightening everybody, baleful and proud, horrid, fateful, and feral, after pretending to be a lover.]

The audience is invited to admire the 'sumptuous stage' on which the action is going to take place. The exhortation to look at World's wealth, Man's joys and Death's deceitful courtship (pretending to be a lover, she brings her beloved's life to an end) is, in fact, a recommendation for the audience to consider carefully the *exemplum* unfolding before their eyes. If the verb 'mirare' ('Mirino gl'occhi nostri') evokes the rhetoric of *evidentia*, the trope is used literally here: the act of looking at the scene merges with the inner consideration of its meaning, for they coincide in the act of attending the performance. The moral suasion promoted by Castellano's

---

manuale di diverse orationi (Venice: Gabriele Giolito, 1568); the Italian translation by Giovanni Miranda was reprinted many times; and *Devotissime meditationi per i giorni della settimana* (Venice: Gabriele Giolito, 1568), translation by Pietro Lauro of Modena, with many reprints over the following decades; on Granada, see Urbano Alonso del Campo, *Vida y obra de fray Luis de Granada* (Salamanca: Editorial San Esteban, 2005).

61   Venice, Biblioteca Nazionale Marciana, MS Ital. IX.316, fol. 3^r; the same poem, with no textual variants in Castellano, *Rime*, fol. B3^v.

madrigal (and possibly achieved through the play) is also at the core of another poem relevant to the performance, 'O miseri mortali'. Not included in the manuscript, it appears alongside the previous one in the print of Castellano's poems.[62] Given that *La Morte innamorata* does not end with a chorus, it is likely that the poem was meant to be delivered as the concluding piece of the performance. While the introductory madrigal addressed the audience as part of a community into which the speaker included themselves, the latter sounds more strictly prescriptive. The addressees are identified as 'miseri mortali' [miserable humans] pursued by the seduction of the World, vividly evoked through the image of a horseman spurring his steed ('e 'l Mondo, oimè, v'aggiunge al fianco sproni'). They are urged to reject earthly pleasures ('fuggite | questi vani diletti') as well as being invited to acknowledge the inevitability of Death ('Morir convien, convien lasciar la salma') and the judgment that comes with her; hence, the need to leave the body, having consecrated one's soul to God ('felice quel ch'a Dio consacra l'alma').

Castellano's madrigals provide the play with a fitting frame, according to which the spectators are first invited to look at what happens on stage and then reminded of the relevance of the plot to their own spiritual lives. The madrigals are thus supposed to contribute to the 'purgation' that I have identified as the main aim of Glissenti's moralities. The same function is performed by Castellano's madrigals for Glissenti's *Il Diligente*, which, differently from *La Morte innamorata*, ends well. The introductory poem ('S'affretti homai, s'affretti, e 'l chiaro albergo') is an invitation to reject idleness and diligently pursue the path of virtue, with a focus on the idea that perseverance is key to the performance and acquisition of virtuous habits.[63] Consistently with the plot of the play, the spiritual conflict is presented here through the opposition of two human types, the 'otioso' [idle] and the 'sollecito' [diligent]. After the successful denouement of the play the concept is reiterated in the conclusive madrigal ('Co'l patir, co'l soffrir'), where the deeds of the protagonist are celebrated as a successful *exemplum* that the audience should follow.[64] He who rejects vanity and pursues the Good is a mirror, which all mortals should contemplate in order to understand that the path of virtue is indeed laborious, yet supremely rewarding ('Tu vero essempio raro | specchio lucido, e chiaro | sei de' mortali; onde ciascun comprende | che con fatica sol virtù s'apprende'). Whereas the metaphor of the mirror is far from uncommon in the literary tradition that Glissenti draws on, it acquires particular significance in this context for two main reasons. First, as is the case with the other metaphors examined in this study, the mirror is returned its literal meaning in Glissenti's dramatic universe (we will see that a mirror appears as a real prop in *La Ragione sprezzata*). Second, the metaphorical image of the mirror reminds us that the semantic field of vision is the one that frames the spiritual experience promoted by allegorical theatre.

The declarations of poetics embedded in the paratext of the performance as witnessed by Castellano's madrigals are consistent with the dynamics that inform

---

62 Castellano, *Rime*, fol. B4^r.
63 Ibid.
64 Castellano, *Rime*, fol. B4^v.

the transition of the *favole morali* from stage to print. The performative dynamic at work in the staging of the plays is conveyed through different textual tools when it comes to the printed editions and their consumption through reading. Alongside dedication letters and notes to the readers, each printed play is introduced by a summary ('argomento') and allegorical explanation of the plot ('allegoria della favola') that convey the pedagogical function of the work. The peculiar features of Glissenti's poetics, though, also come to the fore through poetical pieces that praise the playwright's poetical commitment. This is the case of sonnets included in the prints of *Il Diligente* and *L'Andrio*. In a way, the sonnets replace the paratextual function that, on the occasion of the performance, was taken on by Castellano's madrigals.

In the case of *Il Diligente*, the anonymous sonnet praises the author by highlighting what distinguishes Glissenti's work from that of professional *letterati*. Echoing Glissenti's own statements, the sonnet contrasts his humble style ('parlare humile') and the eloquence of those who seduce the ears of their audience ('Altri con elegante, e vago stile, | Per lusingar l'orecchie').[65] Even if it does not look appealing at first, Glissenti's 'mysterious' manner purges the affections of the audience by presenting good teachings under the cover of poor style ('il bel coprendo sotto mostra vile'). Unlike the Lucretian method, according to which sweetness is used to conceal the bitterness of the medicine, the 'beautiful' content is given here a humble shape. Instead of being concerned with the stylistic issues that usually occupy poets, Glissenti focuses on the goodness of the subject matter. As it happens with a goldmine, whose precious core is hidden by rough stone, the 'poor and humble style' ('negletto e basso') covers the 'great treasure' ('ampio tesoro') of 'moral discipline', where the phrasing 'moral disciplina' is particularly eloquent within the context of Counter Reformation culture, entailing both the private and the public spheres: not only does Glissenti favour a process of catharsis internal to one's conscience ('Purghi [...] i nostri affetti'), but, by doing so, he also prevents his addressees from misbehaving ('l'alme dal mal far arresta').

If the playwright's priority remains the soul's salvation after death, the relevance of such dynamics to everyday life is not negligible either. These include forms of self-discipline that, for instance, were key to the education of the female orphans for whom the plays were originally written. In this respect, the defence of Glissenti's humble style goes beyond the *topos modestiae*. As Giovan Giunio Parisio puts it in the dedication letter of *L'Andrio*, the stylistic qualities of the play ('stile dimesso e umile') fit the humble status and abilities of the girls of the Incurabili, who were supposed to perform it.[66] At the same time, evidence of the author's pedagogical scope, as well as its being part of the broader educational strategies pursued within the orphanages of Venice (specifically in matters of reading), come from within the plays themselves. Through a light-hearted *mise en abyme* of the text, the protagonist of the play *Il Diligente* — whose name is indeed 'Sollecito' (literally, solicitous, with

---

[65] Fabio Glissenti, *Il Diligente overo il Sollecito favola morale* (Venice: Giovanni Alberti, 1608), fol. A4^v.
[66] *L'Andrio*, fol. A3^v.

obvious moral and religious nuance) — stumbles on a booklet, which he begins to read carefully, and which proves key to his journey towards virtue. The booklet is, ironically enough, entitled 'Il Diligente, frottola morale' [The Diligent Man, moral frottola]. Sollecito's engagement with it is indicative of the individual work that every devout reader is meant to be performing on their own:

> Ricolsi ancor queste cartuccie, in cui
> involte fur per sorte alcune merci
> [...]
> apena si scorgean che fosser scritte.
> Io pur le colsi e serviran (mi penso)
> per apprendere qualche avvertimento,
> che potrebbe giovarmi in qualche tempo;
> ché non è storia o favola sì vile
> da cui non possa ogn'uno facilmente
> talhor cavarne qualche buon costrutto.
> Ma vo' veder l'inscrittione hor hora.
> 'Il Diligente, frottola morale,
> per gli otiosi scritta e data in luce'.
> A fè, l'inscrittion non mi dispiace.
> Il contenuto forse ancor sia meglio.
> Io me la tengo cara, e mi fia libro
> da legger quando men sarò occupato,
> che per quant'io n'udì già dir mia madre,
> molto non sa chi molti libri tiene:
> ma chi pochi ne studia e ben l'intende.[67]

> [I just gathered these papers, which were used to wrap some stuff [...] they are barely legible. I picked them up and I believe they will be useful to learn some lessons which might benefit me one day. In fact, there is no history or fable so vile that nothing good cannot be found in it. Let me now consider the title. 'The conscientious man, moral frottola, written and published to the benefit of idlers'. In fact, I quite like the title. I will cherish it and will read it when I am less busy. As I heard from my mother, it is not by owning many books that one knows a lot, but by studying few of them and understanding them well.]

Far from being a mere wink to the audience, the booklet found by Sollecito plays a significant role within the narrative. As a source of wisdom and a moral guide, the book reappears in Act III, where Sollecito explains to his mother, Necessity, that he has studied it thoroughly, finding it rich in 'sentenze' [maxims], 'buoni avisi' [good advice] and 'dotti avvertimenti' [learned warnings].[68] In Act IV, on the occasion of another conversation between Sollecito and Necessity, revolving this time around the opportunity for him to marry Virtue, the protagonist provides a definition of virtue, found in the booklet, that focuses on the studiousness and the good works that make one virtuous.[69] Further references to the benefits of reading works such as the one found by Sollecito are made throughout the play,

---

67 *Il Diligente* 1.6, p. 24–25.
68 *Il Diligente* 3.6, p. 71.
69 *Il Diligente* 4.7, p. 97–98.

with insistence on the importance of keeping their teachings in mind, so as to cultivate virtue and perform it.[70] In a paradoxical turn of events, customary within Glissenti's allegorical dramaturgy, the 'virtuous' worth of the booklet is sanctioned enthusiastically by the character of Virtue herself, who, after coming into possession of the text accidentally, finds its teachings most valuable.

In a productive short circuit between the plot, the booklet mentioned in it, and the actual edition of the play, the very copy of *Il Diligente*, which the reader holds in their hand, includes illustrations that are meant to reinforce the moral teachings of the story. By turning to some of the woodcuts already used in the *Discorsi*, the publisher, possibly advised by the playwright himself, included one image at the beginning of each act. While the scenes represented in the woodcuts do not correspond to the dramatic situations in the text, they are evocative of the broader argument of the play: namely, the looming presence of death in human life and the importance of turning to virtuous deeds rather than following the charm of sensual pleasures [Fig. 3.1].

Differently from the images that illustrate, for instance, Andreini's *L'Adamo*, these woodcuts are not meant to evoke the theatrical context of the performance. Consistently with the iconographic apparatus of the *Discorsi morali*, they are conceived as evocative of the moral teachings of the play. They work as memory aids functional to the reader's individual consumption of the text and possibly conducive to the reader's individual process of moral and spiritual improvement, yet another facet of the 'poetics of purgation' pursued by the morality play.

Spiritual *topoi*

The moral and doctrinal dimension of Glissenti's plays is best illustrated by the thematic threads and dramatic situations that run across the entire corpus. Two of them come to the plays directly from the *Discorsi morali*: the Christian preparation for death and the claim of free will's centrality in all things human. As is the case with the *Discorsi*, one theme is tightly linked to the other; indeed, it is through their own choices that individuals come to face death either prepared or unprepared. While the plays highlight the weakness of Man, specifically his inclination to follow Sense rather than Reason, Glissenti seizes every opportunity to remind the audience that, in the end, Man has complete mastery over his own will, hence his full responsibility when it comes to the handling of morals. In this respect, one of Glissenti's most instructive statements comes from the prologue of *L'Andrio*, which, delivered by the personification of Free Will, outlines the doctrinal core of the entire corpus. According to the most traditional features of allegorical prologues in early modern drama, Free Will does not disclose his identity right away, but plays with the audience's expectations and describes himself through a sort of enigma:

> [...] Per sapere
> forse chi son così ne state attenti?
> Hor ve 'l vo' dir: io son la maggior cosa,

---

70   *Il Diligente* 4.10, pp. 105–07; 5.7, pp. 129–32.

ATTO PRIMO.
SCENA PRIMA.

Necessità madre, Sollecito figliuolo.

Nec. Sollecito figliuol, quātūque io sappia,
Che a quei che son ne le miserie nuol
Posti in humile stato, & anco priui   (si,
De le commodità di questo mondo;
                                    SA-

FIG. 3.1. Glissenti, *Il Diligente* (1608), p. 1

> c'habbi Iddio dato a voi; quella pur dico
> con cui può l'Huom assomigliarsi a lui,
> salir al cielo, e fra beati spirti
> fortunato acquistarsi eccelso loco;
> quella dich'io, con cui può parimente
> (del Demonio seguendo i feri inganni)
> meritar in suo danno acerba morte
> ne l'aspre eterne fiamme dell'Inferno.[71]

[Why are you so attentive? To know who I am? I will tell you: I am the greatest gift that God gave to you; the one through which Man may resemble God, ascend to heaven, and gain a sublime seat among the blessed spirits; the gift by means of which, following Satan's feral deceits, one will deserve untimely death in the harsh eternal flames of hell.]

Just in case the audience does not realise who this is, Free Will eventually makes it explicit ('V'ho detto chi mi sia. Ma se v'aggrada | meglio saperlo ancor, ecco lo scopro. | Libero son de l'Huom Arbitrio e voglia').[72] The following step is an illustration of his appearance in relation to the plot of the play. Upholding the structural function of the theatrical metaphor that we have seen at work in the *Discorsi*, Free Will outlines the two paths of human life (salvation and perdition) as the two terms of a choice that is performed on stage:

> Questo teatro, questa scena, o campo
> è mia habitatione, ed è franchiggia
> sola de l'Huom, che contro i suoi nimici
> può in questo loco vincitor portarsi;
> de l'Intelletto seguendo il consiglio.
> Qui parimente può restar perdente
> il miser Huom e la vittoria in mano
> lasciar a' suoi nemici, se del Senso
> si disporrà seguir gli empi appetiti.[73]

[This theatre, scene or piazza is my home, and it is up to Man to defeat his enemies following Intellect's advice. Miserable Man, he can easily be a loser too when, following Sense's impious desires, he leaves the victory in his enemies' hands.]

The psychomachia that unfolds in the 'campo' of Free Will — the setting of the play is a clear allusion to an exquisitely Venetian urban space — is not simply about angels and demons competing for the control of Man[74]. Rather, it is Man's Will that, helped by Intellect, is expected to choose between Good and Evil.[75] At the

---

71 *L'Andrio*, fol. A6ʳ.
72 Ibid.: 'I told you who I am. But if you wish to know it better, here it is: I am Man's Free Will and desire'.
73 *L'Andrio*, fol. A6ᵛ.
74 *L'Andrio*, fol. A5ᵛ.
75 The trope of the psychomachia is evoked explicitly in the prologue; see *L'Andrio*, fol. A6ᵛ: 'In questa dunque libera campagna | hassi da far, a la presenza vostra, | da demon contro l'Huom aspra battaglia; | che 'l loco franco a tal effetto io presto, | io qui padrin starò (quantunque ascosto)' [In this free land, in your presence, a harsh fight is about to take place between Man and Satan; I offer this free space for the duel, and I will stay here, though hidden, as Man's second].

same time, the role played by divine Grace is not secondary, in that it is Grace herself (a veritable *dea ex machina*) who unveils the misdeeds of World and Pomp, paving the way for Man's salvation.[76]

In his assessment of human nature, Glissenti does not hide the limits of Man: alongside physical vulnerability, which is brought on stage through various allegorical characters, the actual counterpart to Free Will is Inclination ('Inclinazione'). It is Inclination who delivers the prologue of *La Sarcodinamia*, a play in which, differently from *L'Andrio*, man's spiritual component is defeated by Flesh. After stating that it is impossible to recognise anyone based on what they wear (a theme that recurs in most of Glissenti's plays), Inclination introduces herself to the audience, focusing in particular on her desire to experience new things and her ability to manipulate Man's affections.[77] If Free Will is ultimately responsible for making choices, Inclination often pushes towards the wrong ones. In the conflict between Soul and Flesh ('grand'e fier contrasto | fra Spirito e Carne'), Inclination leans towards the latter, revealing an antagonistic stance vis-à-vis those components of the human soul (Discourse, Intellect, Memory) who are instead summoned to support Free Will and defend him from Sense's temptations.

Dichotomies such as those between Free Will and Inclination, good life and sin, mirror those found in Glissenti's *Discorsi*. As recalled above, the plots of the plays draw mostly on the novelle narrated by the Philosopher. Despite obvious generic differences, both the novelle and the plays function as *exempla* conducive to the audience's moral and spiritual enhancement. As such, the storylines, which are rather repetitive, can be divided into two main groups: on the one hand, those that, by having Death as their protagonist, strive to make her presence in human life less unpleasant; and on the other hand, following in the footsteps of the psychomachia tradition, those that stage the conflict between the spiritual component of Man (Soul, Spirit, the intellectual functions) and his earthly dimension (Sense, Flesh, World, Pomp).[78] This bipartition, which does not exclude overlaps, applies to the plays as well. Some of them focus on rejecting the Senses while prioritising spiritual goods (*L'Andrio*, *Il Diligente*, *L'Androtoo*, *Lo Spenserato*, *La Sarcodinamia*); others concentrate instead on the *meditatio mortis* by insisting on the inescapability of death (*La Morte innamorata*, *La giusta Morte*, *Il mercato overo la fiera della Vita humana*). Devoted to a combination of moral and civic allegory is *Il bacio della Giustitia e della Pace*. A dramatisation of the famous line from Psalm 85.10, 'Justice and Peace kiss one another', the play celebrates the harmony that informs the Venetian government, thus echoing the political undertones that characterised Glissenti's description of Venice as 'theatre of the world' in the *Discorsi morali*. More or less *sui generis* is Glissenti's longest and most ambitious play, *La Ragione sprezzata*, which brings together the tropes of the psychomachia and the triumph of Death through a universal eschatological perspective.

76 For the intervention of divine Grace, see the last four scenes of Act v.
77 Fabio Glissenti, *La Sarcodinamia cioè la possanza della carne favola morale* (Venice: Marco Ginammi, 1620), fols A5^v–A6^r.
78 The relationship between the plots of the plays and those of the novelle included in *Discorsi morali* had been summarily illustrated by Neri, 'Le moralità di Fabio Glissenti'.

If the plots stick to straightforward narrative models inherited from the tradition of medieval allegory and sacred drama, the peculiar way in which Glissenti revisits the trope is best exemplified by the settings that he imagines for the plays. With the sole exception of *Il bacio della Giustitia e della Pace*, which takes place in front of Venice's Ducal Palace, all the others shy away from the typically urban locations in which Renaissance drama is traditionally set.[79] Translating the metaphor of the *theatrum mundi* into a truly theatrical space — indeed, a *topos* — Glissenti sets some of the plays on 'the stage of the world'. In *La Ragione sprezzata*, the stage direction 'la scena è il Mondo' [the stage is the World] acquires a special connotation.[80] The play traces the destiny of the human kind by summoning all the components of the universe, from the seven planets to the seven ages of man, from demons and angels, to the holy spirits and those punished in hell. The acceptation of 'World' here is wide, with a fascinating convergence of spatial and temporal perspectives. More strictly focused on the earthly dimension of the world are the settings of *La Morte innamorata* and *Il mercato, overo la fiera della vita humana*. The first one takes place in the 'paese di Lungavita dinanzi l'albergo del Mondo' [land of Longlife, in front of the World's inn], a place where Man mistakenly believes he is safe from Death.[81] The World, a deceitful innkeeper, makes men believe that they will obtain the favours of Fortune, but he then turns them over to Death so as to keep the goods they have accumulated. In a similar vein, *Il mercato* is set 'dinanzi al Palaggio del Mondo nel cui gran cortile si fa la fiera de tutti i viventi' [in front of the Palace of the World, whose courtyard hosts the fair of all humans].[82] In this case, World — the fair's superintendent — first welcomes and later deceives all men, eventually leaving them in Death's hands. Within the perspective created by the trope of the *memento mori*, the space of Renaissance drama is re-functionalised: the 'piazza', a typical setting for both comedies and tragedies, is taken here as a symbolic space, true mirror of the world and its many deceptions. The dynamic is very similar to concurrent uses of architectural metaphors as macro-structures able to house encyclopaedic summaries of human life: one could think of Tomaso Garzoni's *Piazza universale di tutte le professioni del mondo* or Michelangelo Buonarroti the Younger's *La Fiera*, which, despite differences in genre and destination (Garzoni's is a treatise, Buonarroti's is, in principle, a theatrical work, though of its own kind), showcase the correspondence between urban spaces (piazzas, cities, fairs) and human life.[83]

---

79   *Il bacio della Giustitia e della Pace*, p. 4: 'La scena è in Venetia, che da l'un canto rappresenta il Palazzo, da l'altro alcune case di private persone' [The scene is Venice: the Palazzo on one side; a few private households on the other]. On the political relevance of the play, possibly echoing the tensions between Venice and Rome around the 1606 *interdetto*, see Neri, 'Le moralità di Fabio Glissenti', p. 193.
80   *La Ragione sprezzata*, fol. 10^v.
81   *La Morte innamorata*, fol. A4^v.
82   Fabio Glissenti, *Il mercato overo la fiera della Vita humana favola morale* (Venice: Marco Ginammi, 1620), fol. [A7]^v.
83   For Garzoni's *Piazza* (Venice: G. B. Somasco, 1585, with several reprints), see the modern edition Tomaso Garzoni, *La piazza universale di tutte le professioni del mondo*. In Buonarroti's *La Fiera*, the piazza features as a highly ambivalent location in which the actions of 'real' characters

The theatre of the world, then, makes room for the theatre of the soul in those plays that are more directly concerned with the staging of psychomachiae. *L'Andrio*, which, as recalled above, centres on free will, takes place in a rather peculiar setting, the 'campo del Libero Arbitrio'.[84] Given the Venetian context of Glissenti's work, the term 'campo' will likely need to be understood as referring to the open spaces of Venice that, elsewhere, would be called piazzas or squares. As the place hosting the fight between Man (accompanied by his servants, Intellect and Sense) and the demons (who have taken the shape of World, Pomp, and their daughter, Flesh), the 'campo' of Free Will stands out as a double of Man's own conscience, while also echoing, to some extent, the local urban context. In a similar vein, the conflict between Spirit and his wife, Flesh, in *La Sarcodinamia* (which also involves the 'butler' Free Will, the 'secretary' Sense, the 'cupbearer' Intellect, as well as the 'housekeepers' Reason and Conscience) is set in an exquisitely mental space: 'la scena è la propria consideratione di ciascuno' [the scene is one's own consideration], where the word 'consideration' mirrors (and dramatises) the dynamic of purgation described in the preface of *La Ragione sprezzata*.[85] Even more explicit is the description of the scene in the play *L'Androtoo*, which evokes symbolic spaces such as those depicted in Francesco Pona's Christian emblems that I have discussed in the introduction: 'la scena è la casa del cuore di ciascheduno, dove gli affetti interni ed esterni dell'huomo, gareggiando a diverso fine, si risolvono finalmente dove lo stesso huomo vuole' [the scene is one's own heart, where inner and outer affections fight against each other and end up following the choices of man].[86] Consistently with the cardio-centric notion rooted in the Aristotelian tradition, the soul is located by Glissenti in the heart, where all fights between internal and external affections unfold, an inner space which becomes the stage on which human life is played out [Fig. 3.2]. The protagonist of this drama, Androtoo (literally, the 'innocent man'), moves on stage alongside his servants (Discourse, Will, Sense, Intellect, Memory) and is assisted by Conscience and Remorse, always in danger to fall prey of Sin's daughter, Vanity.

These inner settings allow Glissenti to craft a kind of purely allegorical stage upon which human psychology and physiology, deconstructed into their various

---

and allegorical personifications intertwine. On the three redactions of the play, see Michelangelo Buonarroti il Giovane, *La Fiera*, ed. by Pietro Fanfani, 2 vols (Florence: Le Monnier, 1860) (third and last version of the play, whose conspicuous dimension bears witness to the encyclopaedic aim of the work); *La fiera. Redazione originaria (1619)*, ed. by Uberto Limentani (Florence: Leo S. Olschki, 1984); *La fiera. Seconda redazione*, ed. by Olimpia Pelosi (Naples: Liguori, 2003). For an overview of the work, see Bruno Porcelli, *Le misure della fabbrica: studi sull'Adone del Marino e sulla Fiera del Buonarroti* (Milan: Marzorati, 1980); Olimpia Pelosi, *La fiera come gran teatro del mondo: Michelangelo Buonarroti il giovane fra tradizione accademica e prospettiva barocca* (Salerno: Palladio stampa, 1983).
84   *L'Andrio*, p. [10].
85   *La Sarcodinamia*, fol. A4^v.
86   Fabio Glissenti, *L'Androtoo cioè l'huomo innocente favola morale* (Venice: Marco Ginammi, 1616), fol. A5^v. The kind of space evoked by the play is consistent with iconographies such as those found in Pona, *Cardiomorphoseos*, p. 1 ('Liber En ad Te Redeo'), which I have discussed in Chapter 1, p. 10; and p. 21 ('Procul Este Prophani'), in which the heart is indeed depicted as a tower besieged by demons and defended by angels.

A Rcem arduam, inaccessam, multiplici septam muro, ædificauit Rex Deus Cor Hominis, sibique in Domicilium elegit: ac Perduellis Diabolus, pariter inhabitare contendit.
Simul

FIG. 3.2. Pona, *Cardiomorphoseos* (1645), p. 21.

components, are given the opportunity to fully interact with the other characters that determine Man's spiritual successes and failures. Once again, the dialogue between the Philosopher and the Actress in the *Discorsi morali* provides us with insightful remarks into Glissenti's use of the allegorical code. In order to support his argument, the Philosopher turns to the *exemplum* of the fight between Soul and Body. In a novella narrated to the actress, the wife (Soul), worn out by the ungratefulness of her husband (Body), would like to get rid of him; comforted by her maid (Reason), she longs for Death's intervention in order to be freed from the burden of her marriage.[87] The Actress's response to the Philosopher seizes upon the possibility to see through the eyes of the mind ('con gli occhi della mente') what is normally invisible, a feature of the novella that is also key to the rhetorical mechanisms embedded in the morality plays:

> Stette la Recitante molto attenta alla novella del Filosofo [...] e considerando poi come la verità si stava nascosta sotto la morale favola, così disse: 'Non poco obligo habbiamo a quel leggiadro inventore, che ci lasciò scritto così utile dialogo; in cui, come in un bel quadro dipinto, che con colori distinti e varii rappresenti a gli occhi qualche memorabile historia, habbiamo veduto espresso al vivo con gli occhi della mente la natura dell'Anima, l'ufficio della Memoria, la prontezza della Volontà, et i buoni e veri avisi della Ragione.'[88]
>
> [The Actress was very attentive to the Philosopher's novella [...] considering how the truth was hidden underneath the moral fable, she said: 'We are in no small debt to that brilliant author, who left us such a useful dialogue; as in a beautiful painting, which, with various and distinct colours, represents a memorable story, we have seen with the eyes of the mind — and vividly expressed — the nature of the Soul, the function of Memory, the promptness of Will, and the good and truthful advice of Reason.']

Through a simile that evokes the figurative arts, the Actress outlines a reading mode that entails the inner visualisation of the *favola*. The pedagogical import of this spiritual exercise is in full sight when she explains that the novella makes invisible things visible, including the nature of the soul, the function of memory, the readiness of will, and the advice of reason. Thanks to the process of deconstruction and personification pursued by the novella (and re-enacted by the plays), the intellectual functions of Aristotelian psychology are not only adapted to the needs of Christian doctrine, but also vulgarised and made accessible to lay audiences foreign to the sophistications of natural philosophy and metaphysics.

Within this anatomical subdivision of human life, the place of the undisputed protagonist is held by Man. Turning to the medieval tradition of Everyman, embodiment of the human kind and emblem of its universal destiny, Glissenti does not commit to the construction of realistic or plausible characters. Pursuing the abstraction from reality that, as Werner Helmich has suggested, was peculiar to medieval moral drama, Glissenti makes Man interact with personifications that

---

[87] For the novella, see *DM*, 4.10: 'Si lamenta l'Anima della ingratitudine del Corpo suo marito, e desidera di abbandonarlo: viene avvertita dalla Ragione sua camariera. Et ella con patienza sta aspettando la Morte, che venga a farle far divortio'.
[88] *DM*, fol. 356^r.

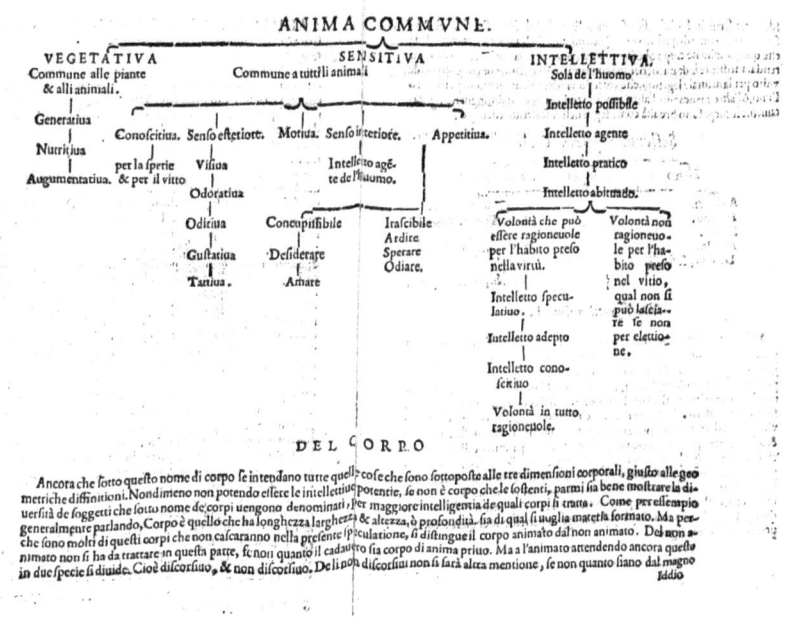

Fig. 3.3. Glissenti, *L'assoluta conclusione dell'humana libertà* (1597), fols B3^v–[B4]^r.

anatomise the subject and unveil its inner mechanisms.[89] The *favole morali* thus make room for the representation of the spiritual and physical components of Man, according to hierarchical dynamics reminiscent of coeval ideas about human psychology and physiology. Particularly illuminating, in this regard, is a comparison between the system of characters laid out by Glissenti in his plays and the reduction of human life into diagrams as outlined by the playwright's relative, Antonio, in his philosophical booklet, *L'assoluta conclusione dell'humana libertà*, printed in Venice in 1597. Within a detailed discussion of free will that minimises the importance traditionally assigned to both Fortune and Inclination, Antonio provides a detailed deconstruction of the human soul and its components that corresponds closely to the dramatisation pursued by Fabio in the plays [Fig. 3.3].[90]

According to this kind of symbolic dissection, Man — whose Greek-sounding names in the plays (Andrio, Androtoo, Antropo) are based on clear etymological roots — is surrounded by his more or less loyal servants and assistants. In the prints, the lists of *dramatis personae* function as didactic summaries of the anatomisation of human life entailed by the dramaturgy. As such, they can be usefully compared to diagrams such as those found in Antonio's work [Fig. 3.4]. *La Ragione sprezzata*, brings all five senses on stage ('Udito', hearing, 'Viso' [seeing], 'Odorato' [smell],

---

89   Werner Helmich, *Die Allegorie im französischen Theater des 15. und 16. Jahrunderts* (Tübingen: Max Niemeyer, 1976); on the notion that 'Everyman' or, simply, 'Man' may be conceived as a 'conceptual name' rather than a character, see Strubel, *Grant senefiance a*, p. 313.
90   Glissenti, *L'assoluta conclusione dell'humana libertà*, fols B3^v–[B4]^r.

Persone, che parlano.

L'Angelo custode fà il Prologo.
Lucifero Prencipe de' Demoni.
Calcabrina,
Malacoda,   } Demoni.
Farfarello,
Schiera di Demoni.
Huomo Monarca del Mondo.
Vdito,
Viso,
Odorato,   } Cinque sensi, serui
Gusto,   dell'huomo.
Tatto,
Anima moglie dell'huomo.
Memoria,
Volontà,   } Serue dell'anima.
Ragione,
Natura madre di tutti.
Tempo.
Atropos,
Cloto,   } Le tre Parche.
Lachesis,
Choro.
Verità.   Giu-

Incantatore.
Giustitia.
Morte.
Genti diuerse.
Anime.
Dannati.
La Scena è il Mondo.
Il Choro è di sette Pianeti,
E delle sette età dell'huomo.
Li sette Pianeti, cioè,
   Luna.
   Mercurio.
   Venere.
   Sole.
   Marte.
   Gioue.   Saturno.
   Le sette età dell'huomo, cioè,
Infantia, retta dalla Luna.
Pueritia,   Da Mercurio.
Adolescenza, Da Venere.
Giouentù,   Dal Sole.
Virilità,   Da Marte.
Vecchiezza,   Da Gioue.
Decrepità,   Da Saturno.

FIG. 3.4. Glissenti, *La Ragione sprezzata* (1606), fol. 10^{r-v}

'Gusto' [taste], 'Tatto' [touch]); in *L'Andrio*, Intellect and Sense (whose names, 'Fronimo' and 'Estesi', offer another example of Glissenti's penchant for inventive etymology) play the roles of Man's footman and servant, respectively; Sense ('Estisi') is instead accompanied by Discourse ('Fradmo') as Man's page in *La Morte innamorata*; Androtoo, in the homonymous play, benefits from the advice given to him by Discourse, Will, Sense, Intellect, and Memory, while also being aided by the housekeeper, Conscience, and her own assistant, Remorse. In *La Ragione sprezzata*, Man, king of the world, is married to Soul, whose maids are Memory, Will, and Reason. Elsewhere (for instance in *La Sarcodinamia*) the conflict between earthly and heavenly concerns is represented through the fight between husband (Spirit) and wife (Flesh): Spirit ('Pneumo') is assisted by the butler, Will ('Procremo'), the secretary, Intellect ('Fronimo'), and the cupbearer, Thought ('Frontido'); Flesh (whose name in the play is 'Sarca'), is accompanied by her servants, Vanity ('Mateota') and Sensuality ('Estesia'). Even in this case, the household is in the hands of two housekeepers, Reason ('Logia') and Conscience ('Sinideta').

The characters of the *favole morali* are not limited to the personifications of the various components of human psychology and physiology. When the setting is specifically mundane, Glissenti turns to personages typical of the medieval allegorical tradition. In *L'Andrio*, the World ('Cosmo') and Pomp ('Pompilia'), are the parents of Flesh (Princess 'Sarcodonta'), and are assisted by servants that embody the earthly temptations ('Idonì' [pleasure], 'Filotimo' [splendour], 'Ergia [sloth], 'Filopotia' [binge]). They all represent the enemies of Man. Similarly, the World appears in *La Morte innamorata* and in *Il mercato*, married to Fraud ('Sofisma') or Comfort ('Commodità'), respectively. These characters embody evil spirits dispatched by Satan to bring his agenda to completion on earth. Occasionally, devils and demons show off their exquisitely Dantesque mould, as is the case with Calcabrina, Malacoda, and Farfarello in *La Ragione sprezzata*; similarly, Cacodemone, Astaroth, Sarcodemone, Asmodeo, and Cosmodemone are Satan's helpers in *L'Andrio* (with Cacodemone and Lucifero appearing in *L'Androtoo* as well).

Another group of characters, though smaller, is made of those who are not allegorical personifications, but are meant to represent human types as well as professional categories. In *Il mercato*, for instance, according to a storyline already deployed in the *Discorsi morali*, various mortals — the Aristocrat, the Baron, the Merchant, the Artisan, the Captain — are deceived by the World, who leads them towards Death as in the *Totentanz* that inspired the illustrations of Glissenti's philosophical dialogue. The universal order is represented by allegorical figures such as Time, Experience, Nature, Justice, and, above all, Death herself, who is constantly about to steal Man's role as the protagonist of the plays.

As suggested by this overview of the characters in Glissenti's *favole morali*, the author bridges between the medieval legacy of dramatic allegories and the classicist rebirth of drama (which provides him with the canonical five-act structure and many features directly imported from the tradition of Renaissance theatre). Alongside the continuity with a theatrical universe that humanism had only partially obfuscated and which had never ceased to exist, erudition is another component of Glissenti's plays, as evidenced by the author's onomastic choices, which, as I recalled at the outset of this chapter, he borrowed from Giovanni Battista Leoni's allegorical plays.[91]

Consistently with the use of Greek-based words in the titles of the dialogues in the *Discorsi morali*, the use of Greek-sounding names for the personages in the plays has a twofold purpose: first, in line with the 'performative' function of the characters, the names reveal (at least to the audience conversant with etymology) what they stand for and what deeds they are supposed to achieve; second, these names make the allegorical framework of the plays less immediately overt, thus bringing the status of personified allegories a bit closer to that of characters. The interplay of 'performativity' and 'characterisation' that informs Glissenti's allegorical plays is pursued in various ways. While an analytical discussion of the *favole morali* go beyond the scope of the present study, in what follows I will offer insights into three areas that are key to the playwright's pedagogical project and spiritual concerns. More precisely, by looking at select examples, I will focus on the ways in which concerns about vanity, conscience, and virtue come to full fruition through Glissenti's dramaturgy.

The Theatre of Vanity

The work that opens the series of Glissenti's plays, *La Ragione sprezzata*, is the only one labelled 'favola *tragica* morale' (my emphasis). The adjective 'tragica' is key to the philosophical framework outlined by the author in the *Discorsi morali*. Indeed, the play offers an emblematic example of the ways in which the metaphorical 'tragedy of human life' is returned its theatrical meaning.[92] With the exception of *Il mercato* and *La Sarcodinamia*, the other plays have happy endings, with Man being brought back to the path of virtue through redemption. Following the legacy of medieval sacred drama, *La Ragione sprezzata* displays instead an eschatological inspiration, which is also reminiscent of concurrent developments in confessional theatre, particularly that of the Jesuits.[93] The work is ambitious not only in its argument, but also as regards its length and impressive number of characters, including choruses and ensemble scenes that, especially towards the end of the play, reach high levels of complexity. While the number of characters was likely due to the need to give all the orphans a chance to take part in the performance, the universal ambition of the script is intrinsic to the author's project. The play reuses materials from various novelle of the *Discorsi morali* and aims to stage the whole world, including the recesses of its earthly spaces and the highest spheres of heaven.[94] Differently from the other plays, which are characterised by simpler structures, *La Ragione sprezzata* merges the two archetypes that inform Glissenti's production: the psychomachia

---

91   On Leoni and his onomastic choices, see pp. 135–37.
92   See my discussion of *Discorsi morali* in Chapter 2.
93   See, on this matter, Gaia Benzi 'La genesi del *Parthenio*: gli influssi della propaganda gesuitica nella drammaturgia confessionale di area veneta', in Selmi and Zucchi, eds, *Allegoria e teatro*, pp. 169–78.
94   For a list of the novelle that provided Glissenti with subject matter to be used in *La Ragione sprezzata*, see Neri, 'Le moralità di Fabio Glissenti', p. 193.

and the triumph of Death. The protagonist, Man, hangs in fact in a precarious balance between the desire to follow Sense and the need to care for his wife, Soul. Within a temporal arch that situates the destiny of each individual within the longer timeframe of eternity, Man navigates the various ages of life, pushing back spiritual concerns. Reason vainly tries to bring him back on the right track. Time flows inexorably and Man, who repents too late, loses himself and makes Soul fall with him. The play closes with a universal judgment that does not spare anyone: the only two souls to be saved are those of a pious woman and a devout hermit. By the end, Nature is left complaining about the tragic fate of her children.

Differently from those reading the play, who have access to the moral of the story right away (indeed the 'argomento' narrates the plot and explains the teachings to be found in it), those who attended the performance were introduced to the play's meaning by the angel delivering the prologue. After recalling the privileged position of Man within the world created by God, the angel reprimands Man's inclination to shy away from spiritual matters. Normally invisible to human eyes, the angel has descended on earth to show the audience what they should learn from the mistakes of others:

> Ond'io di lui buon Angelo Custode
> (visibil però fatto) a voi ne venni
> per farvi noto, che i favori tanti
> dal mio Signor sì largamente havuti
> meritavan gradita ricompensa [...],
> Hor che segua a colui, che ingrato vive,
> che tai favor da Dio non riconosce
> voi vedrete fra poco. [...]
> Voi, che di tale ingrato e tristo essempio
> sarete spettatori, siate accorti,
> che a voi lo stesso non avenga. Udite.
> Saggio è colui, ch'a l'altrui spese impara.[95]

> [I, Man's guardian angel, having been made visible to this purpose, came to you to make you aware that the many gifts copiously received from my Lord deserve some welcome reward [...] You will shortly see what happens to those who live ungratefully, without acknowledging such gifts from God. [...] You, who will be spectators of this ungrateful and miserable example, guard yourselves from incurring the same fate. Listen to me. Wise is the one who learns from the mistakes of others.]

Once the pedagogical scope of the play is declared, the work opens with an infernal council that recalls Tasso's in *Gerusalemme liberata* while also anticipating the vision of hell that concludes the drama itself. The Dantesque demons gathered by Lucifer (Calcabrina, Malacoda, Farfarello) help him assess the current situation on earth. Based on the testimonies of a few souls recently arrived in hell — a courtier, a hypocrite churchman, a heretical philosopher — the council realises that the moment has arrived for Satan to gain hundreds of human souls for the underworld: Justice has left the earth, Truth and Reason have been banned by men, Faith has

---

95 *La Ragione sprezzata*, fol. 10[v].

no place among them anymore. The demons make then room for the appearance of Man. Still in his youth, he comes to the fore surrounded by the Senses, who accompany him throughout the journey that, eventually, will bring him to hell.

The *theatrum mundi* metaphor returns in *La Ragione sprezzata*, where the image's ambivalence stands out. The play represents the world as a stage on which the various characters move according to the iconographic model that we have encountered in Jean-Jacques Boissard's *Theatrum Vitae Humanae*, but theatre is also evoked as an architectural emblem of vanity. The Senses keep reminding Man that he should devote his best years to pleasure, evoking theatre as one of the places that he should attend.[96] Differently from the bitterness associated with the church, the other locations (piazzas, loggias, gardens, and theatres) are deemed suitable for evasion from sombre thoughts. Nature herself, incapable of following Reason's advice, describes Man's sumptuous palace in terms that recall Glissenti's description of the Palazzo Ducale: not only do festive sounds, beautiful decorations, and pomp make the palace look like a theatre, but they also make it look like a starry sphere.[97] When the Senses discuss which one among them brings more joy to Man, Eyesight claims her priority by listing all the marvellous things she is able to show her master. Among them, 'glorious settings' and 'opulent sceneries', which, alongside 'lustful images sculpted and painted', evoke a universe of deceitful appearances destined to betray the expectations of whoever follows them.[98] The insistence with which the Senses recommend that, instead of considering repentance and conversion, Man attend the 'great theatre where games are played and comedies are staged' ('il gran theatro ove solenni | si fanno i giuochi e i comici apparati') stress the negative acceptation of the image.[99]

The splendid theatre of the world, summa of all the pleasures chased by Man, eventually proves (as was the case with the ambiguous Palazzo Ducale) a theatre of vanity. Its real nature is exposed by the Fates: on the occasion of their first appearance in Act III, they describe their function (spinning fibres into yarn, weaving threads on the loom) as integral to the mechanisms that inform the 'theatro immenso de' mortali' [great theatre of men] while also evoking the presence of Death through the image of the 'fair of human life', yet another variation on the *theatrum mundi* trope.[100] Time himself will then recommend that Reason turn to the Fates so as to

---

96 *La Ragione sprezzata*, 1.2, fol. 24^v.
97 *La Ragione sprezzata*, 2.1, fol. 37^v: 'Io stessa i grati, i sontuosi cibi, | i canti, i suoni, et i festevol balli, | et i giuochi de l'armi, e de le giostre, | di contese d'honor, le scene, e gli archi | d'apparati trionfi, e illustri mostre, | tutte veder potei, tutte godere, | sì che questo teatro un picciol cielo | parmi che per arte luminoso splenda' [I myself could admire the pleasant and sumptuous food, the songs, clamours, and festive dances, and duels and jousts, contests of honour, scenes and arches of triumphal apparati, and illustrious decorations; I could enjoy all of them, so that this theatre seemed to me a little heaven, artfully shining].
98 *La Ragione sprezzata*, 2.3, fol. 41^v.
99 *La Ragione sprezzata*, 3.3, fol. 76^v.
100 *La Ragione sprezzata*, 3.7, fols 85^v–86^r; the image of the 'fair' ('la gran fiera humana | dove i mortai dopo fatiche lunghe | ne vanno a far de i loro acquisti il conto' [the great human fair where mortals, after long labours, go to pay for their purchases], 3.7, fol. 86^{r-v}) will be associated with the 'theatre of human life' in *Il mercato*; see, for instance, a passage from the prologue delivered by the

convince Man that it is time to repent and convert. The 'household' of the Fates is described in a way that combines space and time: the structure of their 'spacious theatre' ('spatioso theatro') mirrors that of the solar year, with precise references to months, days, and hours.[101] The complex description, which fits the Baroque predilection for complication and wit, shows that the theatrical metaphor can, at this juncture, be variated in many ways. In this case, the theatre-like structure of the house of the Fates is functional to showing Man the evidence of his imminent death. The episode, narrated in detail by Eyesight to Reason, is of great interest in that it draws on literary tropes that the author reshapes in theatrical terms. The Fates are described in terms that recall the sirens (indeed, like sirens, they attract Man through their 'dolce canto', sweet singing). At the same time, the description of their 'albergo', which centres on the literalisation of the metaphors of the loom and the thread of life, unveils it as a double of the world:

> E quivi tanti stammi, fila e tele,
> orditori, telai, conocchie e fusi,
> arcolai, naspi, navicelle e spole
> con tanta gente ritrovammo e tanta
> ch'un altro mondo di veder ci parve.[102]

[And here we found many fine wools and cloths, warps, looms, distaffs, and spindles, yarn swifts, reels, and spools, and so many people that we seemed to see another world.]

As the description of the Fates demonstrates, the play is a dramatised *memento mori*. One of the scopes of Reason is indeed that of reminding Man of his destiny, so that the invitation to self-examination and repentance may lead to salvation. The tragedy of the psychomachia lies in fact in the impossibility for the Soul to be saved

---

personification of Experience: 'Voi dunque attenti a questo essempio stando, | che qui spiegar fra poco vederete, | potrete per mio mezo farvi accorti | di diportarvi meglio di molt'altri, | quali venuti a questa nobil fiera | che in gratia de la vita è publicata | nel mezo del theatro d'esto mondo', fol. A6ᵛ [By paying attention to the example that you will see unfold here, you will learn, through me, how to behave better than many others who came to this noble fair of human life, which takes place in the middle of this world's theatre]; and a few words by the Nobleman at the beginning of Act 1: 'Mondo cortese, albergator fedele, | nel cui theatro si fa la gran fiera | di questa humana vita' [Courteous World, faithful host, in whose theatre the great fair of this human life unfolds] (*Il mercato*, p. 1).

101 *La Ragione sprezzata*, 4.9, fols 126ʳ–127ʳ: 'Dodici corridori fan corona | a spatioso theatro, Anno nomato, | per cui d'intorno a maraviglia incisi | sono cento quarantaquattro gradi, | per cui s'ascende, e si discende ogn'hora, | da' ministri fatali de le Parche; | ne lo spatio di mezo ovato e grande | stanno i telai de' miseri viventi | dove le tele lor si van tessendo. | Quivi ottomila son sopra sessanta, | e settecento damigelle intente | a trar da le conocchie il loro stame. [...] Tutte queste li stami apparecchiando | a dodici orditoi [...] | e a tessitori ben trecento e cinque | sopra sessanta [...] | le tele prima ordite van porgendo' [Twelve corridors surround a spacious theatre, called Year, around which one hundred and forty-four steps are marvellously carved; through them, the fatal ministers of the Fates ascend and descend all the time. In the middle of this large oval space stand the looms of the miserable mortals, where their cloths are being crafted. Here there are eight thousand seven hundred and sixty maids busy with drawing out the thread from the distaff [...] All these arrange the threads over twelve warpers [...] and they pass the cloths to three hundred and sixty-five weavers].

102 *La Ragione sprezzata*, 4.15, fol. 146ʳ.

if the Body surrenders to the Senses. Reason thus attempts to show Man what it means to die as a sinner. Among the devices used by Reason, special attention must be given to a powerful mirror that she hands over to him. A traditional symbol of vanity, this particular mirror is meant to reveal the fragility of the human condition to whoever looks into it. The prop, which Man's wife, Soul, offers him as a gift, gives him a chance to meditate on death in a way that recalls the visual dynamics at play in the *Discorsi morali*, where the illustrations were meant to visualise the contemplation of death. The mirror — yet another metaphor that is returned to its literal meaning — triggers a kind of spiritual work that resonates with the many books ('specchi') of Christian doctrine, which, conceived around the image of the mirror, were very popular in the period.[103]

Based on Reason's recommendations, Man should keep the mirror always with him and, with remarkable metaphoric shift, he should always keep it fixedly in his mind ('per sempre | lo vi serbate ne la mente fisso').[104] Having raised Man's curiosity, Reason illustrates the nature of the object in intentionally ambiguous terms:

> Egli è un bel terso e luminoso speglio,
> con tal arte construtto e fabricato,
> che chi con gli occhi fissi sta mirando
> scopre in un punto le passate cose
> chiare, come non men fa le presenti.
> Ma di più ancor con meraviglia grande
> le venture dimostra, sempre occulte
> al senso human, e ne fa chiara mostra.
> Specchio che rende l'huom saggio et accorto.[105]

[This is a beautifully terse and bright mirror, made and fabricated with such an art that whoever fixes their gaze upon it will see at once things past as clear as the present ones. But even more marvellously, it reveals the future, which is always concealed from human perception, and shows it plainly. This mirror makes men wise and prudent.]

The mirror, which shows things past, present, and future, is meant to make men wiser and more conscientious. Animated by a somewhat naïve curiosity, Man demands that the Senses unveil it, but the servants hesitate ('Su, Sensi, lo scoprite, e a me si mostri! | Che fate? Che badate? E che temete?').[106] Eyesight, for one thing, is too weak to face the image reflected on the mirror.[107] The protagonist thus resolves to do it himself, unaware that the image returned by the mirror will be a 'putrid skull': 'O debol vista, io scoprirollo, e fisse | terrò le luci in rimirar l'imago. | Ohimè, che veggio? Ahi, qual è questo specchio? | Di putrido defonto

---

103 See, for instance, Luis de Granada's aforementioned *Specchio della vita humana*, among numerous others.
104 *La Ragione sprezzata*, 3.10, fol. 90ᵛ.
105 *La Ragione sprezzata*, 3.10, fol. 91ʳ.
106 *La Ragione sprezzata*, 3.10, fol. 91ᵛ.
107 Ibid.: 'Mirabil luce, che lor gli occhi abbaglia, | Che non ponno mirar tanto splendore' [This wondrous light blinds their eyes, which cannot bear such brilliance].

horrido teschio?'.[108] By fixing his eyes on the mirror, Man faces Death. Once he realises what the mirror is about, Reason unpacks the meaning of the horrifying image and focuses on its macabre details. These draw on the iconography of *vanitas*, specifically the 'Death's head' that, as indicated by Benjamin, is a flagship image of Baroque culture and one of the most powerful icons of the allegorical tradition:[109]

> RAGIONE   Questo è lo specchio de la vita frale,
> del miser huom, che va correndo a morte.
> Qui contemplando le passate cose
> mirar potete, ché cotesto capo
> privo di carne e pelle, e senza spirto
> fu d'un huom, come voi potente al mondo.
> Hor il suo stato sta, come vedete.
> HUOMO   O mondana grandezza dove arrivi!
> Ahi, ahi, che horribil vista!
> RAGIONE   Le presenti
> non men scorger potete, poi che 'l trunco
> d'esto superbo capo in terra giace
> vile, e fracida carne a' vermi in preda.
> HUOMO   Non posso più mirar, ahi fiera vista!
> RAGIONE   Qui le cose future anco mirando
> scorger potete, poi che 'l vostro fasto
> ha in tempo breve a far un tal essempio,
> sì che potete farvi accorto, e saggio.
> HUOMO   Ahimè, che vengo meno![110]

> [REASON: This is the mirror of the frail life of a miserable man who runs towards death. By contemplating things past here, you may recognise that this head with no flesh, skin nor life, belonged to a once powerful man, like you. Here's his current state, as you can see.
> MAN   O mundane greatness, this is what you get! Alas, alas, what a horrible sight!
> REASON   You may see the present too, for the body of that superb head is laid in earth, vile and rotten flesh, food for worms.
> MAN   I cannot look at it anymore, alas, fearful sight!
> REASON   Here you can also see the future, for your current pomp will soon be a similar example to others; so that you may be wise and prudent!
> MAN   Alas, I faint!]

Reason insists on contemplation: by fixing the eyes (both the physical ones and those of the mind) on the image of the skull, Man will be able to meditate on past, present, and future. The dynamic described by Reason is the same at the core of Christian images of *vanitas*, including emblems: once again, Francesco Pona's *Cardiomorphoseos* provides us with a fitting comparison [Fig. 3.5] that merges the iconography of the heart with those of the mirror and Death's Head.[111]

But many other examples could be referenced from the figurative arts, indicating

---

108   Ibid. ('O weak eyesight, I will unveil it, and will fix my eyes onto the image. Alas, what do I see? Alas, what mirror is this? Isn't this a putrid dead skull?').
109   Benjamin, *The Origin of German Tragic Drama*; *Emblems of Death*, ed. by Calabritto and Daly.
110   *La Ragione sprezzata*, 3.10, fols 91^v–92^r.
111   Pona, *Cardiomorphoseos*, p. 17 ('Clavus clavo').

IX.

Clauus Clauo.

L Vteum simulachrum, ferreo Cordi, vulgaris
Amor insculpserat ; fluxam nempe mulie-
bris oris imaginem ; aramque profanam peni-
tùs, fugaci erexerat Pulchritudini : Eiurat mo-
C do

FIG. 3.5. Pona, *Cardiomorphoseos* (1645), p. 17.

that the prop evoked in Glissenti's play is the tangible translation of a widespread iconographic trope: in paintings such as Hans Baldung's *Three Ages of the Woman and the Death* (1510) [Fig. 3.6] and the anonymous *Death and the Maiden* (c. 1570) at Hall's Croft in Stratford-upon-Avon [Fig. 3.7], the mirrors in which the young women look at themselves capture and reflect the looming presence of Death behind the protagonists of the paintings. And if Jacques de Gheyn's *Still Life* (1603) now at the Metropolitan Museum, New York [Fig. 3.8] makes a point about the interconnectedness of mirror and skull, it is Jan van Hemessen's striking *Vanity* (1535–40) of Lille [Fig. 3.9] that seizes upon the same rhetorical strategy dramatised by Glissenti in *La Ragione sprezzata*: an angel holds a plate and points his finger towards the mirroring surface where an anamorphic Death's head responds to the observer's gaze. Just as the bystander is struck when they realise that the image in the plate is a skull, so Man is deeply upset by the vision of Death in Glissenti's play. Luckily (or unluckily...) for the protagonist, the Senses manage to take control once again: they cover his face with a veil so that he may divert his gaze from the mirror.[112]

Since the gift has not worked out in the way in which Reason was hoping, she decides to seek Truth's help. Banned from the world, Truth has taken shelter at Death's place ('l'albergo della Morte'). The place, described by the chorus of the Seven Planets, is peculiar: two different entrances (Truth's and Death's) lead to their common dwelling.[113] The metaphor is straightforward and speaks to the paradoxical commonality of Truth and Death: though both hated by men, they are, in fact, good friends. In order not to be recognised, Truth wears a veil that covers her entirely; before visiting Man, she requires that Justice, who is accompanying her, do the same.[114] They plan on taking Man aback, as Reason did with the mirror. In order to do so, they present him with a judicial case they wish him to rule over. Introducing themselves as sisters, they debate about their mother's inheritance, contained in a mysterious trunk. According to Truth, the trunk contains 'a beautiful idol', skilfully made and provided with a prophetic spirit capable of answering any doubtful question about the future.[115] Not differently from the mirror, the object in the trunk has the power to advise whoever interrogates it. Man's curiosity grows,

112 *La Ragione sprezzata*, 3.10, fol. 92^r: 'Partiam, partiam Signor, sgombriamo quinci, | né vi volgete a dietro, e questo velo | ponetevi su gli occhi, acciò gli incanti | di questa fattucchiera con sue larve | non vi faccian temer. Su presto andiamo' [Let's go, my lord, let's leave from here; do not look behind and put this veil on your eyes, so that the enchantments of this sorceress with her spectres do not frighten you. Hurry, let's go!].
113 *La Ragione sprezzata*, 4.16, fol. 149^v: 'Presso a la Morte s'è ricoverata, | dove non teme de' viventi l'onte. | Quest'è 'l suo albergo. In l'altro sta la Morte. | Commune è dentro poi l'alloggiamento, | Quantunque fuor divisa sia l'entrata. | Entrar tu puoi, ché sempre stassi aperta | A ciascun ch'entrar vuole' [She found shelter at Death's, where she does not fear the offences of men. This is her abode. Death resides in a different one. The entrances are separate, but their lodging inside is the same. You may enter, for the door is always open to those who want to get in].
114 *La Ragione sprezzata*, 5.2, fols 154^v–55^r.
115 *La Ragione sprezzata*, 5.4, fol. 160^r: 'idol vago | fatto per mano d'eccellente mastro, | nel quale spiega le proposte | vaticinante spirto in lui rinchiuso, | sì che ne puote aver certa risposta | ciascun che 'l chiede in ogni dubbia impresa' [a beautiful idol made by an excellent artist; there is a prophetic spirit in it, which gives reliable answers to any questions one might have about doubtful endeavours].

Fig. 3.6. Hans Baldung, *Three Ages of the Woman and the Death* (1510), Vienna, Kunsthistorisches Museum.

Fig. 3.7. Anonymous, *Death and the Maiden* (c. 1570), Shakespeare Trust Birthplace, Hall's Croft, Stratford-upon-Avon.

Fig. 3.8. Jacques de Gheyn II, *Still Life* (1603),
The Metropolitan Museum, New York.

Fig. 3.9. Jan van Hemessen, *Vanity* (1535–1540), Palais Beaux Arts, Lille.

but the two women refuse to open the box in the presence of the Senses, for they would distract Man from contemplating what is inside. Once the Senses walk away, Truth and Justice are ready to open the trunk and reveal their identities:

> VERITÀ   Tenete fissi gli occhi a l'idol prima,
> e poscia noi scoperte mirarete.
> HUOMO   Così farò. E gl'occhi miei son vaghi
> ben l'idol di mirar, ma più 'l bel volto.
> VERITÀ   Scopri, sorella! e voi mirate.
> RAGIONE   Lo scopro.
> HUOMO   Ohimè, ohimè, che fia? Ohimè, che inganno!
> VERITÀ   Sta' cheto, ove è la fede? Attendi alquanto.
> HUOMO   Non posso, no, mirar sì tristo aspetto.[116]

[TRUTH   Fix your gaze on the idol first, then you will see us unveiled.
MAN   I will. My eyes are eager to admire the idol and, even more, the beautiful face.
TRUTH   Uncover it, sister! And you, look!
REASON   I am unveiling it.
MAN   Alas, alas, what is that? Alas, what a deceit!
TRUTH   Be quiet, where is your faith? Wait!
MAN   No, I cannot gaze at such sorrowful face.]

The idol is, in reality, a pile of putrid bones: even more strikingly than with the mirror, Man is forced to face Death ('tenete fissi gli occhi') according to a rhetorical strategy that we have already encountered in the Lyonnais *Simulachres* of 1538.[117] After revealing her identity, Reason invites Man to commit to the *memento mori* he has repeatedly refused to consider:

> Mira qui 'l fasto humano. Ecco, si muore;
> queste son l'ossa d'un monarca estinto,
> come te grande, al mondo havuto in pregio.
> Queste d'un poverel, che gía cercando
> di porta in porta per scacciar la fame.
> Guarda se differenza tu vi scorgi
> fra l'esser del monarca e del mendico.[118]

[Look at the human pomp. Here's the truth, we all die; these are the bones of a dead king, great as you are, praised by the world. These are the bones of a poor man, who went door to door begging for food. See whether you notice any difference between the monarch and the beggar.]

---

116   *La Ragione sprezzata*, 5.4, fol. 161^r.
117   See *Les simulachres et faces historiées de la mort*, fol. Aii^v, where the dedicatee of the volume is invited to consider the function of those 'spiritual mirrors' that, at the entrance of churches and cemeteries, are meant to remind men and women of their weak nature and the equality of everybody in front of Death: 'auiourd'huy sont telz spirituelz miroers mis a l'entrée des Eglises, et Cymitieres [...] pour veoir si entre ces ossemens des mortz pourroit trouver aulcune difference des riches & des pouvres' [nowadays these spiritual mirrors are placed at the entrance of churches and cemeteries [...] to see whether among the bones of the dead one could find any difference between the rich and the poor].
118   *La Ragione sprezzata*, 5.4, fols 161^v–62^r.

'Mira qui', 'Guarda': the orders given by Reason focus on eyesight while also recalling the syntax of preaching, which, over the centuries, had been using the lexicon of image-making in order to facilitate the audience's repentance and conversion ('Ritirati perciò da' Sensi a dietro, | poggia de le virtù per l'erto colle. | Pentiti de' tuoi errori, e aspira al Cielo').[119] Reason, taking advantage of Man's bewilderment, invites him to turn his gaze towards Truth, who is ready to admonish him and encourage him to engage in the examination of his conscience: 'Tu, fra te va' pensando, e fa' giuditio, | come ti trovi ne' l'affetto interno'.[120] The emotional turmoil caused by the sight of the corpse in the trunk and by the words of Reason and Truth prevent Man from reacting. While he describes his own confusion passionately, the Senses convince him that what he has just attended is all made up.[121]

All the attempts to make Man consider the *memento mori* fail: the Senses get the better of him and he is caught by Death. The cautionary inspiration of the narrative becomes even more explicit in the final scenes, which stage a grand macabre dance. Summoned by Justice, Death's equalising endeavour is presented as a way to purify the world corrupted by sin, punish the sinners, and reward those innocent individuals who have deserved salvation. Death invites all mortals to fix their gaze upon her ('sì che avveduti al mio venir lo sguardo | fisso ritengan'), stressing the importance of preparing for her arrival.[122] Man is the first to fall under the grasp of Death, followed by individuals from all layers of society. As in Holbein's *Totentanz*, Death brings together emperors, kings, aristocrats, judges, lawyers, physicians, pedants, soldiers, philosophers, poets, notaries, merchants, artisans, helmsmen, women, lovers, prostitutes, indolent men, gluttons, drinkers and all the other people who play a part in the tragedy of life.[123]

Once all the cloths are severed, Death makes room for Justice, who condemns most of the souls to hell according to a retribution system that recalls the one at work in Dante's *Commedia*. Just to make a few examples, tyrants are devoured,

---

119 *La Ragione sprezzata*, 5.4, fol. 162ʳ ('Reject the Senses, climb the steep hill of virtue. Repent and seek the heavens!').
120 *La Ragione sprezzata*, 5.4, fol. 162ᵛ ('Consider within yourself and judge what your internal affection looks like').
121 *La Ragione sprezzata*, 5.5, fol. 163ʳ⁻ᵛ: 'Soprafatto dal duolo et atterrito | da l'horribil mostra, e fiero aspetto | de' corpi estinti ne la cassa chiusi, | mai non potei fuor dar picciola voce, | ché ne le fauci dal timor rinchiusa | pe' confusi sospir non trovò uscita' [Overwhelmed by grief and terrified by the frightening sight and dreadful aspect of the corpses in the trunk, I was not able to utter a word, for my voice, scared, stayed hidden in my mouth among confused sighs]; as per Eyesight's own words, 'ciò fu d'incanti e magiche apparenze, | crede a me, signor, vano figmento | che per sviar la vostra salda mente, | la perfida Ragion si va inventando' [this was the making of enchantments and magic appearances, believe me, this was a vain fantasy made up by Reason to deviate your firm mind] (5.5, fol. 164ʳ).
122 *La Ragione sprezzata*, 5.15, fol. 181ᵛ.
123 The classification of the sinners, divided according to professional categories and social status, recalls the one at play in the encounters that the Courtier and the Philosopher have with their interlocutors in the *Discorsi morali*. A shortened version of a similar catalogue of human types is also found in *Il mercato overo la fiera della vita humana*, where the incautious victims of World and Death are the Nobleman, the Baron, the Merchant, the Artisan and the Captain.

vomited, and devoured again by Cerberus; lawyers are roasted and oiled with fat so as to make their punishment harsher; physicians are plunged in boiling tar, then rubbed with ice before being boiled again; pedants are flogged and then burnt; notaries have their hands amputated and use their stumps to 'write with large letters the tears of the damned'; various groups of women, derogatorily labelled as 'donnicciuole' (including maids, witches, and the gossipy ones), are condemned to be covered by the faeces of demons ('cacatoi de' mostri de l'Inferno'); idlers, covered with honey, are left to be fed to flies; gluttons are made to swallow the demons' excrements.[124] At the end of the judgment, only two souls are saved: that of a God-fearing hermit ('romito | che nel timor di Dio visse mai sempre') and that of an unpretentious, yet genuinely devout countrywoman ('povera donna | di villa, semplicetta ma devota').[125] The Fates and Death stress the exemplary function of the scene and provide the audience with a set of instructions for effective meditation:

> Attendan tutti mentre ancor son vivi
> a dispensar sua vita in opre sante,
> a seguir la Ragion, fuggir li Sensi,
> e disprezzar ogni mondan diletto,
> che li condanna a sempiterne pene.
> Mirino al Tempo, che lor rubba gli anni.
> Si ricordin di noi, che le lor tele sollecite tessiam.
> Te teman figlia, che rigida a nissun giamai perdoni.
> E si spaventin del tremendo giorno
> che giudicar li dee, con tal essempio
> di tanti, e tanti a sempiterni horrori,
> per fugaci piacer dannati sempre.[126]

[May all mortals focus on spending their life in holy deeds while they are alive, following Reason, rejecting the Senses, and despising all mundane pleasure, which doom them to eternal punishment. May they look at Time, who steals the years from them; may they be reminded of us, who diligently weave their cloths; may they fear you, daughter, who, firm as you are, do not forgive anybody; and may they be frightened by the fearsome day of the judgement, thinking of the example of many who have been condemned to eternal punishment because of fleeting pleasures.]

The scene ends in the 'theatre' of the Fates, which, once bustling and noisy, is now empty and silent, ready to host another cycle of human life doomed to death. Freed from the sinners, the theatre of the Fates becomes a celebratory space, where the 'cloths' of the hermit and the devout woman are exhibited as vivid *exempla* to look at and meditate upon. All other mortals are destined to be forgotten, no matter which hierarchical distinctions characterised them in life.[127] Nature, who joins too late to

---

124 *La Ragione sprezzata*, 5.18, fols 191^r ff. For the organisation of the punishments, see also Glissenti's own *L'horribile e spaventevole inferno*.
125 *La Ragione sprezzata*, 5.17, fol. 182^v.
126 *La Ragione sprezzata*, 5.17, fol. 183^{r-v}.
127 *La Ragione sprezzata*, 5.18, fol. 183^v: 'Le due tele, nutrici, degli eletti | a memoria perpetua risserbate | de' posteri nel vostro ampio theatro. | Ma tutte l'altre (come dissi) [...] | tutte immergete nel corrente Lethe, | sì che di lor mai si ricordi il nome' [O Fates, you should keep the two cloths of

bid farewell to her children, can only try to ascertain what has already happened. The world, a theatre once filled with apparently joyful sounds, dance, and festive gatherings, is now a testament to the vanity of all things earthly.[128] Informed by Time about the punishments that her children are suffering in hell, Nature calls out to them, engaging in a desperate dialogue that, filled with echoes from Dante's *Inferno*, amplifies the harshness of their destiny. Eventually, the *exemplum* brought to the audience's eyes makes them see what they should expect if they do not abandon their sinful ways.[129]

The final judgment at the end of the play is thus meant, in a way, to involve the audience. When the play is performed, the visualisation of the human destiny and, more specifically, of the punishments of hell is concrete: through the bodies and voices of actors, the *exemplum* is made visible to the attendees. As far as we know from the author's account of the performance held at the Derelitti, which I have discussed earlier, the efficacy of the *exemplum* is proved by the audience's sudden desire to turn to self-examination, repentance, and conversion. Through a rhetorical climax, the spectators are gradually made part of the contemplation of Death: the warnings of Reason are, at first, addressed to the characters within the play (this is, for instance, the case of the mirror and the coffin); later, when Man rejects salvation and is dragged to hell, his role as *alter ego* of the audience is made explicit. The final scenes of the play are not for the benefit of the protagonist, whose destiny is inevitably sealed; rather, they are meant to affect the audience, which, by being shown the harshness that comes with the judgment, should aim at repenting.

The dynamic put in motion by Glissenti recalls those of pre-modern figurative cycles such as the triumphs of death, the judgments of the souls, and their punishments in hell. One could think of the frescos in the Camposanto Monumentale of Pisa. The famous Triumph of Death attributed to painter Buonamico Buffalmacco was accompanied by a set of inscriptions that guided the observers through a veritable *meditatio mortis*: invited to fix their gaze (both the physical eyes and those of the

---

the chosen ones in your vast theatre for perpetual memory of future generations. But plunge all the others, as I said [...], in the River Lethe, so that their names may be forgotten forever].

128 *La Ragione sprezzata*, 5.19, fol. 184^{r-v}: 'Ma qual inusitato e novo, | taciturno fia il mondo e cheto il tutto? | Che dove pria di genti il gran susurro, | de' godenti le feste, i suoni, e i canti | facean d'intorno l'aria tintinnire, | hor par che nulla s'oda e taccia il mondo?' [But what unusual and unprecedented silence makes the world so calm and all things noiseless? Where the air was once made resound by the murmurs of people and by the feasts, sounds, and songs of joyful men and women, now it all seems silent and the world is quiet].

129 *La Ragione sprezzata*, 5.19, fol. 186^v: 'NATURA O figli, o figli miei, o cari figli, | che in questa horrenda stanza dimorate, | *lasciate ogni speranza o voi, ch'entrate*, | di cui l'inscrittion m'accresce il pianto. | Scongiurando vi priego, rispondete, | a la Natura cara vostra madre, | e dite dove siete, e come state. | DANNATI Siam condannati, miseri, infelici, | oh che dolor, oh che stridor di denti, | oh che crudele e miserabil pianto, | oh qual horrendo e tenebroso loco, | oh quai tormenti e quai atroci pene, | oh quali stracii ci dilanian l'alme, | oh perché lassi nel rio nascimento | non fummo dati in straccio a' fieri cani?', emphasis mine [NATURE O children, my children, beloved children, who reside in this fearful dwelling, *all hope abandon you who enter here*; the inscription grows my tears. I beg you, please, answer your dear mother, and tell me where you are and how you are. THE DAMNED We are doomed, miserable, wrecked, alas! What pain, alas, what teeth grinding, what cruel and pitiful weeping, what horrid and dark place, what torments and harsh punishments! What tortures tear apart our souls, why weren't we given to ferocious hounds when we were born?].

mind) upon the images, they were expected to recognise themselves in the 'mirror' and find the right path to follow.[130]

When the play is read rather than performed, the mechanisms imagined by the author are similar, though focused on the inner staging of the drama. The final scenes of *La Ragione sprezzata* provide us with a good example of the analogy between theatre and concurrent spiritual practices. Let us turn once again to Loyola, specifically to his instructions on the contemplation of hell: the first step is, as usual in the *Spiritual Exercises*, the 'composition of the place' ('compositione del luogo'), that is to imagine oneself in hell and study carefully the size of the location ('con la vista imaginativa in luogo infernale, et la longezza et largezza et profondità dell'inferno').[131] Once the place is defined and shaped, one has to fill it with images and other sensorial stimuli that make the suffering of the damned vivid and almost tangible:

> Il primo ponto è vedere con la vista imaginativa quelli grandi et spaventosi fuochi dell'inferno, et vedere l'anime come inchiuse in certi corpi de fuochi, come in pregione in quelli tutti abrugiati.
> Il secondo è odire le orrecchie imaginative li grandi pianti et gridi et voci horribile et biasteme spaventose, le quale contra de Christo et suoi santi li dannati dicono.
> Il terzo è odorare interiormente li fumi, sulfuri et sentine, et tutte le altre puzpe [*sic*: the Spanish text reads 'y cosas pútridas'] che patiscono et odorano li miseri dannati nell'inferno.
> Il quarto, gustare interiormente le cose amare, como sonno lagrime, dolori nell'anima, il sinteresin, cioè il verme della conscienza, che patiscono li miseri dannati.
> Il quinto è toccare interiormente quelli fuochi, tormenti, pene insopportabile, con le quale l'anime misere dannate sonno tormentate et afflitte nell'inferno.[132]

[The first point is to see with the sight of the imagination the great and dreadful fires of hell, and the souls as in bodies of fire, all burnt as in a prison. The second is to hear with the ears of the imagination wailings, howlings, cries, and fearful blasphemies uttered by the damned against Christ and all His Saints. The third is to internally smell smoke, sulphur, dregs and putrid things, which the miserable damned suffer and smell in hell. The fourth, to internally taste bitter things, like tears, sorrows of the soul and the *sinteresin*, that is, the worm of conscience, which the miserable damned suffer. The fifth is to internally touch those fires, tortures, and unbearable pains by which the souls are tormented and afflicted in hell.]

The spiritual experience outlined by Loyola involves imagination in all its components. It is not only about *seeing* hell, but also *feeling* it by *hearing* sounds and noises, *smelling* odours, *perceiving* the heat of the flames.[133] The actual meditation will then be completed by the review of the souls punished in hell ('colloquio a Christo, che serrà ridurre a memoria l'anime che sonno nell'inferno'): by revisiting the catalogue

---

130 Bolzoni, *La rete delle immagini*, pp. 3–46.
131 Loyola, *ES*, 65 (trans. by Peruschi, fol. 17^r/p. 667).
132 Loyola, *ES*, 66–70 (trans. by Peruschi, fol. 17^{r-v}/p. 667).
133 On the central role played by the senses in Ignatius's spiritual exercise, see Marty, *Sentir et goûter*.

of sinners, the devout Christian will be able to distance himself from sin and be grateful to God for that.[134] As Loyola puts it in the preamble to the exercise, if God's love does not deflect Man from sin, the 'fear of hell' ('timore dell'inferno') will do it.[135] The vision of hell evoked by Glissenti in the final scenes of *La Ragione sprezzata* makes good use of instructions such as Ignatius's. While the comparison between the two texts remains conjectural (indeed, many other spiritual works could be referenced as possible sources for Glissenti), the analogy does shed light on a kind of dramaturgy that, initially conceived for the actual stage, is adaptable to the needs of individual meditative reading. As Andreini puts it in the preface to *L'Adamo*, once detached from the real occasion of the performance, the dramatic text may function as an effective aid to the staging of the 'theatre of the soul'.

The Theatre of Conscience

If *La Ragione sprezzata* is perhaps the most eloquent example of the ways in which Glissenti turns the meditation on death into a theatrical device, the journey of individuals through the consideration of their own sins, confession, and, eventually, repentance, is best exemplified by those plays in which the working of conscience is translated into dramaturgy. With clear allusion to Adriano Prosperi's 'tribunali della coscienza' [tribunals of conscience], my use of the phrasing 'theatre of conscience' aims to stress two main features at stake in Glissenti's dramatisation of conscience's work.[136] In the playwright's universe, conscience is given the status of a character, if allegorical, while at the same time being conceived as the inner space within which individuals must reckon their actions. By suggesting an analogy between the theatre and the tribunal, I also wish to stress that the theatrical reshaping of conscience entails both the rhetorical mechanisms at work in a trial and the idea of making such mechanisms visible to the targeted audience, no matter whether this audience is made of spectators attending the performance or readers 'performing' the play within their own mind.

Particularly instructive of these dynamics is the play *L'Androtoo* (1616), whose plot revolves around the conflict between Man and Vanity. As mentioned above, the play takes place 'in one's own heart, where the internal and external affections fight against each other and eventually follow Man's will'.[137] The phrasing is of great interest in that, as is the case with other plays (*L'Andrio* and *La Sarcodinamia*, for instance, with 'campo of Free Will' and 'one's own consideration'), it speaks to theatre's ability to open a window onto Man's heart.[138] The heart is taken as the

---

134 Loyola, *ES*, 71 (trans. by Peruschi, fol. 17^v/p. 667).
135 Loyola, *ES*, 65 (trans. by Peruschi, fol. 17^r/p. 667): 'domandare gratia a Dio de sapere et sentire interiormente le pene le quale patiscono li dannati nell'inferno, acciò si l'amore divino non li ritira dalli peccati, almeno il timore dell'inferno li ritira dalli peccati' [to pray God to let me know and internally feel the punishments suffered by the damned in hell, so that if divine love does not move them away from sin, at least the fear of hell may take them away from sin].
136 Adriano Prosperi, *Tribunali della coscienza: inquisitori, confessori, missionari. Nuova edizione* (Turin: Einaudi, 2009).
137 *L'Androtoo*, fol. A5^v.
138 On the metaphor of the windowed soul, Bolzoni, *La stanza della memoria*, pp. 135–86 (pp. 154–64); and *Il cuore di cristallo: ragionamenti d'amore, poesia e ritratto nel Rinascimento* (Turin: Einaudi, 2010);

siege of vital and intellective functions, 'room' par excellence of the human soul, inner space within which both affections and passions move. The widespread *topos* of the window open onto the heart is based on the assumption that the heart is the receptacle of things perceived through the senses. Sticking to the metaphor, to be able to know someone, one should see through their heart.

As suggested by Torquato Accetto's *Della dissimulazione onesta* [The Honest Dissimulation] (1641), Nature has been very careful at concealing man's heart, the crucial role of which is not only about keeping one alive, but also about granting tranquillity ('gran diligenza ha posta la natura per nasconder il cuore, in poter del quale è collocata, non solo la vita, ma la tranquillità del vivere'). Accordingly, when the heart remains hidden, it preserves the good functioning of the external operations ('quando gli occorre di star nascosto [...] serba la salute delle operazioni esterne').[139] The chapter 'Del cuor che sta nascosto' [Of the heart, which is hidden] identifies the heart as an unfathomable and abyssal space, paradoxically wider than the external world, of which man is part. In the same way that powerful men protect themselves by residing in their palaces and secret dwellings ('palagi' and 'camere segrete'), all humans, although visible to one another ('ancorch'esposto alla vista di tutti'), may conceal their concerns in the 'spacious and secret house of the heart' ('nasconder i suoi affari nella vasta ed insieme segreta casa del suo cuore'). Accetto's statement is indicative of the complex relationship between human interiority and its external manifestations that is key to Baroque culture. The theorist of the 'honest dissimulation' stresses the role played by simulation as a form of personal defence. In Glissenti's theatre, the house of the heart is instead an outward-facing space, functioning as a performative mirror for both actors and their audience. Since the scene is meant to represent 'one's own heart' ('il cuore di ciascheduno'), whoever attends the show or reads the play faces the staging of their own interiority. This space is the one in which inner and outer affections fight against each other, a kind of experience that is common to all human beings. If Pona, among others, seizes upon the spatiality entailed by the trope by translating it into emblematic images, how does such a fight actually take shape on the theatrical stage?

L'Androtoo provides us with instructive materials, starting with the plot, which is outlined and explained in the 'Argomento'. The brief text functions as a self-standing *exemplum*. It opens by identifying the two forces at stake in the play and, indeed, in human life, Evil and Good:

> Va procurando il demonio con ogni suo potere la rovina dell'huomo; e perciò col mezo dell'angelo cattivo assistente a lui (che va sempre suggerendo agli sentimenti dell'huomo che i beni apparenti del mondo siano i veri beni, dove consista la felicità humana), lo induce all'amor delle vanità di questo mondo. Acciò che in queste si immerga, e colpevole al fine se ne muoia. All'incontro vuole Iddio che l'huomo si salvi, et acciò da queste fallaci suggestioni del demonio non resti ingannato, gli ha dato il Discorso, la Conscienza, et il

see also Mario Andrea Rigoni, 'Una finestra aperta sul cuore (note sulla metafora della *sinceritas* nella tradizione occidentale)', *Lettere italiane*, 4 (1974), 434–58.
139 Torquato Accetto, *Della dissimulazione onesta*, ed. by Salvatore Silvano Nigro (Turin: Einaudi, 1997), p. 59.

Rimorso interno, come censori acerrimi delle sue operationi. Da i quali avvertito, et ammonito per mezo della Penitenza si riduce nello stato dell'Innocenza, per cui finalmente si viene a salvare, e questa è l'occasione della favola.[140]

[With all his powers, the Devil seeks the fall of man; to this end, through his assistant, the evil Angel (who continuously tells Man that the apparent goods of the world are in fact the real ones in which human happiness resides) pushes man to love the vanities of this world. By plunging himself into them, Man eventually dies as a sinner. On the contrary, God wishes that Man be saved; to prevent Man from being deceived by the Devil's misleading advice, God has gifted him with Discourse, Conscience, and internal Remorse, fierce censors of his actions. Admonished by them and through Penitence, Man returns to the condition of Innocence, through which he is saved. This is the plot of the fable.]

Keen on seeing Man saved, God has provided him with three invaluable aids for self-discipline: alongside the importance of Discourse, who appears in most of Glissenti's plays, *L'Androtoo* highlights the collaboration of Conscience and Remorse. The picture is completed by Penitence, who, by promoting contrition practices, eventually makes it possible for Man to be brought back to Innocence. The second part of the plot is characterised by another attack on the part of the Senses, who try to lead Man towards Vanity. Conscience and Remorse foresee the danger thanks to a peculiar icon whose aspect changes when Man gets closer to the path of sin. Thanks to a miraculous image, they manage to save him:

Persuadono i sentimenti a l'huomo, che voglia prender in moglie la Metamonia, che è la vanità del mondo. Egli non pensando far male vi mette il pensiero, del che avvedutasi la Conscienza, et il Discorso (per mezo d'una immagine miracolosa, la quale cangiava il viso al cangiar dei costumi di chi l'honorava), ritornano l'huomo (aiutandolo in ciò la Penitenza) nella sua prima innocenza. E questa essendogli molto lodata dalla Conscienza, e dalla Penitenza viene ad esser molto stimata da lui.[141]

[The Senses persuade Man to marry Metamonia, that is, the Vanity of the world. Unaware of doing something evil, he considers doing it; once Conscience and Discourse realise it (thanks to a miraculous image, whose face changes with the changing behaviour of those who honour it), they return Man (who is helped in this task by Penitence) to his original innocence. Innocence, being highly praised by Conscience and Penitence, is eventually held in high esteem by Man too.]

The Senses thus turn to deception and make Man believe that Vanity is, in fact, Innocence herself. Once again, the joint efforts of Discourse, Conscience, and Remorse, with the aid of Penitence, rescue him. The moral explanation makes the allegory of the story explicit by stressing the importance of God's help, without which Man falls easily prey to sin:

Dal che si comprende, che quantunque l'huomo habbia voglia di mantenersi Innocente, non può tuttavia senza l'aiuto del soccorso divino. Perché da i propii Sentimenti ingannato, e per la sua fragilità e ignoranza molto debole, facilmente

---

140 *L'Androtoo*, fol. A4^{r-v}.
141 *L'Androtoo*, fol. A4^{v}.

cade nell'amore delli affetti mondani. In tanto che, se col ragionevole Discorso, con la Conscienza, et con la Penitenza non viene soccorso, resta facilmente abbattuto, e vinto. E dove tal volta crede andarsi verso l'Innocenza, ingannato dalli proprii Sentimenti s'accosta alle vanità mondane.[142]

[From these events one learns that, as much as Man wishes to maintain himself innocent, he cannot do it without God's help. Indeed, deceived by his own Senses, and weakened by his frailty and ignorance, he easily falls in love with mundane affections. If he is not helped by Discourse, Conscience, and Penitence, he is easily defeated. And where, at times, he believes to be going towards Innocence, deceived by his own Senses, he gets close to mundane vanities.]

The 'Argomento' provides the readers with all they need to decode the allegory of the *favola*. Its interest does not lie in the summary of the plot, which, made of repetitive patterns, is rather straightforward, but in its being a recapitulation of moral precepts and an abridged illustration of the various components of human psychology, normally invisible to the physical eyes. Alongside Discourse — whose main activity, according to the tautological nature of the character's name, is that of performing the use of reason — a good example of the principle that animates the allegorical characters is the interaction of Conscience (the 'housekeeper') and Remorse (her 'page'). The commonly used metaphor of conscience's remorse is turned into dramatic action. In fact, whenever Man is about to lose Innocence (that is, his spiritual innocence), Conscience and Remorse intervene by performing the duty entailed by their names. Their function is briefly summarised by Conscience herself in a passage from Act v, which provides the audience with the basics of moral discipline. Without conscience or remorse of the 'inner heart', all behaviours become legitimate: 'Ben si può dire, che lecito ogn'hor sia | far ad ogn'un quel che 'l suo cor desia | quando non v'è veruna conscienza, | o rimorso verun nel cor interno' [It is legitimate to do whatever one's heart desires when there is no conscience at work]. Indeed, innocence and goodness are easily lost ('O come facilmente l'huomo cade | da l'innocenza sua, da la bontate) when Man is not eaten away by remorse nor stung by conscience ('quando non ha rimorso che lo rodi, | né conscienza che lo punga o fieda'): once again, the metaphor is taken literally and used to describe the actions of the two personified allegories. Man's fall is not surprising, for he comes to this world vulnerable and ignorant. In order to make him cope with his weakness, God has provided him with Conscience and Remorse:

> Ma non è sì gran fatto, che l'huom cada
> quando che per natura è frale e lieve,
> e per natura ancor nasce ignorante.
> Per questo il grand'Iddio, che ben conobbe
> che tal fragilità, che tal insitia
> potean farlo cader, me col mio paggio
> pose a lui presso; acciò per nostro mezo
> ritornasse innocente, come prima.[143]

---

142 *L'Androtoo*, fol. A5^r.
143 *L'Androtoo*, 5.7, pp. 166–67.

[It is not surprising that Man is prone to falling since he is by nature frail and delicate and is born ignorant too. For this reason, the almighty God, aware of such frailty and knowing that this weakness might make Man fall, put myself and my page next to him, so that, through our assistance, he could become innocent again, as he was before.]

Conscience and Remorse are thus committed to defending their protégé from Vanity's servants, Frailness and Ignorance, who put Man's Innocence to the test over and over again. The concept, clearly outlined in the 'Argomento', is further unpacked in the prologue of the drama delivered by Innocence herself, who symbolises the human condition pursued by Androtoo throughout the play. Recalling the state of grace enjoyed by the progenitors before the Fall, Innocence declares herself eager to welcome Man back. Her presence on stage as an unseen spectator creates a short circuit between the action and the audience's perception of what happens on stage, with particularly ironic implications when Vanity comes in wearing Innocence's clothes.[144]

In the conflict between internal and external affections that unfolds in Man's heart, Conscience's role is substantial. In the first scene of *L'Androtoo*, one of Lucifer's servants, Cacodemone, states that his plans are hindered by shrewd old Conscience more than by Discourse ('questa co 'l suo rimorso l'huom sì assale, | sì lo rode e lo lacera sempre | ch'ei timido s'arretra, quanto io innanzi | lo vo guidando del peccato in grembo').[145] Thanks to 'harsh Penitence' ('l'aspra Penitenza'), Conscience guides Man towards the acquisition of that very Innocence which was once lost ('ad acquistar quell'Innocenza bella | che fu da noi, come tu sai, perduta').[146] In her capacity as housekeeper ('governatrice di casa'), Conscience proves even more important to the plotline than Man's servants (Discourse, Sense, Thought, Memory, and Will), whose functions are outlined on the occasion of Man's first appearance on stage. The ambivalence of the human condition, outstanding and miserable at the same time, makes it difficult for him to grasp both his ultimate goal and what is at stake in his actions and choices.[147] Following a model rooted in medieval allegory, the personifications introduce themselves and give their advice one at a time.

144 *L'Androtoo*, prol., fol. A6ᵛ: 'Qui d'intorno staromi, a la veduta | quantunque ascosta, con pietoso sguardo | a rimirar s'egli la sua salute | provido un tratto ricovrar procuri' [I will be here, though hidden, pitifully seeing whether he will wisely manage to recover his salvation]. According to a feature typical of Renaissance dramaturgy, the characters who deliver the prologues declare that they will remain on stage, though unseen, in Glissenti's other plays as well.
145 *L'Androtoo*, 1.1, p. 15 ('With her remorse she attacks him so forcefully, she consumes and rips him so intensely that he timidly holds back as much as I push him towards sin').
146 Ibid.
147 *L'Androtoo*, 1.2, p. 21: 'Parmi esser cosa tale, e così grande | e nobile, e stupenda, a cui non giunga | al par cosa mortal qua giù creata; | ch'io di me stesso prendo meraviglia. | Ma in fine poi, se meglio volgo il guardo | e fisso mi contemplo, e mi vagheggio, | altro che poca terra, e polve vile | esser mi veggo a lo mio spirto unita. | O se pur carne et ossa, e nervi e vene | son però cose tutte insieme unite | di putre massa e putrescibil sangue' [I seem to be such a great, noble and stupendous thing, with no peer among mortal things created down here, that I am myself astounded. Yet, if I look at myself better and contemplate myself, I see that I am nothing other than a little soil and vile dust united with my spirit. Even my flesh and bones, nerves and veins are kept together by decaying matter and putrefying blood].

The series begins with Thought, who declares that Man would be imperfect if he fell short of any one of the servants. Free Will, consistently with what Glissenti maintains elsewhere in his works, claims the centrality of his decisional power.[148] Sense defends the necessity of making the most of things earthly, while Recollection remains vague, insisting on the priority of mundane preoccupations. The last word is given to Discourse, the wisest among the servants, who reaffirms their complementarity ('Voi sete mio signor con tanti servi | atto a disporvi a voglia, a piacer vostro | al pensar, al sentir, al ricordarvi, | al discorrer ancor disposto e pronto'), and invites Man to consider the contemplation of God as the ultimate goal of life ('acciò possiate con tai mezi il tutto | contemplar d'esso mondo, e la natura | di lui investigar, sì che gli effetti | mirando in lui sì variati e belli, | poggiate a la cagion vivace, e prima, | per conoscerla bene').[149]

Discourse outlines an itinerary towards God that does begin on earth. The 'beautiful world' ('bel mondo') — the scene of human life — does not have a negative acceptation in this case, since it is not taken as valuable in itself, but as a step towards a higher end. Managing a difficult balance between the 'sentimenti esterni' and the 'interior potenze prime', which Nature has provided him with, Man (that is, the microcosm) proves a veritable double of the macrocosm ('un picciol mondo, et un ritratto vivo | del mondo grande sete al fin rimasto').[150] Discourse is the mouthpiece of a distinctively humanist anthropological view, which identifies a spiritual correspondence between 'mondo grande' and 'picciol mondo'.[151] While

---

148 *L'Androtoo*, 1.2, p. 22: 's'io con voi non fossi, | quantunque haveste tutti questi a canto, | nulla sarebbe a voi, nullo profitto | v'apporterebbe il lor servitio o possa, | perché, come potria giovarvi punto | il Discorso, il sentir, l'immaginarvi | se vi mancasse poi la libertade | di poter sempre a vostra voglia pronto | discorrer, o pensar o risentirvi?' [If I weren't with you, despite having all those others next to you, you would have nothing; no benefit would come from their service and power. How could Discourse, sense, and imagination be of any benefit if you were lacking the freedom to be always able to argue, think, and dissent according to your will?].

149 *L'Androtoo*, 1.2, p. 26: 'Thanks to your many servants, you can, my lord, devote yourself, as you wish, to thinking, feeling, remembering; you are also able and ready to argue'; 'So that you can, through these means, contemplate the entirety of the world and investigate nature. By admiring its various and beautiful effects, you may turn to the vivid and primeval cause of things, and get to know it well'.

150 *L'Androtoo*, 1.2, p. 27.

151 Ivi, 1.2, p. 28: 'Il mondo grande, come voi vedete, | egli è composto d'elementi e cieli, | pieno di stelle e di vaganti lumi. | Che son da intelligenze non erranti | retti e guidati ne li corsi loro. | E questi tutti del motore al cenno, | che sopra al mondo a questi è soprastante, | senza interporvi error suo uffitio fanno. | Voi parimente ancor composto sete | d'elementi [...] | Le potenze dell'alma vostra sono | come nel cielo son l'intelligenze. [...] Ma l'alma, che soprasta in libertade | a tutte quelle come nobil forma | da cui dipende tutto l'esser vostro, | di questa humanità, fattura illustre, | è simile al fattor, che tutto il mondo | creò di nulla, e la sua immago serba. [...] Quest'è quel punto dunque, per cui l'huomo | fu fatto un picciol mondo, acciò che un mondo | conosca l'altro mondo' ('The greater world, as you see, is made of elements and heavens, full of stars and moving lights, guided in their movements by higher intelligences. All these, according to the creator's will, who oversees the world, accomplish their function without error. Similarly, you are made of elements [...] The powers of your soul are like the intelligences in the heavens [...] But the soul, whose freedom overpowers all of them, stands above, as the noble form on which your being depends; it is the soul that makes humanity, illustrious accomplishment; in this duty, it is similar to the creator, who created the whole world from scratch in his likeness. [...] This is the principle according to which Man was made a small world, so that one world may know the other').

Man struggles with the very idea of a correspondence between his own finitude ('finito e chiuso | entro brevi confini') and the eternal greatness of God ('non v'è proportion veruna | fra l'infinito, e 'l terminato punto'), Discourse recommends a morally disciplined practice of life as the only way for Man to recover his Innocence and turn his earthly preoccupations into spiritual ones.[152]

According to the process outlined by Discourse, Man is expected to acknowledge God's presence in the world and turn towards him, loving and venerating him with ardour. The spiritual practice outlined by Discourse and enacted within the play by Conscience's behaviour recalls the core principles of the spiritual tradition revamped by Loyola. Given the presence of Ignatius in Venice and the mark left by his apostolate, specifically at the Incurabili and Derelitti, it is not surprising to find echoes of his teachings in Glissenti's works. Indeed, the plays are not only similar, in some respects, to concurrent developments of Jesuit drama, but also, and most importantly, they share the scope of the spiritual practice designed by Ignatius and widely promoted by devotional literature in the vernacular. In line with the founding inspiration of the *Spiritual Exercises* (namely, the invitation to self-examination formulated by Paul in the Second Epistle to the Corinthians), Ignatius offered the devout Christian a guide for meditation, which had an impact on several literary genres.[153] Particularly relevant to the present discussion are Loyola's prescriptions about the inner visualisation of images and their relationship to preaching, the rhetoric of which has much in common with drama.[154] Furthermore, Ignatius's system, which does function as a 'theatre of the soul', deploys rhetorical and compositional devices that build on the notion of theatre as a *locus* for the staging of *imagines agentes*.[155]

By setting the play in the 'house of the heart', the playwright turns to the same kind of inner space in which Ignatius's meditations are meant to unfold. According to Loyola's preliminary remarks, 'con esso nome de esercitii spirituali se intende ciascuno modo de esaminare la propria conscienza, anchora di pensare, di contemplare, di pregare secondo la mente et la parola, et finalmente di fare ciascune altre operationi spirituali' aimed at 'togliere tutte l'affettioni et perturbationi dell'animo male ordinate, e tolte quelle, a cercare et ritrovare la voluntà de Iddio circa la ordinatione della sua vita e salute dell'anima'.[156] These instructions are very

---

152 *L'Androtoo*, 1.2, p. 29.
153 Paul, II Corinthians 13.5 ('vosmet ipsos temptate si estis in fide ipsi vos probate an non cognoscitis vos ipsos quia Christus Iesus in vobis est nisi forte reprobi estis' [Examine yourselves to see whether you are in the faith; test yourselves. Do you not realise that Christ Jesus is in you — unless, of course, you fail the test?', *New International Version*]).
154 On the dynamics at stake in the process described, see Freedberg, *The Power of Images*; Bolzoni, *La stanza della memoria*; Lydia Salviucci Insolera, 'L'uso di immagini come strumento didattico-catechetico nella Compagnia di Gesù', in *I Gesuiti e la Ratio Studiorum*, ed. by Hinz, Righi and Zardin, pp. 191–210.
155 Bologna, *Esercizi di memoria*; and Guaragnella, *Gli occhi della mente*.
156 Loyola, *ES*, 2 (trans. by Peruschi); 'this name of spiritual exercises means to include every way of examining one's conscience, of meditating, of contemplating, of praying vocally and mentally, and finally of performing other spiritual actions'; 'preparing and disposing the soul to rid itself of all the disordered tendencies, and, after it is rid, to seek and find God's will in the management of one's life and salvation of the soul'.

similar to those given by Conscience and Discourse in *L'Androtoo*, and many more can be found in Loyola's work that resonate with the lexicon of Glissenti's morality plays. A few examples will do:

> In tutti li sequenti esercitii debbiamo usare atti de intelletto quando discorremo, ma quando siamo de dispositione, atti de voluntà. [...] L'inimico del'huomo, per più delle volte, per spetie di bene oppugna per nocere quelli li quali avanti habbino dato opera più tosto alla via della vita, la quale è detta illuminativa. [...] Questo modo de esercitatione propriamente se acconviene alli ignoranti, imperfetti, et a quelli li quali sono senza littere, alli quali oltra di questo bisognarà esponerli e narrarli ciascuni precetti de Idio e della Ecclesia e li peccati mortali, insieme con li cinque sensi et opere della misericordia.[157]

> [In the following exercises, we must use acts of the intellect when reasoning, and acts of the will when one's disposition is concerned. [...] Man's enemy often tempts, under the appearance of good, those who have been exercising themselves in the way of life that is called illuminative. [...] This way of exercising is suitable for ignorant people, illiterate and without education, who need to be explained the Precepts of God and the Church, the mortal sins, alongside the Five Senses, and Works of Mercy.]

The operations of intellect and will are the protagonists of the *Exercises* as much as the intellective functions are the protagonists of Glissenti's *favole morali*. Evil temptations are particularly dangerous for the devout, especially at the early stage of the spiritual practice, when it is still easy to be distracted from the meditation's main scope and follow false appearances of good. The same dynamic informs the conflict between world and spirit in Glissenti. Fitting is also the reference to the poor and illiterate, for whom effective pedagogical tools are particularly needed, hence the playwright's choice to use allegory to illustrate doctrinal teachings relevant to Christian life.

Alongside these similarities, the *Spiritual Exercises* display further features that reappear in Glissenti's dramaturgy. The foundational principle of the first week's exercises, for instance, describes the relationship between man and God in terms that are similar to those used by Discourse with regards to Man's love towards God:[158]

> L'huomo è creato a questo fine, che laudi e reverisca il suo Signore, e servendo a quello finalmente pervenga alla gloria eterna; ma l'altre cose che sonno sopra la terra, sonno state create da lui per uso e servitio di quello, acciochè lo aiutino a pervenire et ad acquistare il fine delle sua creatione, per il quale l'huomo è creato; donde sequita che l'huomo deve usare de tutte le creature, quanto lo aiutano per pervenire al suo fine, e quanto lo impediscono e danno impaccio de non potere pervenire a quello, deve lasciarle. Per il che bisogna che l'huomo si facci indifferente in tutte le cose create, de tal maniera che non cerchi della sua parte più presto salute che malatia, ricchezze che povertà, honore che dishonore, vita lunga che breve, ma è cosa conveniente che in tutte l'altre cose finalmente desideri et capi quelle cose, le quale conducono al fine per il quale l'huomo è creato.[159]

---

157 Loyola, ES, 3, 10, 18 (trans. by Peruschi).
158 *L'Androtoo*, 1.2, p. 26.
159 Loyola, ES, 23, 'Principio overo fondamento' (trans. by Peruschi).

[Man is created to praise and revere God our Lord, and, by serving him, to achieve eternal glory; but the other things on earth are created by God to serve man so as to help him in reaching and acquiring the end of his creation, for which he is created; from this it follows that man is to use all creatures as much as they help him on to his end, and ought to rid himself of them so far as they hinder him as to it. For this, it is necessary that man make himself indifferent to all created things, so that, on his part, he does not seek health rather than sickness, riches rather than poverty, honor rather than dishonor, long rather than short life; but it is appropriate that in all other things he should desire and choose those, which are conducive to the end for which he is created.]

The passage describes a practice of life aimed at the salvation of the soul through God's love. Within such perspective, the world is not an end in itself, but a means for reaching a higher goal. According to the same doctrinal premise that we have encountered across Glissenti's *oeuvre*, Man is expected to overcome the worldly obstacle that separates him from God, by making good use of Free Will, distancing himself from earthly goods and turning to spiritual ones.

From the outset of the *Spiritual Exercises*, the priority given to conscience and its examination stands out. What Ignatius has to say about the 'esamina generale della conscienza utilissima a mondare l'anima et a confessarsi delli peccati' [general examination of conscience, very useful to cleanse the soul and confess one's sins] draws a picture that resonates with Glissenti's dramas: 'Prosopongo essere tre li mei pensamenti. Uno il quale procede dalla voluntà e libertà et è dentro di me. Il secondo pensamento nasce dal buon spirito. Il terzo pensamento procede dal mal spirito, e tutti doi questi nascono fuora di me'.[160] Free will, which is responsible for man's actions, is thus represented as hanging in the balance between the 'good spirit' and the 'evil' one. When the recommendations described in the *Exercises* are translated into drama, the spiritual conflict takes the shape of the one between the Good angel and the demons. Ignatius's discipline lays out three main ways to handle such conflict. First, individuals can resist temptations and, when this becomes a habit, they acquire further strength. Second, when the effort made at rejecting a given sin is weak, that makes it a venial one. Third (and worst-case scenario), when one eagerly surrenders to evil thoughts, that is mortal sin.[161] Glissenti's *favole morali* bring all these options to the fore. *L'Androtoo*, for instance, stages several attempts made by Vanity and the Senses to win Man over (it is always thanks to Conscience and Remorse that the protagonist is spared damnation). As illustrated by Loyola, evil takes the shape of good and aims to deceive Man, a situation that, in the play, is embodied by Vanity's plan to disguise herself as Innocence. In plays such as *La Ragione sprezzata* and *Il mercato*, evil thoughts get the better of Man, who dies without any chance of redemption.

The function performed by Conscience in *L'Androtoo* follows Ignatius's instructions closely. In her first appearance, the character illustrates her role alongside that of

---

160 Loyola, ES, 32 (trans. by Peruschi, fol. 10^r/p. 659): 'I presuppose that there are three kinds of thoughts in me. One, which springs from the will and liberty inside me. The second stems from the good spirit. The third from the bad, and both these come from without'.
161 Loyola, ES, 33–35 (trans. by Peruschi, fol. 10^v/pp. 659–60).

Remorse and the awareness of God's benevolence. It all begins with Conscience's 'biting' words, which are meant to engender a strong feeling of bitterness inside man's heart conducive to regeneration ('Io poi con le pungenti mie parole | un tal livor gli imprimo nell'interno, | ch'ei non ha ben, se tosto non rissorge'). In order to then maintain himself in this newly reacquired condition, Man must open his heart to Penitence: his acquaintance with 'such beloved woman' ('donna sì cara') will teach him how to turn mistakes into a tool for spiritual enhancement through repentance and contrition.[162] Finally, by reminding himself of the many benefits received from God, Man will abstain from offending him.[163]

A self-examination of a Jesuit stamp is staged more literally at the end of Act II: following an unexpected alteration in the aspect of the miraculous icon ('la bella immago, | che par ridente in vista, al'hor turbata | ver noi si dimostrò palesemente'),[164] Conscience and Discourse invite Man to scrutinise his soul so that he may identify the sin that has caused the image to change. Conscience, who is the expert on the matter of self-examination, provides Man with clear instructions reminiscent of Loyola's teachings: 'Esaminate ben l'interno vostro, | se in parole, se 'n fatti, se con l'opre, | se col consenso, o col pensier vagante | sete transcorso in qualche grave errore, | acciò tantosto penitenza segue'.[165] The examination of one's errors is the first point of Loyola's second exercise, 'to think about the sins one has committed'.[166] Further instructions given by Conscience brings the self-examination process to completion, which, in fact, coincides with an act of confession:

> Voi mio signor andate discorrendo
> minutamente tutti i vostri affari.
> A fin che facilmente voi possiate
> scoprir l'error, che latitando serpe:
> e per meglio essequir quanto vi lodo,
> farete che l'Arbitrio pronto sia
> ad essequir cotesta voglia mia.
> Indi con diligenza procurate
> che qui 'l Ricordo vi riduca a mente
> ogni vostra andat'opra [...].[167]

---

162 *L'Androtoo*, 1.3, p. 29: 'la Penitenza donna così cara | Gli insegna il vero modo ch'usar deve. | Perché col pentimento de gli errori | commessi a studio, o per fragilitade, | a vera attrition tosto s'appoggia, | e tal appoggio in piedi lo sostenta' [Penitence, such a gracious woman, teaches him how to behave. By repenting the faults, which he committed on purpose or due to weakness, he turns to true contrition and this supports him].
163 *L'Androtoo*, 1.3, p. 29: 'Il ricordarsi appresso tanti e tanti | benefitii che l'huom riceve ogn'hora | da la man liberal del grand'Iddio [...] | lo fa avvertito di non usar offesa | a chi tanta pietade usato gli habbia' [Remembering the many gifts that Man receives every moment from the generous hand of God [...] warns him not to offend the one, who was so pitiful towards him].
164 *L'Androtoo*, 2.8, p. 58.
165 *L'Androtoo*, 2.8, pp. 58–59 ('Carefully examine your soul to see whether you fell into some serious fault in words, actions, deeds, either on purpose or due to lack of attention, so that penitence may follow').
166 Loyola, *ES*, 55–60 (fols. 14^v–15^v/p. 665).
167 *L'Androtoo*, 2.8, p. 59.

[Please, sir, review carefully all your actions, so as to easily uncover the sin that spreads furtively: and in order to better execute what I recommend, you will make sure that your Will be ready to accomplish my wish. So, diligently ensure that Memory will review all your past deeds.]

By remembering both his sins and the benefits received from God, Man joins a conversation with himself that is key to productive meditation. The importance of reviewing them all coincides with Ignatius's recommendation to carefully survey one's sins and remember them by examining every moment of one's life.[168]

The affinity of Glissenti's drama with the legacy of Loyola is also suggested by a curious reference made to the founder of the Jesuits in the play. In one of the several comedic scenes that offer a light-hearted counterpoint to the seriousness of the main topic, Recollection, who has been asked by Sense to keep Conscience away from Man, entrusts the 'housekeeper' with the purchase of a book for their master. Rather clumsy when it comes to telling lies, Recollection is not able to invent a title for the book that she wishes Conscience to buy. In the attempt to identify it, Conscience suggests a series of titles that shed light on the kind of literature she is familiar with:

CONSCIENZA	E che libro è cotesto, ch'egli vuole?
RICORDO	Di quei, di quei... non mi ricordo il nome.
CONSCIENZA	Oh ti possi scordar che ti sia vivo! Forse un offitio?
RICORDO	No.
CONSCIENZA	Forsi leggendario dei santi? O de le vergini volgare?
RICORDO	N'anco questo, egli è un altro. Andate dietro.
CONSCIENZA	Un fiore di virtù?
RICORDO	Né questo ancora.
CONSCIENZA	Le pistole, e Vangeli?
RICORDO	N'anco questo. Egli è un libretto picciolo da vero, di poche carte, ma di gran dottrina.
CONSCIENZA	La dottrina christiana?

---

168 Loyola, *ES*, 56 (fol. 15^r/p. 665): 'Il primo ponto serrà il processo delli peccati, cioè ridurre a memoria et ricordarsi delli miei peccati commessi, pensando di mese in mese e di tempo in tempo, et a fare questo effetto tre cose ce aiutano molto, cioè considerare il luogo dove siamo habitati, e le persone con chi havemo conversato, e li esercitii li quali havemo fatto' [The first Point is the statement of the sins; that is to say, to bring to memory all the sins of life, looking from year to year, or from period to period. For this three things are helpful: first, to look at the place and the house where I have lived; second, the relations I have had with others; third, the occupation in which I have lived]. The individual must proceed in a similar way in the third exercise, which reiterates the previous one in the form of a spiritual dialogue with the Virgin Mary, begging her for three things: 'La prima che impetri che io senta interior cognoscimento delli mei peccati et abominationi. La seconda, che io senti il disordine delli mie operatione, acciochè, havendoli in abominatione, me emendi et mi ordini. La terza domandare gratia d'havere cognoscimento del mondo et della sua vanità, le qual cose fugirle' [first, that I may feel an interior knowledge of my sins, and hatred of them; second, that I may feel the disorder of my actions, so that, hating them, I may correct myself and put myself in order; third, to ask knowledge of the world, in order that, hating it, I may put away from me worldly and vain things], trans. by Mullan (ivi, 62, fol. 16^r/p. 666).

Ricordo	Questa meno.
Conscienza	Il Rosario per sorte?
Ricordo	Né 'l Rosario.
Conscienza	Li sette Salmi, con le Lettanie?
Ricordo	Di cotesta grandezza, ma non questo.
Conscienza	Libro particular de le indulgenze?
Ricordo	Tratta di non so che, ma non di queste.
Conscienza	Modo d'essaminar la conscienza?
Ricordo	Quasi l'havete detto. Egli è un altro.
Conscienza	Modo di confessarsi degnamente?
Ricordo	L'havete al fin trovato, egli è cotesto.[169]

[CONSCIENCE   And what book is the one he wants?
RECOLLECTION   One of those... I don't remember the name.
CONSCIENCE   Oh my, you would forget you are alive! Maybe an order of service?
RECOLLECTION   No.
CONSCIENCE   Maybe a collection of legends of the saints? Or of virgins, in the vernacular?
RECOLLECTION   Not even this one, it's another. Continue.
CONSCIENCE   A Flower of virtue?
RECOLLECTION   Not even that one.
CONSCIENCE   The Epistles and the Gospels?
RECOLLECTION   No. It's a very small booklet indeed, of a few pages, but of great doctrine.
CONSCIENCE   The Christian doctrine?
RECOLLECTION   Not at all.
CONSCIENCE   Perhaps the Rosary?
RECOLLECTION   Not even the Rosary.
CONSCIENCE   The Seven Psalms with the Litanies?
RECOLLECTION   Of that thickness, but not that one.
CONSCIENCE   A particular book of indulgences?
RECOLLECTION   It revolves around something, but it's not that.
CONSCIENCE   Way of examining one's conscience?
RECOLLECTION   Almost there, yet it's another one.
CONSCIENCE   Way of confessing appropriately?
RECOLLECTION   You found it eventually, it's that one!]

The scene is of great interest, especially when one considers its narrative gratuitousness, for the devotional and liturgical books listed by Conscience are not essential to the plotline. Recollection could stop Conscience after the first title, but she does not. In fact, the scene is not only about making fun of Recollection's struggle with memory, but also, and most important, about evoking titles of actual books popular in the market of the period, with which Glissenti's audience was likely familiar. The attention of Recollection is eventually captured by two among the titles referenced by his interlocutor: a handbook for the examination of conscience ('Modo d'essaminar la conscienza') and a guide to confession ('Modo di confessarsi degnamente'). Numerous books of that sort were in high demand in the decades

---

[169] *L'Androtoo*, 2.10, pp. 64–65.

around 1600: one could think of the *Breve modo di esaminare la conscienza* often published alongside the treatise *Della imitatione di Christo*, attributed in Italy to Jean de Gerson;[170] Giovanni Bellarini's *Breve prattica della conscienza*;[171] Alessandro Sauli's *Modo di essaminare la conscienza per sapersi ben confessare*;[172] Modesto Baliotti's *Facilissimo modo di confessarsi*;[173] Giovanni Maria Caneparo's *Modo et regola che si debbe tener per sapersi ben confessarsi*.[174] All these books were widely available to the many vernacular readers interested in the spiritual practices encouraged by the Counter-Reformation.

Persuaded of Man's eventual conversion based on the books that he is supposedly eager to read, Conscience discloses her direct relationship with the Jesuits, whom she mentions explicitly, alongside their founding father:

> Tu in questo mentre, che ritorno indietro,
> ratto ne va, là dove i Gesuiti
> tengon la bella Chiesa, e 'l padre Ignatio
> pregherai da mia parte, che si degni
> quanto prima venir a casa nostra,
> per un servitio mio, molt'importante.
> Guarda non ti scordar da smemorato
> et il loco, e la Chiesa, e 'l nome Ignatio.[175]

[While I go back, you go quickly where the Jesuits have their beautiful church, and, on my behalf, beg father Ignatius to come to our house as soon as possible for a most important service that concerns me. You featherbrain, be careful not to forget the place, the church, and Ignatius's name.]

Father Ignatius is hailed as a veritable *auctoritas*, the mouthpiece of the spiritual practice that Conscience has been fostering. The only 'real' character in the play, he never appears on stage, but his presence is evoked more than once. Conscience later reports having met him in the same bookshop ('bottega') where she was buying the *Modo di confessarsi degnamente*.[176] In Act III, she also declares herself pleased with

---

170 *Incomincia il libro divoto et utile composto per messer Giovanni Gersonne cancelliere di Parisio, della imitatione di Christo Giesù, et del dispreggio di tutte le cose del mondo* (Venice: Francesco Bindoni and Maffeo Pasini, 1545), with a number of editions throughout the following decades; on the tradition of the text across the European vernaculars, see Von Habsburg, *Catholic and Protestant Translations of the Imitatio Christi*.
171 Giovanni Bellarini, *Breve prattica della conscienza raccolta da gravi auttori, nella quale con nuovo compartimento si dà un facil modo di essaminar in poco tempo lo stato di tutta la conscienza, et è opera insieme a i confessori, et a' penitenti accomodata* (Venice: Fioravante Prati, 1597).
172 Alessandro Sauli, *Instruttione compendiosa et breve delle cose più necessarie alla salute, le quali doverebbono essere sapute da ogni fidel christiano [...] Aggiuntovi di nuovo un modo di essaminare la conscienza per sapersi ben confessare* (Pavia: Girolamo Bartoli, 1577).
173 Modesto Baliotti, *Facilissimo modo di confessarsi e specialmente delle persone religiose et altre che spesso si confessano* (Perugia: Pietro Giacomo Petrucci, 1580).
174 Giovanni Maria Caneparo, *Modo et regola che si debbe tener per sapersi ben confessarsi* (Brescia: Giacomo Britannico, 1593).
175 *L'Androtoo*, 2.10, p. 65.
176 *L'Androtoo*, 2.13, p. 69: 'Senza molto cercar il libricciolo | ho ritrovato, che m'è stato imposto. | Ma quel che più mi piace, il padre Ignatio | a caso ho ritrovato, che comprava | anch'egli certo libro; e m'ha promesso | venir fra poco d'hora a ritrovarmi' [Without too much searching around,

Man's penitence, which has been made possible thanks to the joint intervention of Father Ignatius and Remorse.[177] Indeed, the woman is in a close relationship with the priest, a relationship that seems to include mystic experiences:

> Io voglio andarmi a consolar alquanto
> dal padre Ignazio, e trattenermi seco.
> Perché nel vero poco gusto trovo
> se non quando con lui ragiono. Al'hora
> parmi sentir una dolcezza immensa.[178]

[I wish to go and be consoled by Father Ignatius, and stay some time with him. Indeed, I am never happy, but when I speak to him. On those occasions I seem to feel great sweetness.]

Along with turning to Father Ignatius as adviser and, likely, as confessor, Conscience showcases her expertise in the reading and study of those devotional texts that were meant to be pivotal to the training of devout Christians, and which were indeed present in the Venetian hospitals in which Glissenti worked.[179] We do know, for instance, that the library of the Somaschians at the Derelitti contained a copy of Mattia Bellintani's *Pratica dell'oration mentale* (1581), and that Battista da Crema's *Specchio interiore* (1540) included a prologue to the 'Governatrici' of the Incurabili.[180] Alongside the *Modo di confessarsi degnamente*, Conscience wishes to pick up 'certain booklets' ('certi libricciuoli') about the contempt of the world which she deems essential to anyone who desires to gain the salvation of the soul.[181] Confirming her pedagogical and disciplining inclination, Conscience dwells on devotional literature and upholds its priority over those secular writings which lead readers towards Vanity rather than teaching them how to be good Christians. In a curious monologue about the book market (and one should not forget that we are in Venice!) she complains about the fact that most reading material available to

---

I have found the booklet that I was requested to find. Even better is that I found father Ignatius by chance; he was also buying some book; and he promised he would soon come and find me].

177 *L'Androtoo*, 3.1, p. 72.
178 *L'Androtoo*, 4.7, p. 123.
179 On the place of confession as a flagship practice in the Jesuit tradition, see Prosperi, *Tribunali della coscienza*, pp. 485–507.
180 Mattia Bellintani, *Pratica dell'oration mentale* (Venice: Pietro Dusinelli, 1581); Ellero, 'S. Girolamo Miani e i Somaschi all'ospedale dei Derelitti', pp. 48–49, recalls that Bellintani's book was recorded in the 1600 inventory of books at the Derelitti alongside one 'tragicomedia spirituale' by Giovanni Battista Leoni, whose significance to Glissenti I have mentioned above. On Bellintani's work, which focuses on doctrinal themes such as free will, see Giorgio Caravale, *Forbidden Prayer: Church Censorship and Devotional Literature in Renaissance Italy* (London: Routledge, 2012), pp. 100–07. Battista da Crema, *Specchio interiore. Opera divina, per la cui lettione ciascuno devoto potrà facilmente ascendere al colmo della perfettione* (Milan: Francesco Minizio Calvo, 1540), was reprinted through the 1540s; Battista's prologue to the 'venerande come madri M. Maria Gradenica et M. Malipiera, et altre sue coadiutrici, governatrici dell'Hospitale dell'Incurabili, di Venetia in Christo honorande', at fols 1^r–5^v; on *Specchio interiore*, see Caravale, *Forbidden Prayer*, pp. 44–54, 122–24, 152–55.
181 *L'Androtoo*, 3.1, p. 73: 'Andrommi intanto | a ricomprarne certi libricciuoli | che de le vanità di questo mondo | raccontano lo sprezzo, che dovria | ciaschedun far, che al cielo punto aspiri' [Meanwhile I will go buy a few booklets about the contempt of the vanity of this world, which should be pursued by whoever seeks the heavens].

buyers (including books of law, art, and poetry) favours secular concerns, shying away from morality:

> Ho ritrovato al fin quel che cercando
> son ita per più luoghi, in un'angusta
> e vecchia libreria, e quasi appare
> che le famose e più ricche botteghe
> habbino a schifo di tener tal libro.
> Che par lor non sia ben far altra mostra,
> che de i libri di legge, o pur de l'arti,
> o di volgare e celebre poeta.
> Ma sciocchi, qual miglior dottrina od arte
> trovar si può di quella, che la vita
> nostra riduce a moral disciplina?
> Qui sta la sapienza, qui la vera
> Dottrina, che 'l ben vivere ci insegna.[182]

[Eventually, I found in a narrow and old bookshop what I have been looking for in many places. It looks as if the more famous and richer shops disdain having this book, for they do not care exhibiting books other than those of law, art or by some vernacular and famous poet. What fools they are! What better doctrine and art may be found than the one that turns our life into moral discipline? Here is the wisdom, here is the doctrine that teaches us how to live well.]

The main scope of Conscience is the moral disciplining of human life ('moral disciplina'). Accordingly, the good way of living ('ben vivere': a phrasing already used by Glissenti with reference to the subject matter of the *Discorsi morali*) identifies the goal of the good Christian with the preparation for the afterlife through virtuous behaviour. The book bought by Conscience summarises this conduct of life since its title:

> Hor io di questo solo ho fatto scelta,
> come d'ogn'altro più perfetto e degno,
> el titolo rilegger vo di novo:
> 'Dispreggio de le vanità del mondo'.
> Sol questo nome a tutti far dovria
> cognition bastante, onde ciascuno
> del viver suo l'essempio havesse innanzi.[183]

[Now I have chosen this one, which is better and worthier than any other, and I am going to read its title again: 'Contempt of the vanity of the world'. The title itself should be enough to make all aware that they have the example of their life in front of them.]

While the *Modo di confessarsi degnamente* does not seem to allude to a specific title, the *Dispreggio de le vanità del mondo* may likely refer to the homonymous book by the Franciscan friar Diego Estella, translated from Spanish into Italian and printed more than thirty times between 1573 and 1612 in versions by Geremia Foresti, Pietro Buonfanti, and Giovanni Battista Peruschi (who also translated Loyola's

---

182 *L'Androtoo*, 3.10, p. 94.
183 *L'Androtoo*, 3.10, pp. 94–95.

Spiritual Exercises into Italian).[184] The latter, a Jesuit from Rome very close to the Oratoriani, translated not only Estella's *Libro de la vanidad del mundo*, but also Estella's *Meditaciones devotissimas del amor de Dios*, assembling the two works in one voluminous book that fits the description evoked by Conscience:[185]

> Qui la moralità tanta si vede,
> lo specchio di virtù, de l'opre buone,
> e del viver human la meta e 'l fine [...].
> Qui a disprezzar si scopre il mondo infido,
> le lusinghe, gli honor falsi e bugiardi,
> e de l'adulation i vani sogni,
> e d'ogni altro pensier fallace e rio,
> di cui s'usa far stima in questa vita.
> Qui per udir, e per gustar Iddio,
> come sprezzar ogn'altra cosa s'abbia,
> come acquistar del cor un'ampla pace,
> come del vano fin del mondo tutto,
> si debbia haver un ottimo riguardo.[186]

[Here one sees much morality, a mirror of virtue and good works, as well as the scope of human life. [...] Here one learns how to despise the deceitful world, flattery, false and untruthful honours, the frivolous dreams of adulation and any other misleading and sinful thoughts that are normally praised in this life. Here one learns how to listen to God and appreciate him, how to abhor any other thing, gain the peace of the heart, and carefully consider the vanity of the whole world.]

Many of the themes mentioned by Conscience appear in the detailed index of subjects of the 1604 edition of Estella's *Dispregio della vanità del mondo*. Some of the chapter headings give us a sense of the correspondence between Conscience's summary and Estella's book: 'Come per godere Dio bisogna dispregiar le vanitadi del mondo' [How to enjoy God one must despise the vanity of the world], 'Della pace del cuore' [Of the peace of the heart], 'Della vanità che è nelle cose del mondo' [Of the vanity found in the things of the world], 'Del vano fine delle cose mondane' [Of the frivolous scope of mundane matters], 'Dell'inganni e tradimenti del mondo' [Of world's deceits and betrayals], 'Delle false promesse del mondo' [Of world's

---

184 Diego Estella, *Il dispreggio delle vanità del mondo* (Venice: Cristoforo Zanetti, 1575; trans. by Foresti); *Dispregio della vanità del mondo* (Florence: Giorgio Marescotti, 1581; trans. by Buonfanti); *Dispregio della vanità del mondo* (Venice: Giovanni Guerigli, 1601; trans. by Peruschi); on Estella, see Jesús Martinez de Bujanda, *Diego de Estella (1524–1578): estudio de sus obras castellanas* (Rome: Iglesia Nacional Española, 1970); for a modern critical edition of the text, see Diego Estella, *Libro de la vanidad del mundo*, ed. by Pio Sagüés Azcona (Madrid: Editorial Franciscana Aranzazu, 1980); needless to say, works with similar titles did exist, e.g. the aforementioned *Dell'imitatione di Christo, e del dispreggio del mondo*, but also Lorenzo Giustiniani, *Del dispreggio del mondo e delle sue vanità* (Venice: Aldo Manuzio, 1597).
185 Diego Estella, *Dispregio della vanità del mondo [...] Aggiuntevi di nuovo le meditationi dell'Amor di Dio del medesimo autore* (Venice: Giovanni Guerigli, 1604). For some basic information on Peruschi, see Luca Testa, *Fondazione e primo sviluppo del seminario romano (1565–1608)* (Rome: Editrice Pontificia Università Gregoriana, 2002), p. 56.
186 *L'Androtoo*, 3.10, p. 95.

false promises], 'Delli sogni dei mondani' [Of mundane dreams], 'Delle adulationi dei mondani' [Of the adulations of mundane people], 'Dell'inganno dell'allegrezza del mondo' [Of the deceit of world's delight], etc. As Conscience maintains at the end of her summary, what the readers gain from a book such as the *Dispregio* is not in the least comparable to the vain subject matter of secular works, from Ovid to Virgil, from 'foolish' Homer to Ariosto.[187] The booklet ('libricciuolo') is presented as an indispensable aid to meditation, an invaluable guide for a morally disciplined life ('ben viver insegna'), which, alongside penitence and contrition, will keep Man innocent and lead him towards salvation.[188] The positive effects produced by the reading of the devotional text and the observance of Conscience's recommendations are praised by Man at the beginning of the following act. Commending Conscience's role as a mentor ('Donna saggia, e di noi fida maestra, | che al bene ci invitate, e che dal male | ci sottraete coi ricordi vostri'), Man acknowledges his debt towards her and confirms that the 'avvisi del prestato libro' did prove beneficial.[189] As was the case with the ironic *mise en abyme* of the 'frottola morale' read and meditated upon by the protagonist of *Il Diligente*, the very act of reading spiritual literature is presented as a most useful tool for the enhancement of the ability to examine one's conscience, as well as key to the appropriation and 'performance' of Christian virtue.

The Performance of Virtue

The concerns conveyed by Glissenti's dramatisation of self-examination and the playful handling of the reading habits of his allegorical characters dovetail with the idea that drama (be it staged or read) provides a platform for the 'performance' of virtue in the double sense of 'putting on virtue' and 'behaving according to virtue'. 'Putting on virtue' — a phrasing that I borrow from Jennifer Herdt's seminal study of the ways in which the imitation and appropriation of virtuous habits have been conceived, performed, and critiqued — has to do with 'performance', for it entails both the imitation of virtuous behaviours and, as Herdt's own analysis of Jesuit drama indicated, the representation of such behaviours on stage.[190] At the same time, the idea of behaving according to virtue (in other words, the virtuous

---

187 *L'Androtoo*, 3.10, p. 97: 'Da questa lettion si cara e bella, | altro frutto si tragge che da quelli | profani libri c'hora il mondo apprezza. | O sian d'Ovidio favole famose, | o di Virgilio immaginati errori, | d'Homero il folle, o d'Ariosto, o d'altri | poeti ch'al dì d'oggi in vane rime | spendono il tempo in cicalar d'amore' [From this amiable and beautiful reading one obtains more benefit than from those secular books appreciated by the world, be they Ovid's famous fables or the imaginary errors of Virgil, foolish Homer or Ariosto or other poets who spend their time chattering about love in futile poetry].
188 Ibid.: 'Cotesto libricciuolo, al padron mio, | che 'l ben viver insegna, donar voglio; | acciò che in questo legga, e ben contempli | come innocente viver debbia; e come | possa tradur sua vita senza colpa.' [I wish to offer this booklet, which teaches how to live well, to my master; so that, in it, he may read and consider how to live in innocence and conduct his life without sin].
189 *L'Androtoo*, 4.1, p. 104.
190 Jennifer A. Herdt, *Putting on Virtue: The Legacy of the Splendid Vices* (Chicago, IL: University of Chicago Press, 2008), particularly pp. 1–20, 128–70.

behaviours resulting from the acquisition of virtuous habits) relates to 'performance' in that it coincides with the notion of performing virtuous deeds. While the lexical and theoretical clusters connected to performance and performativity are, as I stressed earlier in my study, foreign to the corpus explored here, their clash proves particularly productive when it comes to conceptualising the dynamics at stake in works such as Glissenti's. Indeed, the playwright's concern with the representation of virtue through the staging of virtues and vices is focused not only on issues of subject matter (that is, the core of the teachings that the audience should acquire), but also on the actual mechanisms that inform the process of representation. The point, as we have seen, was made clearly in the *Discorsi morali*. On the occasion of the conversation between the Philosopher and the Actress, the awareness that theatrical performance does not necessarily entail the actual appropriation of the habit performed promoted a form of theatre in which performance becomes a transformative act. By 'putting on' the habit of virtue, the actors should make the 'outer' performance coincide with the 'inner' one.

This dynamic is one of the threads that run across Glissenti's moralities, one that triggers both doctrinal enhancement and comic relief. Crucial to the combination of the two is the idea that deception plays a major role in the ways in which Man may fall prey to evil temptations. Stern warnings about the risk of being misled merge with the dramaturgic potential of deceit, as emblematically shown in the play *L'Androtoo*. Vanity, whose previous attacks were neutralised by Conscience and Discourse, attempts to seduce Man by pretending to be Innocence and 'putting on' her clothes. The trick, a commonplace of the theatrical tradition, aims to deceive Man by meeting his own desires. Indeed, having read and meditated upon the book that Conscience gave to him, he is actively seeking innocence. When Vanity in disguise presents herself as 'Innocence', Man, misguided by the zeal of beginners, falls all too easily for her.

As mentioned above, all the play unfolds under the aegis of the 'real' Innocence, who delivers the prologue and attends the performance, unseen. By disguising herself as Innocence, Vanity triggers a misunderstanding that exposes the meta-theatrical dimension of the situation. The deceiver is instructed by Sense on how to accomplish the plan. The recommendations focus on how to counterfeit Innocence, where the very act of counterfeiting implies both the imitation of someone else's behaviour (as in any comedic situation of mistaken identity) and the hypocritical display of qualities that one does not truly possesses:[191]

> se voi bramate, che 'l padron vi sia
> caro diletto, et amoroso sposo,
> convien che vi cangiate il vostro nome,
> le vesti, il ragionar, il portamento
> e tutti quei costumi usati vostri.
> Anzi che d'imitar voi procuriate
> più che potete l'innocenza stessa

---

[191] Herdt, *Putting on Virtue*, p. 4, recalls the useful distinction between 'counterfeit virtue' and 'semblance of virtue' outlined by Lee Yearley, *Mencius and Aquinas: Theories of Virtue and Conceptions of Courage* (Albany: State University of New York Press, 1990), pp. 20–21.

e le sue serve ancor (se pur inteso
havete mai, come vestita vada,
o come almen da molti si dipinge).[192]

[If you wish the master to be your beloved and lovely spouse, you need to change name, clothes, way of speaking, attitude, and all your habits. Indeed, you need to imitate as closely as possible Innocence herself and her servants too, assuming you ever heard what she wears, or, at least, how she is often depicted.]

Vanity is expected to imitate Innocence in clothing, speech, attitude, and gestures, all outward-facing features that go hand in hand with the appropriation of Innocence's name ('convien che vi cangiate il vostro nome'). The nominalist assumption that the name of a thing conveys its inner essence (hence the idea that the name guarantees the identity of said thing) acquires particular significance in the context of an allegorical play such as *L'Androtoo*, in which the very nature of the personifications hinges upon the presumed correspondence between the names of the characters and their 'performative' functions.

The comedic situation of the travesty exposes the slipperiness of such correspondences and raises questions about the difference between 'being' and 'appearing'; or, to put it more bluntly, how to fake virtue when one is not virtuous at all. In this regard, Sense's recommendation that Vanity take inspiration from the iconographic tradition is illuminating. As Man was recommended by Conscience to meditate carefully on books such as the *Modo di confessarsi degnamente* and the *Dispregio de le vanità del mondo*, Vanity is encouraged to do her own research, iconographic in this case ('se pur inteso | havete mai, *come vestita vada*, | *o come almen da molti si dipinge*', my emphasis). One immediately thinks of depictions of Innocence in allegorical paintings such as Maarten van Heemskerck's [Fig. 3.10] and Lorenzo Lippi's [Fig. 3.11] as well as textual sources such as Ripa's *Iconologia*.[193] Innocence, as detailed by Ripa, is a young woman wearing white ('verginella vestita di bianco'), crowned by a flowery wreath and holding a lamb.[194] As per Ripa's explanation, the whiteness of the costume signals the purity of innocence, comparable to that of a virgin woman ('però dicesi, che l'Innocenza è una libera e pura mente dell'huomo, che senza ignoranza pensi, et operi in tutte le cose con candidezza di spirito, et senza puntura di coscienza').[195] Ripa's description, with its going back and forth between the literal and the metaphorical, relates the condition of innocence to spirit's candour and the absence of conscience's bites, thus outlining the same set of interactions that Glissenti's dramaturgy brings on stage. What the play, however, sheds full light on is the divide between the external features of a

---

192 *L'Androtoo*, 3.12, p. 99.
193 Maarten van Heemskerck (1498–1574), 'Allegory of Innocence and Guile', The Bowes Museum; Lorenzo Lippi (1606–1665), 'An Allegory of Innocence', *c.* 1640, Oxford, The Ashmolean Museum.
194 Ripa, *Iconologia* [1613], p. 381: 'Verginella, vestita di bianco, in capo tiene una ghirlanda di fiori, con un'Agnello in braccio' [Young virgin, dressed in white, a garland of flowers on her heard, a white lamb in her arms].
195 Ibid. ('for this reason it is said that Innocence is a free and pure state of man's mind, considering things without ignorance and operating in all matters with candour of spirit and without conscience's remorse').

FIG. 3.10. Maarten van Heemskerck (1498–1574), *Allegory of Innocence and Guile*, The Bowes Museum, Barnard Castle.

Fig. 3.11. Lorenzo Lippi (1606–1665), *An Allegory of Innocence* (c. 1640), Oxford, The Ashmolean Museum.

given condition (innocence, in this case) and the character's real moral status. This tension comes to the fore when Vanity, who is required to put off her usual clothes in order to be taken for Innocence, questions the very reasons that make Innocence appealing to Man's eyes. Sense explains that this is the fault of the 'housekeeper', Conscience, who has been actively campaigning against Vanity herself. Yet, as Sense cunningly puts it, Conscience's campaign against falsehood and appearance is what will make Vanity's endeavour easier to pursue: if it is true that Conscience forcefully encourages Man to banish all things that might recall Vanity's name, mores, or appearance, it is also true that, in order to win Man over, it will be enough to simply change 'name and clothes' ('la Conscienza, | governatrice de la casa tutta, | lo stimola, lo stringe e quasi sforza | a por in bando qualsivoglia cosa | c'habbia del nome vostro, o de i costumi | vostri, una poca o minima sembianza').[196] By stressing the gap between substance and appearance in terms that resonate with those of the dialogue between the Philosopher and the Actress on matters of theatrical representation, the trick is not about imitating Innocence 'with heart and deeds' ('con lo cor, con l'opre') — a phrasing that, by the way, is consistent with Herdt's notion of 'putting on virtue' — but only in attitude and garment ('sol nel portamento, esterno finto').[197]

Following Sense's instructions, Vanity reappears wearing different clothes: 'Che vi par, serve mie? Parvi ch'io sia | *con questa veste candida e vermiglia* | meno bella di quel che pria mi fossi | vestita ad uso mio, come sapete?' (my emphasis).[198] If the whiteness of Innocence's costume is consistent with the iconography suggested by Ripa, the red component is probably an allusion to the colour of the rose, often associated with the idea of purity (a fitting parallel is found in the prologue of Francesco Farina's 1610 spiritual play, *La Dimne*, which is delivered by the personification of Virginity, 'wearing white, with a red cape', and it may be worth recalling that both allegories of Innocence that I referenced earlier, Heemskerck's and Lippi's, do wear red).[199] Once the clothing is taken care of, Vanity turns to practising (in fact, simulating) the attitude, words, and gestures of Innocence. She is first reassured of her appearance by the servant Epitimia (Lust), who, consistently with her name and identity, does not hide a somewhat morbid attraction to her mistress. The detail is momentous not only because of the markedly gendered context of Glissenti's targeted audience, but also because of the explicitly sexual turn that informs the dichotomy Vanity vs. Innocence.[200] Indeed, as demonstrated

---

196 *L'Androtoo*, 3.12, p. 100 ('Conscience, the housekeeper, spurs him and almost forces him to ban all things that may recall your name or customs').
197 *L'Androtoo*, 3.12, p. 101.
198 *L'Androtoo*, 4.3, p. 109 ('What do you think, my maids? Do you find that this white and red robe makes me less beautiful than I was in my previous attire, which you know well?').
199 Francesco Farina, *La Dimne rappresentatione spirituale* (Venice: Niccolò Misserini, 1610), fol. A8ʳ.
200 *L'Androtoo*, 4.3, p. 110: 'Per dir il vero, quando la mattina | voi vi levate, ancor discinta, e scalza, | inculta ne le chiome, e ne le vesti, | sonnolente talhor, talhor ignuda, | voi così bella, e gratiosa sete, | così vezzosa, così cara e grata, | che struggermi per voi d'ardor mi sento. | E se mi fosse lecito, le braccia | v'annoderei sì strettamente al collo, | che non mi spiccarei fin che satolla | non fossi di baciarvi il caro viso, | con farvi appresso mille cari vezzi' [To tell the truth, when you wake up in the morning, half-dressed and barefoot, your hair uncombed, at times sleepy, at times naked, you

by similar passages in other plays by Glissenti and by archival documents such as the regulations of the Derelitti (which cautioned explicitly about the risks entailed in same-sex friendships), the 'dangers' of homosocial contexts were a concern that drama was able to both voice and, in a way, exorcise.[201] The ambiguous characterisation of Vanity's attempt to fake Innocence's features continues when she enquires about how to imitate innocent 'gestures and words' without truly knowing them. Another servant, Aginona [Pride], cuts her off stating that it will be enough to reverse Vanity's usual behaviour ('riverso usar del rito nostro'):

> [...] dove siam usate
> dal nostro solo naturale istinto,
> o almen da la proclive nostra voglia,
> al vagheggiar, al riso, et agli scherzi,
> c'hora ci stiamo con la testa china,
> col volto assai mesto, e con le labbra
> mormoranti fra noi basse preghiere,
> con l'andar riposato, e con le mani
> incrocicchiate, sospirando appresso,
> talhor mirando di traverso il cielo.[202]

[While our natural instinct or at least our inclination leads us to joy, laughter, and jokes, we now bend our heads down, with sad face, our lips murmuring prayers between us; we shall move slowly, our hands crossed, sighing, occasionally looking at the heavens sideways.]

---

are so beautiful and delicate, so gracious, dear and lovable, that I melt with passion for you. If I were allowed, I would tie my arms around your neck so tightly that I would not detach myself from you until I were satisfied with kissing your beloved face and making you many compliments].
201 Dramatic situations that build on the sexual ambiguity of the interaction among characters (and performers) return in *L'Andrio*, 1.6, 2.2; *Il mercato*, 4.4, 4.11–13; *La Sarcodinamia*, 2.3. Among the statutes regulating the life of the *putte* at the Derelitti, two in particular seem to refer to the risk of intimate relationships; one states that all girls older than twelve should sleep on their own: 'Che tutte le fie che hanno passatto l'età di 12 anni dormino a sola a sola per più honestà' [All girls older than twelve shall sleep on their own for decency's sake]; another, even more explicit, mentions sensual feelings of love as a danger that must be prevented by means of strict discipline: 'Che niuna delle fie parli insieme l'una con l'altra longamente et quando gli occorrerà parlare siano sempre più di due [...] overo in compagnia, acciò non si faccia qualche accordo che causi male e disturbo in casa o scandalo per sugestion del nemico qual è sempre a questo preparato; per oviar a detto scandolo, et quando si vederà una portare disordinato et sensual Amor all'altra, subito si levi la occasione non lassandole conversar insieme' [No girl should speak too long to one of the others, and when they happen to talk, they shall always be more than two [...] that is, in group, so as to prevent connivances that may bring evil and trouble in the house or scandal raised by the enemy [i.e., the devil], who is always ready for this. In order to avoid such scandal, when one girl displays inappropriate and sensual love to another, the matter shall be immediately crushed by preventing them from talking]; both are included in the 'Capitoli dell'Hospedale', Venice, Archivio di Stato, Ospedali e luoghi pii, Busta 910, folder 2, fols 5^r–7^r (fol. 5^v).
202 *L'Androtoo*, 4.3, pp. 110–11.

The posture proposed by Pride coincides with the ethos assigned by Homer to the personification of Prayers, which I have recalled in Chapter 1.[203] However, even more relevant to the moral argument pursued by Glissenti is Vanity's own response. The character recognises the description outlined by Pride as corresponding to the features of both Hypocrisy and her 'sister' Simony ('A quanto dici, par che vogli ch'io | imiti i gesti de l'Hippocrisia | o di quel'altra Simonia sorella'). Eventually, Pride does not recommend imitating Innocence directly, but faking her through the imitation of those who *pretend to be* innocent and God-fearing. As such, the agenda upheld by Vanity and her servants is firmly based on the main currency of their own time, that is, deceitful simulation: 'Poch'altro s'usa al mondo hoggidì tempo. | Quanti sotto cotesto finto manto | con veste vil van ingannando il mondo? | Così a noi far convien, se noi vogliamo | ingannar chi di noi non si fa conto'.[204] Paradoxically critical towards the hypocrisy that informs such behaviour, they claim the sincerity of their usual attitude, which is openly characterised by self-exhibition and the display of earthly goods.[205]

The Senses, emboldened by Conscience's temporary absence, incites Man. Deceived by Vanity, he rejoices about finally meeting the one whom he believes to be Innocence. Discourse is doubtful about the whole situation. Consistently with the main scope of his role — that is, to 'perform' reason — he is not at ease with the very idea that Innocence may be a woman, and specifically, a woman whom one can marry:

> Quantunque habbia più volte udito e inteso
> che l'Innocenza è bella e senza pari,
> degna ch'ognun l'abbracci, e se la prenda
> per cara sua compagna e dolce amica,
> non è perciò ch'io stimi che s'intenda
> che prendere si possa per mogliere,
> come par che dissegni il padron mio.
> Ma stimo ben, che ciò s'intenda in guisa
> che ogn'un dovria (mentre qui nosco vive)
> starsi senza difetto e senza colpa,
> d'ogni mal innocente e senza errore.
> In questo senso stimo che si dica
> ch'ogn'un aspiri a l'Innocenza bella.[206]

[Despite having heard several times that Innocence is beautiful and without

---

203 See Chapter 1, pp. 28, 52–53.
204 *L'Androtoo*, 4.3, p. 112 ('Not much else is used these days. How many go around in that fake attire with humble clothes deceiving the world? We should do the same, if we wish to deceive those who do not care for us').
205 *L'Androtoo*, 4.3, p. 112: 'METAMONIA [...] sotto tali vesti | che dimostrano un disprezzo esterno vile, | si chiudono gran lupi che rapaci | vogliono del sangue altrui farsi satolli. | Ma noi non siam di questi, anzi *mostriamo* | dal pomposo vestir, *d'esser lontane* | *da quella Hippocrisia, che noi biasmamo.* | AGINONA Voi dite troppo il ver, *noi siam sincere*' [METAMONIA [...] under such clothes, which display humble contempt, are hidden voracious wolves eager to be sated by the blood of others. But we are not of that kind; rather, our sumptuous clothes *show that we are far from that Hypocrisy*, whom we despise. AGINONA You tell the truth, *we are sincere*] (my emphasis).
206 *L'Androtoo*, 4.9, p. 127.

peers, worthy of being embraced and taken as a beloved companion and sweet friend, I do not believe this means that she can be taken as wife, as my master seems to be planning. Rather, I think this means that anyone should in life be without faults and sins, innocent of any evil and without errors. It is in this sense that I believe it is said that we all long for beautiful Innocence.]

The allegorical code that structures the entire play is deconstructed from within: Discourse, the personification of rational faculties, unpacks the metaphor rationally. To have Innocence as a mate does not mean that she is a woman; rather, it means that Man ought to live innocently, that is, to be free from sin. The doubts expressed by Discourse are matched by Conscience's reaction when she hears that Man has married Innocence. In a scene that is reminiscent of the slapstick typical of the *commedia dell'arte* (Sense threatens Conscience with a spit), the housekeeper tries to make Man understand his mistake. The passage unfolds as a meta-poetical reflection that, bordering on paradox, challenges the entire allegorical system of personifications on which the play is based. It begins by providing a definition of Innocence as a virtue acquired by men through abstention from sin. As such, she differs significantly from the individual, who pretends to be Innocence, and whom Man is about to marry:

> [...] Ma cotesta
> c'hora volete voi prender in moglie,
> non è *virtù de l'alma* vostra punto,
> né *disposition*. *Habito* è meno
> de l'intelletto vostro in cui s'appogia
> ogni virtù, che l'huomo acquista e prende.
> Questa che voi volete per isposa
> è *cosa esterior*, da voi distinta;
> donna, che in voi non ha che far un punto.
> Hor se costei è donna, come l'altre femine,
> e l'esser suo da sé dipende, com'esser puote
> di quest'alma vostra *habito virtuoso*, ed Innocenza?[207]

[But the one whom you want to take as your wife is not at all a virtue or a disposition of your soul. Even less is she a habit of your intellect, that is, the base of all virtues, which man gains and loses. This one here, whom you want as wife, is an external thing, separate from you; a woman, with whom you have nothing to do. Now, if she is a woman, as all other women, and if her being depends on herself, how can she be a *virtuous habit* of your soul and Innocence?]

Turning to a terminology that recalls phrasings such as those used by Andreini, Bonaventura de Venere, and Bonaventura Morone in order to justify the use of personifications in their works, Glissenti's Conscience shows Man that he has been misled: since Innocence is a virtue and a 'habit' ('habito') of mind, how can she be a tangible object ('cosa esteriore'), distinct ('distinta') — separate — from Man himself? Man acknowledges the point made by Conscience and declares his awareness that virtues such as Justice, Pity, Temperance, and Force are 'gifts of a noble soul' and not real women. Conscience goes even further, for she endorses

---

207 *L'Androtoo*, 5.6, p. 164 (my emphasis).

Man's statement by rejecting the deceitfulness ('equivoco dir e favoloso') of those who speak about the virtues as if they were women. By doing so, she displays an attitude that resonates with discussions of personification's appropriateness such as those of Gabriele Paleotti, which I have reviewed in Chapter 1.[208] Persuaded by Conscience, Man is nonetheless surprised by the fact that the woman who claims to be Innocence has indeed all the features of said virtue. While Conscience asks to meet her in person, so as to check her identity, the actual encounter does not bring to any solution, given Vanity's excellent acting skills. As suggested by Remorse, the only way to settle the issue is to turn to Father Ignatius at once with summoning Penitence, who will eventually be able to clear things up.[209]

Regardless of the somewhat artificial way in which the plot is brought to its happy ending (indeed, Vanity's deceit is unveiled by the joint efforts of Conscience and Remorse), the episode of Vanity's travesty is an instructive example of the paradoxical outcome of Glissenti's handling of the allegorical code. Ultimately, the playwright's reflection on virtues as 'habits' of the soul unveils the artifice of allegorical drama. At the same time, Vanity's successful attempt to be taken for Innocence by 'putting on' Innocence's attributes exposes the tensions embedded in the 'performance' of virtue. If, as Glissenti argues, the acquisition of virtuous habits requires those habits to be appropriated with conviction and performed accordingly, theatre, in spite of its ambiguity, provides a space in which the potentially deceitful nature of the 'performance' may be turned into a 'performative' experience capable of affecting those who consume the text.

---

208 *L'Androtoo*, 5.6, p. 165: 'Così è l'Innocenza; ella è una dote | d'una bell'alma monda e senza colpa. | E se donna talhor alcun la noma | con equivoco dir, o favoloso | così la chiama. E pur è dote sola | del virtuoso che la mette in atto' [Here's what Innocence is: the gift of a beautiful soul without sins. And if occasionally someone calls her a woman, that is metaphorical talk or a fable. Also, it is a gift peculiar to the virtuous individual who puts it into practice]. See what Paleotti argued about the misuse of personifications in Chapter 1, p. 57.
209 *L'Androtoo*, 5.10, pp. 171–72.

CONCLUSION

Death in the Mirror

Despite the successful reception they enjoyed through both performance and print, the morality plays composed by Fabio Glissenti for the female orphans of the Venetian hospitals belong to the wide corpus of early modern dramatic works that fell into oblivion. With very few exceptions, hundreds of plays produced in Italy throughout the sixteenth and the seventeenth centuries lay virtually unexplored. Scholarly attempts to rediscover portions of this corpus have barely scratched the surface. Unsurprisingly, the areas that have been examined more minutely correspond to the generic distinctions that have informed the rhetorical and poetical traditions on which literary criticism has been firmly based since the Renaissance. Studies of early modern Italian drama have thus concentrated on comedy, tragedy, and the pastoral, leaving to one side dramatic forms such as spiritual, allegorical, and religious plays, which challenged the genres canonised by the critical tradition as well as the institutional spaces within which the rebirth of classical theatre had been taking place.[1] Indeed, the number and variety of plays that do not fall within the classicist tripartition of comedy, tragedy, and pastoral is remarkable; it is a variety that increases throughout the late Renaissance and, particularly, in the Baroque age, when the hybridisation of dramatic genres and performative occasions developed on multiple levels, exposing the weakness of traditional generic labels.[2]

Long-standing critical biases against Baroque literary culture are certainly responsible for the neglect that has affected large portions of seventeenth-century literature, including drama, whose case is made more complex by the intrinsically ephemeral nature of its performative status.[3] As a matter of fact, the experience of

---

[1] One could argue, and rightly so, that the pastoral is indeed a hybrid; yet, differently from other forms of generic cross-contamination that have remained on the margins of critical discourses about drama, the pastoral benefited from a direct connection with a homonymous classical genre, which facilitated its modern canonisation through lively debates and discussions. For reassessments of the pastoral and its crucial role in early modern European theatre, see Robert Henke, *Pastoral Transformations: Italian Tragicomedy and Shakespeare's Late Plays* (Newark: University of Delaware Press, 1997); Lisa Sampson, *Pastoral Drama in Early Modern Italy: The Making of a New Genre* (Oxford: Legenda, 2006); Eric Nicholson, 'Crossing Borders with Satyrs, the Irrepressible Genre-Benders of Pastoral Tragicomedy', *Italian Studies*, 40.3 (2020), 342–61.

[2] Goethals and Refini, 'Genre-Bending in Early Modern Performative Culture'.

[3] For an overview of the questions raised by the very notion of Baroque, see Jon R. Snyder, *L'estetica del Barocco* (Bologna: il Mulino, 2005); and, for a recent assessment of the main trends in studies of the Baroque, see *Rethinking the Baroque*, ed. by Helen Hills (Farnham: Ashgate, 2011), and Claire Farago, Helen Hills, Monika Kaup, Gabriela Siracusano, Jens Baumgarten, and Stefano

early modern drama has left us with a handful of indirect traces. Written records of performances, scripts, libretti, and scores have gradually lost the energy that enlivened their performative presentation. In a way, they turned into 'dead pages', to borrow Emanuele Tesauro's phrasing. If it were not for serendipitous pieces of evidence, which occasionally remind us that those texts were indeed performed and consumed through the active involvement of communities, they would remain totally lost to us. Given that, in most cases, the literary quality of the plays is not sufficient to make them stand out as textual products worthy of critical study, it is by reassessing their performative nature that we may have a chance to make the texts speak to us again.

Without underestimating the findings that come from thorough analysis of the eminently textual features of the plays (indeed, my own study has unveiled the multiple layers that inform the textual fabric of moralities such as those by Fabio Glissenti), the most productive way to revive their 'dead pages' is to look at them through the lens of their performative dimension. By surveying the theoretical premises of early modern uses of personification in drama and by considering both staging and reading practices as forms of performance, I have shown that the notion of 'performative' may be applied in flexible and revealing ways to the production and consumption of allegorical theatre in the period. If performance refers, in the first place, to the actual staging of a play — as is the case with the *favole morali* staged at the Venetian hospitals — I have suggested that the performative quality of the plays themselves goes beyond the act of performing them on stage. By comparing the plays to concurrent developments in spiritual and devotional literature, I have shown that allegorical theatre provides the audience with rhetorical tools that allow not only for the inner staging and performance of the plays, but also for the pursuit of forms of spiritual practice (e.g., self-examination and repentance) conducive to self-discipline and spiritual reform.

Differently from seminal accounts of performativity such as Austin's, which tended to exclude theatrical performance from the discussion of performatives, throughout this study I have argued that early modern drama can be better understood when one attempts to read performance as deeply imbued with performativity.[4] Allegorical drama offers, in this respect, a particularly fruitful case study, especially when personified allegories are involved in the action. As my analysis of the *favole morali* has indicated, the performative function of personifications is explicitly exposed by the allegorical context, in which 'performance' and 'performative act' merge. Instead of considering early modern drama as quintessentially meta-theatrical, as most scholarship has done, I have turned to the lexicon of performativity in order to stress its extra-theatrical repercussions.

By focusing on the dramatic reappropriation of metaphors such as the *theatrum mundi*, and by stressing the relevance of the allegorical code to the use of such metaphors, I have endeavoured to show that key to early modern, and specifically

Jacoviello, 'Conceptions and Reworkings of Baroque and Neobaroque in Recent Years', *Perspective: actualité en histoire de l'art*, 1 (2015), 43–62.
4   Austin, *How to Do Things with Words*; Bauman and Briggs, 'Poetics and Performance', p. 65; Egginton, *How the World Became a Stage*, pp. 17–18.

Baroque, theatricality is not merely the idea of exposing theatre's features through theatre itself, but the idea that theatre functions as a framing device for approaching both the outward and inward dynamics, which inform human life: in other words, the external world in which men and women conduct their lives, and the deepest recesses of the human mind, in which the spiritual life of men and women unfold. Accordingly, I argue that theatre, allegorical drama most prominently, is not only concerned with the self-referential exhibition of the mirroring function that informs it as a representational device, but also, and most importantly, with providing both performers and audiences with an actual mirror through which to stage (i.e., construct) their identities.

★ ★ ★ ★ ★

My analysis of Glissenti's morality plays has suggested that the performative context is what allows for the understanding of theatre as a mirror. Indeed, the performance is the moment when (and the space where) such feature comes to the fore. Having chased serendipitous connections among authors, texts, and ideas throughout this book, one further instance of serendipity will help me assess both the reach of my argument and possible ways of making remote experiences such as Glissenti's speak to modern notions of theatricality and performativity. Curiously enough, the only play by Glissenti for which we do have a substantial set of information about the original staging — *La Morte innamorata*, which the English ambassador, Sir Henry Wotton, attended at the Derelitti in 1607 — is the only play that has been revived on stage in modern times. Most likely unaware of the circumstances witnessed by the manuscript copy held in the Marciana Library, Italian director Luca Ronconi unearthed the play in 1987, when he staged it in Rome as the end-of-year student production of the Accademia Nazionale d'Arte Drammatica.[5] The play was given in a non-canonical location: the by then newly created Teatro di Documenti, a multi-level space recovered by scenographer Luca Damiani in the heart of the Roman neighbourhood of Testaccio [Fig. C.1].[6] Devoid of clear-cut distinctions between on-stage and off-stage, the Teatro di Documenti was conceived as a space in which performers and audience would merge while also allowing for multiple actions to unfold at the same time.

This feature, which Ronconi had been particularly fond of since his highly experimental adaptations of Ludovico Ariosto's *Orlando furioso*, provided him with a most fertile context for an exploration of Baroque theatricality.[7] In fact, it

5   The production is documented by the original poster and a series of pictures now available at <https://lucaronconi.it/scheda/scuola/accademia-silvio-d-amico-la-morte-innamorata> [accessed 30 August 2021], which includes digital reproductions of the relevant press review.
6   On the Teatro di Documenti, located in Rome, Via Zabaglia 42, see the overview provided on the theatre's website at <http://www.teatrodidocumenti.it/> [accessed 30 August 2021] and: Fernando Bevilacqua, *Teatri di Roma, 1980–2008* (Rome: Gangemi Editore, 2008), p. 17–18; *Lo spazio della musica: flessibilità e nuove configurazioni spaziali*, ed. by Donatella Radogna and Francesca Castagneto (Rome: Gangemi Editore, 2016), p. 37; for a profile of Luciano Damiani, see *Dizionario dello spettacolo del '900*, ed. by Felice Cappa, Piero Gelli, and Marco Mattarozzi (Milan: Baldini & Castoldi, 1998), p. 302–03.
7   On Ronconi's treatment of Ariosto in theatre and television, see Sandro Bernardi, 'From Poem

Fig. C.1. Scene from *La Morte innamorata*, Rome, Teatro di Documenti, Rome, June 1987

fitted Ronconi's interest in pre-modern theatre, whose heterogeneous nature he perceived as able to challenge the theatrical canons imposed by the dominant neo-classicist aesthetics of modern dramaturgy.[8]

If texts such as Glissenti's morality plays, in spite of significant progress in the critical reassessment of seventeenth-century culture, remain niche repertory today, the choice to stage *La Morte innamorata* was all the more peculiar in the 1980s, especially when one considers that the little-known 'favola morale' was chosen for a student performance. The scope of Ronconi's choice emerges when the broader project is examined, as do both its pedagogical import and its consistency with the specific location in which the show was produced. After almost four hundred years, *La Morte innamorata* returned to the stage as part of a diptych that included Giovan Battista Andreini's comedy *Amor nello specchio* [Love in the Mirror] (1622) [Fig. C.2].

---

to Theatre to Cinema: Luca Ronconi's *Orlando furioso*', in *Ariosto Today: Contemporary Perspectives*, ed. by Massimo Ciavolella and Roberto Fedi (Toronto: University of Toronto Press, 2003), pp. 195–210; and Claudio Longhi, *Orlando Furioso di Ariosto-Sanguineti per Luca Ronconi* (Pisa: ETS, 2006).

8   For an introduction to the life, works, and poetics of Luca Ronconi, see *Luca Ronconi: prove di autobiografia*, ed. by Giovanni Agosti (Milan: Feltrinelli, 2019); but also *Luca Ronconi e il suo teatro*, ed. by Isabella Innamorati (Rome: Bulzoni, 1996); *Luca Ronconi: un'idea di teatro. Conversazioni e testimonianze*, ed. by Maddalena Lenti (Milan: Mimesis, 2011); *Luca Ronconi: il palcoscenico dell'utopia*, ed. by Massimo Luconi (Florence: Edizioni Clichy, 2016).

ACCADEMIA NAZIONALE D'ARTE DRAMMATICA « SILVIO D'AMICO »

00198 ROMA - VIA VINCENZO BELLINI, 16 - TEL. 853860

COD. FISC.: 80218590588

"LA MORTE INNAMORATA"

FAVOLA MORALE

di Fabio GLISSENTI

"AMOR NELLO SPECCHIO"

COMMEDIA

di Gian Battista ANDREINI

ESERCITAZIONE DEGLI ALLIEVI DEL II ANNO DEI CORSI DI RECITAZIONE E REGIA - Anno Accademico 1986/87 -

DIRETTI DA

LUCA RONCONI

con la collaborazione di

ANGELO CORTI

Teatro, Scene e Costumi di

LUCIANO DAMIANI

Musica a cura di

PAOLO TERNI

Lo spettacolo si svolge in due tempi, con inizio alle ore 18,00 "La Morte Innnamorata" ed alle ore 21,00 "Amor nello Specchio".

TEATRO DI DOCUMENTI DELLO STUDIO DAMIANI

Via Nicola Zabaglia 42

ROMA

FIG. C.2. *La Morte innamorata* and *Amor nello specchio*, poster of Luca Ronconi's production for the Accademia Nazionale d'Arte Drammatica (1987)

Considered today a signature work of Baroque theatre, Andreini's play, which has gained substantial attention over the years (including annotated editions, translations, and critical studies, as well as revivals on both stage and screen) was not a mainstream piece at the time of Ronconi's production.⁹ In fact, it was one of those early modern dramatic works that were being rediscovered and appreciated, not only as objects of scholarly consideration, but also as texts viable for the performance. Ronconi himself was a pioneer in this respect, having already revived Baroque plays such as Giordano Bruno's *Il Candelaio* in 1968 and Andreini's own *La Centaura* and *Le due commedie in commedia* in 1972 and 1984, respectively. The reasons for Ronconi's interest in *Amor nello specchio* are not difficult to grasp. The refined, yet diverse quality of Andreini's dramatic language, which spanned the divide between literary sophistication and the bawdy gestural universe inherited from the *commedia dell'arte*, went hand in hand with a cluster of topics and tropes that resonated with the cultural and social debates of the time.

First, as had been the case with both *La Centaura* and *Le due commedie in commedia*, the play *Amor nello specchio* is indeed meta-theatrical in the sense that informed Ronconi's poetics throughout his career. One can read Florinda's narcissistic love for herself and her fixation with her own image reflected in the mirror as emblems of the narcissistic work of the performer, always aware of the tension between fiction and reality. But Florinda's falling in love with the image of Lidia, which she sees reflected on the same mirror that had previously facilitated her own masturbatory phantasy, also echoes — and subverts — the actual tension that animated the relationship (both on and off stage) between the real Florinda (Virginia Ramponi, the playwright's wife) and the real Lidia (Virginia Rotari, the playwright's lover).

Second, the overtly homoerotic bond that solidifies the alliance of the two women against their male counterparts challenges not only assumed notions of 'nature' but also the norms enforced by the patriarchal order upheld by the male characters. Although the order of things is re-established at the end of the comedy, the damage, so to speak, is done, and the tension produced by the homosocial tie of Lidia and Florinda (which builds on appearance, gender confusion, cross-dressing, and sexual misunderstandings) keeps lurking beyond the plot's closure.

Third, the mirror (that is, the medium through which the plot is set in motion) functions both as a prop (Florinda admires herself on it, but the mirror is also the framing device that allows Lidia's face to capture Florinda's attention) and as a multivalent metaphor. It is conducive to self-knowledge as well as being, at the same time, a misleading creator of images that can be easily taken for something else

---

9   The play was printed in Paris by Nicolas della Vigna in 1622; for a modern edition of the text, see Giovan Battista Andreini, *Amor nello specchio*, ed. by Salvatore Maira and Anna Michela Borracci (Rome: Bulzoni, 1997); see also the bilingual edition Giovan Battista Andreini, *Love in the Mirror*, ed. and trans. by Jon R. Snyder (Toronto: Iter, 2009). A modern production of the play by Luca Ronconi himself was given at Ferrara in 2002: see details at <https://lucaronconi.it/scheda/teatro/amor-nello-specchio> [accessed 30 August 2021]; the play was also the object of a filmic adaptation: *Amor nello specchio*, dir. by Salvatore Maira (Italy, 1999). For a fine reading of the play, with insightful remarks on the metaphoric values of the mirror and their place within Andreini's dramaturgy, see Emily Wilbourne, 'Amor nello specchio (1622): Mirroring, Masturbation, and Same-Sex Love', *Women and Music*, 13.1 (2009), 54–65.

(thus Florinda takes Lidia for a man, before realising that she is, in fact, a woman). Likewise, according to the unstable and deceitful epistemology emblematised by the mirror, Florinda's perception of gender is fluid: who cares whether Lidia is a woman? Florinda falls in love with the image seen in the mirror, and the satisfaction of her desire is the only thing that matters. Accordingly, when Lidia's brother, Eugenio, appears on stage, Florinda does not bat an eyelid: she takes him for Lidia, and makes the most of the sexual encounter anyway. Needless to say, the fact that the roles of Eugenio and Lidia may be performed by the same person — a trick that would be immediately clear to the knowing audience now as then — spotlights the troubles playfully triggered by what, in the aftermath of Judith Butler's provocative work (which appeared only a few years after Ronconi's production of *Amor nello specchio*), we today call 'performance of gender'.[10]

Given the features of *Amor nello specchio* that resonated with Ronconi's own poetics, one might wonder where the sensual world of the libertine *capocomico* Giovan Battista Andreini meets with the spiritually inflected universe of the doctor-turned-playwright Fabio Glissenti. Apparently, nowhere. The body and its needs are the driving forces of *Amor nello specchio*, whereas concerns about the salvation of the soul lay at the core of *La Morte innamorata*. The senses and the satisfaction of one's desires lead the plot of Andreini's comedy, while their rejection is the scope that justifies the dramaturgy of Glissenti's morality play. Yet, Andreini's apology of love and Glissenti's reminder of death's inescapability have more in common than their most prominent features would suggest. As observed by theatre critic Enzo Siciliano in his review of the double bill presented at the Teatro di Documenti, both plays bear witness to a moment in the history of Italian theatre when 'the language of drama grows into text independently from the concurrent improvisations of the performers' ('la lingua teatrale si fa testo indipendentemente dalle parallele improvvisazioni degli attori'), a kind of textuality, made of gestures, dramatic situations, psychological tangles, spectacular conflict ('gesto, situazione scenica, viluppo psicologico, conflitto spettacolare'), that can only be brought to full fruition through the performance.[11] According to Siciliano, Ronconi seized the priority of the 'word' and made the young performers learn how to handle it through rigorous 'expressive discipline': not only is the critic's remark interesting in that it stresses the centrality of the verbal text vis-à-vis the other components of the show, but also because the term 'discipline' with reference to Ronconi's training of the actors invites comparison with the notion of 'discipline' that I have indicated as key to Glissenti's poetical agenda. Ronconi's 'expressive discipline', Siciliano continues, entails two different approaches to the 'word': symbolic, when it comes to Glissenti's allegory; realistic when it comes to Andreini's comic game ('una parola usata sul versante simbolico con Glissenti, sul versante del parlar quotidiano con Andreini').[12]

---

10   Butler, *Gender Trouble*.
11   Enzo Siciliano, *Corriere della sera*, 10 June 1987.
12   Ibid.

As suggested by Siciliano's distinction between the 'versante simbolico' and the 'versante del parlar quotidiano', Ronconi conceived the two plays as two interrelated facets of the Baroque theatrical imagination. In an interview with the Catholic newspaper *Il Sabato* released on the occasion of the production, Ronconi himself acknowledged a feature of his approach to Andreini that, in unexpected ways, seizes upon some of the dynamics that I have identified in my discussion of Glissenti's moralities. Speaking about the actors and actresses he worked with — young men and women in their twenties — the director found that they lacked any awareness of their human experience.[13] To his eyes, they were not even able to 'represent' themselves. While working on universal themes such as death, deception, and love, they displayed an 'empty conscience' and the inability to relate to — and look into — themselves ('vuoto di coscienza, un'impossibilità a paragonarsi, a pescare dentro se stessi').[14] As if they did not have any connection with real life, they were only able to identify as part of relational interactions (in other words, they acknowledged their own existence and identities only in relation to those of others).

The situation described by Ronconi is obviously very different from that of the original performers for whom both Andreini and Glissenti wrote their plays: the members of a widely known professional theatre company and the orphan schoolgirls of the Venetian hospitals. However, similarities between Ronconi's description of his students and their seventeenth-century predecessors are noteworthy. Such affinities come to light when one focuses on the tension between the inward and outward dynamics that, as I have shown, was at the core of the plays performed, read, and consumed by Glissenti's targeted audience. If Andreini's kaleidoscopic theatre, conceived for a company of professionals, played with the uncatchable mutability of life and human desires, the disciplining scope of Glissenti's *favole morali* was built on the idea that the performers would indeed construct their identities through the performance. Faced with the transience of the human experience, Andreini and Glissenti both turned to drama as a way to illustrate the challenges that come with the definition of one's role in the play of human life — a struggle that, under other circumstances, returned in Ronconi's students.

It goes without saying that the word 'coscienza' [conscience] does not bear the same meaning in Glissenti and Ronconi. Yet, the apparently unbridgeable clash between the post-Tridentine 'consideration of oneself' and the modern incapability of introspection exposes striking commonalities under the aegis of performativity. In this respect, the modern re-enactment of the double bill Glissenti/Andreini proves particularly instructive, for the two seventeenth-century playwrights and the twentieth-century director shared the idea that the performance is the space where the performers find themselves. Ultimately, the common ground on which Glissenti, Andreini, and Ronconi met was the idea that the stage functions as a mirror, taken here as both a material object and a powerful metaphor. If, as we have seen, the mirror comes up as a prop in *La Ragione sprezzata*, it is the lexicon of vision

---

13 Riccardo Bonacini, 'Un sogno contro il vuoto. Intervista con Luca Ronconi', *Il Sabato*, 13–19 June 1987.
14 Ibid.

that, throughout Glissenti's dramatic corpus, captures its function: as much as the protagonist, Man, is required to look into Death's face in order to acknowledge that they belong with each other, so is the audience asked to fix their gaze upon what they see on stage in order to learn the same lesson.

Death is, after all, the other pervasive image that — through the looking glass — connects Glissenti and Andreini. The rhetorical process that I have described as the anatomisation of man's spiritual life, and which is effectively captured by Glissenti's presentation of the uneasy relationship between Man and Death in *La Morte innamorata*, returns in the form of a comical sketch in Andreini's *Amor nello specchio*. Among the prodigious events made to happen by the magician (who is meant to help the male protagonists fulfil their desires, but turns magic into *beffa*), the appearance of Death herself is of particular interest.[15] Let out from a bag, whose hidden content should facilitate Guerindo's pursuit of Florinda, Death frightens the lover and his servant, Coradella. The scene reminds us not only of Death's role in Glissenti's plays, but also of her pervasive presence in the *Discorsi morali*, where the iconographic apparatus warned the reader that life is but a *Totentanz*. In *Amor nello specchio*, Coradella is terrified by the sinister shape of the Grim Reaper and exorcises his fear by turning to colourful appellations: called 'testa pelata' [hairless head] and 'culo senza natiche' [butt without buttocks], the appearance of Death is at once a reminder of the caducity of human life and a laughable cameo. With the servant kidnapped by four more players dressed as Death, who come out of the flames that invade the stage, the scene turns into a mixture of slapstick comedy and bewildering special effects, making the audience laugh and shudder at the same time.

If it is likely that the Gelosi performances of Andreini's play did not trigger mass repentance, confession, and conversion as was allegedly the case with the moralities staged at the hospitals of Venice, Ronconi's modern presentation of *Amor nello specchio* and *La Morte innamorata* highlighted the cultural interrelatedness of the two plays. By considering them as part of the same theatrical universe and by trying them out together on stage, the director captured — perhaps inadvertently — a key feature of any allegorical discourse, as well as one of the reasons for modernity's fascination with allegory: namely, its reflective nature, its being concerned with the communication of messages in distorted ('other') forms. On close inspection, the process is not much different from that of anamorphosis: in order to appreciate the essence of a given anamorphic image — for instance, a skull in the mirror as in Jan van Hemessen's *Vanity* that I recalled in Chapter 3 — it is necessary to decode it by fixing one's gaze on it. Similarly, Man in *La Ragione sprezzata* is asked to recognise the Death's Head reflected in the mirror and Coradella in *Amor nello specchio* faces the personification of Death coming out of the bag. Both encounters with Death are meant to reflect upon the spectators, who are expected to appreciate the *memento mori* entailed by these scenes. As much as the allegorical discourse implied in the texts is brought to life through the performance of the actors, so does the audience join the performative effort by taking an active part in the unpacking of

---

15   Andreini, *Amor nello specchio*, 3.9 (p. 111).

the allegory. Be it for fun or for soul's salvation, the spectators' involvement with the performance reveals that they are part of the same *theatrum mundi* that unfolds before their eyes.

* * * * *

Ronconi's staging of *La Morte innamorata* and *Amor nello specchio* brings us back to where this study began. By bridging across the performative culture of the early Seicento and its modern rediscovery, it illuminates the broader implications of the case studies discussed in this book while at the same time providing a fruitful lens through which to review my claims. Indeed, the questions raised by the pairing of Glissenti and Andreini shed further light on the intersections of theatricality, performance, and allegorical discourse that I have explored through both theoretical and literary sources from the period. By testing the performative potential of these undeniably peculiar plays, Ronconi reminds his modern audience that allegory (be it conveyed through personifications, embedded in the plotline, or assigned to specific signifiers such as the mirror) does come to fuller fruition through acts of performance. Indeed, one could go so far as to say that any act of performance is inevitably allegorical, for performance shares the transactional nature of allegorical discourse. Furthermore, the double bill Glissenti/Andreini exposes the interrelatedness of performance and performativity that I have identified as key to the scope of early modern allegorical drama: namely, to make the invisible visible in order to affect the minds and souls of those involved in the consumption of drama itself, an ambition that comes close to coeval forms of spiritual practice.

A play such as *La Morte innamorata* does this by adopting, as all moralities do, personification as its very idiom: in these works, the rhetorical features of personification as a figure of speech and thought, which I have discussed in Chapter 1, gain centre stage, providing both performers and viewers with a tool to visualise the inner workings of their spiritual lives. Andreini's *Amor nello specchio* stages instead the other side of the allegorical mirror, the one in which personification is reduced to a purely comedic device. By doing so, the play unveils the ambiguous status of allegorical discourse that Glissenti himself was clearly aware of: if, as we have seen, Vanity's 'performance of virtue' in *L'Androtoo* exposes the risks of taking allegory too literally, the appearance of Death's personification in Andreini's comedy ridicules man's inability to unmask the rhetorical trick.

These different takes on allegory and drama contribute to framing the numerous tensions that inform Glissenti's broader production. As recalled in Chapter 2, the 'tragedy of human life' was introduced in the *Discorsi morali* as a metaphor to signify man's spiritual struggles on the stage of the world; yet, as further suggested by Glissenti's systematic references to theatre throughout his philosophical work, it is by acknowledging the truly performative nature of man's life that tragedy may be turned into an opportunity for spiritual growth. Ultimately, what the *Discorsi morali* aim to achieve by means of dialogical exchange, *exempla*, and visual prompts, is eventually returned to dramatic shape in Glissenti's morality plays. As I suggested in Chapter 3, the *favole morali* offer an instructive example of the ways in which allegory could be used to serve educational projects built on the idea that if the world is conceived as a stage, then it is on and through the stage that human life takes shape and can be disciplined.

BIBLIOGRAPHY

Manuscripts

Florence, Biblioteca Nazionale Centrale, MS Magl. IX.125
Florence, Biblioteca Riccardiana, MS 2237
Venice, Archivio di Stato, Ospedali e luoghi pii, Busta 910
Venice, Biblioteca Nazionale Marciana, MS Ital. IX.316

Printed sources

ACCETTO, TORQUATO, *Della dissimulazione onesta*, ed. by Salvatore Silvano Nigro (Turin: Einaudi, 1997)
AGOSTI, GIOVANNI, ed., *Luca Ronconi: prove di autobiografia* (Milan: Feltrinelli, 2019)
AIKEMA, BERNARD, and DULCIA MEIJERS, eds, *Nel regno dei poveri: arte e storia dei grandi ospedali veneziani in età moderna, 1474–1797* (Venice: Arsenale editrice, 1989)
ALONSO DEL CAMPO, URBANO, *Vida y obra de fray Luis de Granada* (Salamanca: Editorial San Esteban, 2005)
ANDREINI, GIOVAN BATTISTA, *L'Adamo sacra rapresentatione* (Milan: Girolamo Bordone, 1613)
—— *Amor nello specchio*, ed. by Salvatore Maira and Anna Michela Borracci (Rome: Bulzoni, 1997)
—— *L'Adamo*, ed. by Alessandro Ruffino (Trento: La finestra, 2007)
—— *Love in the Mirror*, ed. and trans. by Jon R. Snyder (Toronto: Iter, 2009)
APHTHONIUS, *Aphthonii Sophistae Progymnasmata partim a Rodolpho Agricola, partim a Ioanne Maria Cataneo latinitate donata* (Paris: Jean Mace, 1573)
—— *Progymnasmata*, ed. by H. Rabe (Leipzig: Teubner, 1926)
ARISTOTLE, *On the Soul. Parva Naturalia. On Breath*, trans. by W. S. Hett (Cambridge, MA: Harvard University Press, 1957)
—— *Art of Rhetoric*, trans. by J. H. Freese, revised by Gisela Striker (Cambridge, MA: Harvard University Press, 2020)
—— LONGINUS, DEMETRIUS, *Poetics. Longinus: On the Sublime. Demetrius: On Style*, trans. by Stephen Halliwell, W. Hamilton Fyfe, Doreen C. Innes, W. Rhys Roberts; revised by Donald A. Russell (Cambridge, MA: Harvard University Press, 1995)
ARNOLD, DENIS, 'L'attività musicale', in Aikema and Mejiers, *Nel regno dei poveri*, pp. 99–108
Arte e musica all'Ospedaletto: schede d'archivio sull'attività musicale degli ospedali dei Derelitti e dei Mendicanti di Venezia (sec. XVI–XVIII) (Venice: Stamperia di Venezia, 1978)
AUSTIN, JOHN L., *How to Do Things with Words* (Cambridge, MA: Harvard University Press, 1962)
BALIOTTI, MODESTO, *Facilissimo modo di confessarsi e specialmente delle persone religiose et alter che spesso si confessano* (Perugia: Pietro Giacomo Petrucci, 1580)
BARATTO, MARIO, *La commedia del Cinquecento: aspetti e problemi* (Vicenza: Neri Pozza, 1977)
BARBIERI, NICOLÒ, *La Supplica: Discorso famigliare a quelli che trattano de' comici*, ed. by Ferdinando Taviani (Bologna: Cue Press, 2015)
BAROCCHI, PAOLA, ed., *Trattati d'arte del Cinquecento tra Manierismo e Controriforma* (Bari: Laterza, 1961)

BARONCINI, RODOLFO, 'Gli Ospedali, la nuova pietas e la committenza musicale cittadinesca a Venezia (1590–1620): i casi di Bartolomeo Bontempelli dal Calice e di Camillo Rubini', in *Atti del Congresso internazionale di musica sacra in occasione del centenario di fondazione del PIMS: Roma, 26 maggio–1 giugno 2011*, ed. by Antonio Addamiano and Francesco Luisi (Vatican City: Libreria Editrice Vaticana, 2013), pp. 569–85

——, and MARCO DI PASQUALE, *Monteverdi a San Marco. Venezia 1613–1643* (Lucca: LIM, 2020)

BÄTSCHMANN, OSKAR, and PASCAL GRIENER, *Hans Holbein* (Princeton, NJ: Princeton University Press, 1997)

BATTISTA DA CREMA, *Specchio interiore. Opera divina, per la cui lettione ciascuno devoto potrà facilmente ascendere al colmo della perfettione* (Milan: Francesco Minizio Calvo, 1540)

BAUMAN, RICHARD, and CHARLES L. BRIGGS, 'Poetics and Performance as Critical Perspectives on Language and Social Life', *Annual Review of Anthropology*, 19 (1990), 59–88

BEDA, 'De schematibus et tropis' in Beda, *Opera didascalica. 1. De orthographia; De arte metrica et de schematibus et tropis; De natura rerum*, ed. by C. W. Jones and C. B. Kendall, *Corpus Christianorum, Series Latina*, 123A (Turnhout: Brepols, 1975), pp. 59–171

BELLARINI, GIOVANNI, *Breve prattica della conscienza raccolta da gravi auttori, nella quale con nuovo compartimento si dà un facil modo di essaminar in poco tempo lo stato di tutta la conscienza, et è opera insieme a i confessori, et a' penitenti accomodata* (Venice: Fioravante Prati, 1597)

BELLINTANI, MATTIA, *Pratica dell'oration mentale* (Venice: Pietro Dusinelli, 1581)

BENASSI, ALESSANDRO, 'Lo "scherzevole inganno": figure ingegnose e argutezza nel "Cannocchiale aristotelico" di Emanuele Tesauro', *Studi secenteschi*, 47 (2006), 9–55

BENJAMIN, WALTER, *The Origin of German Tragic Drama* [1925], trans. by John Osborne (London and New York: Verso, 2003)

BENZI, GAIA, 'La genesi del Parthenio: gli influssi della propaganda gesuitica nella drammaturgia confessionale di area veneta', in Selmi and Zucchi, eds, *Allegoria e teatro*, pp. 169–78

BERNARD OF CLAIRVAUX, *On Consideration*, trans. by George Lewis (Oxford: Clarendon, 1908)

BERNARDI, CLAUDIO, 'Censura e promozione del teatro nella Controriforma', in *Storia del teatro, 1: La nascita del teatro moderno Cinquecento–Seicento*, ed. by Roberto Alonge and Guido Davico Bonino (Turin: Einaudi, 2000), pp. 1023–42

BERNARDI, SANDRO, 'From Poem to Theatre to Cinema: Luca Ronconi's *Orlando furioso*', in *Ariosto Today: Contemporary Perspectives*, ed. by Massimo Ciavolella and Roberto Fedi (Toronto: University of Toronto Press, 2003), pp. 195–210

BERNHEIMER, RICHARD, 'Theatrum Mundi', *The Art Bulletin*, 38.4 (1956), 225–47

BEVILACQUA, FERNANDO, *Teatri di Roma, 1980–2008* (Rome: Gangemi Editore, 2008)

BHASIN, CHRISTINE S., 'Nuns on Stage in Counter-Reformation Venice (1570–1750)' (unpublished PhD dissertation, Northwestern University, 2012)

—— 'Prostitutes, Nuns, Actresses: Breaking the Convent Wall in Seventeenth-Century Venice', *Theatre Journal*, 66.1 (2014), 19–35

BINO, CARLA MARIA, '"Lo Spiritual Teatro" e la "Sacra Scena": una prima indagine negli scritti di Federico Borromeo', *Studia Borromaica*, 20 (2002), 263–82

BISI, MONICA, 'Visione e invenzione: la conoscenza attraverso la metafora nel Cannocchiale aristotelico', *Studi secenteschi*, 47 (2006), 57–87

BLAIR, ANN, *The Theater of Nature: Jean Bodin and Renaissance Science* (Princeton, NJ: Princeton University Press, 1997)

BLOOMFIELD, MORTON W., 'A Grammatical Approach to Personification Allegory', *Modern Philology*, 60 (1963), 161–71

BOISSARD, JEAN-JACQUES, *Theatrum Vitae Humanae* (Metz: Abraham Faber, 1596)

BOLOGNA, CORRADO, 'Esercizi di memoria: dal *Theatro della sapientia* di Giulio Camillo agli

Esercizi spirituali di Ignazio di Loyola,' in *La cultura della memoria*, ed. by Lina Bolzoni e Pietro Corsi (Bologna: il Mulino, 1992), pp. 169–221

BOLZONI, LINA, *Il teatro della memoria: studi su Giulio Camillo con un'appendice di testi* (Padua: Liviana, 1984)

—— *La stanza della memoria: modelli letterari e iconografici nell'età della stampa* (Turin: Einaudi, 1995) [English trans. by Jeremy Parzen: *The Gallery of Memory: Literary and Iconographic Models in the Age of the Printing Press* (Toronto: University of Toronto Press, 2000)]

—— *La rete delle immagini: predicazione in volgare dalle origini a Bernardino da Siena* (Turin: Einaudi, 2002) [English trans. by Carole Preston and Lisa Chien: *The Web of Images: Vernacular Preaching from its Origins to St Bernardino da Siena* (Aldershot: Ashgate, 2004)]

—— 'Le tecniche della memoria e la costruzione degli spazi interiori fra Medioevo e Rinascimento', *Lettere italiane*, 55.1 (2003), 26–46

—— *Il cuore di cristallo: ragionamenti d'amore, poesia e ritratto nel Rinascimento* (Turin: Einaudi, 2010)

BONACINA, GIOVANNI, *Origine della congregazione dei Padri Somaschi: la compagnia pretridentina di San Girolamo Miani elevata ad ordine religioso* (Rome: Curia Generale Padri Somaschi, 2009)

BONACINI, RICCARDO, 'Un sogno contro il vuoto. Intervista con Luca Ronconi', *Il Sabato*, 13–19 June 1987

BONAVENTURA DI VENERE [ROMITO PELLEGRINO], *Rappresentatione spirituale dell'anima, et del corpo, con alcune laudi, et altre ottave, fatte dal Pellegrino Romito* (Rome: Guglielmo Facciotti, 1608) (Rome and Perugia: Bartoli e Lorenzi, 1644)

BONCIANI, FRANCESCO, *Lezione della prosopopea* [Florence, Biblioteca Riccardiana, MS 2237, ff. 96–109], in Weinberg, ed., *Trattati di poetica e retorica*, vol. III, pp. 237–53

BONUZZI, LUCIANO, 'Medicina e sanità', in *Storia di Venezia* (Rome: Istituto della Enciclopedia Italiana, 1991–2002), vol. V, pp. 407–40

BORSELLINO, NINO, 'Prologo', in *Enciclopedia dello Spettacolo* (Rome: Le Maschere, 1954–1968), vol. VIII, pp. 526–34

BRADSHAW, MURRAY C., 'Salvation, Right Thinking, and Cavalieri's *Rappresentatione di anima, et di corpo* (1600)', *Musica Disciplina*, 52 (1998–2002), 233–50

BRITTAN, SIMON, *Poetry, Symbol, and Allegory: Interpreting Metaphorical Language from Plato to the Present* (Charlottesville and London: University of Virginia Press, 2003)

BUONARROTI, MICHELANGELO 'il Giovane', *La Fiera*, ed. by Pietro Fanfani, 2 vols (Florence: Le Monnier, 1860)

—— *La fiera. Redazione originaria (1619)*, ed. by Uberto Limentani (Florence: Leo S. Olschki, 1984)

—— *La fiera. Seconda redazione*, ed. by Olimpia Pelosi (Naples: Liguori, 2003)

BURROUGHS, CATHERINE, ed., *Closet Drama: History, Theory, Form* (London: Routledge, 2018)

BUSSELS, STIJN, *The Animated Image: Roman Theory on Naturalism, Vividness and Divine Power* (Leiden: Leiden University Press, 2012)

BUTLER, JUDITH, *Gender Trouble: Feminism and the Subversion of Identity* [1990] (New York: Routledge, 2007)

CALABRITTO, MONICA, and PETER DALY, eds, *Emblems of Death in the Early Modern Period* (Geneva: Droz, 2014)

CALDERÓN DE LA BARCA, PEDRO, *Obras completas* (Madrid: Aguilar, 1991)

CAMILLO, GIULIO, *L'idea del theatro con 'L'idea dell'eloquenza', Il 'De transmutatione' e altri testi inedita*, ed. by Lina Bolzoni (Milan: Adelphi, 2015)

CAMPANELLA, TOMMASO, *Le poesie*, ed. by Francesco Giancotti (Turin: Einaudi, 1998)

CANEPARO, GIOVANNI MARIA, *Modo et regola che si debbe tener per sapersi ben confessarsi* (Brescia: Giacomo Britannico, 1593)

CANTAGALLI, ROBERTO, 'Francesco Bonciani', in *Dizionario Biografico degli Italiani*, 11 (1969), pp. 673–74

CAPPA, FELICE, PIERO GELLI, and MARCO MATTAROZZI, eds, *Dizionario dello spettacolo del '900* (Milan: Baldini & Castoldi, 1998)

CAPUTO, VINCENZO, 'Gli abusi dei pittori e la norma dei trattatisti: Giovanni Andrea Gilio e Gabriele Paleotti', *Studi rinascimentali*, 6 (2008), 99–110

CARAVALE, GIORGIO, *Forbidden Prayer: Church Censorship and Devotional Literature in Renaissance Italy* (London: Routledge, 2012)

CARLIN, CLAIRE L., and KATHLEEN WINE, eds, *Theatrum mundi: Studies in Honor of Ronald W. Tobin* (Charlottesville, VA: Rookwood Press, 2003)

CARLSMITH, CHRISTOPHER, *A Renaissance Education: Schooling in Bergamo and the Venetian Republic, 1500–1650* (Toronto: University of Toronto Press, 2010)

CARPANI, ROBERTA, 'Hermenegildus/Ermegildo: la tragedia cristiana nell'opera di Emanuele Tesauro', *Comunicazioni sociali*, 19.2 (1997), 181–220

CARRUTHERS, MARY, *The Book of Memory: A Study of Memory in Medieval Culture* (Cambridge: Cambridge University Press, 1990)

—— *The Craft of Thought: Meditation, Rhetoric, and the Making of Images, 400–1200* (New York: Cambridge University Press, 1998)

CASOLARI, SILVIA, 'Allegorie nella *Rappresentatione di anima et di corpo* (1600): testo e immagine', *Rivista Italiana di Musicologia*, 33.1 (1998), 7–40

CASONI, GUIDO, *Il giuoco di fortuna* (Venice: Tommaso Baglioni, 1622)

CASSINI, GIOCONDO, *Piante e vedute prospettiche di Venezia, 1479–1855* (Venice: Istituto federale delle Casse di Risparmio delle Venezie, 1971)

CASTELLANO, GIACOMO, *Rime spirituali et morali* (Venice: Evangelista Deuchino and Giovan Battista Pulciani, 1608)

CASTELVETRO, LUDOVICO, *Poetica d'Aristotele vulgarizzata et sposta* (Vienna: Caspar Stainhofer, 1570)

—— *Poetica d'Aristotele vulgarizzata et sposta*, ed. by W. Romani, 2 vols (Bari: Laterza, 1978–1979)

CASTIGLIONE, BALDASSAR, *Il libro del Cortegiano*, ed. by Walter Barberis (Turin: Einaudi, 1998)

CASTIGLIONE, GIOVANNI BATTISTA, *Sentimenti di S. Carlo Borromeo intorno agli spettacoli* (Bergamo: Lancellotti, 1759)

CHIABÒ, MARIA, and FEDERICO DOGLIO, eds, *I gesuiti e i primordi del teatro barocco in Europa* (Viterbo: Centro studi sul teatro medioevale e rinascimentale, 1995)

CHRISTIAN, LYNDA G., *Theatrum Mundi: The History of an Idea* (New York: Garland, 1987)

CICERO, *Brutus. Orator*, trans. by G. L. Hendrickson, H. M. Hubbell (Cambridge, MA: Harvard University Press, 1939)

—— *On Invention. The Best Kind of Orator. Topics*, trans. by H. M. Hubbell (Cambridge, MA: Harvard University Press, 1949)

—— *On the Orator: Books 1–2*, trans. by E. W. Sutton, H. Rackham (Cambridge, MA: Harvard University Press, 1942)

—— *On the Orator: Book 3. On Fate. Stoic Paradoxes. Divisions of Oratory*, trans. by H. Rackham (Cambridge, MA: Harvard University Press, 1942)

—— *Topica*, ed. by Tobias Reinhardt (Oxford: Oxford University Press, 2003)

CLARK, D. R., 'The Rise and Fall of Progymnasmata in Sixteenth and Seventeenth Century Grammar Schools', *Speech Monographs*, 19 (1952), 159–263

CONSTABLE, M. V., 'The Venetian "figlie del coro": Their Environment and Achievement', *Music & Letters*, 63.3 (1982), 181–212

—— 'The Education of the Venetian Orphans from the Sixteenth to the Eighteenth Century: An Expression of Guillaume Postel's Judgement of Venice as a Public Welfare State', in Kuntz, ed., *Postello, Venezia e il suo mondo*, pp. 179–202

Constitutioni et Regole della Casa delle Cittelle di Venezia (Venice: Girolamo Albrizzi, 1701)

COPELAND, RITA, and PETER STRUCK, eds, *The Cambridge Companion to Allegory* (Cambridge: Cambridge University Press, 2010)

COSTANTINI, MASSIMO, 'Le strutture dell'ospitalità', in *Storia di Venezia* (Rome: Istituto della Enciclopedia Italiana, 1991–2002), vol. v, pp. 881–912

COSTANZO, MARIO, *Il 'Gran Theatro del Mondo': schede per lo studio dell'iconografia letteraria nell'età del Manierismo* (Milan: All'insegna del pesce d'oro, 1964)

COX, VIRGINIA, 'Re-Thinking Counter-Reformation Literature', in McHugh and Wainwright, eds, *Innovation in the Italian Counter-Reformation*, pp. 15–55

COZZANDO, LEONARDO, *Libraria bresciana* (Brescia: Giovanni Maria Rizzardi, 1694)

CURTIUS, ERNST R., *European Literature and the Latin Middle Ages* [1953], trans. by Willard R. Trask (Princeton, NJ: Princeton University Press, 2013)

DAMIANO, GIANFRANCO, 'Il Collegio gesuitico di Brera: festa, teatro e drammaturgia tra XVI e XVII sec.', in *La scena della gloria: drammaturgia e spettacolo a Milano in età spagnola*, ed. by Annamaria Cascetta and Roberta Carpani (Milan: Vita e Pensiero, 1995), pp. 473–506

D'ANGELO, ROSA MARIA, 'Rutilio Lupo 2,6: un tormentato esempio di prosopopea', *Museum Helveticum*, 62 (2005), 133–44

DAOLMI, DAVIDE, *Le origini dell'opera a Milano (1598–1649)* (Turnhout: Brepols, 1998)

DAVIS, TRACY C., and THOMAS POSTLEWAIT, eds, *Theatricality* (Cambridge: Cambridge University Press, 2005)

DE BUJANDA, JESÚS M., *Diego de Estella (1524–1578): estudio de sus obras castellanas* (Rome: Iglesia Nacional Española, 1970)

Della imitatione di Christo, e del disprezzo del mondo (Venice: Altobello Salicato, 1580)

DEMETRIUS, *Demetrii Phaleri De elocutione liber a Stanislao Ilovio Polono Latinitate donatus et annotationibus illustrates* (Basel: Johannes Oporinus, 1552)

DIONYSIUS OF HALICARNASSUS, *Critical Essays, Volume I: Ancient Orators. Lysias. Isocrates. Isaeus. Demosthenes. Thucydides*, trans. by Stephen Usher (Cambridge, MA: Harvard University Press, 1974)

DUTTON, RICHARD, '*Hamlet, An Apology for Actors*, and The Sign of the Globe', in *Shakespeare Survey*, ed. by Stanley Wells (Cambridge: Cambridge University Press, 1989), pp. 35–44

EGGINTON, WILLIAM, *How the World Became a Stage: Presence, Theatricality, and the Question of Modernity* (Albany: State University of New York Press, 2003)

ELLERO, GIUSEPPE, 'Origini e sviluppo storico della musica nei quattro grandi ospedali di Venezia', *Nuova Rivista Musicale Italiana*, 13.1 (1979), 160–67

——'San Girolamo Miani e i Somaschi all'Ospedale dei Derelitti', in Scarabello, ed., *San Girolamo Miani*, pp. 39–54

——*L'archivio IRE. Inventari dei fondi antichi degli ospedali e luoghi pii di Venezia* (Venice: I. R. E., 1987)

——'Guillaume Postel e l'ospedale dei Derelitti (1547–1549)', in Kuntz, ed., *Postello, Venezia e il suo mondo*, pp. 137–62

——'Personaggi e momenti di vita', in Aikema and Mejiers, eds, *Nel regno dei poveri*, pp. 109–20

——, and SILVIA LUNARDON, *Guida all'Ospedaletto: itinerario storico, artistico e musicale della Chiesa e Ospedale dei Derelitti* (Venice: I. R. E., 2005)

ESTELLA, DIEGO, *Il dispreggio delle vanità del mondo*, trans. by Geremia Foresti (Venice: Cristoforo Zanetti, 1575)

——*Dispregio della vanità del mondo*, trans. by Pietro Buonfanti (Florence: Giorgio Marescotti, 1581)

——*Dispregio della vanità del mondo*, trans. by Giovanni Battista Peruschi (Venice: Giovanni Guerigli, 1601)

—— *Dispregio della vanità del mondo [...] Aggiuntevi di nuovo le meditationi dell'Amor di Dio del medesimo autore* (Venice: Giovanni Guerigli, 1604)

—— *Libro de la vanidad del mundo*, ed. by Pio Sagüés Azcona (Madrid: Editorial Franciscana Aranzazu, 1980)

FABRE, PIERRE-ANTOINE, *Ignace de Loyola. Le Lieu de l'image: Le Problème de la composition de lieu dans les pratiques spirituelles et artistiques jésuites de la seconde moitié du XVIe siècle* (Paris: Vrin — EHESS, 1992)

FANO, FABIO, 'Bassano, Giovanni', *Dizionario Biografico degli Italiani*, 7 (1970), pp. 112–13

FARAGO, CLAIRE, HELEN HILLS, MONIKA KAUP, GABRIELA SIRACUSANO, JENS BAUMGARTEN and STEFANO JACOVIELLO, 'Conceptions and Reworkings of Baroque and Neobaroque in Recent Years', *Perspective: actualité en histoire de l'art*, 1 (2015), 43–62

FARINA, FRANCESCO, *La Dimne rappresentatione spirituale* (Venice: Niccolò Misserini, 1610)

FENARIO, PANFILO, *Discorsi sopra i cinque sentimenti; ne i quali si dimostrano le varie lor potenze, et effetti, e fin dove per lor mezo arriva l'intelletto humano. Con un trattato del medesimo delle virtù morali, dove con brevità si dichiara quale sia il vero loro fine* (Venice: Giovan Battista Somasco, 1587)

FILIPPI, BRUNA, '"...Accompagnare il diletto d'un ragionevole trattenimento con l'utile di qualche giovevole ammaestramento...". Il teatro dei gesuiti a Roma nel XVII secolo', *Teatro e storia*, 9 (1994), 91–128

FIORANI, MALVINA, 'Aristotelismo e innovazione barocca nel concetto di ingegno del Cannocchiale aristotelico di Tesauro', *Studi secenteschi*, 46 (2005), 91–129

FLETCHER, ANGUS, *Allegory: The Theory of a Symbolic Mode* (Ithaca, NY: Cornell University Press, 1965)

FONTANIER, PIERRE, *Les figures du discours* [1821–27], ed. by Gérard Genette (Paris: Flammarion, 1968)

FORD, PHILIP, 'Conrad Gesner et le fabuleux manteau', *Bibliothèque d'Humanisme et Renaissance*, 47 (1985), 305–20

FRANCO, GIACOMO, *Habiti delle donne venetiane* (n.p.: n.pub., n.d.); see the facsimile edition edn by Lina Urban (Venice: Centro internazionale della grafica, 1990)

FREEDBERG, DAVID, *The Power of Images: Studies in the History and Theory of Response* (Chicago, IL: University of Chicago Press, 1989)

FREGOSO, ANTONIO FILEREMO, *Opere*, ed. by Giuliano Dilemmi (Bologna: Commissione per i testi di lingua, 1976)

FUMAROLI, MARC, *L'Âge de l'éloquence: rhétorique et "res literaria" de la Renaissance au seuil de l'époque Classique* (Geneva: Droz, 1980)

—— *Héros et Orateurs: Rhétorique et dramaturgie cornéliennes* (Geneva: Droz, 1990)

GAETA BERTELÀ, GIOVANNA, and ANNAMARIA PETRIOLI TOFANI, eds, *Feste e apparati medicei da Cosimo I a Cosimo II: mostra di disegni e incisioni* (Florence: Leo S. Olshki editore, 1969)

GALLINARO, IRENE, 'Il "Cardiomorphoseos' di Francesco Pona', *Lettere italiane*, 56.4 (2004), 570–601

GAMBA, BARTOLOMEO, *Delle novelle italiane in prosa, bibliografia* (Florence: All'insegna di Dante, 1835)

GARBERO ZORZI, ELVIRA, *Teatro e spettacolo nella Firenze dei Medici: modelli dei luoghi teatrali* (Florence: Leo S. Olschki, 2001)

GARZONI, TOMASO, *L'ospidale de' pazzi incurabili*, ed. by Stefano Barelli (Rome and Padua: Antenore, 2004)

—— *La piazza universale di tutte le professioni del mondo*, ed. by Paolo Cherchi and Beatrice Collina (Turin: Einaudi, 1996)

—— *Theatro de' vari e diversi cervelli mondani* (Venice: Paolo Zanfretti, 1583)

GHILINI, GIROLAMO, *Teatro d'huomini letterati* (Venice: Guerigli, 1647)

GIAMBULLARI, PIER FRANCESCO, *Regole della lingua fiorentina*, ed. by Ilaria Bonomi (Florence: Accademia della Crusca, 1986)
GIARDA, CRISTOFORO, *Bibliothecae Alexandrinae Icones Symbolicae* (Milan: Melchiorre Malatesta, 1626)
GILIO, GIOVANNI ANDREA, *Dialogo nel quale si ragiona degli errori e degli abusi de' pittori circa l'istorie* (Camerino: Antonio Gioioso, 1564)
—— *Dialogue on the Errors and Abuses of Painters*, ed. by Michael Bury, Lucinda Byatt, and Carol M. Richardson, trans. by Michael Bury and Lucinda Byatt (Los Angeles: Getty Research Institute, 2018)
GILIO, PIER GIUSEPPE, *L'attività musicale negli ospedali di Venezia nel Settecento: quadro storico e materiali documentari* (Florence: Leo S. Olschki, 2006)
GIOVANNI PAOLO DA COMO, *Ordini et capitoli della Compagnia dell'Oratorio il quale è nell'Hospitale de gli Incurabili in Venetia, circa il governo delle Schole de Putti, che sono in detta città* (Venice: Gabriel Giolito de' Ferrari, 1568)
GIOVIO, PAOLO, *Dialogo dell'imprese militari e amorose*, ed. by Maria Luisa Doglio (Rome: Bulzoni, 1978)
GIUSTINIANI, LORENZO, *Del dispreggio del mondo e delle sue vanità* (Venice: Aldo Manuzio, 1597)
GLISSENTI, ANTONIO, *Trattato del regimento del vivere, et delle altre cose che deveno usare gli huomini per preservarsi sani nelli tempi pestilenti. Continuato alla cognitione delle cause che producono la peste* (Venice: Rutilio e Camillo Borgominieri, 1576)
—— *Il summario delle cause che dispongono i corpi de gli huomini a patire la corrottione pestilente del presente anno 1576. Quelle che producono la peste, quelle che gli prestano aiuto, & fauore nel aggrandirla, & quelle che la fanno parere piu crudele*, [n.d.: n.pub., 1576]
—— *Risposta fatta per il sumario della cause pestilenti alla apologia dell'eccell. m. Anibal Raimondo veronese* [n.d.: n.pub., 1576]
—— *Oratione divotissima per ringratiare il nostro Signore Iddio, nella liberatione del male contagioso di Venetia* [n.d.: n.pub., 1576]
—— *Elogio per il serenissimo principe dell'illustrissima republica Venetiana, il signor Sebastian Veniero* (Venice: n.pub., 1577)
—— *Dialogo del Gobbo da Rialto, et Marocco dalle pipone dalle colonne di S. Marco, sopra la cometa alli giorni passati apparsa su nel cielo* (Venice: n.pub., 1577)
—— *Risposta al modo d'irrigare la campagna di Verona* (Venice: n.pub., 1594)
—— *Replica in proposito della risposta de m. Christoforo Sorte* (Venice: n.pub., 1594)
—— *L'assoluta conclusione dell'humana libertà* (Venice: Giovanni Antonio Rampazzetto, 1597)
GLISSENTI, FABIO, *In quinque praedicabilia Porphyrij. In sex principia Gilberti Porretani. In Praedicamenta Aristotelis. In perihermenias Aristotelis. In priora, et posteriora Aristotelis. Per methodicas Divisiones brevissima commentaria* (Venice: Giovan Battista Ciotti, 1594)
—— *Discorsi morali [...] contra il dispiacer del morire. Detto Athanatophilia* (Venice: Domenico Farri, 1596)
—— *La Ragione sprezzata, favola tragica morale* (Venice: Marco Claseri, 1606)
—— *Il bacio della Giustitia e della Pace. Favola morale* (Venice: Giovanni Alberti, 1607) [2nd edn, Venice: Angelo Salvadori, 1629]
—— *L'Andrio, cioè l'Huomo virile favola morale* (Venice: Giovanni Alberti, 1607) [second edition, Venice: Tommaso Ginammi, 1634]
—— *Il Diligente overo il Sollecito favola morale* (Venice: Giovanni Alberti, 1608) [second edition, Venice: Bartolomeo Ginammi, 1643]
—— *La Morte innamorata favola morale* (Venice: Giovanni Alberti, 1608) [second edition, Venice: Marco Ginammi, 1643]

——— *L'Androtoo cioè l'Huomo innocente favola morale* (Venice: Marci Ginammi, 1616) [second edition, Venice: Marco Ginammi, 1643]
——— *La giusta Morte, favola morale* (Venice: Marco Ginammi, 1617)
——— *L'Horribile e spauenteuole inferno, dove si discorre della poca consideratione che si ha d'intorno alle tremende pene di lui* (Venice: Marco Ginammi, 1617)
——— *Lo Spensierato fatto pensoroso [...] avvenimento morale* (Venice: Marco Ginammi, 1617) [second edition, Venice: Antonio Ginammi, 1634]
——— *Il mercato overo la fiera della Vita humana favola morale* (Venice: Marco Ginammi, 1620) [second edition, Venice: Bartolomeo Ginammi, 1643]
——— *La Sarcodinamia cioè la possanza della Carne favola morale* (Venice: Marco Ginammi, 1620) [second edition, Venice: Bartolomeo Ginammi, 1644]
——— *Breve trattato nel quale moralmente si discorre qual sia la pietra di filosofi* [facsimile edn] (Brescia: F.lli Gerolli, 1987)
GLIXON, JONATHAN E., *Mirrors of Heaven or Worldly Theaters? Venetian Nunneries and their Music* (Oxford: Oxford University Press, 2017)
GOETHALS, JESSICA, 'Worth Its Salt: Margherita Costa's Ridiculous Defence of Buffoonery', *The Italianist*, 40.3 (2020), 362–81
———, and EUGENIO REFINI, 'Genre-Bending in Early Modern Performative Culture', *The Italianist*, 40.3 (2020), 317–26
GOGGIO, EMILIO, 'The Prologue in the *Commedie Erudite* of the 16th Century', *Italica*, 18.3 (1941), 124–32
GOMBRICH, ERNST H., 'Personification', in *Classical Influences on European Culture, A.D. 500–1500*, ed. by Robert R. Bolgar (Cambridge: Cambridge University Press, 1971), pp. 247–57
——— *Symbolic Images: Studies in the Art of the Renaissance* (London: Phaidon Press, 1972)
——— 'Icones Symbolicae. Philosophies of Symbolism and their Bearing on Art', in Gombrich, *Symbolic Images*, pp. 123–91
GREEN, HENRY, ed., *Les Simulachres et historiées faces de la mort, commonly called The Dance of death* (Manchester: A. Brothers, 1869)
GROSSER, HERMAN, *La sottigliezza del disputare: teorie degli stili e teorie dei generi in età rinascimentale e nel Tasso* (Florence: La Nuova Italia, 1992)
GUARAGNELLA, PASQUALE, *Gli occhi della mente: stili del Seicento italiano* (Bari: Palomar, 1997)
GUARINO, RAIMONDO, *Teatro e mutamenti: Rinascimento e spettacolo a Venezia* (Bologna: il Mulino, 1995)
GUICCIARDINI, LODOVICO, *L'ore di ricreazione*, ed. by Anne-Marie Van Passen (Rome: Bulzoni, 1990)
HAUG, WALTER, ed., *Formen und Funktionen der Allegorie* (Stuttgart: J. B. Metzlersche Verlagsbuchhandlung, 1979)
HELMICH, WERNER, *Die Allegorie im französischen Theater des 15. und 16. Jahrunderts* (Tübingen: Max Niemeyer, 1976)
HENDRIX, JOHN SHANNON, and CHARLES H. CARMAN, eds, *Renaissance Theories of Vision* (Burlington, VT: Ashgate, 2010)
HENKE, ROBERT, *Pastoral Transformations: Italian Tragicomedy and Shakespeare's Late Plays* (Newark: University of Delaware Press, 1997)
HERACLITUS, *Allegoriae in Homeri fabulas de diis [...] Conrado Gesnero interprete* (Basel: Oporinus, 1544)
——— *Homeric Problems*, ed. by D. A. Russell and David Konstan (Leiden and Boston, MA: Brill 2005)
HERDT, JENNIFER A., *Putting On Virtue: The Legacy of the Splendid Vices* (Chicago, IL: University of Chicago Press, 2008)

HILLS, HELEN, ed., *Rethinking the Baroque* (Farnham: Ashgate, 2011)
HINZ, MANFRED, *Die menschlichen und die göttlichen Mittel: Sieben Kommentare zu Baltasar Gracián* (Bonn: Romanistischer Verlag, 2002)
—— 'Agudeza e Progymnasmata', in *I Gesuiti e la Ratio Studiorum*, ed. by Manfred Hinz, Roberto Righi and Danilo Zardin (Rome: Bulzoni, 2004), pp. 293–314 (on Hermogenes, pp. 295–96; on Aphthonius, pp. 296–97)
HOXBY, BLAIR, 'Allegorical Drama', in Copeland and Struck, eds, *The Cambridge Companion to Allegory*, pp. 191–208
IGNATIUS OF LOYOLA, *Exercitia spiritualia* (Rome: Antonio Blado, 1548)
—— *Esercitii spirituali*, trans. by Giovanni Battista Peruschi (Rome: Collegio Romano, [1555])
—— *Exercitia spiritualia. Textuum antiquissimorum nova editio*, ed. by José Calveras s.i. and Cándido de Dalmases s.i. (Rome: Istituto Storico della Società di Gesù, 1969)
—— *Esercizi spirituali*, ed. by Giuseppe De Gennaro s.i., in Ignatius of Loyola, *Gli scritti*, ed. by Mario Gioia (Turin: UTET, 1977), pp. 65–184
Il tema della fortuna nella letteratura francese e italiana del Rinascimento (Florence: Leo S. Olschki, 1990)
Incomincia il libro divoto et utile composto per messer Giovanni Gersonne cancelliere di Parisio, della imitatione di Christo Giesù, et del dispreggio di tutte le cose del mondo (Venice: Francesco Bindoni and Maffeo Pasini, 1545)
INNAMORATI, ISABELLA, ed., *Luca Ronconi e il suo teatro* (Rome: Bulzoni, 1996)
KENNEDY, GEORGE A., *Progymnasmata: Greek Textbooks of Prose Composition and Rhetoric* (Atlanta, GA: Society of Biblical Literature, 2003)
—— *Invention and Method: Two Rhetorical Treatises from the Hermogenic Corpus* (Leiden: Brill, 2005)
KING, PAMELA M., 'Morality Plays', in *The Cambridge Companion to Medieval English Theatre*, ed. by Richard Beadle (Cambridge: Cambridge University Press, 1994), pp. 240–64
KUNTZ, MARION LEATHERS, ed., *Postello, Venezia e il suo mondo* (Florence: Leo S. Olschki, 1988)
KURTZ, BARBARA ELLEN, *The Play of Allegory in the 'Autos Sacramentales' of Pedro Calderón de la Barca* (Washington, DC: Catholic University of America, 1991)
KURTZ, LEONARD P., *The Dance of Death and the Macabre Spirit in European Literature* (New York: Columbia University, 1934)
LANCETTA, TROILO, *La scena tragica d'Adamo e d'Eva, estratta dalli primi tre capi della sacra Genesi, et ridotta a significato morale* (Venice: Giovanni Guerigli, 1644)
LASOCKI, DAVID, and ROGER PRIOR, *The Bassanos: Venetian Musicians and Instrument Makers in England, 1531–1665* (Brookfield, VT: Ashgate, 1995)
LAUSBERG, HEINRICH, *Handbook of Literary Rhetoric: A Foundation for Literary Study*, trans. by R. Dean Anderson (Leiden and Boston, MA: Brill, 1998)
LAVEN, MARY, *Virgins of Venice: Broken Vows and Cloistered Lives in the Renaissance Convent* (London: Viking, 2002)
LEE, RENSSELAER W., *'Ut pictura poesis*: The Humanistic Theory of Painting', *The Art Bulletin*, 22.4 (1940), 197–269
LENTI, MADDALENA, ed., *Luca Ronconi. Un'idea di teatro. Conversazioni e testimonianze* (Milan: Mimesis, 2011)
LEONI, GIOVANNI BATTISTA, *La conversione del peccatore a Dio, tragicomedia spirituale* (Venice: Francesco de' Franceschi, 1591)
—— *La falsa riputatione della fortuna favola morale* (Venice: Giovan Battista Ciotti, 1596)
Les simulachres et historiées faces de la mort, autant élégamment pourtraictes que artificiellement imaginées (Lyon: Trechsel, 1538)

LIONARDI, ALESSANDRO, *Dialogi della inventione poetica* (Venice: Plinio Pietrasanta, 1554)
LONGHI, CLAUDIO, *Orlando Furioso di Ariosto–Sanguineti per Luca Ronconi* (Pisa: ETS, 2006)
LUCONI, MASSIMO, ed., *Luca Ronconi: il palcoscenico dell'utopia* (Florence: Edizioni Clichy, 2016)
LUIS DE GRANADA, *Specchio della vita humana, nel quale si contiene il libro della contemplatione, et il manuale di diuerse oration* (Venice: Gabriele Giolito, 1568)
—— *Devotissime meditationi per i giorni della settimana* (Venice: Gabriele Giolito, 1568)
MAGGI, ARMANDO, 'Visual and verbal communication in Francesco Pona's *Cardiomorphoseos* (1645)', *Word & Image*, 16.2 (2000), 212–24
MAJORANA, BERNADETTE, 'Governo del corpo, governo dell'anima: attori e spettatori nel teatro italiano del XVII secolo', in Prodi, ed., *Disciplina dell'anima*, pp. 437–90
MANENTI, GIOVANNI, *Opera nuova in versi volgare, intitulata Specchio de la Giustitia. Nel quale se dimostra lo Inferno, il Purgatorio, et il Paradiso del Mondo* (Venice: Giovanni Antonio Nicolini da Sabbio, 1539)
MANIERI, ALESSANDRA, *L'immagine poetica nella teoria degli antichi: phantasia ed energeia* (Pisa: IEPI, 1998)
MANNI, AGOSTINO, *Rappresentatione di anima et corpo nuovamente posta in musica dal sig. Emilio del Cavaliere per recitar cantando* (Rome: Niccolò Muzi, 1600)
MARITI, LUCIANO, *Commedia ridicolosa: comici di professione, dilettanti, editoria teatrale nel Seicento. Storia e testi* (Rome: Bulzoni, 1978)
MAROTTI, FERRUCCIO, and GIOVANNA ROMEI, *La commedia dell'arte e la società barocca, Volume 2: La professione dell'attore* (Rome: Bulzoni, 1991)
MARTY, FRANÇOIS, *Sentir et goûter: les sens dans les "Exercices spirituels" de saint Ignace* (Paris: Les Éditions du cerf, 2005)
MASUCCIO SALERNITANO, *Il Novellino*, ed. by Alfredo Mauro (Bari: Laterza, 1940)
MAZZONI, STEFANO, *Atlante iconografico: spazi e forme dello spettacolo in Occidente dal mondo antico a Wagner* (Pisa: Titivillus, 2003)
MCCLURE, GEORGE, 'The "Artes" and the "Ars moriendi" in Late Renaissance Venice: The Professions in Fabio Glissenti's *Discorsi morali contra il dispiacer del morire, detto Athanatophilia* (1596)', *Renaissance Quarterly*, 51.1 (1998), 92–127
—— *The Culture of Profession in Late Renaissance Italy* (Toronto and Buffalo, NY; London: University of Toronto Press, 2004)
MCHUGH, SHANNON, and ANNA WAINWRIGHT, eds, *Innovation in the Italian Counter-Reformation* (Newark: University of Delaware Press, 2020)
MEERE, MICHALE, 'Introduction', in *French Renaissance and Baroque Drama: Text, Performance, Theory*, ed. by Michael Meere (Newark: University of Delaware Press, 2015), pp. xv–xxxi
MOLANUS, JOHANNES, *De picturis et imaginibus sacris, liber unus: tractans de vitandis circa eas abusibus, et de ea earundem significationibus* (Leuven, Hieronymus Welleus, 1570)
MONTAGNE, VÉRONIQUE, 'La Notion de prosopopée au XVIe siècle', *Seizième Siècle*, 4 (2008), 217–36
MONTAIGNE, MICHEL DE, *Discorsi morali, politici, et militari [...] Tradotti dal sig. Girolamo Naselli dalla lingua francese nell'italiana* (Ferrara: Bendetto Mammarello, 1590)
—— *Essays. Livre premier*, ed. by Jean Céard (Paris: Le Livre de poche, 2002)
MONTGOMERY, ROBERT L., 'Allegory and the Incredible Fable: The Italian View from Dante to Tasso', *Proceedings of the Modern Language Association*, 81.1 (1966), 45–55
MORONE, BONAVENTURA, *Il mortorio di Christo, tragedia spirituale* (Venice: Sebastiano Combi, 1615)
MOSSE, RAMONA, 'Thinking Theatres beyond Sight: From Reflection to Resonance', *Anglia*, 136.1 (2018), 138–53
MOY, CHARLOTTE C., 'The Enclosed Renaissance: Intellectual and Spiritual Learning

in Early Modern Venetian Convents' (unpublished PhD dissertation, Northwestern University, 2018)

NAPOLI, MARIA, *L'impresa del libro nell'Italia del Seicento: la bottega di Marco Ginammi* (Naples: Guida, 1990)

NERI, FERDINANDO, 'Le moralità di Fabio Glissenti', in *Scritti vari di erudizione e di critica in onore di Rodolfo Renier*, ed. by Arturo Graf (Turin: Bocca, 1912), pp. 187–96

NEWBIGIN, NERIDA, *Making a Play for God: The Sacre Rappresentazioni of Renaissance Florence* (Toronto: Centre for Renaissance and Reformation Studies, 2021)

NEWMAN, SARA, 'Aristotle's Notion of "Bringing-Before-the-Eyes": Its Contributions to Aristotelian and Contemporary Conceptualizations of Metaphor, Style, and Audience', *Rhetorica*, 20.1 (2002), 1–23

NICHOLSON, ERIC, 'Crossing Borders with Satyrs, the Irrepressible Genre-Benders of Pastoral Tragicomedy', *Italian Studies*, 40.3 (2020), 342–61

NORMAN, JOANNE S., *Metamorphoses of an Allegory: The Iconography of the Psychomachia in Medieval Art* (New York: Peter Lang, 1988)

OTTONELLI, GIOVANNI DOMENICO, *Della christiana moderatione del theatro*, 5 vols (Florence: Luca Franceschini and Alessandro Logi, 1648–1652)

PALEOTTI, GABRIELE, *Discorso intorno alle imagini sacre et profane* (Bologna: Alessandro Benacci, 1582)

—— *Discourse on Sacred and Profane Images*, trans. by William McCuaig (Los Angeles: Getty Research Institute, 2012)

PAPANTI, GIOVANNI, *Catalogo dei novellieri italiani in prosa* (Livorno: Francesco Vigo, 1871)

PARKER, ANDREW, and EVE KOSOFSKY SEDGWICK, eds, *Performativity and Performance* (New York: Routledge, 1996)

PASERO, CARLO, 'Giacomo Franco, editore, incisore e calcografo nei secoli XVI e XVII', *La Bibliofilia*, 37 (1935), 332–45

PASSANO, GIAMBATTISTA, *I novellieri italiani in prosa. Parte I* (Turin: Stamperia Reale, 1878)

PATTERSON, ANNABEL M., *Hermogenes and the Renaissance: Seven Ideas of Style* (Princeton, NJ: Princeton University Press, 1970)

PATTINI, DANTE, 'Un percorso dantesco all'interno del Palazzo Ducale di Venezia : lo Specchio de la Giustitia di Giovanni Manenti (1539)', *Studi veneziani*, 61 (2010), 109–56

PAXSON, JAMES J., *The poetics of Personification* (Cambridge and New York: Cambridge University Press, 1994)

PELLEGRINO, CAMILLO, *Il Carrafa, o vero della epica poesia* (Florence: Iacopo Sermartelli, 1584)

PELOSI, OLIMPIA, *La fiera come gran teatro del mondo: Michelangelo Buonarroti il giovane fra tradizione accademica e prospettiva barocca* (Salerno: Palladio stampa, 1983)

PERONA, BLANDINE, *Prosopopée et 'persona' à la Renaissance* (Paris: Garnier, 2013)

PERONI, VINCENZO, *Biblioteca bresciana* (Brescia: Nicolò Bettoni, 1818)

PESENTI, GIULIANO, 'Libri censurati a Venezia nei secoli XVI–XVII', *La Bibliofilia*, 58 (1956), 15–30

PHILOSTRATUS, *Apollonius of Tyana, Volume II: Life of Apollonius of Tyana, Books 5–8*, ed. and trans. by Christopher P. Jones (Cambridge, MA: Harvard University Press, 2005)

PIANTONI, LUCA, 'Morte a Venezia: l'"Athanatophilia" di Fabio Glissenti, 1596', in *Visibile teologia: il libro sacro figurato in Italia tra Cinque e Seicento*, ed. by Erminia Ardissino and Elisabetta Selmi (Alessandria: Edizioni dell'Orso, 2012), pp. 221–50

PIERGUIDI, STEFANO, *'Dare forma humana a l'Honore et a la Virtù': Giovanni Guerra (1544–1618) e la fortuna delle figure allegoriche da Mantegna all'Iconologia di Cesare Ripa* (Rome: Bulzoni, 2008)

PIRROTTA, NINO, *Li due Orfei: da Poliziano a Monteverdi* (Turin: Einaudi, 1975)

PONA, FRANCESCO, *Cardiomorphoseos sive ex corde desumpta emblemata sacra* (Verona: 1645)

PONTANI, FILIPPOMARIA, 'From Budé to Zenodotus: Homeric Readings in the European Renaissance', *International Journal of the Classical Tradition*, 14.3–4 (2007), 375–430

PORCELLI, BRUNO, *Le misure della fabbrica: studi sull'Adone del Marino e sulla Fiera del Buonarroti* (Milan: Marzorati, 1980)

POSTLEWAIT, THOMAS, 'Theatricality and Antitheatricality in Renaissance London', in *Theatricality*, ed. by Tracy C. Davis and Thomas Postlewait (Cambridge: Cambridge University Press, 2005), pp. 90–126

PRODI, PAOLO, ed., *Disciplina dell'anima, disciplina del corpo e disciplina della società tra medioevo ed età moderna* (Bologna: il Mulino, 1994)

—— 'Introduction', in Paleotti, *Discourse on Sacred and Profane Images*, pp. 1–42

PROSPERI, ADRIANO, *Tribunali della coscienza: inquisitori, confessori, missionari. Nuova edizione* (Turin: Einaudi, 2009)

PROSPERI, VALENTINA, *Di soavi licor gli orli del vaso: la fortuna di Lucrezio dall'Umanesimo alla Controriforma* (Rome: Aragno, 2004)

PULLAN, BRIAN, *Rich and Poor in Renaissance Venice: The Social Institutions of a Catholic State, to 1620* (Oxford: Blackwell, 1971)

—— 'La nuova filantropia nella Venezia cinquecentesca', in Aikema and Mejiers, eds, *Nel regno dei poveri*, pp. 19–34

QUINTILIAN. *The Orator's Education*, ed. and trans. by Donald A. Russell, 5 vols (Cambridge, MA: Harvard University Press, 2002)

QUIRING, BJÖRN, ed., *'If Then the World a Theatre Present...': Revisions of the Theatrum Mundi Metaphor in Early Modern England* (Berlin and Boston, MA: De Gruyter, 2014)

QUONDAM, AMEDEO, *Forma del vivere: l'etica del gentiluomo e i moralisti italiani* (Bologna: il Mulino, 2010)

RADOGNA, DONATELLA, and FRANCESCA CASTAGNETO, eds, *Lo spazio della musica: flessibilità e nuove configurazioni spaziali* (Rome: Gangemi Editore, 2016)

RAIMONDO, ANNIBALE, *Apologia intorno alcuni amorevoli avisi mandateli, et per la risolutione di varii, et diversi dubii. Indirizzata a tutti quelli che si dilettarano di leggerla, overo di udirla leggere* (Venice: Domenico Nicolini da Sabbio, 1576)

RAMAKERS, BART, and WALTER MELION, eds, *Personification: Embodying Meaning and Emotion* (Leiden: Brill, 2016)

RAO, CESARE, *Invettive, orationi, et discorsi fatte sopra diverse materie, et a diversi personaggi dove si riprendono molti vitii, et s'essortano le persone all'esercitio delle virtù morali, et alle scienze, et arti liberali* (Venice: Damiano Zenaro, 1587)

RAUSEO, CHRIS, *Mœurs et maximes: personnification, représentation et moralisation théâtrales, du 'Gran teatro del mundo' au 'Malade imaginaire'* (Heidelberg: Universitätsverlag C. Winter, 1998)

REFINI, EUGENIO, 'Prologhi figurati: rappunti sull'uso della prosopopea nel prologo teatrale del Cinquecento', *Italianistica*, 35.3 (2006), 3, 61–86

—— *Per via d'annotationi: le glosse inedite di Alessandro Piccolomini all''Ars poetica' di Orazio* (Lucca: Pacini Fazzi, 2009)

—— '"Quasi una tragedia delle attioni humane": le tragique entre allégorie et édification morale dans l'œuvre de Fabio Glissenti (1542–1615)', *Cahiers d'études italiennes*, 19 (2014), 185–98

—— 'The Courtier and the Philosopher's Stone: Dialogue and Conflict in Fabio Glissenti's *Discorsi morali*', in *Forms of Conflict and Rivalries in Renaissance Europe*, ed. by David A. Lines, Marc Laureys, and Jill Kraye (Bonn: Bonn University Press, 2015), pp. 207–22

—— 'Reforming Drama: Theater as Spiritual Practice in the Works of Fabio Glissenti', in McHugh and Wainwright, eds, *Innovation in the Italian Counter-Reformation*, pp. 169–89

REGIO, PAOLO, *Discorsi intorno le virtù morali ove con sentenze, et esempi di detti, et fatti degli antichi da diversi illustri autori raccolti, si tratta della giustizia, prudenza, temperanza, et fortezza.*

Con molti avertimenti utili così per la vita humana, come per il governo de' i prencipi, et delle repubbliche (Naples: Orazio Salviani, 1576)
REINIS, AUSTRA, *Reforming the Art of Dying: The 'ars moriendi' in the German Reformation (1519–1528)* (Aldershot: Ashgate, 2007)
Rhetorica ad Herennium, trans. by Harry Caplan (Cambridge, MA: Harvard University Press, 1954)
RHODES, DENNIS E., *Giovanni Battista Leoni, diplomatico e poligrafo* (Manziana: Vecchiarelli, 2013)
RIGONI, MARIO ANDREA, 'Una finestra aperta sul cuore (note sulla metafora della *sinceritas* nella tradizione occidentale)', *Lettere italiane*, 4 (1974), 434–58
RIPA, CESARE, *Iconologia* (Rome: Giovanni Gigliotti, 1593)
—— *Iconologia* (Siena: Matteo Florimi, 1613)
RIPOSIO, DONATELLA, *Nova comedia v'appresento: il prologo nella commedia del Cinquecento* (Turin: Tirrenia Stampatori, 1989)
ROMANO, DENNIS, 'L'assistenza e la beneficenza', in *Storia di Venezia* (Rome: Istituto della Enciclopedia Italiana, 1991–2002), vol. V, pp. 355–406
RONCONI, ALESSANDRO, 'Prologhi "plautini" e prologhi "terenziani" nella commedia italiana del '500', in *Il teatro classico italiano nel '500* (Rome: Accademia Nazionale dei Lincei, 1971), pp. 197–217
ROSSI, NICOLÒ, *Discorsi intorno alla tragedia* (Vicenza: Giorgio Greco, 1590)
SALVIUCCI INSOLERA, LYDIA, 'L'uso di immagini come strumento didattico-catechetico nella Compagnia di Gesù', in *I Gesuiti e la Ratio Studiorum*, pp. 191–210
SALZBERG, ROSA, *Ephemeral City: Cheap Print and Urban Culture in Renaissance Venice* (Manchester: Manchester University Press, 2014)
SAMPSON, LISA, *Pastoral Drama in Early Modern Italy: The Making of a New Genre* (Oxford: Legenda, 2006)
SANGALLI, MAURIZIO, *Cultura, politica e religione nella Repubblica di Venezia tra Cinque e Seicento: Gesuiti e Somaschi a Venezia* (Venice: Istituto Veneto di Scienze, Lettere ed Arti, 1999)
SANSOVINO, FRANCESCO, *Venetia città nobilissima, et singolare* (Venice: Stefano Curti, 1663)
SASO, ANNA LAURA, 'Fabio Glissenti', in *Dizionario Biografico degli Italiani*, 57 (2001), pp. 406–08
SAULI, ALESSANDRO, *Instruttione compendiosa et breve delle cose più necessarie alla salute, le quali doverebbono essere sapute da ogni fidel christiano [...] Aggiuntovi di nuovo un modo di esaminare la conscienza per sapersi ben confessare* (Pavia: Girolamo Bartoli, 1577)
SCALIGER, JULIUS CAESAR, *Poetices libri septem*, ed. by Luc Deitz and Gregor Vogt-Spira, 5 vols (Stuttgart: Fromman, 1993–2003)
SCARABELLO, GIOVANNI, ed., *San Girolamo Miani nel V Centenario della nascita* (Venice: Studium Cattolico Veneziano, 1986)
—— 'Le strutture assistenziali', in *Storia di Venezia* (Rome: Istituto della Enciclopedia Italiana, 1991–2002), vol. VI, pp. 863–74
SCARPATI, CLAUDIO, and ERALDO BELLINI, *Il vero e il falso dei poeti: Tasso, Tesauro, Pallavicino, Muratori* (Milan: Vita e Pensiero, 1990)
SCORRANO, LUIGI, 'Gabriele Paleotti e il catechismo dei pittori "teologi mutoli"', *Studi rinascimentali*, 3 (2005), 113–27
SEBASTIANI MINTURNO, ANTONIO, *L'arte poetica* (Venice: Giovanni Andrea Valvassori, 1564)
SELMI, ELISABETTA, 'Prolegomeni all'allegoria teatrale: "Nel labirinto delle idee confuse". Alcune considerazioni', in Selmi and Zucchi, eds, *Allegoria e teatro*, pp. i–xxx
——, and ENRICO ZUCCHI, eds, *Allegoria e teatro tra Cinque e Settecento: da principio compositivo a strumento esegetico* (Bologna: Emil, 2016)
SEMI, FRANCA, *Gli ospizi di Venezia* (Venice: Edizioni Helvetia, 1983)

SHAKESPEARE, WILLIAM, *The Oxford Shakespeare. The Complete Works*, ed. by John Jowett, Stanley Wells, Gary Taylor, and William Montgomery (Oxford: Oxford University Press, 2005)

SHAPIRO, HARVEY A., *Personifications in Greek Art: The Representation of Abstract Concepts, 600–400 B.C.* (Zürich: Akanthus, 1993)

SIFAKIS, G. M., 'The Misunderstanding of *opsis* in Aristotle's *Poetics*', in *Performance in Greek and Roman Theatre*, ed. by George Harrison and Vayos Liapis (Leiden and Boston, MA: Brill, 2013), pp. 45–62

Simolachri, historie, e figure de la morte (Venice: Vincenzo Valgrisi, 1545)

SNYDER, JON R., *L'estetica del Barocco* (Bologna: il Mulino, 2005)

SORTE, CRISTOFORO, *Modo d'irrigare la campagna di Verona e d'introdur più nauigationi per lo corpo del felicissimo Stato di Venetia trovato* (Verona: Girolamo Discepolo, 1593)

STÄUBLE, ANTONIO, *La commedia umanistica del Quattrocento* (Florence: Istituto Nazionale di Studi sul Rinascimento, 1968)

STEADMAN, JOHN M., 'Image-Making in the Verbal and Visual Arts: A Renaissance Obsession', *Huntington Library Quarterly*, 61.1 (1998), 53–80

STERN, TIFFANY, 'Was *Totus Mundus Agit Histrionem* ever the motto of the Globe Theatre?', *Theatre Notebook*, 51.3 (1997), 122–27

STRUBEL, ARMAND, *'Grant senefiance a': allégorie et littérature au Moyen Âge* (Paris: Champion, 2002)

TAMBLING, JEREMY, *Allegory*, The New Critical Idiom (London: Routledge, 2010)

TAVIANI, FERDINANDO, *La commedia dell'arte e la società barocca*, Volume 1: *La fascinazione del teatro* (Rome: Bulzoni, 1991)

TENENTI, ALBERTO, *La vie et la mort à travers l'art du XVe siècle* (Paris: Cahiers des Annales, 1952)

—— *Il senso della morte e l'amore della vita nel Rinascimento (Francia e Italia)* (Turin: Einaudi, 1957)

TENTORIO, MARCO, *Saggio storico sullo sviluppo dell'ordine Somasco dal 1569 al 1650* (Rome: Archivio Storico Padri Somaschi, 2011)

TESAURO, EMANUELE, *Il cannocchiale aristotelico, o sia idea dell'arguta et ingeniosa elocutione che serve a tutta l'arte oratoria, lapidaria et simbolica esaminata co' principii del divino Aristotele* (Turin: Bartolomeo Zavatta, 1670)

TESTA, LUCA, *Fondazione e primo sviluppo del seminario romano (1565–1608)* (Rome: Editrice Pontificia Università Gregoriana, 2002)

TESTAVERDE MATTEINI, ANNA MARIA, *L'officina delle nuvole: il teatro mediceo nel 1589 e gli Intermedi del Buontalenti nel Memoriale di Girolamo Seriacopi* (Milan: Edizioni Amici della Scala, 1991)

TREADWELL, NINA K., *Music and Wonder at the Medici Court: The 1589 Interludes for La Pellegrina* (Bloomington: Indiana University Press, 2008)

TRISSINO, GIAN GIORGIO, *La quinta et la sesta divisione della Poetica* (Venice: Giovanni Bonadio, 1562)

TUCCI, UGO, 'Bontempelli (Bontempello) dal Calice (Calese) Bartolomeo', in *Dizionario Biografico degli Italiani*, 12 (1970), pp. 426–27

TYDEMAN, WILLIAM, *The Theatre in the Middle Ages: Western European Stage Conditions, c. 800–1576* (Cambridge: Cambridge University Press, 1978)

VAGLIA, UGO, 'Fabio Glisenti e la sua opera letteraria', *Memorie dell'Ateneo di Salò*, 16 (1952–54), 143–51

—— *L'arte del ferro in Valle Sabbia e la famiglia Glisenti* (Brescia: Geroldi, 1959)

VALESIO, PAOLO, 'Esquisse pour une étude des personnifications', *Lingua e stile*, 4 (1964), 1–21

VENIERO, ANGELO, *Teatro de' viventi e trionfo della morte diviso in due parti raccolte da i Discorsi morali dell'eccellentiss. Sig. Fabio Glissenti, dove si ragiona e discorre con molto profitto della salute di tutta la somma della morale, e Christiana filosofia, che insegna il bene e il virtuoso vivere, e come si possa e sappia santamente morire* (Venice: Fioravante Prati, 1605)

VENTRONE, PAOLA, ed., *Le Temps revient — 'l tempo si rinuova. Feste e spettacoli nella Firenze di Lorenzo il Magnifico* (Milan: Silvana editoriale, 1992)

VETTORI, PIETRO, *Petri Victorii Commentarii in librum Demetrii Phalerei De elocutione positis ante singulas declarationes Graecis vocibus auctoris, iisdemque ad verbum Latine expressis* (Florence: Bernardo Giunta, 1562)

VON HABSBURG, MAXIMILIAN, *Catholic and Protestant Translations of the Imitatio Christi, 1425–1650: From Late Medieval Classic to Early Modern Bestseller* (London: Routledge, 2011)

WARBURG, ABY, 'The Theatrical Costumes for the Intermedi of 1589', in Aby Warburg, *The Renewal of Pagan Antiquity*, trans. by David Britt (Los Angeles: Getty Research Institute for the Research of Arts and Humanities, 1999), pp. 349–401

WEAVER, ELISSA, *Convent Theatre in Early Modern Italy: Spiritual Fun and Learning for Women* (Cambridge: Cambridge University Press, 2007)

WEBSTER, T. B. L., 'Personification as a Mode of Greek Thought', *Journal of the Warburg and Courtauld Institutes*, 17 (1954), 10–21

WEINBERG, BERNARD, *A History of Literary Criticism in the Italian Renaissance* (Chicago, IL: University of Chicago Press, 1961)

——, ed., *Trattati di poetica e retorica del Cinquecento* (Bari: Laterza, 1970–1974)

WHITMAN, JON, *Allegory: The Dynamics of an Ancient and Medieval Technique* (Cambridge, MA: Harvard University Press, 1987)

WILBOURNE, EMILY, 'Amor nello specchio (1622): Mirroring, Masturbation, and Same-Sex Love', *Women and Music*, 13.1 (2009), 54–65

WITCOMBE, CHRISTOPHER, *Copyright in the Renaissance: Prints and the Privilegio in Sixteenth-Century Venice and Rome* (Leiden and Boston, MA: Brill, 2004)

WOLFE, JESSICA, 'Homer in Renaissance Europe (1488–1649)', in *The Cambridge Guide to Homer*, ed. by Corinne Ondine Pache (Cambridge: Cambridge University Press, 2020), pp. 490–504

WOTTON, HENRY, *Reliquiae Wottonianae. Or, a collection of lives, letters, poems; with characters of sundry personages: and other incomparable pieces of language and art. By the curious pensil of the ever memorable Sir Henry Wotton* (London: Thomas Maxey, 1651)

YATES, FRANCES A., *The Art of Memory* (London: Routledge and Paul, 1966)

—— *Theatre of the World* (Chicago, IL: University of Chicago Press, 1969)

YEARLEY, LEE, *Mencius and Aquinas: Theories of Virtue and Conceptions of Courage* (Albany: State University of New York Press, 1990)

ZAMPELLI, MICHAEL, '"Lascivi spettacoli": Jesuits and Theatre (from the Underside), in *The Jesuits II. Cultures, Sciences and the Arts, 1540–1773*, ed. by John William O'Malley *et al.* (Toronto: University of Toronto Press, 2006), pp. 550–71

ZANLONGHI, GIOVANNA, *Teatri di formazione: actio, parola e immagine nella scena gesuitica del Sei-Settecento a Milano* (Milan: Vita e Pensiero, 2002)

ZARDIN, DANILO, 'Libri e biblioteche negli ambienti monastici dell'Italia del primo Seicento', in *Donne filosofia e cultura nel Seicento*, ed. by P. Totaro (Rome: Consiglio Nazionale delle Ricerche, 1999), pp. 347–83

ZORZI, LUDOVICO, *Il teatro e la città: saggi sulla scena italiana* (Turin: Einaudi, 1977)

INDEX

Accademia degli Alterati 46
Accademia Fiorentina 46
Accademia Nazionale d'Arte Drammatica 17, 211
Accetto, Torquato:
   Della Dissimulazione onesta 184
Aeschylus:
   Prometheus Bound 45
Alamanni, Luigi 42
Alberti, Bartolomeo 84
Alberti, Giovanni 85
Alberti, Leon Battista 121
Alighieri, Dante 92
   Commedia 123, 165, 167, 179, 181
      Inferno 17.10–15: 52
      Paradiso 4.40–48: 47
   'Tre donne intorno al cor' [canzone] 41–42
allegory 14–15, 22–28, 29–31, 52–53, 95, 135, 137, 158–59, 185–87, 190, 215, 217–19
Andreini, Giovan Battista 16
   Adamo, L' 63–69, 70, 72, 76, 78, 147, 155, 183, 207
   Amor nello specchio 17–18, 212–18
   Centaura, La 214
   Due commedie in commedia, Le 214
Andreini, Isabella 127
Anselm of Aosta 75
Aphthonius of Antioch:
   Progymnasmata 38, 39, 41–42, 50
Ariosto, Ludovico 92, 199
   Orlando furioso:
      14.76–84: 53
      27.35: 54
      27.38: 54
      staged by Ronconi 211–12
Aristophanes:
   Plutus 43–44
Aristotle:
   De an.:
      427b 15–20: 48
      427b 20–21: 23
      428a 10–16: 23
      428b 11–14: 23
      429a 1–5: 23
   Poetics:
      1448a 19–24: 44, 49
      1449b 24–29: 149
      1449b 31–32: 6

      1450b 9–11: 39
      1454a 16–36: 40, 52
   Rhetoric:
      1389a ff.: 40
      1410b 35: 48
      1411a 28: 20, 24, 30
      1411b 32 ff.: 48
      1411b 34–35: 30
      1412a 1–3: 30
art of memory 12, 23–24, 51, 53, 59, 143, 155
Augustine of Hippo 75
Austin, John L. 21, 210

Baldung, Hans:
   Three Ages of the Woman and the Death 173–74
Baliotti, Modesto:
   Facilissimo modo di confessarsi 195
Barbieri, Nicolò:
   Supplica 127
Barnabites [religious order] 15, 142–43
Barocchi, Paola 56
Bassano, Giovanni 141
Bätschman, Oskar 101
Battista of Crema:
   Specchio interiore 196
Bede the Venerable:
   Liber de schematibus et tropis 2.1.8–10: 41
Bellarini, Giovanni:
   Breve prattica della conscienza 195
Bellintani, Mattia:
   Pratica dell'oration mentale 196
Benjamin, Walter 101, 171
Bernard of Clairvaux:
   On consideration 150
Bernheimer, Richard 2
Boccaccio, Giovanni 120
Boethius:
   Consolation of Philosophy 13
Boileau, Henri 30, 31
Boissard, Jean-Jacques:
   Theatrum Vitae Humanae 9–10, 13, 168
Bologna, Corrado 78
Bolzoni, Lina 12
Bonaventure of Bagnoregio 75
Bonciani, Francesco 16
   Lezione della prosopopea 46–54, 59

Borromeo, Carlo 127, 135
Borromeo, Federico 135
Breve modo di esaminare la conscienza 195
Bruno, Giordano:
   Candelaio, Il 214
Buffalmacco, Buonamico:
   Trionfo della Morte 181–82
buffoonery 127
Buonarroti the Younger, Michelangelo:
   Fiera, La 159
Buonaventura de Venere 16
   Rappresentatione spirituale dell'Anima e del Corpo 71–73, 207
Buonfanti, Pietro 197
Buontempelli dal Calice, Bartolomeo 139, 146
Butler, Judith 215

Calderón de la Barca, Pedro 2, 61
   Gran mercado del mundo, El 2
   Gran teatro del mundo, El 2
Camillo, Giulio:
   Idea del theatro, L' 10–12
Campanella, Tommaso:
   'Cosa stupenda ha fatto il Senno eterno' [madrigal] 121–22
Caneparo, Giovanni Maria:
   Modo et regola che si debbe tener per sapersi ben confessarsi 195
Casoni, Guido:
   Giuoco di Fortuna, Il 121
Castellano, Giacomo:
   Rime spirituali et morali 140–42, 151–53
Castelvetro, Lodovico:
   Poetica d'Aristotele volgarizzata e sposta 44–45, 48
Castiglione, Baldassar:
   Libro del Cortegiano 121
Castiglione, Giovanni Battista:
   Sentimenti di S. Carlo Borromeo intorno agli spettacoli 127, 135
catachresis 28, 47
catechism 142, 143, 150
catharsis 149, 153
Cavalieri, Emilio de':
   Rappresentatione di Anima et Corpo 69–70
character 31–33, 35–40, 46, 52, 58, 61, 63, 129–30, 132, 137, 165–66
Christian, Lynda G. 2
Cicero:
   De inv.:
      1.107: 34
      1.109: 34
   De off. 1.5: 57
   De or.:
      1.57.245: 34
      2.87.357: 23, 33
      2.87.358: 24
      3.53.204–05: 33, 34, 40
   De part. or. 16.55: 34
   Or.:
      85: 34
      138: 34
   Top.:
      27: 25
      45: 34
Claudian: 58
Coccina, Maria Francesca 147
commedia dell'arte 124, 207
Compagnia dell'Oratorio at the Incurabili 143
Compagnie del Divino Amore 142
confession 143, 144, 150, 183, 192, 194, 217
conformatio 23, 25, 33, 43
consideratio 150
Contarini, Pietro 160
contemptus mundi 150
contrasto [dramatic genre] 71, 95
Costa, Margherita 127
Costanzo, Mario 2
Council of Trent 54, 131, 142, 150
Curtius, Ernst R. 2

Damiani, Luca 211
Daolmi, Davide 67
De Gennaro, Giuseppe 77
Demetrius 6, 35
   De eloc.:
      81: 20, 24, 30, 48
      265–66: 32
Denores, Giason:
   Breve trattato dell'oratore 42
Dionysius of Halicarnassus:
   Thucyd. 37: 40
discipline 4, 5, 71, 82, 113, 134, 145, 153, 185–86, 189, 199, 210, 215
Donati, Baldassarre 141

Eden, garden of 63, 68, 101
effictio 33
Egginton, William 3, 21
eidolopoiia 25, 39, 113
enargeia 20, 26
energeia 20, 24, 30, 32
Ennius 38, 43, 44
Erasmus of Rotterdam 10, 121
   Encomium Moriae 42
Estella, Diego:
   Libro de la vanidad del mundo [*Dispregio della vanità del mondo*] 197–98
   Meditaciones devotissimas del amor de Dios 198
ethopoeia 39–40
ethos 39–40, 206

Everyman 1, 162
evidentia 20, 26, 34, 40, 70, 89, 93, 113, 151

fabulation 31
Farina, Francesco:
   Dimne, La 204
Farri, Domenico 84, 86
Fenario, Panfilo:
   Discorsi sopra i cinque sentimenti 87, 93
festivals 51, 59
figura 23
Fludd, Robert 10
Fontanier, Pierre 29–32
Foresti, Geremia 197
Francis of Assisi 78
Francis Xavier 142
Franco, Giacomo:
   Habiti delle donne venetiane 86, 114–16, 118
free will 84, 95–97, 137, 155, 157–58, 160, 163, 183, 188, 191
Fregoso, Antonio Fileremo:
   Dialogo di Fortuna 121
Fumaroli, Marc 32, 61

Garzoni, Tomaso:
   Hospidale de' pazzi incurabili, L' 122
   Piazza universale di tutte le professioni del mondo, La 122, 159
   Theatro de' vari e diversi cervelli mondani, Il 122
Gelli, Giovan Battista 130
Gelosi [commedia dell'arte company] 217
Gerson, Jean 195
   De scientia mortis 88
Gessner, Konrad 27
Gheyn, Jacques de:
   Still Life 173, 175
Giambullari, Pier Francesco:
   Regole della lingua Fiorentina 41–42, 44
Giarda, Cristoforo:
   Icones symbolicae 15, 56
Gilbert of Poitiers 84
Gilio, Giovanni Andrea 16
   Degli errori e degli abusi de' pittori 54–56, 59
Ginammi, Bartolomeo 85–86, 146
Ginammi, Marco 85
Giordani, Bernardo 146
Giovanni Paolo of Como 143–44
Giovio, Paolo:
   Dialogo dell'imprese militari e amorose 90
Glissenti, Antonio 83–84
   Assoluta conclusione dell'humana libertà, L' 163
Glissenti, Cornelio 84, 86
Glissenti, Elisabetta Serenella 1, 140, 146
Glissenti, Fabio:
   life 82–86
   works:
      Andrio cioè l'uomo virile, L' 85, 139, 141, 145, 146, 153, 155, 157–58, 160, 163, 165, 183, 205
      Androtoo, L' 85, 86, 142, 145, 146, 158, 160, 163, 165, 183–208, 218
      Bacio della Giustizia e della Pace, Il 85, 122, 145, 146, 158, 159
      Diligente overo il Sollecito 85, 139, 142, 145, 146, 151–56, 158, 199
      Discorsi morali contra il dispiacer del morire 4, 16, 17, 81–134, 135–37, 145, 147, 149, 155, 158, 162, 165, 166, 170, 197, 200, 217, 218
      Giusta Morte, La 85, 146, 158
      Horribile e spaventevole inferno, L' 85, 180
      Mercato overo la fiera della vita humana, Il 85, 146, 158, 159, 165, 166, 168, 169, 179, 191, 205
      Morte innamorata, La 1–2, 4, 9, 13–14, 17, 18, 85, 138, 140–42, 145, 146, 149, 151–52, 158, 159, 165, 211–12, 215, 217, 218
      Ragione sprezzata, La 85, 97, 128, 138–39, 145, 147–52, 158–60, 163–65, 166–83, 191, 216, 217
      Sarcodinamia cioè la possanza della Carne, La 85, 146, 158, 160, 165, 183, 205
      Spensierato fatto pensoroso, Lo 85, 146, 147
      Theatro de' viventi e trionfo della morte 85
Glissenti, Glissentia 84, 89–91, 146
Glixon, Jonathan 145
Globe Theatre 3, 12
Goethals, Jessica 127
Gombrich, Ernst H. 15
Griener, Pascal 101
Guicciardini, Lodovico:
   Ore di ricreazione, Le 121

Helmich, Werner 162–63
Heemskerck, Maarten van:
   Allegory of Innocence and Guile 201, 202, 204
Hemessen, Jan Sanders van:
   Vanity 173, 177, 217
Heraclitus 27–28, 52
   Quaest. Hom.:
      29.4–7: 27
      37.2–3: 28
      37.6: 28
Herdt, Jennifer 199–200, 204
Hermogenes 38–40
   De inv.:
      3.10: 40
      3.15: 40
   Progymn.:
      9.20.7–9: 39
      9.20.14–18: 39
      9.21.6–9: 40
Hesiod 26–27
   Scutum 267: 26

Holbein, Hans:
    Totentanz 98, 101, 109, 179
Homer 30, 42, 46, 52, 92, 199, 206
    Il.:
        4.442–43: 26–28
        9.502–03: 28
Horace 67, 92, 134
    Ars poet. 180–81: 23

Ilovius, Stanislaus 32
imago 23, 36
imago agens 14, 16, 19, 24, 59, 189
Imitation of Christ 97, 150, 195, 198
impersonation 33, 36, 38, 132–33
Isidore of Seville:
    Etym. 2.13.1–2: 38–39

Jesuit drama 61, 72, 134, 189, 199
Jesuits 142–43, 166, 193, 195
John Chrysostom 58
John of Salisbury:
    Policraticus 3

Lancetta, Troilo 16
    Scena tragica d'Adamo e d'Eva 78–80
Laven, Mary 145
lectio 35
Leoni, Contarina 146
Leoni, Giovanni Battista 166, 180
    Conversione del peccatore a Dio, La 135–36
    Falsa riputatione della Fortuna, La 136–37
Lionardi, Alessandro:
    Dialogi della inventione poetica 42
Lippi, Lorenzo:
    Allegory of Innocence 201, 203, 204
Lodrone, Paride 83, 96
Longinus (ps.) 6, 26, 27
    De subl.:
        9.4–5: 26
        9.7: 27
        15.1: 25
Lorenzo the Magnificent 50–51
Lorich, Reinhard 42
Loyola, Ignatius 72, 142
    Spiritual Exercises 74–78, 150, 182–83, 189–93, 197–98
Lucan 58
Lucian 58
Luis de Granada:
    Devotissime meditationi 150
    Specchio della vita humana 150, 170
Lützelberger, Hans 98, 101

Manenti, Giovanni:
    Opera nuova in versi volgare, intitulata Specchio de la Giustitia 122–24

Manni, Agostino 16
    Rappresentatione di Anima et Corpo 69–70
Mantovano, Battista 58
Maria Perpetua da Camoro 146
mascherata 50–51
Mazzucchi, Carlo Maria 27
McClure, George 82, 83, 88
Medici, Eleonora de' 138–39, 147
Medici, Maria de' 67
Menander 39, 42, 50
meraviglia 51
metaphors:
    'active' metaphors 20, 24, 30, 48
metonymy 29
Miani, Girolamo 143
mimesis ('icastic' and 'phantastic') 22, 48
mnemotechnics, *see* art of memory
Molanus, Johannes:
    De picturis et imaginibus sacris 56
Montaigne, Michel de:
    Essays 86–87, 90
Morone, Bonaventura 16, 147
    Mortorio di Christo, Il 72–78

Naselli, Girolamo:
    Discorsi morali, politici et militari 86–87
Newbigin, Nerida 145
notatio 33

Ospedale degli Incurabili 85, 139, 142–43, 153, 189, 196
Ospedale di San Giovanni e Paolo (Derelitti, Ospedaletto) 85, 139–45, 148, 151, 181, 189, 196, 205, 211
Ottonelli, Giovanni Domenico:
    Della christiana moderatione del theatro 135
Ovid 30, 42, 43, 44, 58, 199
    Met. 11.592–649: 53

Paleotti, Gabriele 16, 208
    Discorso intorno alle immagini sacre et profane 56–59
Palmi, Benedetto 144
Parisio, Giovan Giunio 139, 146, 153
Patillon, Michel 40
Paul the Apostle:
    II *Corinthians* 13.5: 189
    Romans 1.19–20: 112
Paxson, James 44
Pellegrino, Camillo:
    Carrafa, o vero della epica poesia, Il 42
performance 5, 12, 16–18, 20–21, 59, 67, 70, 80, 82, 134, 136, 147–55, 166–67, 199–208, 210–12, 214–18
performativity 3–5, 13–18, 20–22, 24, 28, 44, 56, 59, 80, 82, 134, 137, 153, 166, 184, 200–01, 208, 209–11, 216, 218
Perona, Blandine 41

persona 32–33, 37–38, 42–43, 46, 54
personification 2, 14–17, 19–80, 137, 162, 165, 201, 207–08, 210, 218
   as figure of speech 29–30
   as figure of thought 30–31
Peruschi, Giovanni Battista 72, 197
Petrarch (Francesco Petrarca) 42, 43, 44, 92, 120
   Canzoniere:
      53.10–14: 49
      117.5–8: 52
      151.9–12: 49
   Triumphi 44
Petrella, Bernardino 84
Petronius 3
phantasia 25–28, 48–49
Philostratus, Flavius:
   Vita Apoll. 6.19.2: 22–23
Piantoni, Luca 82
Piccolomini, Alessandro 48
Pico della Mirandola, Giovanni 130
Plato 3, 22
   Menex. 32
   Phaedr. 250d: 57
   Soph. 235d–236c: 22, 48
Plautus:
   Trinummus 35, 50
Pona, Francesco:
   Cardiomorphoseos 10–11, 160–61, 171–72, 184
Porphyry 84
Priscian:
   Inst. gram. 12.18: 38–39
prosopopoeia 28, 31–36, 38–40, 41–54, 60
Prosperi, Adriano 183
Prudentius:
   Psychomachia 9, 13, 58
psychomachia 9–10, 38, 95, 136, 137, 157–58, 166, 169
Pullan, Brian 143
purgation 147–55
putte 1, 138–40, 144

Quintilian:
   Inst. or.:
      1.8.3: 35
      3.8.49: 35
      3.8.50: 36
      3.8.51–52: 36
      4.1.28: 36
      4.2.103: 36
      4.2.107: 36
      6.1.25: 36
      6.1.26: 36
      6.1.30–32: 37
      6.2.29–32: 26
      9.2.29–32: 38
      9.2.36: 38, 43
      9.2.40: 40

Raimondo, Annibale 83
Raleigh, Walter 3
Rao, Cesare:
   Invettive, orationi e discorsi 87
Rauseo, Chris 61
Regio, Paolo:
   Discorsi intorno le virtù morali 87
Reinhardt, Tobias 25
Rhetorica ad Herennium 33, 41, 47
   3.37: 14
   4.63: 33
   4.66: 33
Ripa, Cesare:
   Iconologia 19–22, 25, 45, 201
Rivarola, Ottavio 146
Roman de la Rose 13
Ronconi, Luca 17, 211–18
Rossi, Nicolò:
   Discorsi intorno alla tragedia 42
Rutilius Lupus, Publius 39, 42, 50
   Schem. lex. 2.6: 34–35

sacred drama 17, 59–80, 81, 132, 145, 159, 166
Sansovino, Francesco 85
Sauli, Alessandro:
   Modo di essaminare la conscienza per sapersi ben confessare 195
Scaliger, Julius Caesar:
   Poetices libri septem 3.47: 42–43, 50
school drama 2, 17, 60, 61, 138–45
Schools of Christian Doctrine 142
Scippa Bhasin, Christine 145
Sebastiani Minturno, Antonio:
   Arte poetica 43–45
   De poeta 43
self-examination 78, 82, 128, 143–44, 150, 169, 179, 181, 189, 191–94, 199, 210
Seminario Patriarcale of Venice 136
sense perception 23, 30, 49, 55, 68, 93, 94
sermocinatio 33, 38, 47
Shakespeare, William 1, 3, 12
   As You Like It 2
   Macbeth 2, 13
   Othello 14
Siciliano, Enzo 215, 216
Silius Italicus 58
simulacrum 113
Somaschians [religious order] 142–43, 196
Soranzo, Camilla 96
Sorte, Cristoforo 83
Stanauser, Giovanni 146
Stringa, Giovanni 85
Strubel, Armand 13–14
suasoria 35
symbol 15
synecdoche 29

Tasso, Torquato 92, 121
   Gerusalemme liberata 167
Teatro di Documenti, Rome 211–12, 215
Terence:
   Eunuchus 132
Tesauro, Emanuele:
   Cannocchiale aristotelico 60, 210
Theatines [religious order] 142–43
theatrum mundi [theatre of the world] 2–6, 9–12, 16, 82, 89, 92, 116, 119, 124, 129, 131, 137, 159, 168, 210, 218
Theophrastus 36
Totentanz 88, 98, 165, 179, 217
Trissino, Gian Giorgio:
   Quinta et la sesta divisione della Poetica, La 42
triumph of Death 88, 158, 167, 181

vanitas 102, 171
Valgrisi, Vincenzo 98, 101
Venier, Angelo 84–85
Venier, Sebastiano 84
Vettori, Pietro:
   Commentarii in librum Demetrii Phalerei De elocutione 32, 35

Viglius [Wigle Aytta van Zwichem] 10, 12
Virgil 38, 42, 43, 44, 53, 92, 199
   Aen. 6.236 ff.: 53
visualisation 14, 22–23, 26, 37, 70, 75, 113–14, 162, 181, 189
Vivaldi, Antonio 144
Voltaire [François-Marie Arouet] 30, 31

Weaver, Elissa 145
Wotton, Henry 1, 3, 9, 13, 140, 146, 211
   Reliquiae Wottonianae:
   'De Morte' 3–4

Yates, Frances A. 2, 3, 12

Zabarella, Jacopo 84
Zane, Marino 146
Zitelle [religious shelter in Venice]:
   Constitutioni et regole 144
Zorzi, Marino 96

www.ingramcontent.com/pod-product-compliance
Lightning Source LLC
Chambersburg PA
CBHW080223170426
43192CB00015B/2732